During the last twenty years our understanding of expertise has dramatically increased. Laboratory analyses of chess masters, experts in physics and medicine, musicians, athletes, writers, and performance artists have included careful examination of the cognitive process mediating outstanding performance in very diverse areas of expertise. These analyses have shown that expert performance is primarily a reflection of acquired skill resulting from the accumulation of domain-specific knowledge and methods during many years of training and practice. The importance of domain-specific knowledge has led researchers on expertise to focus on characteristics of expertise in specific domains.

In *Toward a General Theory of Expertise* many of the world's foremost scientists review the state-of-the-art knowledge about expertise in different domains, with the goal of identifying characteristics of expert performance that are generalizable across many different areas of expertise. These essays provide a comprehensive summary of general methods for studying expertise and of current knowledge about expertise in chess, physics, medicine, sports and performance arts, music, writing, and decision making. Most important, the essays reveal the existence of many general characteristics of expertise.

Toward a general theory of expertise

Toward a general theory of expertise
Prospects and limits

Edited by
K. ANDERS ERICSSON AND JACQUI SMITH
Max Planck Institute for Human Development and Education
Berlin, Germany

The right of the University of Cambridge to print and sell all manner of books was granted by Henry VIII in 1534. The University has printed and published continuously since 1584.

CAMBRIDGE UNIVERSITY PRESS
Cambridge
New York   Port Chester   Melbourne   Sydney

Published by the Press Syndicate of the University of Cambridge
The Pitt Building, Trumpington Street, Cambridge CB2 1RP
40 West 20th Street, New York, NY 10011, USA
10 Stamford Road, Oakleigh, Melbourne 3166, Australia

First published 1991

Library of Congress Cataloging-in-Publication Data
Toward a general theory of expertise: prospects and limits / edited
by K. Anders Ericsson, Jacqui Smith.
    p. cm.
Includes index.
ISBN 0-521-40470-3. – ISBN 0-521-40612-9 (pbk.)
1. Expertise. I. Ericsson, K. Anders (Karl Anders), 1947–
II. Smith, Jacqui.
BF431.T69 1991
153 – dc20   90-20029
                                                                  CIP

British Library Cataloguing in Publication Data
Toward a general theory of expertise: prospects and limits.
1. Psychology. Theories
I. Ericsson, K. Anders II. Smith, Jacqui
150.1

ISBN 0-521-40470-3 hardback
ISBN 0-521-40612-9 paperback

Transferred to digital printing 1999

100560496X

Contents

vi   *Contents*

Preface

One of the most exciting challenges in cognitive science today is to understand the mechanisms mediating the superior performance of experts in various domains, such as chess, physics, medicine, sports, dance, and music. Recent advances in describing the structure of expert performance in specific domains naturally raise the issue of whether expert performance in general across domains can be accounted for by a common set of theoretical principles. But major obstacles to uncovering general characteristics of expert performance across different domains are the complexity and the domain-specific nature of expertise. Moreover, extracting general principles of expert performance requires in-depth knowledge of expertise in two or more domains, whereas leading investigators of expertise generally have firsthand knowledge about only one domain.

In response to this challenge, Jacqui Smith and I arranged a conference in West Berlin in June 1989 at the Max Planck Institute for Human Development and Education, with the goal of extracting general theoretical principles of expertise. With financial support from the Max Planck Society, we invited the best representatives of each of the major domains of expertise in which expert performance had been extensively studied empirically. The participants were asked to summarize the state-of-the-art research on expert performance in their respective domains, as well as to suggest theoretical principles that might generalize across domains. The conference presentations were followed by a lively discussion and exchange of ideas and suggestions concerning the presentations. Later, in response to the suggestions, the presentations were converted into chapters, which were circulated among the participants for further comments. The end result of this process is the current book before you.

I thank Paul Baltes, Director at the Max Planck Institute for Human Development and Education, and Julia Hough, our editor at Cambridge University Press, for all their help in completing this project.

K. Anders Ericsson

Boulder, Colorado
March 11, 1991

Contributors

Fran Allard
Department of Kinesiology
University of Waterloo
Waterloo, Ontario
Canada

Yuichiro Anzai
Department of Electrical Engineering
Keio University
Yokohama
Japan

Carl Bereiter
Center for Applied Cognitive Science
Ontario Institute for Studies in
  Education
Toronto, Ontario
Canada

Kevin J. Biolsi
Computer Information Systems
Business Graduate School
University of Michigan
Ann Arbor, Michigan
USA

Colin F. Camerer
Department of Marketing
Wharton School
University of Pennsylvania
Philadelphia, Pennsylvania
USA

Neil Charness
Department of Psychology
University of Waterloo
Waterloo, Ontario
Canada

Dietrich Dörner
Max-Planck Gesellschaft
Projektgruppe für kognitive
  Anthropologie
Berlin
Germany

K. Anders Ericsson
Department of Psychology
University of Colorado at Boulder
Boulder, Colorado
USA

Guy J. Groen
Centre for Medical Education
Faculty of Medicine
McGill University
Montreal, Quebec
Canada

Keith J. Holyoak
Department of Psychology
University of California, Los Angeles
Los Angeles, California
USA

Eric J. Johnson
Department of Marketing
Wharton School
University of Pennsylvania
Philadelphia, Pennsylvania
USA

Judith Reitman Olson
Computer Information Systems
Business Graduate School
University of Michigan
Ann Arbor, Michigan
USA

x   *Contributors*

Vimla L. Patel
Centre for Medical Education
Faculty of Medicine
McGill University
Montreal, Quebec
Canada

Timothy A. Salthouse
School of Psychology
Georgia Institute of Technology
Atlanta, Georgia
USA

Marlene Scardamalia
Center for Applied Cognitive Science
Ontario Institute for Studies in
   Education
Toronto, Ontario
Canada

Julia Schölkopf
Universität Bamberg
Lehrstuhl für Klinische Psychologie
Bamberg
Germany

John Sloboda
Department of Psychology
University of Keele
Keele
England

Jacqui Smith
Max Planck Institute for Human
   Development and Education
Berlin
Germany

Janet L. Starkes
School of Physical Education
McMaster University
Hamilton, Ontario
Canada

1 *Prospects and limits of the empirical study of expertise: an introduction*

K. ANDERS ERICSSON AND JACQUI SMITH

Research on expertise may be one of the most rapidly expanding areas within cognitive psychology and cognitive science. Typically, when a topic becomes popular in psychology, the research approach and the methodology associated with it are also accepted, and the pressure to demonstrate the utility and feasibility of the approach diminishes. Efforts are directed instead toward the theoretical integration of research findings. Furthermore, popularity of a new approach nearly always means that many investigators will adopt it. An even larger number of investigators, however, will adopt only the terminology and will attempt to modify other research approaches to encompass the new concepts. That, in turn, leads to diffusion of the defining characteristics of the "new" approach, making straightforward attempts to integrate published research findings difficult. Because of this process of diffusion, often the new approach will no longer be readily distinguishable from previous alternative research approaches.

In this introductory chapter we attempt to provide a conceptual framework for distinguishing important characteristics of the *original expertise approach*. Our chapter consists of three sections. The first section attempts to characterize the study of expertise in the most general and domain-independent manner so that we can compare the expertise approach with a number of alternative approaches that had similar objectives. The focus of this section is on briefly reviewing some of the outcomes and failures of the earlier approaches. Our goal is to show that the expertise approach can account for these failures at the expense of greater empirical and theoretical complexity. In the second section we specify the nature of the original expertise approach and methodology. Here the pioneering work on chess expertise by de Groot (1978) and Chase and Simon (1973) is used to exemplify the sequence of research steps that characterized the original expertise approach. In the final section we elaborate criteria for these steps and use these criteria to discuss and review the prospects for, and limits of, more recent research on expertise.

1

DEFINITION OF OUTSTANDING PERFORMANCE AND EXPERTISE: A COMPARISON

On the most general level, the study of expertise seeks to understand and account for what distinguishes outstanding individuals in a domain from less outstanding individuals in that domain, as well as from people in general. We deliberately use the vague term "outstanding" because by not specifying more detailed criteria we are able to point to a number of distinctly different scientific approaches that have addressed the same problem.

In nearly all human endeavors there always appear to be some people who perform at a higher level than others, people who for some reason stand out from the majority. Depending on the historical period and the particular activity involved, such individuals have been labeled exceptional, superior, gifted, talented, specialist, expert, or even lucky. The label used to characterize them reflects an attribution of the major factor responsible for their outstanding behavior, whether it is intended to or not. Scientific efforts to understand the sources of such outstanding behavior have been guided by similar conceptions and attributions.

We limit our discussion to those cases in which the outstanding behavior can be attributed to relatively stable characteristics of the relevant individuals. We believe that stability of the individual characteristics is a necessary condition for any empirical approach seeking to account for the behavior with reference to characteristics of the individual. This constraint does not distinguish whether the characteristics are inherited or acquired. It does, however, eliminate a large number of achievements due to unique immediate environmental circumstances.

The most obvious achievements to be excluded by the stability constraint are those that involve events of fair games of chance, such as winning a large amount of money in a single lottery. More interestingly, the same criterion rules out achievements that occur only once in a lifetime, such as a single scientific discovery, a major artistic creation, a historically significant decision or prediction, or a single victory in a sport. This, of course, does not mean that we reject the possibility of defining criteria for outstanding performances in the arts, sciences, and sports arenas. It does mean, however, that a single achievement in a unique situation does not allow us to infer that the achievement was solely due to the particular individual's characteristics.

In order to support an attribution to the stable characteristics of a person, ideally one would require a series of outstanding achievements under different circumstances. Furthermore, one would like to have a larger group of other individuals (a "control" group of sorts) who have experienced similar opportunities to make contributions or to achieve. In the case in which many other individuals would be equally likely to achieve in similar situations, there is no need to attribute the achievement to special personal characteristics. Almost by definition the numbers of individuals given opportunities in some life realms to achieve and to stand out from the majority are small (e.g., heads of state, army generals, people with vast economic resources). In such cases, even a stable series of achievements cannot unambiguously be linked to stable personal characteristics, because of the confounding influence of a unique stable situation.

Examination of our simple stable-characteristic constraint indicates that many achievements popularly acknowledged as evidence for expertise must be questioned and carefully scrutinized. Another important consequence of this constraint is more indirect and concerns the validity of social evaluation and perception of outstanding performance or ability. One would expect social evaluation to be greatly influenced by observations of previous performances (not all by the same individual) occurring under unique circumstances. A social judgment, then, might not be the most precise evaluation of an individual's current ability to perform. Ideally, one needs to determine the unique situation of the individual and to observe performances in standardized situations that allow interindividual comparisons (e.g., laboratory tasks or tests). Once it is possible to measure superior performance under standardized conditions, there is no need to rely on social indicators. Attuned to some of the difficulties of definition and assessment, let us now proceed to discuss some scientific approaches that have been directed toward accounting for outstanding or superior performance.

SCIENTIFIC APPROACHES TO ACCOUNTING FOR OUTSTANDING PERFORMANCE

Several different scientific approaches have been used to investigate outstanding performance. The constructs that have been investigated have primarily reflected popular attributions regarding the source of the outstanding behavior. These conceptualizations, in turn, have directly influenced what empirical evidence has been considered and collected. Table 1.1 summarizes the different types of stable personal characteristics that have been hypothesized to underlie outstanding performance and links those attributions to associated theoretical constructs and research methods. The attributed personal characteristics noted in Table 1.1 reflect a basic belief that behavior either is predominantly influenced by inherited qualities or is a function of learning and acquisition. Further, outstanding performance is attributed either to some general characteristic of the individual or to a specific aspect. The associated theoretical constructs and methodologies reflect these dimensions: *inherited* versus *acquired, general* versus *specific*. So, for example, the researcher will focus either on the effects of general traits (e.g., intelligence, personality), specific abilities (e.g., musical ability, spatial ability), and general life and educational experience (e.g., language, study strategies) or on domain-specific training and practice.

One's conception of the likely origins of outstanding performances will greatly influence the group of people selected for study, as well as the type of information sought concerning these individuals. For example, investigators

Table 1.1. *Different approaches to accounting for outstanding performance*

Attribution	Construct	Research approach
Primarily inherited		
General abilities	Intelligence, personality	Correlation with personality profile, general intelligence
Specific abilities	E.g., music ability, artistic ability, body build	Correlation with measures of specific ability
Primarily acquired		
General learning and experience	General knowledge and cognitive strategies	Investigation of common processing strategies
Domain-specific training and practice	Domain- or task-specific knowledge	Analysis of task performance, i.e., the expertise approach

pursuing an account in terms of general inherited capacities would be likely to consider individuals regardless of their domains and would be particularly interested in information allowing assessment of the genetic contribution. A longitudinal study of individuals identified as having exceptionally high intelligence, by Terman and his associates (Oden, 1968; Stanley, George, & Solano, 1977; Terman & Oden, 1947), illustrates this approach. A focus on domain-specific acquired characteristics would lead investigators to constrain themselves to one domain or task and to try to assess what was acquired (e.g., specific memory strategies), as well as the process of acquisition.

On a priori grounds one can argue that the most parsimonious theoretical account of outstanding performance is in terms of general, predominantly inherited characteristics. Indeed, in the history of scientific research on superior performance, that approach was initially preferred. It was primarily because of inability to explain certain empirical observations that accounts based on more specific abilities and acquired characteristics came to be seriously considered. We shall briefly consider some of those failures before turning to a consideration of the expertise approach that exemplifies the belief that specific acquired characteristics underlie outstanding performance.

Accounts in terms of general and specific inherited characteristics

If one wants to attribute outstanding performance to general inherited characteristics, it is reasonable to rely on readily available criteria to identify instances of outstanding behavior and of individuals who exhibit that behavior, criteria such as social evaluation and recognition by one's peers. In the first major study in that area, Galton (1869) used social recognition to identify eminent individuals in a wide range of fields and then studied their familial and genetic origins. Galton argued that individuals gained eminence in the eyes of others because of a long-term history of achievement. Such achievement, he suggested, was the product of a blend of intellectual (natural) ability and personal motivation. He reported strong evidence for eminence's being limited to a relatively small number of families stemming from common ancestors, and he inferred that eminence was genetically determined.

Contemporary work in Galton's time and subsequent studies were directed at uncovering the loci of individual differences in general ability. The genetic nature of those general capacities led investigators to search for differences in basic characteristics of processes, such as the speed of mental processes as reflected by reaction time. In subsequent studies, however, individual differences in performance of simple tasks showed disappointingly low correlations, both among tasks and between performance and indices of ability, such as grade in school (Guilford, 1967).

More recent effort to uncover general basic cognitive processes that could account for individual differences have been inconclusive (Baron, 1978; Carroll, 1978; Cooper & Regan, 1982; Hunt, 1980). For example, research on individual differences in general memory ability has found low correlations of memory performance across different types of material and methods of testing, leading investigators to reject the idea of a general memory ability (Kelley, 1964). More direct evidence against stable basic memory processes comes from repeated demonstrations that memory performance for specific types of material can be drastically improved even after short periods of practice (Ericsson, 1985; Kliegl, Smith, & Baltes, 1989). Moreover, as Cooper and Regan noted (1982, p. 163), inadequacies in the definition and design of both cognitive tasks and intelligence measures create serious problems for interpreting correlations between measures of basic cognitive processes and ability.

Tests measuring general intelligence have been extremely useful for prediction and diagnosis in a wide range of situations, although there is considerable controversy about what they actually measure (Resnick, 1976; Sternberg, 1982). IQ tests, however, have been remarkably unsuccessful in accounting for individual differences in levels of performance in the arts and sciences and advanced professions, as measured by social indicators (e.g., money earned, status) and judgments (e.g., prizes, awards) (Tyler, 1965).

There were other lines of research that examined subjects with reliably superior performances and compared them with control groups. Much of that research was similarly motivated by the belief that exceptionally high levels of performance would reflect some basic exceptional ability involving attention (power or concentration), memory, general speed of reaction, or command of logic. Some investigators, however, focused on other stable individual characteristics, such as features of personality, motivation, and perceptual style (e.g., Cattell, 1963; Roe, 1953).

In the 1920s, three Russian professors examined the performance of eight grand masters (world-class chess players) on a wide range of laboratory tests for basic cognitive and perceptual abilities (de Groot, 1946/1978). Surprisingly, the grand masters did not differ from control subjects in those basic abilities, but they were clearly superior in memory tests involving chess positions.

In the case of exceptional chess performance, superior spatial ability often is assumed to be essential (Chase & Simon, 1973; Holding, 1985). Doll and Mayr (1987) compared the performances of about thirty of the best chess players in what was then West Germany with those of almost ninety normal subjects of similar ages, using an IQ test with seven subscales. Only three of the subscales showed reliable differences, and somewhat surprisingly the largest difference between the two groups concerned higher scores for numeric calculation for the chess masters. Doll and Mayr (1987) found no evidence that chess players were selectively better on spatial tasks. In accounting for the unexpected superiority of the chess players on two of the subscales, Doll and Mayr (1987) argued that one reason could be that elite chess players had prior experience in coping with time pressure because of their past chess competitions. When the analysis was restricted to the group of elite chess players, none of the subscales of the IQ test was found to have a reliable correlation with chess-playing performance.

Of the research that has focused not on intelligence but on other relatively stable characteristics of individuals, that by Cattell (1963; Cattell & Drevdahl, 1955) is probably the best example. Cattell sought to determine whether the personality profiles for eminent researchers in physics, biology, and psychology could be distinguished from those of teachers and administrators in the same fields and from those of the general population. Compared with all other groups, top researchers were found to exhibit a consistent profile, being more self-sufficient, dominant, emotionally unstable, introverted, and reflective. Such a profile supports Galton's earlier opinion that eminence and outstanding achievement in a field are products not only of ability but also of aspects of personal motivation. Motivation and striving for excellence often are focused on a small number of domains or even a single domain, suggesting that aspects of motivation may well be acquired.

Despite these hints at possible personality patterns, the research approach of accounting for outstanding and superior performance in terms of general inherited characteristics has been largely unsuccessful in identifying strong and replicable relations. The search for links to specific inherited abilities has been similarly inconclusive. Indeed, as the specific characteristics proposed to account for the superior performance become integral to that performance, it becomes difficult to rule out the possibility that such characteristics have not been acquired as a result of many years of extensive training and practice. Investigators have therefore focused their attention on characteristics that appear in children and that reflect basic capacities for which a genetic origin is plausible. We shall briefly consider two examples of such basic capabilities, namely, absolute pitch among musicians and physiological differences among elite athletes.

A recent review of the research on absolute pitch shows that most of the empirical evidence favors an account in terms of acquired skill (Ericsson & Faivre, 1988). The ability to recognize musical pitch is not an all-or-none skill, and many musicians have it to various degrees. They display the best performance on their own instruments, and their performance decreases as artificial tones from a tone generator are presented (Bachem, 1937). The ability to name pitches correctly is closely related to the amount of one's formal musical training (Oakes, 1955). Furthermore, pitch recognition can be dramatically improved with training, and one musician has documented how he acquired absolute pitch through long-term training (Brady, 1970).

Similarly, a recent review shows that many anatomical characteristics of elite athletes, such as larger hearts, more capillaries for muscles, and the proportions of different types of muscle fibers, are acquired during years of practice (Ericsson, 1990). Such findings showing the far-reaching effects of training do not, however, rule out possible genetic constraints. An individual's height and overall physique are determined by genetic factors (Wilson, 1986). Height and physique, for example, impose important constraints in many physical and sports domains, such as basketball, high jumping, gymnastics, ballet, and professional riding. It is also conceivable that genetic factors might influence the rate of improvement due to training. Nevertheless, training and preparation appear to be necessary prerequisites and important determinants of outstanding performance. We turn to a brief discussion of accounts of outstanding and superior performance based on acquired characteristics.

Accounts in terms of specific acquired characteristics: the expertise approach

In this brief review we have seen that the more parsimonious theoretical approaches relying on stable inherited characteristics seem inadequate to account for outstanding and superior performance. It is therefore necessary to consider accounts based on acquired characteristics. Here we need to identify not only what the acquired characteristics are but also the process by which they are acquired.

How long is the acquisition period, and over what time frame do we need to observe and monitor changes in performance? Simon and Chase (1973) were the first to observe that 10 years or more of full-time preparation are required to attain an international level of performance in chess. Studies by Hayes (1981) and Bloom (1985) revealed that a decade of intensive preparation is necessary to become an international performer in sports or in the arts or sciences. In a recent review, Ericsson and Crutcher (1990) found consistent support for the requirement of 10 years of intensive preparation in a wide range of studies of international levels of performance. Furthermore, Ericsson and Crutcher (1990) found for many domains that most international-level performers had been seriously involved in their domains before the age of 6 years. The period of preparation for superior performance appears to cover a major proportion of these individuals' development during adolescence and early adulthood.

A detailed analysis of acquisition processes extending over decades under widely different environmental circumstances is extraordinarily difficult to conduct. Without a theoretical framework to outline the relevant aspects, the number of possible factors that could be critical to attain superior performance is vast. One can, of course, gain some idea of the range of factors by reading biographies and analyses of unusual events or circumstances in the lives of outstanding scientists and artists (Albert, 1983; McCurdy, 1983). It is unlikely, though, that descriptive studies seeking correlations between ultimate performance of individuals and information about their developmental histories will ever be able to yield conclusive results. A much more promising approach is offered by a careful analysis of the attained performance. This is the crux of the expertise approach.

The expertise approach differs from the approaches discussed earlier in some important respects. The other approaches were attempts to measure independently the constructs hypothesized to be the sources and bases of outstanding performance. In contrast, the expertise approach is an attempt to describe the critical performance under standardized conditions, to analyze it, and to identify the components of the performance that make it superior.

Two features distinguish the expertise approach from other approaches: first, the insistence that it is necessary to identify or design a collection of representative tasks to capture the relevant aspects of superior performance in a domain and to elicit superior performance under laboratory conditions; second, the proposal that systematic empirical analysis of the processes leading to the superior performance will allow assessment of critical mediating mechanisms. Moreover, it is possible to analyze the types of learning or adaptation processes by which these mechanisms can be acquired and to study their acquisition in real life or under laboratory conditions.

The expertise approach is more limited in its application than the other approaches reviewed earlier. Whereas the other approaches can use social indicators as criterion variables of outstanding performance, the expertise approach requires the design of a set of standardized tasks wherein the superior performance can be demonstrated and reliability reproduced. With this important limitation in mind, we now turn to a closer examination of the original expertise approach.

The original expertise approach: the pioneering work on chess

There is no consensus on how the expertise approach should be characterized. If one takes the original work on chess expertise by de Groot (1978) and Chase and Simon (1973), however, it is possible to extract three general characteristics. First, the focus is on producing and observing outstanding performance in the laboratory under relatively standardized conditions. Second, there is a theoretical concern to analyze and describe the cognitive processes critical to the production of an outstanding performance on such tasks. Finally, the critical cognitive processes are examined, and explicit learning mechanisms are proposed to account for their acquisition.

If one is interested in reproducing superior performance under standardized conditions, one should give preference to domains in which there are accepted measures of performance. Chess provides such a domain. It is possible to measure an individual's chess-playing ability from the results of matches against different opponents in different tournaments (Elo, 1978). It is easy to select groups of chess players who differ sufficiently in chess ability that the probability of one of the weaker players beating one of the stronger players in a particular game is remote.

A critical issue in the expertise approach is *how to identify standardized tasks* that will allow the real-life outstanding performance to be reproduced in the laboratory. Because of the interactive nature of chess games and the vast number of possible sequences of moves, the same sequences of chess moves are hardly ever observed in two different chess games. Better chess players will consistently win over weaker chess players employing a wide variety of chess-playing styles. One could therefore argue that the better chess players consistently select moves as good as, or better than, the moves selected by weaker players. De Groot (1978) argued that it is possible to develop a collection of well-defined tasks capturing chess expertise by having chess players select the "best next move" for a number of different chess positions. Measurement of performance in this task requires that it be possible to evaluate qualitatively, on a priori grounds, the dependent variable, that is, the next chess move selected for a given chess position. It is not currently possible to evaluate the quality of chess moves for an arbitrary chess position. In fact, one international chess master claims to have spent a great part of his life unsuccessfully seeking to determine the best move for one particular chess position (Saariluoma, 1984).

De Groot (1978) collected think-aloud protocols from chess players of widely differing levels of expertise while they selected their best next moves for several chess positions. After extended analysis of these classic positions, however, he found that only *one* of them differentiated between grand masters and other chess experts who differed greatly in chess ability: All of the very best chess players selected better moves than did any of the comparatively weak players (nonoverlapping). Hence, he inferred that the task of selecting moves for that chess position must elicit cognitive processes that differentiate chess players at different levels of expertise.

Another pioneering aspect of de Groot's study was his use of verbal protocols. He was able to localize differences in cognitive processes between the grand masters and the other class experts by analyzing think-aloud protocols from his best-next-move task. He found that both masters and experts spent about 10 minutes before deciding on a move. In the beginning, the players familiarized themselves with the chess position, evaluated the position for strengths and weaknesses, and identified a range of promising moves. Later they explored in greater depth the consequences of a few of those moves. On average, both masters and experts considered more than thirty move possibilities involving both Black and White and considered three or four distinctly different first moves.

De Groot (1978) first examined the possibility that, compared with chess experts, the grand masters were able to explore longer move combinations and thereby uncover the best move. He found, however, that the maximum depth of the search (i.e., the length of move combinations) was virtually the same for the two groups. When de Groot then focused his analysis on how the players came to consider different moves for the position, he did find differences. Few of the chess experts initially mentioned the best move, whereas most of the grand masters had noticed the best move during the familiarization with the position. More generally, de Groot argued, on the basis of his analysis of the protocols, that the grand masters perceived and recognized the characteristics of a chess position and evaluated possible moves by relying on their extensive experience rather than by uncovering those characteristics by calculation and evaluation of move possibilities. In some cases the discovery of promising chess moves was linked to the verbal report of a localized weakness in the opponent's chess position. Other grand masters discovered the same move without any verbal report of a mediating step (de Groot, 1978, p. 298). The superior chess-playing ability of more experienced chess players, according to de Groot, is attributable to their extensive experience, allowing retrieval of direct associations in memory between characteristics of chess positions and appropriate methods and moves. De Groot (1978, p. 316) argued that mastery in "the field of shoemaking, painting, building, [or] confectionary" is due to a similar accumulation of experiential linkings.

To examine the critical perceptual processing occurring at the initial presentation of a chess position, de Groot (1978) briefly showed subjects a middle-game chess position (2–10 seconds). Shortly after the end of the presentation the chess players gave retrospective reports on their thoughts and perceptions during the brief presentation and also recalled the presented chess position as best they could. From the verbal reports, de Groot found that the position was perceived in large complexes (e.g., a pawn structure, a castled position) and that unusual characteristics of the position (such as an exposed piece or a far-advanced pawn) were noticed. Within this brief time, the chess masters were found to integrate all the characteristics of the position into a single whole, whereas the less experienced players were not able to do so. The chess masters also often perceived the best move within that short exposure time. The analysis of the amount recalled from the various chess positions was consistent with the evidence derived from the verbal reports. Chess masters were able to recall the positions of all the 20–30 chess pieces virtually perfectly, whereas the positions recalled by the less experienced chess experts ranged from 50 to 70 percent.

The classic study of Chase and Simon (1973) followed up on this superior memory performance by chess masters for briefly presented chess positions.

They designed a standardized memory task in which subjects were presented with a chess position for 5 seconds with the sole task of the subjects being to recall the locations of as many chess pieces as possible. We shall later review more carefully to what extent this new task can be viewed as capturing the cognitive processes underlying superior chess-playing performance.

With that memory task, Chase and Simon (1973) were able to corroborate de Groot's earlier finding that chess players with higher levels of expertise recalled the correct locations of many more pieces for representative chess positions. They also went a significant step farther and experimentally varied the characteristics of the presented configurations of the chess pieces. For chessboards with randomly placed pieces, the memory performances of the chess masters were no better than those of novice chess players, showing that the superior memory performance of the master depends on the presence of meaningful relations between the chess pieces, the kinds of relations seen in actual chess games.

Chase and Simon (1973) found that a player's ability to reproduce from memory the previously presented chess position proceeded in bursts in which chess pieces were rapidly placed, with pauses of a couple of seconds between bursts. The pieces belonging to a burst were shown to reflect meaningfully related configurations of pieces (i.e., chunks) that corresponded well to the complexes discovered by de Groot (1978). The chess masters were found to differ from other chess players primarily in the number of pieces belonging to a chunk, that is, the size of the chunk. In support of the hypothesis that memory and perception of chess positions rely on the same encoding processes, Chase and Simon (1973) demonstrated that the recall process had a structure similar to that of the process of reproducing perceptually available chess positions. Rather than discuss the large number of additional empirical studies by Chase and Simon (1973), we shall change the focus and consider their theoretical effort to specify the detailed processes underlying superior memory performance and the relation of these processes to general constraints on human information processing.

One of the most severe constraints on an account that is based on acquired knowledge and skill involves explicating what has been acquired and showing that the acquired characteristics are sufficient to account for the superior performance without violating the limitations of the general capacities of human information processing (Newell & Simon, 1972). The superior recall of 15–30 chess pieces by chess masters would at first glance seem to be inconsistent with the limited capacity of short-term memory in humans, which allows storage of around 7 chunks (Miller, 1956). Chase and Simon (1973) found that the number of chunks recalled by chess players at all skill levels was well within the limit of around 7 ± 2. They attributed the difference in memory performance between strong and weak players to the fact that the more expert chess players were able to recognize more complex chunks, that is, chunks with a larger number of chess pieces per chunk.

On the basis of computer simulations of the encoding and recall of middle-game chess positions, Simon and Gilmartin (1973) were able to show that 1,000 chunks were sufficient to reproduce the memory performance of a chess expert. They estimated that simulation of the performance of a chess master would require between 10,000 and 100,000 chunks. Assuming that the superior performance of the expert depends on the recognition of familiar patterns that index previously stored relevant knowledge of successful methods (actions), the time-consuming process of becoming an expert would consist in acquiring those patterns and the associated knowledge. Simon and Chase (1973) estimated that around 3,000 hours are required to become an expert, and around 30,000 hours to become a chess master. They also commented that "the organization of the Master's elaborate repertoire of information takes thousands of hours to build up, and the same is true of any skilled task (e.g., football, music). That is why *practice* is the major independent variable in the acquisition of skill" (p. 279). Whether or not one agrees with the Chase and Simon theory of expertise, it would be unwise to confound the methodology of their research with the theoretical assumptions of their specific theory. Indeed, Chase and Simon (1973) were rather cautious when they proposed their theory, describing it as simply a rough first approximation.

THE THREE STEPS OF THE ORIGINAL EXPERTISE APPROACH

From our review of the pioneering research on chess expertise we have extracted three steps. The first step involves capturing the essence of superior performance under standardized laboratory conditions by identifying representative tasks. In the following sections we try to distinguish between collections of tasks that capture the superior performance and collections of tasks that measure a related function or ability. In our review of the initial work on chess, we argued that only the task that required that subjects consistently select the "best moves" meets the criterion of capturing the nature of superior performance. Two other tasks, one involving perception and the other measuring memory for briefly presented chess positions, assess related functions but do not directly represent chess-playing skill.

The second step involves a detailed analysis of the superior performance. The pioneering research on chess nicely illustrates the use of refined analyses of sequences of verbal reports and placement of chess pieces to infer the underlying cognitive processes mediating the superior performance, as well as the use of experimental manipulation of stimulus materials.

The third and final step involves efforts to account for the acquisition of the characteristics and cognitive structures and processes that have been found to mediate the superior performances of experts. A persistent failure to identify conditions under which the critical characteristics could be acquired or improved would provide strong evidence that those characteristics are unmodifiable and hence basic and most likely inherited.

Our explication of the original expertise approach imposes clear limits for its successful application. Unless the essence of the superior performance of the expert can be captured in the laboratory (satisfying the criterion for the first step), there will not be a performance to be further analyzed in terms of its mediating processes. Similarly, failure to identify mediating processes that can account for the superior performance during the second step will leave the investigator with only the original differences in overall performance and will make the third step essentially superfluous.

At the same time, our explication of the expertise approach is applicable to any phenomenon involving reliably superior performance that can be captured in the laboratory. We believe that an attempt to encompass phenomena normally labeled as perceptual (e.g., chicken sexing), motoric (e.g., typing), or knowledge-based (e.g., physics) within the same overall approach will allow us to identify common methodological and theoretical issues and to consider a common and more differentiated set of learning mechanisms in accounting for achievement of superior performance in any one of these different domains. Such an approach will have the additional advantage of allowing us to consider the many different perceptual, memory, motoric, and knowledge-based aspects of superior performance in domains like chess (Charness, chapter 2, this volume), physics (Anzai, chapter 3, this volume), medicine (Patel & Groen, chapter 4, this volume), performing arts and sports (Allard & Starkes, chapter 5, this volume), and music (Sloboda, chapter 6, this volume).

Capturing superior performance: the first step

The first step in the expertise approach involves finding or designing a collection of tasks to capture the superior performance in the appropriate domain. If one is able to identify such a collection of tasks, the following important advantages will accrue: First, the performance of the designed tasks will reflect the stable characteristics of the superior real-life performance. More important, the availability of such a collection of tasks will allow us to study the performance of the experts extensively in order to accumulate sufficient information on the mediating processes to make a detailed assessment and analysis. During these extensive observations of performance, we should not expect significant changes due to learning and practice, as we shall be monitoring stable processes that have been adapted and perfected over a long period of time. The period during which performance will be observed will be negligible in comparison.

Finally, these collections of tasks will provide us with an excellent testing ground for studying how rapidly the various identified characteristics can be acquired through practice. In fact, one could argue that with an adequate collection of tasks, the rates of acquisition should be comparable for practice with the collection of tasks and in real life. If, on the other hand, the collection of designed tasks does not elicit the mechanisms that mediate superior real-life performance, or does so only partially, then we are likely to see substantial learning and changes in the processes as a result of further practice. Collections of tasks that lead to rapid rises in levels of performance by experts with further practice are unlikely to yield an adequate representation of superior performance. Even more devastating evidence against the claim that such a collection can capture superior performance comes from situations in which novices have matched or surpassed the performance levels of experts after only a few weeks or months of practice.

For some types of expertise it is easy to identify such a collection of tasks, but in most cases it is the most difficult step. We shall first describe some simple cases and then turn to the difficult issues involved in designing a collection of tasks to characterize real-life expertise. We shall also consider the advantages and problems of designing a collection of memory tasks to study superior memory performance by experts, as opposed to studying directly the superior performance of experts.

Tasks capturing real-life expertise. There are few instances of real-life expertise in which superior performance can be demonstrated under relatively standardized conditions. Mental calculators and memory experts provide such instances. They often exhibit their performance under conditions similar to those used in traditional experiments. In both of these cases it is easy to define a large pool of different stimuli (e.g., 10 billion possible multiplications of two 5-digit numbers, or 100 trillion digit sequences of 14 digits). Drawing on this pool of items, the experimenter can observe the performance in a large number of different trials and accumulate information on the cognitive processes underlying the expertise. Similarly, some types of psychomotor performance, such as typing, and some sporting events can easily be imported into the laboratory.

Apart from the preceding cases, the design of standardized tasks to capture real-life expert performance is difficult. The problem is somewhat similar to that of isolating phenomena in the natural and biological sciences. By careful analysis of the expert performance in real life, we try to identify recurrent activities that can be reproduced under controlled conditions. In those domains in which expertise can be measured, it is important to restrict the focus to those activities that are involved in producing the relevant performance or resulting product. One should search for goal-directed activities that result in overt behavior that can be reproduced by presentation of the appropriate stimuli.

A nice illustration of this procedure comes from the previously described research on chess, in which de Groot (1978) designed the task of selecting the best next move for a given middle-game position. It should be possible to collect a large number of such positions with which even top-level chess players would be unfamiliar. In extracting out a single chess position from a chess game, one is faced with a problem that is common in research on expertise, namely, the determination of the correct response, or the reliable evaluation of selected moves. Given that currently there was no method available that could have provided that information objectively, de Groot (1978) spent an extended period carefully analyzing the selected chess position to evaluate the relative merits of different moves. A different method of dealing with this problem was offered in a recent study by Saariluoma (1984), who selected chess positions that had clearly discernible best next moves. Both of these methods are oriented toward finding or designing a small set of tasks, and they cannot easily be extended into specifying a large population of tasks that could be claimed to capture the chess expertise.

In most other complex task domains, such as physics and medical diagnosis, investigators tend to select a small number of tasks without specifying the population from which those tasks were chosen to be a representative sample. One reason for this is that a detailed task analysis of even a single complex problem is difficult and extraordinarily time-consuming. More important, our knowledge of complex domains of expertise is incomplete, and it would not at this time be possible to specify a population of tasks to capture such expertise. Many scientists, however, are working on building expert systems in which the tasks and prerequisite knowledge must be specified, and other researchers are working on describing the formal characteristics of various task environments (see Charness's analyses of chess in chapter 2).

In many domains, experts produce complex products such as texts on a given topic or performances of a given piece of music. Although judges can reliably assess the superior quality of the product, it is difficult to analyze such products in order to identify the measurable aspects capturing the superior quality of the product. Hence, in their analysis of expertise in writing, Scardamalia and Bereiter (chapter 7, this volume) focus on systematic characteristics of the cognitive processes involved in designing and writing a text in an effort to differentiate expert from novice writers.

It is, of course, possible to give up the hope of designing a collection of tasks that could capture the full extent of the superior performance and focus instead on one or more well-defined activities involved in the expertise or measuring knowledge about the task domain. In adopting such an approach, one no longer can be certain that one is examining cognitive structures and processes essential to the superior performance. Occasionally, expected differences between the performance of novices and that of experts in component activities are not found. For example, Lewis (1981) found no reliable differences in performance on algebra problems between expert mathematicians and the top third of a group of college students. The most frequently studied activity related to expert performance is memory for meaningful stimuli from the task domain.

Tasks focusing on domain-specific memory performance. In the context of the difficulties of identifying a collection of tasks that can capture the expertise, it is easy to see the attractiveness of studying memory performance. It is possible to evaluate memory performance for presented information by means of recognition and reproduction of literal details (e.g., correct placement of chess pieces), which does not involve any in-depth analysis of tasks or prior knowledge in the given domain. Large samples of different meaningful stimuli can relatively easily be extracted from a given domain even though no formal description of the corresponding population of stimuli is given. Similarly, it is relatively easy to assemble unrepresentative or even meaningless stimuli by recombining stimulus elements in an arbitrary or random manner.

In a wide range of different domains, experts have been shown to display superior memory performance for representative stimuli from their domains of expertise when adaptations of Chase and Simon's (1973) original procedure have been used: chess (for a review, see Charness, chapter 2 this volume); bridge (Charness, 1979; Engle & Bukstel, 1978); go (Reitman, 1976); music notation (Sloboda, 1976); electronic circuit diagrams (Egan & Schwartz, 1979); computer programming (McKeithen, Reitman, Rueter, & Hirtle, 1981); dance, basketball, and field hockey (Allard & Starkes, chapter 5, this volume). Other studies have shown superior retention of domain-related information as a function of the subject's amount of knowledge of the domain, such as baseball (Chiesi, Spilich, & Voss, 1979; Spilich, Vesonder, Chiesi, & Voss, 1979; Voss, Vesonder, & Spilich, 1980) or soccer (Morris, Gruneberg, Sykes, & Merrick, 1981; Morris, Tweedy, & Gruneberg, 1985). Hence, many studies have found evidence supporting a monotonic relation between recall performance for a domain and expertise in that domain. There are, however, several lines of research that have questioned the generality of that relation. Sloboda (chapter 6, this volume) points out the striking similarity in accuracy and structure of recall of presented melodies between musicians and nonmusicians, which he attributes to shared extensive experience with music. Allard and Starkes (chapter 5, this volume) show that superior recall of briefly presented game situations by elite players, as compared with intramural players, is not always found in sports with speed stress, such as volleyball. Finally, Patel and Groen (chapter 4, this volume) demonstrate that levels of medical expertise have nonmonotonic relations to the amounts of information recalled from presented medical cases, which they attribute in part to the ability of experts to efficiently identify the information relevant to the medical diagnosis. These findings show that superior memory performance is not an inevitable consequence of attaining expertise.

It is thus questionable that a collection of tasks to measure the superior memory of experts can be claimed to really capture the expertise in question. With the exception of experts on memory tasks, superior performance by experts in many domains does not include explicit tests of memory performance. Moreover, there is no reason to believe that experts explicitly train with the goal of increasing their memory performance. It is therefore unlikely that their memory performance would have reached a stable maximum. We shall later discuss in more detail the cognitive processes relating memory performance and expertise.

An issue shared by studies of superior memory performance and studies of superior performance in other realms is the problem of determining the stimulus characteristics necessary to evoke performance in the laboratory analogous to real-life expertise.

Finding the appropriate stimuli to evoke superior performance. In capturing
expert-level performance, one attempts to create a situation that is maximally
simple and yet sufficiently similar to the real-life situation to allow the reproduction of the expertise under laboratory conditions. The mere demonstration that an expert-level performance can be reproduced under controlled
laboratory conditions reveals something important about the mechanisms underlying the corresponding expertise. It reduces the number of possible stimulus variables that are critical to performance, and it can also eliminate a
number of systematic covariations that would make the real-life performance
much easier than it would initially appear. Despite the critical importance of
the process of finding appropriate stimuli to evoke superior performance, that
process has rarely been documented. Ericsson and Polson (1988a, 1988b)
investigated the ability of expert waiters and waitresses to match meal orders
to customers. They reproduced under laboratory conditions the superior memory performance related to dinner orders by simulating actual customers with
photos of faces. Similarly, Bennett (1983) reproduced the superior memory
performance related to drink orders by cocktail waitresses in a simulated
situation with dolls representing customers. Hence, highly schematic stimuli
are sufficient to elicit the perceptual and representational mechanisms that
mediate superior memory performance. Similarly, Chase and Simon (1973)
found that the memory performance of two chess experts did not differ for
chessboards with real pieces and schematic diagrams of chess positions,
whereas a beginner at chess showed poorer recall with schematic diagrams
because of lack of familiarity with the diagram notation. When they exposed a
chess expert to an unfamiliar type of letter diagram representing the chess
positions, his memory performance was only half as good as his performance
with a real board. But after only 16 trials, his performance with the unfamiliar
diagrams had improved to the level of his performance with the real board.
Charness (chapter 2, this volume) provides a review of the current research
using different visual representations of chess positions.

There is some evidence that there are limits to the extent to which stimuli
can be abstracted. Gilhooly, Wood, Kinnear, and Green (1988) demonstrated
that the lack of superior memory performance by expert map users, as compared with the novices studied by Thorndyke and Stasz (1980), could be
attributed to their use of schematic maps (mainly used by tourists) as stimuli.
By studying recall of both schematic maps and more advanced contour maps
by expert and novice map users, Gilhooly et al. (1988) found, as expected,
superior memory of contour maps by the experts, but no differences between
experts and novices for the commonly available schematic maps. The fact that
superior performances can be reproduced in the laboratory with schematic
stimuli is important not only for practical purposes but also for theoretical
analyses of the mediating mechanisms.

The issues of how to design representative laboratory tasks are discussed in
many chapters in this volume. For example, Patel and Groen (chapter 4, this
volume) consider the differences between medical diagnoses based on written

texts presenting medical cases and diagnoses based on interviews with real patients. Dörner and Schölkopf (chapter 9, this volume) report on the management of simulations of very complex systems.

Summary. The essential first step of the study of expert performance involves identifying a collection of standardized tasks that can capture the superior performance under controlled conditions. It is a necessary condition for further analysis that superior performance by experts be reliably shown for the designed tasks. In complex domains it is often especially difficult to identify a population of tasks to capture the expertise; it may be possible to identify instead a small number of representative tasks to elicit superior performance. Nonetheless, it may be useful to think of expertise in terms of a corresponding population of tasks. Various experts may, however, require different populations of tasks. Patel and Groen (chapter 4, this volume) show that with increasing expertise in medicine, experts become more specialized in particular areas of medicine. Similar specialization is to be expected in most complex domains. To capture specialized expertise adequately, it is necessary to design special populations of tasks appropriate for a small group of experts or even individual experts (case studies). Superior memory performance by an expert is a legitimate subject for study as long as we keep in mind that the processes underlying the superior memory performance may only partially overlap with those that generally underlie the superior performance of experts.

The fact that it is possible to reproduce expert performance in a laboratory task has important theoretical implications. It reduces the significance of large numbers of factors that influence complex real-life situations. Furthermore, it indicates a fair degree of generalizability, especially concerning the detailed stimulus representation. Let us now turn to further analysis of the processes that mediate superior performance.

Analysis of expert performance: the second step

After identifying collection of tasks that can capture the superior performance of experts, one can apply the full range of methods of analysis in cognitive psychology to examine the phenomena associated with a particular type of expertise. In the following sections we present a brief outline of the wide range of observations that can be made to infer information about the processes mediating superior performance. We then discuss different research paradigms, such as comparisons of performance by experts and novices in a small number of tasks, and extended analysis of individual experts. Finally, we report on analyses of particular types of superior performance, such as superior memory performance.

Performance analysis: methods of inferring mediating processes. It is clear that one cannot directly observe mediating cognitive processes, but what can be

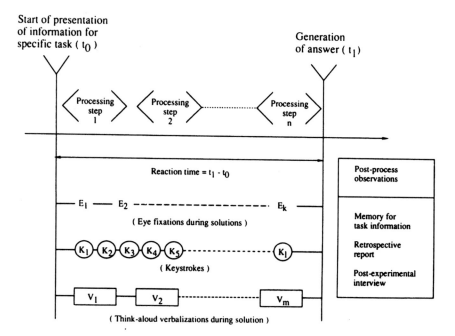

Figure 1.1. An overview of different types of observations on cognitive processes mediating performance on a task, adapted from a figure in Ericsson and Oliver (1988).

observed concurrently with cognitive processes can be related to the underlying cognitive processes within the information-processing theory of cognition. Figure 1.1 shows a number of different types of observations that can be collected on any cognitive process. At the top of Figure 1.1, cognitive processing is represented schematically as a series of internal processing steps, as proposed by the information-processing theory of human cognition. These internal processing steps cannot, of course, be observed directly, but it is possible to specify hypotheses about the relations between the internal processing steps and observable behavior. For example, when a subject fixes his or her gaze on a specific item in a visually presented table of information, we can infer that the corresponding internal steps involve processing that information. On the basis of veridical recall of the presented information after the task has been completed and the presented information is no longer available to the subject, one can infer that that information was processed during the completion of the task. In research on transcription typing, it is possible to determine what part of the text the typist is looking at and what part of the text is simultaneously being typed. The general finding is that the higher the skill level of the typist, the farther ahead in the text the typist looks during typing. Being able to look ahead in the text appears to be critical to the superior typing speeds of expert typists, because when their freedom to look ahead is experimentally restricted, their typing speeds are reduced to levels approaching those for novice typists (Salthouse, 1984, chapter 11, this volume).

It is possible to extend our analysis beyond the processing of presented information and consider one's access of preexisting knowledge and procedures. In that case, a *task analysis* of the particular task should be performed before the data collection. A task analysis involves specifying a number of different sequences of processing steps that could generate the correct answer for a specific task given the subjects' preexisting knowledge. In well-defined task domains, such as mental multiplication or problem solving in logic, it is relatively easy to specify nearly exhaustively the different sequences of processing steps leading to a correct answer in an efficient manner. In more complex domains, the a priori task analysis makes explicit the pool of hypothesized processing sequences that is being considered. On the basis of the think-aloud verbalizations of subjects, one can determine only that the verbalized information was accessed. A task analysis is critical for relating the verbalized information to the underlying cognitive processes leading to its access or generation (Ericsson & Simon, 1984).

Analysis of think-aloud verbalizations is time-consuming, and therefore researchers in expertise using these types of data tend to collect data on many subjects for a small number of tasks (expert–novice comparisons) or to collect data on individual subjects for a large number of tasks (case studies).

Expert–novice comparisons. Comparison of think-aloud verbalizations by experts and novices is the best-known method of assessing differences in the mediating processes as functions of the subjects' levels of expertise: Subjects at different levels of expertise are asked to think aloud while carrying out a small number of representative tasks. The number of tasks usually is not sufficient for assessing stable characteristics of individual subjects; the focus is on comparing the groups of subjects to identify salient differences in regard to mediating knowledge and processes.

The types of differences found in a wide range of domains of expertise are remarkably consistent with those originally noted by de Groot (1978) in the domain of chess. Expert performers tend to retrieve a solution method (e.g., next moves for a chess position) as part of the immediate comprehension of the task, whereas less experienced subjects have to construct a representation of the task deliberately and generate a step-by-step solution, as shown by research on physics problems (Anzai, chapter 3, this volume; Chi, Glaser, & Rees, 1982; Larkin, McDermott, Simon, & Simon, 1980; Simon & Simon, 1978) and algebra-word problems (Hinsley, Hayes, & Simon, 1977). Medical experts generate their diagnoses by studying the symptoms (forward reasoning), whereas less experienced medical students tend to check the correctness of a diagnosis by inspecting relevant symptoms (backward reasoning) (Patel & Groen, chapter 4, this volume).

On the same theme, expert performers have a body of knowledge that not only is more extensive than that for nonexperts but also is more accessible (Feltovich, Johnson, Moller, & Swanson, 1984; Johnson et al., 1981; Voss, Greene, Post, & Penner, 1983). Whenever knowledge is relevant, experts appear to access it efficiently (Jeffries, Turner, Polson, & Atwood, 1981). The experts are therefore able to notice inconsistencies rapidly, and thus inconsistent hypotheses are rejected rapidly in favor of the correct diagnosis (Feltovich et al., 1984; Johnson et al., 1981). On presentation, information in the problem is integrated with the relevant domain knowledge (Patel & Groen, 1986, chapter 4, this volume).

Similar characteristics of expert performance are found across different domains of expertise. The studies cited earlier suggest several important characteristics that can be more effectively studied in relation to tasks particularly designed to elicit them in a more controlled manner. We shall consider such research shortly.

Extensive case studies of single subjects. In contrast to the group studies discussed earlier, in which small numbers of tasks were used to elicit the cognitive processes of experts, we shall briefly consider two examples of research efforts that have used detailed case studies in order to describe the cognitive processes underlying superior performance.

The first example draws on several case studies of calendar calculations. Calendar calculation is the rather astounding ability to name the day of the week on which a given date falls. For example, when asked on what day of the week August 5, 1934, fell, such a subject would be able to say, correctly, that it was a Sunday. A major interest in this curious ability derives from the fact that several individuals with this skill have been severely mentally retarded, and little is known about how the ability emerged or was acquired. Analysis of this performance is further complicated by the low intelligence of the subjects. On the basis of a task analysis, where no knowledge about calculation can be assumed for these mentally retarded subjects, one is led to assume that the subjects must have memorized the information for all dates.

Investigators have examined a fairly large number of individuals for whom the ability of calendar calculation has been substantiated (for reviews, see Ericsson & Faivre, 1988, and Howe & Smith, 1988). Most calendar calculators can demonstrate that ability for only a limited range of years. All such subjects examined have been unable to explain how they know the correct answers. Some investigators, however, have been able to assess mediating steps by analyzing these subjects' mumblings prior to reporting an answer. Other investigators have been able to obtain informative retrospective reports on mediating steps. The most reasonable conclusion seems to be that the detailed structures of these subjects' processes differ from subject to subject and rely on a combination of memory for specific dates and some limited specialized calculation (Howe & Smith, 1988). The rare calendar calculators whose abilities extend from A.D. 0 to A.D. 999,999 appear to use a version of known algorithms that can be mastered by a graduate student within a couple of weeks to reach a comparable level of performance (Addis & Parson, described in Ericsson & Faivre, 1988).

A second example of single-subject research to analyze expert performance draws on the many case studies of memory experts. Studies of expert memory performances are particularly suited for the laboratory and can capitalize on the long tradition of experimental research on memory. The same research tradition has primarily used stimuli that have been selected to be meaningless, or at least has minimized the role of knowledge in order to capture basic memory processes. It has, however, been difficult to account for vastly superior memory performance within this tradition, and occasionally investigators have suggested that such exceptional individuals are endowed with structurally different memory systems (Luria, 1968; Wechsler, 1952). Analysis of expert memory performance is difficult even in the information-processing tradition, because it is virtually impossible to conduct an a priori task analysis specifying the mediating processing steps and the relevant knowledge used to store information efficiently in memory.

One of the methods available is to use think-aloud and retrospective verbal reports to identify the knowledge used by an individual memory expert and experimentally evaluate hypotheses about the mediating role of that knowledge. For each individual expert it is possible to hypothesize which stimuli could and could not be successfully encoded using the uncovered mediating knowledge. By comparing memory performances for compatible and incompatible stimuli, it is possible to validate hypotheses about the mediating knowledge using the general method developed by Chase and Simon (1979). In a study of a long-distance runner who acquired an exceptional digit span through extended training, Chase and Ericsson (1981) found that the runner encoded sequences of three digits (513) as familiar running times (5 minutes and 13 seconds in a mile race) whenever possible. When the runner was presented with experimentally prepared sequences of triplets of digits that could not be encoded as running times (483 would be 4 minutes and 83 seconds), his digit-span performance was dramatically reduced, and for prepared sequences of triplets all of which could be encoded as running times, his performance was reliably improved over his performance with random digit sequences. Similarly, Sloboda (chapter 6, this volume) shows that superior memory performance for classical music by idiots savants is mediated by knowledge of that type of music and cannot be generalized to modern atonal music.

Case studies of memory experts have revealed that the knowledge used to encode the presented information varies greatly from expert to expert. Similarly, the details of the acquired cognitive structures (retrieval structures) to store information in retrieval form in long-term memory also differ. Chase and Ericsson (1982; Ericsson, 1985), however, found three principles of skilled memory that described the general characteristics of essentially all memory experts who have been systematically studied.

Studies of particular aspects of expert performance. Up to this point we have discussed studies of expert performance using tasks selected to capture the essence of that performance. It was pointed out that in many cases particular cognitive activities associated with expertise could be identified that could be more effectively examined in tasks designed to focus on those particular cognitive activities. For example, in their study of experts in physics, Chi et al. (1981) focused on the initial encoding of physics problems to account for these experts' immediate availability of plans for complete solutions to those problems. They asked experts and novices to sort a large number of physics problems into categories of similar problems. Consistent with the hypothesis that experts' encodings would incorporate information about solution methods, the experts' categories of problems reflected the physical principles underlying the solutions, whereas the novices' categories were based on the situations and objects mentioned in the problem text. In this case, the knowledge uncovered stands in close correspondence to the knowledge evoked during the solution of the physics problems. Several other investigators have used similar sorting methods to assess the immediate encodings of mathematical problems (Berger & Wilde, 1987; 1981), as well as encodings of pictures of situations in team sports (Allard & Starkes, chapter 5, this volume). It is, of course, possible to examine the knowledge of experts more generally. In their study of representation of expert knowledge, Olson and Biolsi (chapter 10, this volume) discuss a wide range of methods. Attempts to measure knowledge about chess directly with psychometric tests have been quite successful, and scores on these tests show a clear correlation with rated chess performance (Charness, chapter 2, this volume).

During a study of the selection of the best move for an unfamiliar chess position, de Groot (1978) also found that the critical differences in cognitive processes relating to chess expertise occurred within the initial perception of the chess position. After a brief exposure to an unfamiliar chess position, the chess masters could give very informative verbal reports about the perceived characteristics of the presented chess position, along with virtually perfect recall of the locations of all chess pieces. In subsequent research, superior memory performance and superior perceptual performance of experts have been studied in specially designed tasks.

As reported earlier, Chase and Simon (1973) accounted for the superior memory performance of chess masters in terms of their storage of chess positions in short-term memory using complex independent chunks of chess pieces. The assumptions of storage in short-term memory and of independence of chunks have been seriously questioned by more recent investigators. Carefully designed studies of superior memory performance for chess positions, as reviewed by Charness (chapter 2, this volume), showed that chess experts store information about chess positions in long-term memory, not solely in short-term memory as Chase and Simon (1973) originally proposed.

Subsequent researchers have questioned Chase and Simon's (1973) assumption that chunks of chess pieces were distinct and that a given chess piece could therefore belong to only a single chunk. Chi (1978) showed that occasionally a chess piece can belong to more than one chunk, a finding that suggests relations between the chunks from a given chess position. On the basis of retrospective verbal reports of grand masters and masters after brief exposures to chess positions, de Groot (1978) found clear evidence of perception of chess pieces in chunks, or complexes, as well as of encodings relating chunks to one another to form a global encoding of the position. It appears necessary to assume that global and integrating encodings account for the ability of chess experts to recall accurately more than one briefly presented chess position at a single trial (Frey & Adesman, 1976).

In analyses of superior memory performance in domains other than chess, evidence of global integration of the presented information has also been found (Egan & Schwartz, 1979; Reitman, 1976). Studies in other domains, however, have also revealed differences from the findings regarding chess experts. In domains with complex stimuli, such as medicine (Patel & Groen, chapter 4, this volume) and computer programming (Adelson, 1984), it is clear that part of the integration of the presented information involves identification of the relevant and critical information, and any analysis of subsequent recall must distinguish between relevant and irrelevant information. For different domains of expertise, the processes of encoding presented information will be quite different, depending on the demands of the particular type of expertise (Allard & Starkes, chapter 5, this volume). Expert dancers display superior memory for presented dance sequences, whereas skilled volleyball players can detect the location of the volleyball with superior speed. Superior perceptual processing has also been demonstrated as a function of chess expertise for tasks involving simple perceptual judgments about critical aspects of presented chess positions (Charness, chapter 2, this volume).

General comments on the analysis of expert performance. Once the expert performance can be elicited by a collection of tasks in the laboratory, the full range of methods in cognitive science can be applied to assess the mediating cognitive structures and processes. The mediating mechanism for an expert performance should be stable and not much influenced by the additional experience in the laboratory, as the laboratory experience will constitute only a minor fraction of the experts' total experience of tasks in their domains. In fact, an absence of further improvement during extended laboratory testing should provide a nice index for evaluating our ability to capture the mechanisms underlying the real-life expertise.

On the basis of this argument, one immediately realizes some potential dangers of studying aspects of "real" expert performance with tasks not encountered in the normal environments of the experts. If we provide an expert with unfamiliar tasks, we need to consider the possibility that the expert may resort to nonoptimal and unstable strategies that can be rapidly improved even during just a couple of sessions. With respect to memory for briefly presented chess positions, Ericsson and Oliver (Ericsson & Staszewski, 1989) found substantial improvement in the memory performance of a candidate chess master during a few months of testing. They found no evidence of changes in the mediating processes, however, only a marked speedup of the processes.

We have been unable to find much evidence concerning the effects of extended testing of experts. Ericsson (1985) reported several instances of marked improvements in the performance of memory experts when they were observed on several test occasions. In several cases the tests were separated by several years, and one cannot distinguish between the effects of testing and the improvement due to accumulated experience outside the laboratory. Ericsson and Polson (1988b) found continual improvements in their expert waiter's performance of their standard task during about two years of weekly testing. It is likely that part of the observed speedup resulted from the particular constraints of the dinner orders studied. A more important determinant of the speedup, however, was the fact that the real-life task of memorizing dinner orders was not constrained by speed, because the customers required more time to decide on their dinner selections than the waiter needed to memorize them. Only in the laboratory situation with preselected dinner orders did the time required for memorization become critical.

In sum, differences between real-life situations and analogous laboratory tasks with respect to demands for maximum speed and the presented perceptual information are likely to lead to practice effects, even for experts, during extended testing. But as long as the practice effects for the experts remain comparatively small and the performance of the experts remains reliably superior to those for novices even after extended practice, we would claim that such a collection of tasks can successfully capture the superior expert performance.

The effects of extended practice for novices will provide a major source of empirical evidence as we now turn to a review of theoretical accounts of how the superior performance of experts can be acquired through extensive training.

Accounting for superior performance by experts: the third step

In all the studies discussed earlier, the assessed mechanisms mediating superior performance implicated cognitive structures that were specific to the relevant task domains. The nature of the mediating cognitions allows us to infer that they reflect acquired knowledge and previous experiences in the domain. In order to account for those aspects of superior performance that are acquired, it is critical to understand the role of knowledge acquisition and the important effects of practice and training for their acquisition.

When we restrict ourselves to those task domains in which superior performance has been adequately captured, the empirical findings can be summarized relatively easily. The superior performance consists of faster response times for the tasks in the domain, such as the superior speed of expert typists, pianists, and Morse code operators. In addition, chess experts exhibit superior ability to plan ahead while selecting a move (Charness, 1981). In a wide range of task domains, experts have been found to exhibit superior memory performance.

What is acquired by experts? Superior performance in different domains reflects processes and knowledge specific to the particular domain. The challenge is to account for the widest range of empirical phenomena with the smallest of learning mechanisms and processes responsible for changes as a function of long-term practice. Because it is not possible to observe subjects during a decade of intensive practice, most of the empirical evidence is based on extrapolation of changes in performance found as a result of practice at laboratory tasks over much shorter terms. Another important constraint is that the proposed descriptions cannot posit performance capacities that would violate the known limits of human information processing.

In this section we shall consider various accounts concerning the processes and knowledge that experts have acquired. We shall first briefly describe the Chase and Simon theory of expertise. Then we shall briefly review some of the empirical evidence concerning speedup of performance, superior memory performance, and superior ability to plan, with the intent of pointing to issues requiring further attention and elaboration.

The Chase and Simon theory. Chase and Simon (1973) argued that the main differences among masters, experts, and novices in a wide range of domains were related to their immediate access to relevant knowledge. Chase and Simon's (1973) elegant theoretical account of chess expertise provided an account of how the masters rapidly retrieved the best move possibilities from long-term memory. The recognized configurations of chess pieces (chunks) served as cues to elicit the best move possibilities, which had been stored in memory at an earlier time. The chess masters' richer vocabulary of chunks thus played a critical role in the storage and retrieval of superior chess moves.

Within the same theoretical framework, the speedup in selecting moves can be accounted for in terms of recognition of chess configurations and direct retrieval of knowledge about appropriate move selections. Similarly, Chase and Simon (1973) proposed that the superior memory performance for the briefly presented chess positions was due to recognition of familiar configurations of chess pieces by the masters. The near-perfect recall by the chess masters, involving more than twenty chess pieces, was assumed to be mediated by approximately seven chunks or configurations – within the postulated limits of short-term memory.

Finally, with respect to planning, Chase and Simon (1973) outlined a mechanism whereby the experts' chess knowledge could be accessed in response to internally planned moves in the mind's eye. Given that no evidence was available to show that the depth of planning increased with a rise in the level of expertise (Charness, 1981), they did not consider the acquisition of such a mechanism.

Accounts focusing on practice and learning. Across a wide range of tasks, an improvement in performance is a direct function of the amount of practice, and this relation can be remarkably accurately described by a power function (Newell & Rosenbloom, 1981). This consistent relation between performance and practice has been given a theoretical account by Newell and Rosenbloom (1981) using a uniform mechanism of learning chunks, which they explicitly relate to Chase and Simon's (1973) analysis of chess expertise.

It is possible to describe skill acquisition in a broader range of tasks and domains in which the subject at the outset does not have the prerequisite knowledge to produce error-free performance. In systematizing a large body of data on the acquisition of skills, Fitts (1964) proposed three different acquisition stages: The "cognitive stage" is characterized by an effort to understand the task and its demands and to learn to what information one must attend. The "associative stage" involves making the cognitive processes efficient to allow rapid retrieval and perception of required information. During the "autonomous stage," performance is automatic, and conscious cognition is minimal. More recently, Anderson (1982) provided a theoretical model with three different learning mechanisms, each corresponding to a stage of the Fitts model. Anderson was able to derive a power law for relating performance to the amount of practice.

It is clear that the learning mechanisms that mediate increasing improvements from repeated practice trials must play important roles in the acquisition of expertise. It may even be useful to consider such mechanisms with an eye to identifying some limits to their applicability.

First, it is important to distinguish between practice and mere exposure or experience. It is well known that learning requires feedback in order to be effective. Hence, in environments with poor or even delayed feedback, learning may be slow or even nonexistent. Making predictions and forecasts for complex environments that are dynamically changing can present difficult information-extraction problems, which may, at least in part, account for the poor performance of expert consultants and decision-makers (Camerer & Johnson, chapter 8, this volume). In addition, merely performing a task does not ensure that subsequent performance will be improved. From everyday experience, anyone can cite countless examples of individuals whose performance never appears to improve in spite of more than 10 years of daily activity at a task. These observations deserve to be considered in more detail, but we shall limit ourselves to one issue relevant to research on expertise: On the basis of the foregoing considerations, one should be particularly careful about accepting one's number of years of experience as an accurate measure of one's level of expertise.

Second, the learning mechanisms discussed can account only for making the initial cognitive processes more efficient and ultimately automatic. In real-life perceptual motor skills, there exist a wide range of motor movements that can allow realization of a given goal. There is good evidence from sports that the beginner's spontaneously adopted baseline strokes in tennis or basic strokes in swimming are nonoptimal and that it is impossible to improve their efficiency by iterative refinement. Hence, the first thing a coach will do when beginners start training is to have them relearn their basic strokes to achieve correct form. Only then can the basic motor patterns be perfected through further training. It is thus possible that the final performance levels may reflect differences in the initial representations used by different subjects.

Third, once we are willing to consider the effects that result from weeks, months, and years of daily practice, it is likely that we cannot limit the consideration to purely cognitive effects on the central nervous system. Research on sports performance shows that extensive and intensive training is associated with a full range of changes related to the blood supply and the efficiency of muscles (Ericsson, 1990). Such changes will influence the speed of performance. It is possible that the correlations concerning speed of movements, as measured by maximum rate of tapping and speed of typewriting (Keele & Hawkins, 1982; Salthouse, 1984), should be considered not only as reflections of inherited characteristics but also as adaptations of the motor system during years of practice.

Finally, and most important, these types of learning mechanisms focus only on how performance can be made faster and more efficient; they do not take into account the acquisition of new cognitive structures, processes that are prerequisites for the unique ability of experts to plan and reason about problem situations.

Accounts focusing on memory functioning. The Chase-Simon hypothesis that the superior memory of the expert reflects storage of more complex independent chunks in short-term memory has been seriously questioned, and most of the empirical evidence also suggests storage of interrelated information in long-term memory, as mentioned earlier. Even without the constraints of independence of chunks and storage in a limited-capacity short-term memory, human information-processing theory suggests a number of limits and processing constraints that must be taken into consideration in any acceptable account. But let us first review some of the empirical characteristics of the superior memory of experts.

Over a broad range of domains, experts have superior memory restricted to information in their domains of expertise. Furthermore, de Groot (1978) and Chase and Simon (1973) found that chess skill among a small number of subjects was monotonically related to their memory performance, which would suggest a high correlation between skill level and memory performance. Subsequent studies with representative samples involving large numbers of subjects found reliable correlations, but the strength of the association was lower than would have been expected from the Chase-Simon theory (Charness, chapter 2, this volume; Holding, 1985).

Although experts with decades of experience nearly always exhibit memory performance superior to that of subjects lacking expertise, there is at least one intriguing counterexample: Even though experts in mental calculation show far better memory performance for numbers than do normal subjects, their performance is far inferior to that of subjects who have practiced memorizing digits over extended periods (Chase & Ericsson, 1982; Ericsson, 1985). Whereas the mental-calculation experts rely predominantly on their vast mathematical knowledge of numbers, the trained subjects draw on a variety of knowledge essentially unrelated to mathematics. The most important difference between mental calculators and memory experts is that mental calculators require years and decades of practice to achieve memory performance comparable to what can be achieved by normal subjects after 50–100 hours of practice in a memory task. Hence, it is possible that the superior memory performance of experts has only a weak association with their expert knowledge.

Similarly, superior memory for briefly presented chess positions can be trained. Ericsson and Harris (1989) found that after 50 hours of practice, a subject without chess-playing experience was able to recall chess positions at a level of accuracy approaching that of some chess masters. In similarity to the digit-span experts, a close examination of the mediating processes revealed that the subject's performance was mediated by perceptually salient configurations of chess pieces, without implications for playing chess. Hence, it appears that by means of practice directed toward improving memory of performance, subjects without expertise can, after a couple of months of daily practice, match or surpass the superior memory performance of experts.

To account for the results concerning memory experts and long-term training studies, Chase and Ericsson (1981, 1982; Ericsson, 1985, 1988; Ericsson & Staszewski, 1989) proposed a skilled-memory theory to account for how memory performance can be improved within the known limits of human information processing. Chase and Ericsson proposed that experts can develop skilled memory to rapidly store and retrieve information using long-term memory for information in their domains of expertise. Building on the distinction between a limited short-term memory and a vast long-term memory, this theory sees the key problem to be selective access to information stored in long-term memory. Skilled-memory theory postulates that at the time of encoding, experts acquire a set of retrieval cues that are associated in a meaningful way with the information to be stored. At a later time, the desired information can be retrieved from long-term memory by using the appropriate retrieval cue. After extensive practice using a stable set of retrieval cues with meaningful information in the domain, one's speed of encoding and retrieval is assumed to approach that for short-term memory. The best empirical evidence regarding the structure and operation of skilled memory comes from studies of subjects who achieved exceptional levels of performance on the digit-span task (Chase & Ericsson, 1981, 1982; Staszewski, 1987). The retrieval cues used for rapid storage of meaningful encodings of three- and four-digit groups (up to a total of more than a hundred digits) can be used to access digits in presented matrices in a manner earlier believed to require a raw visual image (Ericsson & Chase, 1982). Studies of other types of expertise have given clear evidence for retrieval cues indexing content (e.g., specific intermediate products in mental calculation) (Ericsson & Staszewski, 1989; Staszewski, 1988).

The most direct evidence suggesting the use of retrieval structures in chess comes from a series of studies with a candidate chess master by Ericsson and Oliver (Ericsson & Staszewski, 1989). They found that the chess master could read the description of the sequence of chess moves in a game and mentally generate the sequence of intermediate chess positions almost as fast as he could play out similar chess games by actually moving the pieces on a chess-board. During the process of mentally playing out the chess games, sometimes they would interrupt him and test his ability to name the piece on a given square for the current chess position, which he could do within a few seconds. In other experiments, his speed of access to different types of information for a briefly presented middle-game chess position was examined. The chess master could name the piece located on a given square within a second, and within seconds he could report the number of his opponent's pieces that were attacking a given square, which suggests remarkable availability of many different types of information about the presented chess position. Ericsson and Oliver (Ericsson & Staszewski, 1989) found evidence for rapid and flexible retrieval using a retrieval structure. This research raises the possibility that acquisition of expert-level chess skill involves the development of skilled memory for chess positions.

Once it is accepted that mediating mechanisms are acquired, that raises a number of challenging issues. One can no longer assume that superior performance is automatically achieved merely as a function of practice. The history of expert memory performance provides a number of cases in which individuals who have had extensive practice and experience have settled for suboptimal methods. Crutcher and Ericsson (Ericsson & Polson, 1988b) found that several waiters and waitresses who on a daily basis memorized dinner orders relied on less effective encoding methods than did the expert waiter JC, who exhibited vastly superior performance. Chase and Ericsson (1981, 1982) documented extended problem-solving efforts by digit-span experts to identify strategies and encoding methods to increase their digit-span performance, as well as similar efforts by other subjects, whose performance never improved or did not improve beyond a certain level. When that evidence is considered together with studies of other memory experts (Ericsson, 1985; 1988) past and present, it appears that all memory experts rely on the same limited set of mechanisms (Chase & Ericsson, 1982). Given that most memory experts have not been instructed but have themselves discovered the structures necessary for their memory skills over extended periods, the importance of problem solving for their ultimate performance can hardly be overestimated. Similarly, studies of the development of a number of perceptual motor skills suggest the importance of discovered methods and strategies for performing tasks such as juggling (Norman, 1976). There appears to exist a wealth of phenomena such that successful performance in the future cannot be predicted on the basis of current performance. Similarly, there is no reason to believe that such problem solving is limited to the early stages in the development of expert performance.

Accounts focusing on the ability to plan and reason. Analyses in several different domains of expertise have revealed that experts engage in a number of complex mental activities involving reasoning that relies on mental models and internal representations. The most frequently studied activity has been the planning of chess moves. Charness (1981) found that the depth to which a possible move sequence for a chess position was explored was closely related to the level of chess skill, at least for chess players at or below the level of chess experts. Mental planning and evaluation of possible move sequences place greater demands on memory as the depth increases, and such a cognitive activity will be particularly tractable using acquired skilled memory to represent chess positions.

As noted earlier, de Groot (1978) found no reliable differences in regard to depth of search among advanced chess players with differing levels of chess ability. Holding (1985) suggested that the differences were too small to be detected, because of the small number of subjects. Charness (1989), however, presented a case study suggesting that the depth of search may increase with chess skill only up to some level of chess skill and then level off. One should also keep in mind that the task of searching for a move for a middle-game chess position is not designed to measure the capacity to make deep searches and hence may well reflect pragmatic criteria for sufficient depth of exploration to evaluate a prospective move.

In support of the findings of remarkable capacities to explore chess positions mentally, it is well known that chess players at the master level can play while blindfolded with only a minor reduction in chess capability without any prior specialized practice (Holding, 1985). In the absence of a strict time constraint, there appears to be no clear limit to the depth to which a chess master can explore a position. Ericsson and Oliver (Ericsson & Staszewski, 1989) found that a candidate chess master was able to access all the information about a mentally generated chess position rapidly and accurately, and they showed that the memory representation of the chess position was consistent with the characteristics of skilled-memory theory (Chase & Ericsson, 1982; Ericsson & Staszewski, 1989).

The need to represent and integrate large amounts of presented information internally is common to a wide range of different types of expertise. Charness (1989) showed that expertise at the game of bridge was closely linked with the capacity to generate successful plans for playing the cards in the optimum order. In medical diagnosis, the medical expert has to integrate many different pieces of information that are not simultaneously available perceptually. The internal representation of the presented medical information must be sufficiently precise to allow extensive reasoning and evaluation of consistency, but also must be sufficiently flexible to allow reinterpretation as new information becomes available (Lesgold et al., 1985; Patel & Groen, chapter 4, this volume). Anzai (chapter 3, this volume) reviews the critical role of effective representations in solving physics problems and how methods of generating such representations can be developed through practice. In order to account for expertise, it is essential to describe emerging skills for managing extended memory demands, as well as their efficient processing and manipulation.

Comments on the problem of accounting for expert performance. Chase and Simon (1973) may have been correct in their claim that access to aggregated past experience is the single most important factor accounting for the development of expertise. More recent research, however, shows that to describe the structure of expertise accurately, several other factors must be considered, ranging from acquired skill allowing for an extended working memory to increased physiological efficiency of the motor system due to adaptation to intensive practice. We believe that the research on superior expert performance is benefited more by the development of a taxonomy of different types of mechanisms acquired through different types of learning and adaptation processes than by restricting the definition of expertise to a specific type of acquisition through learning.

SUMMARY AND CONCLUSION

In this chapter we initially contrasted the study of expertise with a number of other approaches studying outstanding and superior performance, and we found that one distinguishing feature was the claim that the superior performance was predominantly acquired. Drawing on the pioneering work on chess, we identified three important steps in the study of expertise: first, identification of a collection of representative tasks by means of which the superior performance of experts can be reproduced; second, analysis of the cognitive processes mediating that performance, followed by design of experimental tasks to elicit the critical aspects of such performance in a purer form; third, theoretical and empirical accounts of how the identified mechanisms can be acquired through training and practice.

The most effective approach to organizing the results across different domains of expertise is to propose a small number of learning mechanisms that can account for the development of similar performance characteristics in different domains within the limits of human information capabilities. There is now overwhelming empirical support for the theory of acquisition of skill with mechanisms akin to those originally proposed by Chase and Simon (1973). They proposed their account as "simply a rough first approximation" (p. 252), and it would therefore make sense to seek a fuller account, both looking for the conditions limiting those principles and supplying other principles that can account for the complete range of performance capacities. Next we looked at some of those additional mechanisms. It would seem that one of the strengths of a generalized study of superior performances lies in a careful consideration of learning mechanisms and associated acquired characteristics uncovered across different domains.

We believe that both the excellent prospects and the clear-cut limitations of the expertise approach lie in its exacting methodological criteria, particularly the criterion that superior performance should be demonstrated as well as captured by a collection of laboratory tasks. To the extent that we are studying mechanisms and phenomena that have emerged as a result of intensive preparation during years or decades, we can be certain that tens or hundreds of hours of laboratory testing are not likely to alter their structure seriously. This affords excellent opportunities to examine and to describe carefully the mechanisms mediating the observed superior performance. In this regard, the superior expert performance is a phenomenon that is particularly well suited for laboratory study and experimental analysis.

A major limitation of the approach is the fact that many types of expertise have not yet been adequately captured. In some cases, the lack of success in capturing the essence of an expertise is so well documented that there may not be a legitimate phenomenon to study. Perhaps the most important limitation concerns the difficulty of studying the development of superior performance in real-life expertise. To understand the many factors underlying why some individuals attain the highest levels of performance whereas others do not, we need to broaden our approach. Indeed, in many cases we may well be forced to rely on correlational methods. As our ability to describe the structures of different types of expert performance improves, we shall be able to focus on the essential aspects, which can be monitored in longitudinal studies.

On the most general level, the study of expert performance provides us with a range of capacities and associated characteristics that can be acquired. A careful systematization of those should allow us to map out the potential for human performance that can be acquired through experience.

ACKNOWLEDGMENTS

The thoughtful suggestions and comments on earlier drafts of this chapter by Ralf Krampe, Natalie Sachs-Ericsson, Herbert Simon, and Clemens Tesch-Römer are gratefully acknowledged.

REFERENCES

Adelson, B. (1984). When novices surpass experts: The difficulty of the task may increase with expertise. *Journal of Experimental Psychology: Learning, Memory, and Cognition, 10,* 483–495.

Albert, R. S. (1983). Family positions and the attainment of eminence. In R. S. Albert (Ed.), *Genius and eminence* (pp. 141–154). Oxford: Pergamon Press. (Original work published 1980.)

Allard, F. & Burnett, N. (1985). Skill in sport. *Canadian Journal of Psychology, 39,* 294–312.

Anderson, J. R. (1982). Acquisition of cognitive skill. *Psychological Review, 89*, 369–406.

Bachem, A. (1937). Various types of absolute pitch. *Journal of the Acoustical Society of America, 9*, 146–151.

Baron, J. (1978). Intelligence and general strategies. In G. Underwood (Ed.), *Strategies in information processing* (pp. 403–450). London: Academic Press.

Bennett, H. L. (1983). Remembering drink orders: The memory skill of cocktail waitresses. *Human Learning, 2*, 157–169.

Berger, D. E., & Wilde, J. M. (1987). A task analysis of algebra word problems. In D. E. Berger, K. Pezdek, & W. P. Banks (Eds.), *Application of cognitive psychology: Problem solving, education and computing* (pp. 123–137). Hillsdale, NJ: Erlbaum.

Bloom, B. S. (Ed.). (1985). *Developing talent in young people*. New York: Ballantine Books.

Brady, P. T. (1970). The genesis of absolute pitch. *Journal of the Acoustical Society of America, 48*, 883–887.

Carroll, J. B. (1978). How shall we study individual differences in cognitive abilities? Methodological and theoretical perspectives. *Intelligence, 2*, 87–115.

Cattell, R. B. (1963). The personality and motivation of the researcher from measurements of contemporaries and from bibliography. In C. W. Taylor & F. Barron (Eds.), *Scientific creativity: Its recognition and development* (pp. 119–131). New York: Wiley.

Cattell, R. B., & Drevdahl, J. E. (1955). A comparison of the personality profile (16 PF) of eminent researchers with that of eminent teachers and administrators, and of the general population. *British Journal of Psychology, 46*, 248–261.

Charness, N. (1976). Memory for chess positions: Resistance to interference. *Journal of Experimental Psychology: Human Learning and Memory, 2*, 641–653.

Charness, N. (1979). Components of skill in bridge. *Canadian Journal of Psychology, 33*, 1–6.

Charness, N. (1981). Search in chess: age and skill differences. *Journal of Experimental Psychology: Human Perception and Performance, 7*, 467–476.

Charness, N. (1989). Expertise in chess and bridge. In D. Klahr & K. Kotovsky (Eds.), *Complex information processing: The impact of Herbert A. Simon* (pp. 183–208). Hillsdale, NJ: Erlbaum.

Chase, W. G., & Ericsson, K. A. (1981). Skilled memory. In J. R. Anderson (Ed.), *Cognitive skills and their acquisition* (pp. 141–189). Hillsdale, NJ: Erlbaum.

Chase, W. G., & Ericsson, K. A. (1982). Skill and working memory. In G. H. Bower (Ed.), *The psychology of learning and motivation* (Vol. 16, pp. 1–58). New York: Academic Press.

Chase, W. G., & Simon, H. A. (1973). The mind's eye in chess. In W. G. Chase (Ed.), *Visual information processing* (pp. 215–281). New York: Academic Press.

Chi, M. T. H. (1978). Knowledge structures and memory development. In R. S. Siegler (Ed.), *Children's thinking: What develops?* (pp. 73–96). Hillsdale, NJ: Erlbaum.

Chi, M. T. H., Feltovich, P. J., & Glaser, R. (1981). Categorization and representation of physics problems by experts and novices. *Cognitive Science, 5*, 121–152.

Chi, M. T. H., Glaser, R. & Rees, E. (1982). Expertise in problem solving. In R. S. Sternberg (Ed.), *Advances in the psychology of human intelligence* (Vol. 1, pp. 1–75). Hillsdale, NJ: Erlbaum.

Chiesi, H. L., Spilich, G. J., & Voss, J. F. (1979). Acquisition of domain-related information in relation to high and low domain knowledge. *Journal of Verbal Learning and Verbal Behavior, 18,* 257–273.

Cooper, L. A., & Regan, D. T. (1982). Attention, perception and intelligence. In R. J. Sternberg (Ed.), *Handbook of human intelligence* (pp. 123–169). Cambridge: Cambridge University Press.

de Groot, A. (1978). *Thought and choice in chess.* The Hague: Mouton. (Original work published 1946.)

Doll, J., & Mayr, U. (1987). Intelligenz und Schachleistung – eine Untersuchung an Schachexperten. [Intelligence and achievement in chess – a study of chess masters]. *Psychologische Beiträge, 29,* 270–289.

Egan, D. E., & Schwartz, B. J. (1979). Chunking in recall of symbolic drawings. *Memory and Cognition, 7,* 149–158.

Elo, A. E. (1978). *The rating of chessplayers, past and present.* London: Batsford.

Engle, R. W., & Bukstel, L. H. (1978). Memory processes among bridge players of differing expertise. *American Journal of Psychology, 91,* 673–689.

Ericsson, K. A. (1985). Memory skill. *Canadian Journal of Psychology, 39,* 188–231.

Ericsson, K. A. (1988). Analysis of memory performance in terms of memory skill. In R. J. Sternberg (Ed.), *Advances in the psychology of human intelligence* (Vol. 5, pp. 137–179). Hillsdale, NJ: Erlbaum.

Ericsson, K. A. (1990). Peak performance and age: An examination of peak performance in sports. In P. B. Baltes & M. M. Baltes (Eds.), *Successful aging: Perspectives from the behavioral sciences* (pp. 164–195). Cambridge: Cambridge University Press.

Ericsson, K. A., & Chase, W. G. (1982). Exceptional memory. *American Scientist, 70,* 607–615.

Ericsson, K. A., Chase, W. G., & Faloon, S. (1980). Acquisition of a memory skill. *Science, 208,* 1181–1182.

Ericsson, K. A., & Crutcher, R. J. (1990). The nature of exceptional performance. In P. B. Baltes, D. L. Featherman, & R. M. Lerner (Eds.), *Life-span development and behavior* (Vol. 10, pp. 187–217). Hillsdale, NJ: Erlbaum.

Ericsson, K. A., & Faivre, I. (1988). What's exceptional about exceptional abilities? In L. K. Obler & D. Fein (Eds.), *The exceptional brain: Neuropsychology of talent and special abilities* (pp. 436–473). New York: Guilford.

Ericsson, K. A., & Harris, M. (1989). *Acquiring expert memory performance without expert knowledge: A case study in the domain of chess.* Unpublished manuscript.

Ericsson, K. A., & Oliver, W. (1988). Methodology for laboratory research on thinking: Task selection, collection of observation and data analysis. In R. J. Sternberg & E. E. Smith (Eds.), *The psychology of human thought* (pp. 392–428). Cambridge University Press.

Ericsson, K. A., & Polson, P. G. (1988a). An experimental analysis of a memory skill for dinner-orders. *Journal of Experimental Psychology: Learning, Memory, and Cognition, 14,* 305–316.

Ericsson, K. A., & Polson, P. G. (1988b). Memory for restaurant orders. In M. Chi, R. Glaser, & M. Farr (Eds.), *The nature of expertise* (pp. 23–70). Hillsdale, NJ: Erlbaum.

Ericsson, K. A., & Simon, H. A. (1984). *Protocol analysis: Verbal reports as data.* Cambridge, MA: Bradford Books/MIT Press.

Ericsson, K. A., & Staszewski, J. (1989). Skilled memory and expertise: Mechanisms of exceptional performance. In D. Klahr & K. Kotovsky (Eds.), *Complex informa-*

tion processing: The impact of Herbert A. Simon (pp. 235–267). Hillsdale, NJ: Erlbaum.

Feltovich, P. J., Johnson, P. E., Moller, J. H., & Swanson, D. B. (1984). LCS: The role and development of medical knowledge in diagnostic expertise. In W. J. Clancey & E. H. Shortliffe (Eds.), *Readings in medical artificial intelligence* (pp. 275–319). Reading, MA: Addison-Wesley.

Fitts, P. M. (1964). Perceptual-motor skill learning. In A. W. Melton (Ed.), *Categories of human learning* (pp. 243–285). New York: Academic Press.

Frey, P. W., & Adesman, P. (1976). Recall memory for visually presented chess positions. *Memory and Cognition, 4,* 541–547.

Galton, F. (1869). *Hereditary genius.* New York: Macmillan.

Gilhooly, K. J., Wood, M., Kinnear, P. R., & Green, C. (1988). Skill in map reading and memory for maps. *Quarterly Journal of Experimental Psychology, 40A,* 87–107.

Guilford, J. P. (1967). *The nature of human intelligence.* New York: McGraw-Hill.

Hayes, J. R. (1981). *The complete problem solver.* Philadelphia: Franklin Institute Press.

Hinsley, D. A., Hayes, J. R., & Simon, H. A. (1977). From words to equations: Meaning and representation in algebra word problem. In M. A. Just & P. A. Carpenter (Eds.), *Cognitive processes in comprehension* (pp. 89–108). Hillsdale, NJ: Erlbaum.

Holding, D. H. (1985). *The psychology of chess skill.* Hillsdale, NJ: Erlbaum.

Howe, M. J. A., & Smith, J. (1988). Calendar calculating in "idiot savants": How do they do it? *British Journal of Psychology, 79,* 371–386.

Hunt, E. (1980). Intelligence as an information processing concept. *Journal of British Psychology, 71,* 449–474.

Jeffries, R., Turner, A. A., Polson, P. G., & Atwood, M. E. (1981). The processes involved in designing software. In J. R. Anderson (Ed.), *Cognitive skills and their acquisition* (pp. 255–283). Hillsdale, NJ: Erlbaum.

Johnson, P. E., Duran, A. A., Hassebrock, F., Moller, J., Prietula, M., Feltovich, P. J., & Swanson, D. B. (1981). Expertise and error in diagnostic reasoning. *Cognitive Science, 5,* 235–283.

Keele, S. W., & Hawkins, H. L. (1982). Explorations of individual differences relevant to high level skill. *Journal of Motor Behavior, 14,* 3–23.

Kelley, H. P. (1964). Memory abilities: A factor analysis. *Psychometric Society Monographs, 11,* 1–53.

Kliegl, R., Smith, J., & Baltes, P. B. (1989). Testing-the-limits and the study of adult age differences in cognitive plasticity of a mnemonic skill. *Developmental Psychology, 25,* 247–256.

Larkin, J., McDermott, J., Simon, D. P., & Simon, H. A. (1980). Expert and novice performance in solving physics problems. *Science, 208,* 1335–1342.

Lesgold, A., Rubinson, H., Feltovich, P., Glaser, R., Klopfer, D., & Wang, Y. (1985). *Expertise in a complex skill: Diagnosing X-ray pictures.* LRDC, University of Pittsburgh Technical Report.

Lewis, C. (1981). Skill in algebra. In J. R. Anderson (Ed.), *Cognitive skills and their acquisition* (pp. 85–110). Hillsdale, NJ: Erlbaum.

Luria, A. R. (1968). *The mind of a mnemonist.* New York: Avon.

McCurdy, H. G. (1983). The childhood pattern of genius. In R. S. Albert (Ed.), *Genius and eminence* (pp. 155–169). Oxford: Pergamon Press. (Original work published 1957.)

McKeithen, K. B., Reitman, J. S., Rueter, H. H., & Hirtle, S. C. (1981). Knowledge organization and skill differences in computer programmers. *Cognitive Psychology, 13,* 307–325.

Miller, G. A. (1956). The magical number seven, plus or minus two. *Psychological Review, 63,* 81–97.

Morris, P. E., Gruneberg, M. M., Sykes, R. N., & Merrick, A. (1981). Football knowledge and the acquisition of new results. *British Journal of Psychology, 72,* 479–483.

Morris, P. E., Tweedy, M., & Gruneberg, M. M. (1985). Interest, knowledge and the memorization of soccer scores. *British Journal of Psychology, 76,* 415–425.

Newell, A., & Rosenbloom, P. S. (1981). Mechanisms of skill acquisition and the law of practice. In J. R. Anderson (Ed.), *Cognitive skills and their acquisition* (pp. 1–55). Hillsdale, NJ: Erlbaum.

Newell, A., & Simon, H. A. (1972). *Human problem solving.* Englewood Cliffs, NJ: Prentice-Hall.

Norman, D. A. (1976). *Memory and attention* (2nd ed.). New York: Wiley.

Oakes, W. F. (1955). An experimental study of pitch naming and pitch discrimination reaction. *Journal of Genetic Psychology, 86,* 237–259.

Oden, M. H. (1968). The fulfillment of promise: Forty-year follow-up of the Terman gifted group. *Genetic Psychology Monographs, 77,* 3–93.

Patel, V. L., & Groen, G. L. (1986). Knowledge based solution strategies in medical reasoning. *Cognitive Science, 10,* 91–116.

Reitman, J. (1976). Skilled perception in go: Deducing memory structures from inter-response times. *Cognitive Psychology, 8,* 336–356.

Resnick, L. B. (Ed.). (1976). *The nature of intelligence.* Hillsdale, NJ: Erlbaum.

Roe, A. (1953). A psychological study of eminent psychologists and anthropologists, and a comparison with biological and physical scientists. *Psychological Monographs, 67,* 1–55.

Saariluoma, P. (1984). *Coding problem spaces in chess: A psychological study.* Helsinki: Societas Scientiarum Fennica.

Salthouse, T. A. (1984). Effects of age and skill in typing. *Journal of Experimental Psychology: General, 113,* 345–371.

Silver, E. A. (1981). Recall of mathematical information: Solving related problems. *Journal for Research and Mathematical Education, 12,* 54–64.

Simon, D. P., & Simon, H. A. (1978). Individual differences in solving physics problems. In R. S. Siegler (Ed.), *Children's thinking: What develops?* (pp. 325–348). Hillsdale, NJ: Erlbaum.

Simon, H. A., & Chase, W. G. (1973). Skill in chess. *American Scientist, 61,* 394–403.

Simon, H. A., & Gilmartin, K. (1973). A simulation of memory for chess positions. *Cognitive Psychology, 8,* 165–190.

Sloboda, J. (1976). Visual perception of musical notation: Registering pitch symbols in memory. *Quarterly Journal of Experimental Psychology, 28,* 1–16.

Spilich, G. J., Vesonder, G. T., Chiesi, H. L., & Voss, J. F. (1979). Text processing of domain-related information for individuals with high and low domain knowledge. *Journal of Verbal Learning and Verbal Behavior, 18,* 275–290.

Stanley, J. C., George, W. C., & Solano, C. H. (1977). *The gifted and creative: A fifty-year perspective.* Baltimore: Johns Hopkins University Press.

Staszewski, J. J. (1987). *The psychological reality of retrieval structures: An investiga-*

tion of expert knowledge. Unpublished doctoral dissertation, Cornell University, Ithaca, NY.

Staszewski, J. J. (1988). Skilled memory and expert mental calculation. In M. T. H. Chi, R. Glaser, & M. J. Farr (Eds.), *The nature of expertise* (pp. 71–128). Hillsdale, NJ: Erlbaum.

Sternberg, R. J. (Ed.). (1982). *Handbook of human intelligence.* Cambridge University Press.

Terman, L. M., & Oden, M. H. (1947). *Genetic studies of genius. Vol. 4: The gifted child grows up.* Stanford, CA: Stanford University Press.

Thorndyke, P. W., & Stasz, C. (1980). Individual differences in procedures for knowledge acquisition from maps. *Cognitive Psychology, 12,* 137–175.

Tyler, L. E. (1965). *The psychology of human differences.* New York: Appleton-Century-Crofts.

van Dijk, T. A., & Kintsch, W. (1983). *Strategies of discourse comprehension.* New York: Academic Press.

Varon, E. J. (1935). The development of Alfred Binet's psychology. *Psychological Monographs, 46* (Whole No. 207).

Voss, J. F., Greene, T. R., Post, T. A., & Penner, B. C. (1983). Problem-solving skill in the social sciences. *Psychology of Learning and Motivation, 17,* 165–213.

Voss, J. F., Vesonder, G. T., & Spilich, G. J. (1980). Text generation and recall by high-knowledge and low-knowledge individuals. *Journal of Verbal Learning and Verbal Behavior, 19,* 651–667.

Wechsler, D. (1952). *The range of human capacities.* Baltimore: Williams & Wilkins.

Wilson, R. S. (1986). Twins: Genetic influence on growth. In R. M. Malina & C. Bouchard (Eds.), *Sports and human genetics* (pp. 1–21). Champaign, IL: Human Kinetics Publishing.

2 Expertise in chess: the balance between knowledge and search

NEIL CHARNESS

Chess is a deceptively simple two-player game that involves alternation of moves of chess pieces on a chessboard. The player with the white pieces moves first, the player with the black pieces replies, and they continue to alternate moves until either one player is defeated or the position is agreed to be drawn.

The rules of chess are simple enough to be learned by children; yet to be able to play chess skillfully a player must practice and study for years. Simon and Chase (1973) suggested that no one reaches Grandmaster-level strength (a rating of approximately 2500–2600 points) in fewer than 9 or 10 years. (Recently, however, the young Hungarian star Judith Polgar achieved her first Grandmaster result by age 12.) The Elo chess rating system (Elo, 1978) rank-orders chess players with high accuracy. The skill scale (an interval scale of measurement) runs from a theoretical score of zero upward, with the highest-rated players in history reaching the 2700–2800 range. The mean rating in a large national chess organization usually is around 1500, with the standard deviation around 250 rating points.

Because of its unique properties – particularly its rating scale and its method of recording games – chess offers cognitive psychologists an ideal task environment in which to study skilled performance. It has been called a *Drosophila,* or fruit fly, for cognitive psychology (Charness, 1989; Simon & Chase, 1973).

In this chapter, I shall summarize some of the findings on expertise in chess. The theme being stressed is the opportunity for trading off knowledge and search to reach a single goal: skilled play. First, the extensive search capabilities of nonhuman chess players, computer chess programs, will be examined. Psychological investigations of human chess skill will then be reviewed to contrast the ways in which the two "species" achieve expertise. Then the knowledge base that humans have developed about chess will be assessed, using encyclopedic sources concerning the three phases of chess: the opening, the middle game, and the endgame. Some speculations will be advanced regarding what portion of this knowledge base the chess master may possess, and how such knowledge may be acquired. Finally, I shall look at whether knowledge accumulation and training in chess have meant better play, both over time and across chess federations. In closing, the extent to which an

39

understanding of chess skill can be of assistance in understanding other types of human skill will be briefly discussed.

COMPUTER CHESS SKILL

Because it is an intellectual activity, chess playing has been a subject of intensive investigation by those in the field of artificial intelligence (AI). Many predictions and wagers have been advanced concerning the possibility of getting a computer chess program to equal or exceed the performance of the best human practitioners. In the past ten years there has been steady improvement in the performances of chess programs. At the time of this writing, there are commercially available dedicated microcomputer programs that play at Master strength (2200+ rating points), meaning that these programs rank alongside the top 1 percent of human chess players. Top-level research programs, such as *Deep Thought* and *Hitech*, two programs developed at Carnegie-Mellon University, play at International Master strength (2300+) and have beaten human Grandmasters (2500+) in tournament games. (*Deep Thought* tied for first place in a strong tournament in 1988, playing at Grandmaster-level strength.) Current predictions (*Chess Life*, September 1989) suggest that world champion–level programs will be seen before the end of the century. Hsu, one of the programmers for *Deep Thought*, hopes to reach a search speed of a billion nodes per second in a few years (translating to a 14-ply full-width search).

Although much of the work in AI has been focused on finding ways to search the tree of move possibilities more quickly and efficiently, occasionally there have been projects that have explored more humanlike ways of choosing moves. Wilkins (1983) used a production-system knowledge base as the engine for his program PARADISE (PAttern Recognition Applied to DIrecting SEarch). It formed pattern-oriented, knowledge-driven plans about middle-game positions that were tactically active. The PARADISE program was able to find winning moves that were too deep to be discovered with standard search techniques. The intriguing aspect of his program is that knowledge enabled PARADISE to solve tactical problems with very small search trees (20–100 nodes), quite comparable to those generated by humans.

PARADISE notwithstanding, most programmers in chess AI have endorsed the idea of improving search techniques and have been concerned only minimally with embedding new knowledge into their programs. With the exception of the addition of more lines to already large libraries of opening moves, most programs have been improved through the use of faster or specialized hardware. Such programs can generate a 10-ply (or greater) full-width search tree in the middle game, by grinding out close to a million plies per second. (I think it is fair to say that in the battle between knowledge and search, PARADISE lost.) See Berliner (1981), Berliner and Ebeling (1989), and Schaeffer (1986) for discussion of the trade-offs between knowledge and search in computer chess.

Noteworthy is the strong showing of Berliner and Ebeling's (1989) *Hitech* program, which has moved somewhat in the direction of using chess knowledge to guide search. *Hitech* carries out an extensive full-width search, examining 175,000 positions per second, but does so by combining clever procedures for move generation and evaluation. Move generation and basic aspects of evaluation are implemented in fast hardware, though evaluation is also guided by chess knowledge in the form of down-loaded pattern recognizers that help order moves for search.

The information-processing demands imposed by extensive search place severe limits on how expertise can be achieved when humans are confronted with the problem of choosing the best move.

Anderson (1988) has argued that the information-retrieval demands that face an organism shape the cognitive architecture that evolves to meet those needs. His rational analysis of memory suggests that many memory phenomena – "signature" phenomena such as the fan effect, power-law learning, and massed versus spaced practice effects – can be explained by appealing to a simple model of an information-retrieval system. The system attempts to minimize computational costs. It aims to answer queries (the environment can be seen to pose the queries) and must balance the cost of searching for an item against the probability that a search attempt will retrieve the item.

Problem solving can also be cast in this light. The key feature driving human problem solving when the goal is not well defined is balancing search with evaluation. Evaluation demands knowledge. (Although chess is not typically thought of as an ill-defined problem-solving situation, it seems to qualify. What exactly is a "good move" or the "best move"? Much like judging creativity in art, determining the best move in chess in many situations requires asking the top practitioners in the discipline, Grandmasters, for their opinions.)

Consider search in chess, in which a player examines either the base position as it stands on the chessboard or a potential future position, generated in the mind's eye (Chase & Simon, 1973a). When "looking" at a chess position, humans and programs have to decide on the basis of a set of evaluation dimensions (piece balance, mobility, pawn structure, etc.) whether the position is favorable or unfavorable and, more important, whether it is quiescent (no obvious captures and checks remain) or whether more search is needed to reach a quiescent position. Humans use knowledge of chess relations to pinpoint the relevant features of a given position and to narrow the search to a few relevant lines. In some cases, particularly in the opening and endgame, the best move may simply be retrieved from memory in response to the pattern description that the players build up. But because few chess games follow identical paths beyond the opening phase, a search will almost always be necessary to verify a player's intuition concerning the best move.

Computer programs use very little evaluative information (some use little more than material balance), but develop enormous search trees to compensate for lack of sophistication in evaluation. Slate and Atkin (1983) put it aptly when discussing a chess program's evaluation function, f, applied to successively deeper plies in a search: "The point is that if f contains a particular chess concept such as material gain, then the depth operator in a peculiar way transforms, enriches, and extends the concept, by expressing the result of projecting this concept out to the end points of an n-ply search" (p. 114). That is, if f at ply 2 "understands" that it is good to fork two pieces, then f at ply 3 "understands" that it is good to prevent a forking maneuver by the opponent. Search can be seen as a reasoning process that derives deep understanding by extending shallow knowledge out into the problem space.

Feigenbaum (1989) argued that "Knowledge is Power." I would argue, with Newell (1989), that Power/Skill = f(Knowledge, Search). Determining how a system copes with the trade-offs possible in that space is an appropriate goal for cognitive science.

Newell and Simon (1972) pointed out that the basic problem-solving processes are recognition, generate and test, and heuristic search. Heuristic search can be conceptualized as a knowledge-accumulation process. (Newell & Simon's choice of the term "knowledge state" to refer to a point in the problem space was particularly appropriate.) Even experts cannot usually rely solely on recognition. Experts have to search for solutions to problems, though they can recognize solutions more often than novices.

A striking finding in the general problem-solving literature is that people do not look far ahead when evaluating a course of action. Even moderately skilled chess players may look only one or two plies deep (Charness, 1981b; Saariluoma, 1990a). People working on Missionaries and Cannibals, the Tower of Hanoi, and other puzzles of that ilk also fail to look far ahead. Humans have the capacity to search quite a bit deeper (skilled chess players often look 8–10 plies deep, or more); so why do they not normally do so? One possibility is that humans "satisfice" (Simon, 1981); that is, they look for good-enough solutions, not optimal solutions. It is only when they discover that a limited search has led to a poor result that problem solvers will expend the effort necessary to search deeply.

There is another possibility. Much searching may be goal-directed, rather than haphazard information seeking. Players often may be attempting to implement a strategic goal. When playing chess, a player may search for ways to have a knight reach a good outpost, or try to initiate a promising sacrificial attack. That is, search in chess may resemble that for proof justification in theorem proving. Weaker players may not have such plans. Saariluoma (1990a) has argued for precisely this point based on protocol analyses of one tactical position by eleven chess players. Holding (1989a) also has argued that plans are important for directing search.

In short, chess can well fulfill the role of *Drosophila* for investigation of the trade-off between search and knowledge in human problem solving.

CHESS SKILL: A SUMMARY OF THE PSYCHOLOGICAL LITERATURE

The two current views about skill in chess date from the early 1970s (Chase & Simon, 1973a, 1973b; Simon & Chase, 1973) and middle 1980s (Holding, 1985). Chase and Simon (1973a, 1973b) drew on earlier work by de Groot (1978) showing that there were virtually no differences between Grandmasters and strong club players in the way in which they conducted search through the problem space. Chase and Simon followed up de Groot's finding that there were major skill differences in regard to recall of briefly shown game positions. They introduced an important control condition, showing players structured, gamelike positions as well as random arrangements of pieces. The advantage in recall with structured positions disappeared when random positions were reconstructed. They showed that the recall advantage depended on the Master's ability to recognize familiar patterns or chunks. That is, the Master had a nearly normal short-term memory capacity (7 ± 2 chunks), but he was able to recall pieces more effectively because groups of pieces, rather than single pieces, formed his chunks.

From this finding of no search differences, but perceptual/recall differences, they advanced the hypothesis that chess skill depended on a large knowledge base indexed through thousands of familiar chess patterns. They theorized that recognition drives move generation in search, enabling the skilled player to examine promising paths, but leaving the less skilled to wander down less productive paths. A corollary to this view is that evaluation processes (responsible for controlling search) will be more accurate for players with greater skill. Both Holding (1988; Holding & Pfau, 1985) and I (Charness, 1981a) have shown the latter to be true: The more skilled players can evaluate a given position more accurately, whether it is a middle-game position (Holding, 1988) or an endgame position (Charness, 1981a).

Nonetheless, further research has revealed some apparent flaws in a strictly recognition-based theory. Other studies have brought into question the notion that recall of briefly seen chess positions would depend on the type of short-term memory system simulated by Simon and Gilmartin (1973). Holding and Reynolds (1982) showed that despite a lack of skill differences for recall of disorganized but legal chess positions, the more skilled players subsequently chose better moves from those positions. I showed (Charness, 1981c) that older chess players recalled structured chess positions less well than did equivalently skilled younger players. Saariluoma (1985) also failed to show a skill-by-board-type interaction for detecting a check or enumerating minor pieces with structured and random positions. Better players were superior to less skilled players in both types of positions. In short, a simple recognition-association theory was inadequate to account for all the data.

Both I (Charness, 1976) and Frey and Adesman (1976) demonstrated that when chess players recalled briefly seen positions, information was not retrieved from short-term memory. My study showed virtually no interference when players had to perform interpolated processing between exposure to the chess position and recall. Frey and Adesman showed little interference when a second chess positions was memorized before the first one was recalled. Clearly, a more sophisticated view of skilled memory, such as that proposed by Chase and Ericsson (1982), Ericsson (1985), and Ericsson and Staszewski (1989), is needed to account for recall effects. These theorists have stressed the importance of domain-specific, easily activated, long-term-memory retrieval structures in recall performance.

Holding (1985) argued that search efficiency was a major component that differentiated stronger and weaker chess players. He suggested a tripartite model of skill differences (SEarch, Evaluation, Knowledge: SEEK). For the importance of search, he drew on a study I had conducted (Charness, 1981a, 1981b) showing that as skill increased, the depth of search increased, a finding contrary to that of de Groot (1978). A major problem with reconciling the two studies is that de Groot used 5 Grandmaster-level and 5 Master-level players with only 1 position, whereas I used 34 players varying from weak amateurs to expert-level players with 4 positions.

The problem with Holding's SEEK model is that it fails to describe the theoretical underpinnings linking search and skill level. What enables stronger players to search more deeply? What enables move-generation processes to operate, or evaluation processes to be executed? Clearly, telling amateurs to search more deeply is not likely to lead them to equal Grandmasters in proficiency. Pattern-recognition processes are intimately related to move generation and position evaluation.

Two recent studies (Charness, 1989; Saariluoma, 1990a) cast doubt on the importance of depth or extent of search as a determinant of skill. I retested DH, a subject in the initial 1981 study, after a 9-year interval, when DH had climbed to International Master strength (2400 rating points) from average tournament-level strength (1600 points). DH showed virtually no change in search (depth, extent), but did show major changes in recall, evaluation, and chunking. In short, this longitudinal study indicated that there were few skill-related differences in search once players reached intermediate (1600) skill levels. The major changes seemed to be pattern-related. Saariluoma did protocol analysis of strong players (Grandmaster, International Master) and weaker players. He showed that the former searched *less* extensively than did Master-level players, who searched more extensively than did second-class and novice players. Again, it seems that the significant factor in skilled chess play at the top levels is what is searched, now how extensively or deeply the search is conducted.

But Saariluoma (1989, 1990a, 1990b) also showed that simple chunking explanations encountered problems when players were given a significant amount of time to remember aurally presented chess positions that were either structured or random and were presented randomly or in a consistent order. He showed that stronger players recalled both types and orders better than weaker players did, although they performed less well on random positions and orders. They apparently could organize the input more effectively for recall when given enough encoding time. Lories (1987) reported a similar finding for 1-minute visual exposures to structured and random chess positions (no interaction of position type with skill level). Unfortunately, ceiling effects in accuracy made interpretation of that result difficult.

Calderwood, Klein, and Crandall (1988) examined move-selection processes under time pressure. Three Masters (2401, 2403, and 2500 ratings) and three Class B players (1729, 1736, and 1786 ratings) played two-game round-robin matches within their rating groups under both normal and speeded time controls. As expected, better players chose better moves. (The authors analyzed "complex" moves primarily, eliminating those that were obvious. Moves were rated by a Grandmaster for type and quality.) Also, the quality of move choice deteriorated when players played at blitz speed (5 minutes per game) rather than regular speed (40 moves in 90 minutes), but Masters were much less affected by time pressure than Class B players. The authors interpreted their results as indicating that Masters rely more on pattern recognition than on search and therefore are affected less when time is short. Nonetheless, it is also possible that the Masters searched more quickly than the Class B players and showed less deterioration because search was less severely curtailed for them under time pressure. That possibility received some support from Holding (1989c).

Where does skill begin to have an impact? An early tachistoscopic study by Ellis (1973) showed that better players could make same–difference judgments of quarter boards faster than less skilled players. If the piece symbols were replaced by disks, however, no skill differences were evident. That work suggested that skilled players carried out their match by using larger clusters of pieces to make the same difference judgments, but that worked only for chess pieces.

In my lab, Kevin Waghorn (1988) attempted to extend a finding by Church and Church (1983) concerning check detection. They had shown, with a single subject, that the time to detect (yes/no decision) a checking relation between a king and a rook, bishop, or queen varied linearly with distance, with the slope being about 10 times as great for diagonal checks as for horizontal or vertical checks. Milojkovic (1982) had replicated that finding with a capture-prediction task and had found that a Master was faster than novices. When the task was done as an imagery task, rather than as a perceptual task, there were no distance effects for the Master. Waghorn attempted to replicate the linear function and looked at skill differences by including nine rated chess players (1352–2133 rating points) and ten unrated players. Perhaps surprisingly, there were no skill differences in speed of simple check detection or in errors on the check-present trials.

It seems probable that once players reach modest levels of skill, they are quite effective at the type of low-level pattern recognition needed for a two-piece check-detection task. More troublesome, however, was Waghorn's failure to replicate the Church and Church finding of a steep slope difference between diagonal checks and vertical/horizontal checks. Part of the difference may have had to do with the sizes of the displays and the kinds of symbols.

Waghorn used a VDT with a relatively large display area and used piece icons similar to those found in chess publications, whereas Church and Church used letters (k, q, r, b) on an oscilloscope to represent chess pieces. Milojkovic used standard chess symbols on cards in a tachistoscope.

There is another source of evidence that strong players have an early perceptual processing advantage. Saariluoma (1990b) showed that on a piece-enumeration task, strong chess players announced their counts more quickly than did weaker players. They demonstrated an advantage even with randomly arranged arrays. Unfortunately, because Saariluoma did not report accuracy for this task, the possibility of speed–accuracy trade-offs cannot be discounted. In short, it is unclear whether strong players have an advantage at perceptual identification of pieces.

The findings regarding the search process suggest that functions relating psychological variables to skill levels may not be linear and may even depart from monotonicity. Studies of skilled performers in other domains, such as abacus calculation (Hatano, Miyake, & Binks, 1977), typing (Gentner, 1989), and medical diagnosis (Patel & Groen, chapter 4, this volume), support the notion that the nature of the representation underlying skilled performance can change radically as one moves up the skill scale. It is clear that future chess research should include exploration of the full range of skill whenever possible.

Age effects

Complicating the picture of chess skill presented earlier is the finding that there are pronounced age effects on a player's developmental trend (Elo, 1965, 1978). Grandmasters show a steady rise in performance from their teens until their thirties, with modest decline thereafter. Nonetheless, performance at 63 years of age is about equivalent to that at 21 years. Recent research provides evidence of declines in memory processes that could support chess playing. I have shown (Charness, 1981a, 1981b, 1981c) that older chess players do not recall briefly presented chess positions as effectively as do equally skilled younger players. This disadvantage increases as exposure duration increases from 1 to 2 to 4 seconds. A simple slowing model of aging can account for this effect (Charness, 1988). Similarly, when incidental recall is tested for positions that were shown in a choose-a-move task, older players show poorer recall than younger players. Pfau and Murphy (1988) have also shown age deficits in memory for chess positions for an intentional 5-second recall task.

Somewhat surprisingly, few age effects have been shown for search, where, if anything, older chess players search less extensively than equivalently skilled younger players, though equally deeply (Charness, 1981b). Work on aging and skill suggests that the models of skill based on young adults need to be extended to model skill differences across the life span.

In short, the theoretical explanations of chess skill need further development. It is clear that neither theoretical position – neither recognition-association theory nor Holding's (1985) SEEK model – is well enough developed to make strong experimental predictions. All would agree that human experts know more than human novices. The nature of the knowledge differences has not been adequately delimited. My goal for the rest of this chapter is to outline potential avenues of exploration for getting at knowledge differences.

How big is the task environment?

One advantage of using chess as a task environment is that it provides a stable game environment. As Hooper and Whyld (1984) noted, the rules of chess play have remained essentially the same since changes in two pieces in the fifteenth century (queen and bishop replacing the *fers* and *aufin,* respectively). Chess notation, a system to record chess positions and games, has allowed chess knowledge to be codified succinctly in books (and, more recently, in chess database programs). Thus, there exist copious records of games played in tournaments by strong players, and numerous treatises have been written advising chess players of the best ways to make their opening moves, plan strategy for their middle games, and play their endings.

Chess books have a long history, with early primers published in the 1600s, and "modern" works on openings and endgames appearing in the late nineteenth century. (A typical 1988 chess-book catalogue by the *Chess Federation of Canada* listed about 320 entries, with 177 on opening theory, 63 on middle-game strategy, and 23 on endgame strategy. Most of those books had publication dates in the 1980s, but one listed a publication date of 1901.) The historical success of chess as a game undoubtedly derives as much from its notation system as from its intrinsic properties as a game of skill.

During the past twenty years, the "Chess Promotion Centre" in Belgrade and the World Chess Federation (FIDE, Fédération International des Echecs) have conducted a project to develop encyclopedic sources of opening knowledge, middle-game combinations, and endgame knowledge by having the world's best chess theoreticians and practical players collaborate on books. These volumes provide an opportunity to try to delimit the contribution of one's knowledge base to one's chess skill, in much the same way that large dictionaries provide an opportunity to estimate the vocabulary size of a native speaker (Oldfield, 1963).

I shall next attempt to assess the extent of the knowledge base in chess for opening theory and suggest procedures for estimating what is known by players at difficult skill levels. I shall then look at middle-game knowledge and, finally, endgame knowledge.

Opening theory

The body of knowledge distilled from the writings of chess Masters and Grand Masters concerning how to begin a chess game is known as *open-*

ing theory. It is highly developed. Among Grandmasters, the first 10–20 moves usually are played fairly rapidly because they consist of memorized variations. (A *move* in chess usually refers to a move for each side: White playing a pawn from the e2 square to the e4 square and Black replying by moving a pawn from the e7 square to the e5 square would constitute the first move of a King pawn opening. The term *ply* is used to refer to the move of one side.) It is worth noting that the number of distinct legal openings is immense. There are 400 unique positions possible after one move (ply 2), given the 20 possible moves available to both White and Black. Three moves from the opening position (ply 6) can lead to more than 9 million distinct positions (Hooper & Whyld, 1984, p. 232). It has been estimated that the number of unique chess games (though mostly senseless ones) falls in the range of 10^{120}, though sensible master games fall in the range of 4×10^{20} (Charness, 1983). It is little wonder that even when only plausible openings are considered, a thorough treatment of opening theory requires a five-volume reference set (Chess Informant's *Encyclopedia of Chess Openings*). Hooper and Whyld (1984) noted that there are distinct names for 701 different opening variations (their Appendix A). Much like their human counterparts, strong chess-playing programs often contain a great deal of opening knowledge. By looking up moves in their libraries, programs can save time for search in the middle game. Another technique borrowed from human play is the practice of predicting the opponent's most probable move and searching the consequences while the opponent is thinking.

Although many opening variations have been published in the literature, it is not clear how many of those a typical Grandmaster will know, nor is it known how strong is the relation between opening knowledge and skill in chess. A recent investigation by Pfau and Murphy (1988) showed that a questionnaire that tapped a number of dimensions, including knowledge of openings, was a better predictor of chess skill ($r = .69$) than was the de Groot/Chase and Simon rapid recall task ($r = .44$). Although the questionnaire contained 25 items that Pfau and Murphy classified as pertaining to openings, 18 additional items classified as "specific middlegames" also required knowledge of openings for successful completion. An example was item 4: "In the main line of the Two Knights' Defense, Black obtains compensation for his pawn by having. . . ." (I thank Martin Murphy for providing the questionnaire.) By my breakdown, 43 of the 74 items tested opening knowledge. Two choose-a-move tests (one tactical, one positional) correlated even more highly with chess rating ($r = .72, .76$, respectively).

Humans face a clear trade-off between knowledge and search. Knowledge is used to constrain search to manageable levels. Rarely do human players overtly examine more than 100 nodes in the game tree during a typical 10-minute search episode (Charness, 1981b). The earliest and least skilled chess-playing programs clearly searched more extensively than that, and current Senior Master–level programs (ratings of 2300+) will examine millions of nodes in a 3-minute search episode (e.g., *Deep Thought*). Knowledge enables human players to search the problem space *selectively*.

Given these dimensions, there is a choice to be made: Should a player memorize opening variations or try to perfect planning and search skills in the hope that search will compensate for knowledge? Because chess is a timed game, with each side constrained to make its first 40 moves in 2 hours, there is a severe cost to any player who must search, relative to those who merely recall. (The time limit of 3 minutes per move is being challenged by those who want to speed up the pace of tournament games. They are promoting so-called active chess, with a time limit of about 30 seconds per move.) Holding (1979, 1988) has shown that even strong players will form inaccurate evaluations of unfamiliar game positions until they reach moderate depths of search. To get around the problem of an opponent known for opening knowledge, many players will intentionally depart from the more conventional lines of play in order to reach positions that will have been less thoroughly analyzed.

I take the *Encyclopedia of Chess Openings* as a conservative source of opening knowledge. It provides underestimates, because since the earliest volume was published in 1979 (Volume A), much additional opening knowledge has been developed, appearing in chess magazines, *Chess Informant* game collections, and so forth. Openings are given in groupings that vary somewhat in their depth (number of plies that the analysis covers). A typical entry in the *Encyclopedia* gives a header of moves, followed by about a dozen branching lines that proceed to between moves 10 and 20, with footnotes indicating alternative lines. That is, analysis is given to a minimum depth of about ply 20 and to a maximum depth of around ply 40. Footnotes usually refer to specific tournament games in which the opening line under discussion was played. Advertisements for this series claim that there are examples from 120,000 tournament games.

We have tried to estimate the number of unique lines of opening analysis at different depths. We sampled two of the five volumes and counted the main lines to ply 10 and ply 20. We also estimated the number of additional lines of analysis contained in the footnotes. On average, estimated for the five-volume set, there are about 2,900 different main lines in the tables at ply 10 and about 6,300 at ply 20. Much of the analysis is in the footnotes, however. Tracing through a small sample of footnotes, we estimated that there are 45,500 additional lines at ply 10 and 35,300 lines at ply 20. In short, around 48,000 different opening sequences are analyzed to 5 moves, and 40,000 to 10 moves.

It is worth recalling that just three moves (ply 6) into a game, about 9 million different continuations are possible. The sampling I report does not come close to exhausting the possible openings and, indeed, does *not* show the exponential growth with depth that occurs in the objective game tree. (To see what happens at ply 30, we counted through Volume B and found 351 main variations at ply 10, 1,197 at ply 20, and 696 at ply 30.) Still, learning opening theory is a formidable task for human players. Even though virtually all of the possible continuations remaining at ply 20 develop from those at ply 10, it is clear that there is a great deal to master. Also, sheer memorization obviously is not sufficient for skilled opening play. More important is understanding the themes of different openings, because at some point one of the opponents will depart from the "book" line. At any rate, even if memorization were the path to mastery, it would take a very long time to memorize 40,000 distinct opening sequences.

Also, it is not clear that Grandmasters prepare more than a few opening lines for tournament play. Botvinnik, the first world champion in the post-World War II era, put it this way (Botvinnik, 1960, p. 10): "Here I must remark that in my view a player should not, and indeed cannot attempt to play all the openings known to theory. For one competition three or four opening systems for White and the same for Black are quite sufficient." If we take Botvinnik's term "opening system" to mean main lines to ply 20, then we collapse the 40,000 to about 1,200 distinct lines, a large but manageable chore for an experienced player. Obviously, experimental probing of the relation between chess skill and opening knowledge is a necessary next step. We plan to sample opening positions from this set in order to estimate how opening knowledge varies with skill.

Combinational themes for the middle game

A chess *combination* usually is a sequence of attacking moves that results in the winning of more pieces (or value-equivalent pieces) than the attacker initially sacrificed, or else results in checkmate (or occasionally forces a draw from an inferior position). As Alekhine, a world champion in the 1940s, is reputed to have said, "the combination is the heart of chess." Chess experts have chosen to categorize combinational themes into a relatively small (in comparison with openings) number of categories. Popular chess books typically use labels such as "pin," "double attack," "x-ray," and "deflection." *Chess Informant*'s *Encyclopedia of Chess Middlegames: Combinations* (1980) illustrates 16 basic categories via 1,817 examples. All these themes are organized around stereotyped patterns of attack, which in turn spring from specific piece relations. Again, it would be interesting to see how many of the examples are known to chess players at different skill levels.

Endgame knowledge

In similarity to the case of openings, knowledge of how to play endings is well systematized. The first three volumes (published in 1982, 1985, and 1986) of a planned five-volume series on the endgame by *Chess Informant* contain 5,083 diagrams, with accompanying analysis. Assuming a similar pattern in the next two volumes, about 8,500 cases will have been detailed. The earlier major English-language resource book, Fine's *Basic Chess Endings*

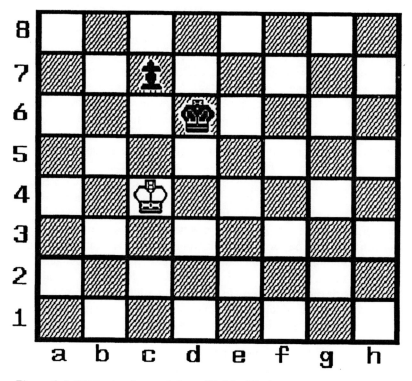

Figure 2.1. White to play and draw (K-d4); Black to play and win (K-c6).

(1941), discussed 607 main cases, although he often elaborated on a, b, or c versions of the main cases.

Knowing specific endgame cases is critical to skilled play. First, knowledge of the outcome of a particular configuration (win, lose, or draw) is critical to evaluating move choices in the opening and middle game. An inaccurate evaluation can be the difference between a draw and a win. Second, when playing endgames, a slight difference in piece configurations can make a major difference in the outcome. Search generally will not be a feasible way of choosing between two plausible moves, one of which loses and one of which draws. As seen in Figure 2.1, it would take more than a 20-ply search to find the correct move to lead to a new queen for Black if Black is on move, and a similar deep search to find how to prevent Black from queening if White is on move.

Although players need not know all endgame positions and the appropriate methods of play, at the least they need to know major classes and heuristics of play. If one knows a rule such as "to win with a bishop, knight, and king arrayed against a king, one must drive the opposing king to a corner of the *same color* as one's bishop," one can do a fairly focused search to determine how to reach that subgoal. Similarly, knowing the principle of the "opposition" (Hooper & Whyld, 1984, p. 232) helps to make pawn endings (such as that in Figure 2.1) manageable with little search.

Fine (1941) concluded his book *Basic Chess Endings* with a two-page summary. The first page outlines three principles: how much material is needed to win when no pawns are present, why a two-pawn advantage makes a win routine, how a one-pawn advantage is to be converted into a win. These principles guide planning and can be used in the evaluation process when players search for moves to make. On the second page, he outlines 15 rules, although 2 are redundant. Again, these rules are general and can serve only for planning and evaluation purposes (e.g., "The easiest endings to win are pure Pawn endings." "The King is a strong piece: Use it!"). In short, there are no specific algorithms for winning specific endings; such algorithms are available only when discussing the six hundred or so basic ending positions.

It will be useful to examine to what extent endgame knowledge consists in memorizing move sets for given positions and to what extent it consists in knowing specific patterns and principles of play for those patterns. We can make a rough estimate from some of my earlier data on endgame evaluation accuracy (Charness, 1981a). I showed 20 of Fine's 607 positions to chess players, with the instructions to try to evaluate the position as a win, loss, or draw as quickly as possible. The regression equation predicting accuracy (percentage correct evaluations) from chess rating was

$$\text{accuracy} = 0.032(\text{rating}) + 5.8 \quad (SE = 10.8)$$

Unfortunately, positions were not randomly sampled from the text but were chosen partly to contain relatively few pieces in order to minimize the expected encoding advantages for more skilled players. Thus, only a ballpark figure can be given for knowledge of endings for these players. Extrapolating (linearly) to Fine's 607 diagrams suggests that a Master (2200 rating points) can accurately evaluate about 76 percent of the catalogued endings, or about 460 of the positions. This estimate probably is on the high side, given the selection biases. Further, it indicates only how many can be *classified* accurately, not how many can be *played* accurately.

It is worth checking how well the regression equation extrapolates outside the range of skill for this sample (the highest-rated player had 2004 rating points). DH, one of the players in the sample (Charness, 1989), was tested again nine years later, when his rating had risen to 2423. His predicted score for that rating was 83 percent. His actual score was 75 percent, within one standard-error unit of the predicted score. Nonetheless, this result suggests that a linear relation may not characterize knowledge acquisition. Rather, a power function (Newell & Rosenbloom, 1981) may provide a better fit.

One constraint I have ignored thus far concerns the frequencies of appearance of openings, middle-game combinations, and endings. Much like word frequencies in natural languages, positions in chess do not occur equally often. Often there are fads regarding openings. King pawn openings (such as King's Gambit and Giuoco Piano) predominated in the 1800s, when open games and sacrificial attacks were in vogue. More recently, players seem to prefer closed positions, where subtle maneuvering for a space advantage becomes an important skill. As the general level of proficiency has risen, it has become less likely that one can expect to succeed by sacrificing material in an attack, awaiting an error in the opponent's defense, and then bludgeoning the opponent into submission. It may be useful to catalogue the frequencies of openings and endings in master play to arrive at a finer estimate of the extent of a player's knowledge base.

How much does the Master need to know?

Do Grandmasters know all 8,500 specific endgame cases, all 50,000 opening variations, all 1,817 middle-game combinations? Although no studies have been conducted to establish the vocabulary of a Grandmaster, we can safely conclude that the answer is no. A good parallel is the case for skill at arithmetic calculation. Humans usually memorize a small set of facts (e.g., the multiplication tables from 1×1 to 12×12) and learn a few powerful rules (the rules for multiplying by 1 and by 0, the multidigit multiplication and division algorithms) in order to perform well in the domain of arithmetic. It is likely that chess Masters know many specific facts but also rely on a set of general principles, or heuristics, to guide their search when playing chess.

How do general principles apply to specific cases? A problem with general rules is that more than one may apply, or none may be relevant to an individual case. As mentioned earlier, the recall advantage for more skilled players has been taken as evidence that Masters know many specific patterns. There are many exceptions to any general rule, and Masters tend to know how to deal with them. They are likely to have *schematized* their knowledge of chess patterns, much as experts in physics represent their knowledge via physics diagrams (Anzai, chapter 3, this volume) or as physicians represent their diagnostic knowledge (Patel & Groen, chapter 4, this volume). The debate over whether knowledge consists of abstracted prototypes or memory for instances (or some combination) still continues in the concept-formation literature in general experimental psychology (e.g., McClelland & Rumelhart, 1985).

How is the knowledge base acquired?

Chess players have almost always had access to chess books or manuscripts. Early manuscripts date from the thirteenth century, although the main flow of chess books for the modern version of the game started in the middle of the eighteenth century (Hooper & Whyld, 1984). A great deal of knowledge probably is acquired through study of these sources. It is one of the standard features of most human cultures that hard-won knowledge is stored in such "nonvolatile" forms, to enable future generations of practitioners to benefit from the experiences of their predecessors. The study of written sources is a way of life for most apprentices, and that explains, in part, the zeal with which the modern world embraces literacy. The reason is that the real world often presents important exemplars in too haphazard a way.

A tournament game lasts, on average, forty moves and takes about three to four hours to play. It is clear that players can achieve only limited exposure to opening theory and endgame theory through their own games. The greatest number of rated tournament games by a player in Canada during 1987–8 was 172 (as reported in *En Passant*, 1988, No. 92, p. 48). The most active fifteen players all played a hundred games or more. A typical "Swiss" weekend tournament usually comprises four to six games, so these players are playing in a tournament every two weeks. Even assuming that such active players play roughly the same numbers of unrated chess-club games, they cannot personally experience more than about four hundred unique openings and endings per year solely through tournament play. (Opening experience is likely to be even more circumscribed because players often heed Botvinnik's advice and specialize in only a few lines.)

The opportunity to learn about combinations is exercised at practically every move past the early stages of the opening, with about 30 moves × 400 games × 12,000 opportunities in this same interval. (This assumes that players do not conduct analysis while their opponents plan their moves.) Assuming that a maximum of 100 positions are examined with each move (Charness, 1981a), very active players will have analyzed a maximum of 1,200,000 positions over a year of play. (Contrast that search value with the figures for some computer chess programs, which can reach that total in a few seconds of analysis of a single move.) To build an effective knowledge base concerning chess openings and endings, players need to supplement their tournament experience by studying chess books and magazines. Printed sources have the virtue of making rare situations more common, in addition to providing analysis and indicating how to play specific chess positions more astutely.

It is safe to assume that most knowledge acquisition takes place away from the tournament room, though modest levels of skill may be attainable with little more than game-playing experience if play is frequent enough. Child prodigies obviously depend on such playing experience, because many reach moderate skill levels long before they can study book sources. Still, it is not clear how much information is retained from playing a single game.

Good players are reputed to be able to reconstruct an entire game (to around ply 80 from memory shortly after the game's conclusion), and Grandmasters have occasionally been reported to be able to recall games played months or years earlier. This is a wonderful example of "incidental"serial-recall memory, because players are required to record their moves in tournament play and hence have no need to memorize the sequence of moves. No empirical tests of either of these reported memory performances are available to me, although personal experience, as well as Chase and Simon's (1973a) study of recall of short move sequences, suggests that these phenomena do occur. Moves in a tournament game are meaningful, organized in terms of opening type (and how the game departs from opening theory), surprises encountered, piece exchange sequences, and so forth. The 40 moves (80 plies) undoubtedly collapse into a much smaller number of chunks. Players also will have been analyzing for several minutes per move, though probably not with the intent of remembering the move.

If book knowledge is important in acquiring skill, then the ever increasing number and easier availability of chess books should be raising the general level of chess play in the population of serious players.

Evidence of generational improvement

One way to assess the influence of the recorded knowledge base of chess is to look at historical trends. My assumption is that if knowledge leads to skill improvement, then the best players in the world (leading Grandmasters, world champions) will receive significantly higher ratings over time. Elo (1978) noted that the average rating for the world's top players increased from 2485 rating points for fifteen top players in 1860 to 2575 rating points for the top fifty players in 1960. There is a competing explanation, however, for such skill increase: population growth. As Elo (1978) commented, the base population of chess players has been increasing. He likened the situation to that of a pyramid with an increasing base, where the maximal height (top chess rating) increases as the base widens.

A more formal argument evolves from probability theory. Suppose that chess talent (potential skill) is approximately normally distributed in the population. Then the most extreme member of a large sample of active players will have a higher rating than the most extreme member of a smaller sample. An informal proof is that as sample size increases from 1 to N, the probability of including the top player in the sample increases from $1/N$ to 1. (The assumption of a normal distribution of chess performance is questionable. Chess ratings are *not* normally distributed – they are positively skewed [Elo, 1978, p. 115]. Apparently a Maxwell-Boltzmann function provides a good fit.)

Elo corrected somewhat for the growing population of chess players by using larger samples to base the mean rating for the world's top players. (The chess population may approximate the exponential growth of the world's population.) With no proper estimate of the number of chess players in any era, however, no formal evaluation of the adequacy of that correction can be made.

The hypothesis of skill's being related to sample size can be checked by examining the number of titled players as a function of a country's chess-playing population. Elo (1978, pp. 108–10) examined the chess-playing populations of a sample of countries in 1977. I used his data to derive the scattergram shown in Figure 2.2. It excludes (for scaling purposes) the special case of the Soviet Union, which reports nearly a hundred times as many registered chess players as its nearest rival. The larger the number of registered players, the larger is the number of titled players, those earning the FIDE designations

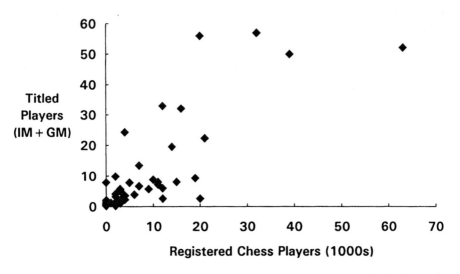

Figure 2.2. FIDE 1977 statistics on player populations and titled players for 71 countries, USSR excluded. From Elo (1978).

of International Master (IM) and Grandmaster (GM) by playing in FIDE-rated international events. The relation is quite linear ($r = .82$), modestly supporting a "pyramid" explanation of skill.

There are within-generation checks that have been taken to show that training makes a difference beyond the number of those playing. Elo (1978, p. 110) cited the ratios of Grandmasters and International Masters among one thousand chess players in the top five Western countries (.14, .39) and the top five Socialist countries (.30, .47) as evidence of the effectiveness of state support for chess. The critical test, however, involves using the entire sample of countries to see if there is any additional prediction from nation type after taking into account the relation between number of titled players and number of registered chess players. I coded countries, as did Elo, into five categories: Western, Socialist, Developing, Special Statistical Cases (USSR, Iceland, Mongolia, Singapore), and Other. I regressed the number of titled players (IM + GM) on registered chess players (1,000s) and country type, excluding countries with chess-player populations of fewer than two thousand. The only significant predictor was the number of registered chess players (1,000s), with $R^2 = .546$, $df = 36$, $F(2, 36) = 21.68$, $p < .001$. The equation was

total titled players = 0.019 (registered players) − 2.95(country type) + 16.469

Country type just missed significance ($p < .07$).

If we select only for Western and Socialist countries, again the only significant predictor is the number of registered chess players: titled players = 0.522(registered players) + 5.649(country types) − 2.577. Here, for 32 countries, $R^2 = .634$, $F(2, 29) = 25.07$, $p < .001$. Country type is still not a significant predictor ($p < .14$), though the direction (Western coded 1, Socialist coded 2) is as Elo suggested.

It is clear that the number of players registered with a national chess organization is more significant than training in predicting the occurrence of top-level talent. Chess is an individual enterprise that demands thousands of hours of practice and study to reach high levels of proficiency. It may be true for chess, as in education more broadly, that one does not teach it; rather, players are afforded the opportunity to acquire skill.

A case in point is that of the two highest-rated players in history, Robert Fischer (best 5-year average = 2780) and Gary Kasparov (2800 in January 1990). The American, Fischer, had little formal support (coaching or financial) in his efforts to become world champion. The current world champion, Kasparov, a player who was identified early on as a player of great promise, received careful supervision, coaching, and financial support within the Soviet Chess Federation.

There is little question that national differences in success influence whether or not people join chess federations. The case of whether or not there are significant national training effects in chess attainment must be tendered the Scottish verdict of "unproven."

Unfortunately, the FIDE chess rating system has not been run totally according to Elo's original formulation, and so it would be difficult to look at generational (time of measurement) trends to see how the tournament performance of top players has changed over the past few decades. FIDE reportedly inflated the rating system a few years ago by providing artificial ratings to entry-level players and bonuses to women.

So, does increased knowledge and easier access to it through books and magazines result in generational improvements in play? Chess ratings have clearly moved upward over the past century. It seems, however, that most of the gain can be attributed to increasing numbers of people playing chess, with the concomitant probability that the best of these current players will be better than the best of the smaller number who competed in the past. Similarly, state interventions to train chess players seem not to have had much impact beyond increasing the number of serious participants. It is also problematic to work out the impact of increases in numbers of players on the Elo rating system. The rating system itself may mask improvements because of deflation, although monitoring over the 1970–6 period, when the FIDE pool expanded tenfold, showed little evidence of deflation (Elo, 1978). Also, it is not clear how far we can trust the figures supplied by national chess federations to FIDE concerning their player populations. If such statistics are inflated to impress others, successful state training programs may be obscured.

It is worth considering that computer chess programs, which generally do not benefit much from increased chess knowledge, have also improved tremendously over the past twenty years or so. They have better "knowledge" of how to search (better search algorithms), but, as mentioned earlier, most of the improvement in play results from running these algorithms faster than ever before. Given the stability of chess skill associated with a given program, there exists the intriguing possibility of tracking any generational changes in the rating system: Assume that a stable rating of 2000 is achieved by a program via play against humans in 1990. It will be possible to calibrate future generations of human players with 2000 ratings by having them play matches against that program.

CONCLUSIONS

The ancient homily "a dwarf on a giant's shoulders sees the farther" applies well to chess when considering the relation between search and knowledge. Computer programs rest on the shoulders of technological advances that make gigantic search capabilities with dwarflike chess knowledge go a long way. In essence, such programs generate "knowledge" on the fly. Human players have capitalized on literally centuries of slowly accumulated knowledge of openings and endings, heuristics for planning, together with much more modest ability to search, to reach the highest levels of chess skill. Individual players can count on both public knowledge (book sources) and private knowledge (acquired through their own analysis) to help them through the enormous maze of possibilities defined by the rules of chess.

Our prospects for understanding expertise in chess are fairly good, aided by projects launched by chess players to categorize chess knowledge. We need to concentrate on finding ways to describe and catalogue the vocabulary of patterns and associated playing methods that players possess. There is still room to expand on our knowledge of how the search process varies along the skill continuum, because too few players and chess positions have been subjected to examination with think-aloud procedures. In short, we have come a long way since the earliest forays (Binet, 1966; Cleveland, 1907), but still have quite a distance to travel.

As some of the chapters in this volume point out, chess skill was one of the first skills to undergo intensive psychological investigation, and models of skill in chess have strongly influenced investigations of expertise in other domains. Chess playing still presents a model environment, in the sense that Salthouse (chapter 11, this volume) has indicated. Skill can be measured with remarkable precision, unlike the case for other forms of decision making (e.g., Camerer & Johnson, chapter 8, this volume) in which there are no clear markers for expertise. There is also the opportunity to tap into theoretical work in artificial intelligence to guide our understanding of search mechanisms, although it is clear that humans do not conduct search in the same fashion as most chess programs.

Nonetheless, chess has its limitations as a model environment. A major hurdle to investigation is the difficulty of obtaining skilled chess players for research projects. In Canada, for instance, there are only about three thousand active rated chess players. If one wants to do studies that involve the top players, one has but a small population from which to sample; only about fifty players in Canada have ratings over 2300. It is a nontrivial task to reach modest sample sizes. Almost by definition, the highly skilled practitioner is a rare commodity. Other skill domains share this problem.

Another challenge is posed for experimenters because much of the knowledge base probably is represented in nonverbal, spatial patterns. The choice of the term "spatial" instead of "visual" is motivated by findings that strong players can play skillfully without sight of the board (so-called blindfold play, where moves are announced orally). Ericsson and Staszewski (1989) reported that the characteristics of such mentally generated representations closely resembled those derived from perception. It is not as easy to present experimental probes to the chess lexicon as to the word lexicon. Fortunately, chess players have a well-developed language for communicating about chess positions. Chess diagrams and chess notation allow for precise communication. Data-intensive experimental techniques such as protocol analysis work reasonably well; see, for instance, Holding's (1989b) use of written protocols to examine how counting interferes with search.

Nonetheless, another limitation is that knowing about skill in chess may not tell us much about skill in a verbal activity, such as writing or medical diagnosis, though it may provide constructs useful in characterizing expertise in other domains that rely on spatial representations, such as physics (e.g., diagram knowledge). There may also be some interesting parallels between learning how to "read" chess positions and learning how to "read" other pictorial materials, such as medical X rays, PET and CAT scans, ultrasound pictures, and maps. Further, there are some intriguing similarities between the extent of search in chess and the number of relevant propositions inferred and recalled in medical diagnosis (Patel & Groen, chapter 4, this volume). Saariluoma reported *less* searching by the very top players than by Master players, who searched more extensively than weaker players. Patel and Groen reported an inverted U-shaped function as well for recall and inference propositions in case descriptions as a function of medical experience. Such functions argue for *qualitative* differences in the way information is processed as high skill levels are achieved.

It is probably fair to characterize much of human learning as pattern learning. An unanswered question is that of whether certain patterns are easier to learn (and model) than others. Both psychometric investigations and neuropsychological research provide evidence that all processing is not the same: Some people are better at spatial tasks; others, at verbal tasks. Damage in specific parts of the cortex impairs some skills but leaves others intact. Whether processes essential for chess playing fall into this category is unclear. Neuropsychological investigations have not shown strong cerebral localization for chess, though there is weak evidence for right-hemisphere involvement (Cranberg & Albert, 1988).

Another unexplored issue is that chess playing is an emotional activity (see Sloboda, chapter 6, this volume, for the case of music). Aside from such homilies as "sit on your hands" or "when you find a good move, look for a better one," there is little formal instruction about how to control the emotional arousal that is evoked in the heat of battle. It is not unusual to be surprised by an opponent's move. There have been few systematic investigations of the influence of emotion on move choice. An early Russian study (Tikhomirov & Vinogradov, 1970) needs replication and extension.

Although intentional book learning apparently is critical for the development of world-class expertise in chess, it is not even an available route for other domains. As Sloboda (chapter 6, this volume) points out, much knowledge of musical scale structure is acquired by children at a very young age, long before intentional memorizing strategies are evident. A significant challenge faced by all theorists regarding skill is to describe the incidental learning process (implicit memory) that is responsible for most of the knowledge that experts possess. One of the expectations about studying expertise is that it will lead to better instruction. Yet we know little about how to translate implicit knowledge into explicit and effective instructional techniques, particularly for the case of nonverbal patterns.

Chess has proved to be a durable task for psychological investigation. The microcosm of 64 squares and 2 opposing sets of 16 chess pieces has attracted the interest of psychologists for the past century. The judgment is not yet in regarding whether the models developed to account for skill in chess can be extended to cover other domains. Nonetheless, chess undoubtedly will continue to be an informative domain to explore in the quest for better understanding of expertise.

ACKNOWLEDGMENTS

This work was supported by a grant from the Natural Sciences and Engineering Research Council of Canada, NSERC A0790. I am grateful to Kim Dawson for helping with the count of opening variations. Address correspondence to Neil Charness, Psychology Department, University of Waterloo, Waterloo, Ontario, Canada N2L 3G1.

REFERENCES

Anderson, J. R. (1988). The place of cognitive architectures in a rational analysis. In *Program of the Tenth Annual Conference of the Cognitive Science Society,* 17–19 August 1988, Montreal, Quebec, Canada (pp. 1–10). Hillsdale, NJ: Erlbaum.

Berliner, H. J. (1981). *Search vs. knowledge: An analysis from the domain of games.* Paper presented at the NATO Symposium on Human and Artificial Intelligence, Lyon, France, October 1981. (Available as CMU-CS-82-103 from Computer Science Department, Carnegie-Mellon University.)

Berliner, H., & Ebeling, C. (1989). Pattern knowledge and search: The SUPREM architecture. *Artificial Intelligence, 38,* 161–198.

Binet, A. (1966). Mnemonic virtuosity: A study of chess players. *Journal of Genetic Psychology, 74,* 127–162. (Translated from *Revue des Deux Mondes,* 1893, *117,* 826–859.)

Botvinnik, M. M. (1960). *One hundred selected games* (S. Garry, Trans.). New York: Dover.

Calderwood, B., Klein, G. A., & Crandall, B. W. (1988). Time pressure, skill, and move quality in chess. *American Journal of Psychology, 101,* 481–493.

Charness, N. (1976). Memory for chess positions: Resistance to interference. *Journal of Experimental Psychology: Human Learning and Memory, 2,* 641–653.

Charness, N. (1981a). Aging and skilled problem solving. *Journal of Experimental Psychology: General, 110,* 21–38.

Charness, N. (1981b). Search in chess: Age and skill differences. *Journal of Experimental Psychology: Human Perception and Performance, 7,* 467–476.

Charness, N. (1981c). Visual short-term memory and aging in chess players. *Journal of Gerontology, 36,* 615–619.

Charness, N. (1983). Human chess skill. In P. W. Frey (Ed.), *Chess skill in man and machine* (2nd ed., pp. 34–53). New York: Springer-Verlag.

Charness, N. (1988). The role of theories of cognitive aging: Comment on Salthouse. *Psychology and Aging, 3,* 17–21.

Charness, N. (1989). Expertise in chess and bridge. In D. Klahr & K. Kotovsky (Eds.), *Complex information processing: The impact of Herbert A. Simon* (pp. 183–208). Hillsdale, NJ: Erlbaum.

Chase, W. G., & Ericsson, K. A. (1982). Skill and working memory. In G. H. Bower (Ed.), *The psychology of learning and motivation* (Vol. 16, pp. 1–58). New York: Academic Press.

Chase, W. G., & Simon, H. A. (1973a). The mind's eye in chess. In W. G. Chase (Ed.), *Visual information processing* (pp. 215–281). New York: Academic Press.

Chase, W. G., & Simon, H. A. (1973b). Perception in chess. *Cognitive Psychology, 4,* 55–81.

Church, R. M., & Church, K. W. (1983). Plans, goals, and search strategies for the selection of a move in chess. In P. W. Frey (Ed.), *Chess skill in man and machine* (2nd ed., pp. 131–56). New York: Springer-Verlag. (Original work published 1977.)

Cleveland, A. A. (1907). The psychology of chess and of learning to play it. *American Journal of Psychology, 18,* 269–308.

Cranberg, L., & Albert, M. L. (1988) The chess mind. In L. K. Obler & D. Fein (Eds.), *The exceptional brain. Neuropsychology of talent and special abilities* (pp. 156–190). New York: Guilford.

de Groot, A. D. (1978). *Thought and choice in chess* (2nd ed.). The Hague: Mouton.

Ellis, S. H. (1973). *Structure and experience in the matching and reproduction of chess patterns.* Unpublished doctoral dissertation, Carnegie-Mellon University. (*Dissertation Abstracts,* 73-26, 954.)

Elo, A. E. (1965). Age changes in master chess performances. *Journal of Gerontology, 20,* 289–299.

Elo, A. E. (1978). *The rating of chessplayers, past and present.* New York: Arco.

Encyclopedia of chess middlegames: Combinations (1980). Belgrade, Yugoslavia: Chess Informant.

Encyclopedia of chess openings, Vol. E (1978). Belgrade, Yugoslavia: Chess Informant.

Encyclopedia of chess openings, Vol. A (1979). Belgrade, Yugoslavia: Chess Informant.

Encyclopedia of chess openings, vol. C (1981). Belgrade, Yugoslavia: Chess Informant.

Encyclopedia of chess openings, Vol. B (1984). Belgrade, Yugoslavia: Chess Informant.

Encyclopedia of chess openings, Vol. D (1987). Belgrade, Yugoslavia: Chess Informant.

Ericsson, K. A. (1985). Memory skill. *Canadian Journal of Psychology, 39*, 188–231.
Ericsson, K. A., & Staszewski, J. J. (1989). Skilled memory and expertise: Mechanisms of exceptional performance. In D. Klahr & K. Kotovsky (Eds.), *Complex information processing: The impact of Herbert A. Simon* (pp. 235–267). Hillsdale, NJ: Erlbaum.
Feigenbaum, E. A. (1989). What hath Simon wrought? In D. Klahr & K. Kotovsky (Eds.), *Complex information processing: The impact of Herbert A. Simon* (pp. 165–182). Hillsdale, NJ: Erlbaum.
Fine, R. (1941). *Basic chess endings.* New York: McKay.
Frey, P. W., & Adesman, P. (1976). Recall memory for visually presented positions. *Memory and Cognition, 4*, 541–547.
Gentner, D. R. (1989). Expertise in typewriting. In M. T. H. Chi, R. Glaser, & M. J. Farr (Eds.), *The nature of expertise* (pp. 1–21). Hillsdale, NJ: Erlbaum.
Hatano, G., Miyake, Y., & Binks, M. G. (1977). Performance of expert abacus operators. *Cognition, 5*, 47–55.
Holding, D. H. (1979). The evaluation of chess positions. *Simulation and Games, 10*, 207–221.
Holding, D. H. (1985). *The psychology of chess skill.* Hillsdale, NJ: Erlbaum.
Holding, D. H. (1988). Evaluation factors in human tree search. *American Journal of Psychology, 102*, 103–108.
Holding, D. H. (1989a). Adversary problem solving by humans. In K. J. Gilhooly (Ed.), *Human and machine problem solving* (pp. 83–122). New York: Plenum.
Holding, D. H. (1989b). Counting backward during chess move choice. *Bulletin of the Psychonomic Society, 27*, 421–424.
Holding, D. H. (1989c). *Search during speech chess.* Paper presented at the Psychonomic Society meetings, Atlanta.
Holding, D. H., & Pfau, H. D. (1985). Thinking ahead in chess. *American Journal of Psychology, 98*, 271–282.
Holding, D. H., & Reynolds, R. I. (1982). Recall or evaluation of chess positions as determinants of chess skill. *Memory and Cognition, 10*, 237–242.
Hooper, D., & Whyld, K. (1984). *The Oxford companion to chess.* Oxford University Press.
Lories, G. (1987). Recall of random and nonrandom chess positions in strong and weak chess players. *Psychologica Belgica, 27*(2), 153–159.
McClelland, J. L., & Rumelhart, D. E. (1985). Distributed memory and the representation of general and specific information. *Journal of Experimental Psychology: General, 114*, 159–188.
Milojkovic, J. D. (1982). Chess imagery in novice and master. *Journal of Mental Imagery, 6*, 125–144.
Newell, A. (1989). Putting it all together. In D. Klahr & K. Kotovsky (Eds.), *Complex information processing: The impact of Herbert A. Simon* (pp. 399–440). Hillsdale NJ: Erlbaum.
Newell, A., & Rosenbloom, P. S. (1981). Mechanisms of skill acquisition and the power law of practice. In J. R. Anderson (Ed.), *Cognitive skills and their acquisition* (pp. 1–55). Hillsdale, NJ: Erlbaum.
Newell, A., & Simon, H. A. (1972). *Human problem solving.* Englewood Cliffs, NJ: Prentice-Hall.
Oldfield, R. C. (1963). Individual vocabulary and semantic currency: A preliminary study. *British Journal of Social and Clinical Psychology, 2*, 122–130.

Pfau, H. D., & Murphy, M. D. (1988). Role of verbal knowledge in chess skill. *American Journal of Psychology. 101*, 73–86.

Saariluoma, P. (1985). Chess players' intake of task-relevant cues. *Memory and Cognition, 13*, 385–391.

Saariluoma, P. (1989). Chess players' recall of auditorally presented chess positions. *European Journal of Psychology, 1*, 309–320.

Saariluoma, P. (1990a). Apperception and restructuring in chess players' problem solving. In K. Gilhooly, M. T. G. Keane, R. H. Logie, & G. Erdos (Eds.), *Lines of thinking: Reflections on the psychology of thought* (Vol. 2, pp. 41–57). London: Wiley.

Saariluoma, P. (1990b). Chess players' search for task relevant cues: Are chunks relevant? In D. Brogan (Ed.), *Visual search* (pp. 115–121). London: Taylor & Francis.

Schaeffer, J. (1986). *Experiments in search and knowledge* (Technical Report TR 86-12, Department of Computing Science, University of Alberta). (Ph.D. thesis at University of Waterloo, May 1986.)

Simon, H. A. (1981). *The sciences of the artificial* (2nd ed.). Cambridge, MA: MIT Press.

Simon, H. A., & Chase, W. G. (1973). Skill in chess. *American Scientist, 61*(4), 394–403.

Simon, H. A., & Gilmartin, K. (1973). A simulation of memory of chess positions. *Cognitive Psychology, 5*, 29–46.

Slate, D. J., & Atkin, L. R. (1983). Chess 4.5 – The Northwestern University chess program. In P. W. Frey (Ed.), *Chess skill in man and machine* (2nd ed., pp. 82–118). New York: Springer-Verlag.

Tikhomirov, O. K., & Vinogradov, Y. E. (1970). Emotions in the heuristic function. *Soviet Psychology, 8*, 198–203.

Waghorn, K. (1988). *Chess players' use of task-specific processes in a perceptual classification task.* Unpublished honors thesis, University of Waterloo.

Wilkins, D. (1983). Using chess knowledge to reduce search. In P. W. Frey (Ed.), *Chess skill in man and machine* (2nd ed., pp. 211–242). New York: Springer-Verlag.

3 *Learning and use of representations for physics expertise*

YUICHIRO ANZAI

WHAT IS PHYSICS EXPERTISE?

Physics is a domain of thought for understanding and explaining the physical world in scientific terms. Its history has included the integration of new theories with old ones for thinking about the physical world in more general, compact, consistent, and complete terms. Such new theories emerge not from scratch but from the heritage of forerunners' knowledge and various facets of general intelligence.

Expertise in physics comprises the abilities of acquiring and possessing those theories, exploiting them for understanding and predicting new phenomena, developing new theories to explain the physical world from novel points of view, and devising new experiments to reveal unknown facts about the physical world, with the capacity of learning to acquire knowledge underlying these abilities.

The recent development of cognitive studies on physics problem solving has clarified some part of the complex process of acquiring physics expertise. The goal of this chapter is to provide a concise scientific account of physics expertise from this modern cognitive viewpoint, with a new interpretation of the process of learning to draw physics diagrams.

This chapter has three parts. The first presents an overview of cognitive work on physics problem solving and expertise. It aims at summarizing the current status of this field and predicting the future directions of our research, particularly from the standpoint of cognitive representations. The second part analyzes one particular issue underlying physics expertise, namely, the acquisition of knowledge for drawing and using physics diagrams. The topic is adopted here as an instance of an important accomplishment worthy of pursuit. Though apparently too narrow a subject to cover our whole enterprise, the process of learning how to draw and use diagrams could be at the heart of acquisition of physics expertise, not only for novice learners but also for expert physicists, because physics expertise necessitates abstract knowledge quite different from naive knowledge about the physical world, and diagrams are powerful tools for representing and solving problems based on such abstract knowledge. These first two parts are concerned only with physics expertise. In the last part of this chapter we turn to relations between physics expertise and expertise in other domains, chess and medical diagnosis in particular, based on the earlier analysis. In the third part we not only compare the differences between physics and the other two domains but also try to extract some generalities encompassing expertise in all three domains. Note that this chapter is concerned solely with the cognitive point of view, although there are a variety of different approaches to research on physics expertise.

COGNITION AND PHYSICS EXPERTISE

First, let us divide the recent cognitive research on physics expertise into three categories, (1) expert–novices differences, (2) cognitive representations and their shifts, and (3) general problem-solving knowledge and self-monitoring, and take a brief look at each of them. Note that these divisions are made principally for concise description. Actually, most of the work to be summarized here was directed toward more than one category. Also, the list of studies cited here, though representative, is not exhaustive, even in cognitive science. There have been many other programs of research that are not cited here but have been related more or less to the research progress.

Expert–novice differences

Work on differences between experts and novices in physics problem solving flourished in the late 1970s and early 1980s. In particular, such work revealed the qualitative differences in their problem representations: Experts tend to represent physics problems in abstract terms, speaking, for example, of point-masses, massless strings, and frictionless surfaces, whereas novices often use naive concepts, such as those of blocks, ropes, and slopes, that are more directly related to the real world. The latter, more concrete concepts can result in misconceptions of the physical world and can lead to problem-solving failure. The extensive work on misconception in physics reported in the 1970s and early 1980s shed much light on this characteristic of expert–novice differences in physics problem solving (Anzai & Yokoyama, 1984; Clement, 1982; diSessa, 1982; McClosky, Caramazza, & Green, 1980; McClosky & Kohl, 1983; Trowbridge & McDermott, 1980, 1981; Viennot, 1979; White, 1983, 1984). Particularly, those studies revealed that novices tend to interpret physical phenomena not on the basis of the underlying physics principles but by direct observations based on common sense.

For example, suppose that a yo-yo, made by connecting the centers of two circular disks with an axle, is on a table, as illustrated in Figure 3.1, where the yo-yo's disks can roll but cannot slide. Then, consider the problem of telling whether the yo-yo will roll to the left (counterclockwise), will roll to the right (clockwise), or will not move, when one pulls the end of the string wound round the yo-yo's axle to the left, as shown in Figure 3.1.

For this problem, even though the correct solution is that the yo-yo will roll

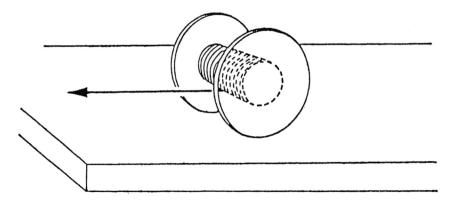

Figure 3.1. A yo-yo on a table for the yo-yo problem.

to the left (thus the released part of the string will be wound round the axle), naive learners in physics are likely to answer that the yo-yo will roll to the right, the direction opposite to the direction in which the string is pulled. Even with a real yo-yo and a real table it is not easy for a novice to decide that it will move in the same direction as the hand pulling the string. Experts, however, tend to think in terms of momentum or force equilibrium for solving the problem (Anzai & Yokoyama, 1984). This result suggests that novices may fall into misconceptions by generating naive causal representations based on common sense (if one pulls the string, then the yo-yo will move farther from one) quite different from experts' abstract representations. (Experts' representations of the yo-yo problem will be discussed in the next section.)

The differences in problem representations between physics experts and novices were also suggested by an elegant experiment by Chi, Feltovich, and Glaser (1981). They demonstrated that experts and novices in physics differ in their categorizations of physics problems: Experts are good at classifying physics word problems, and those with diagrams, with respect to underlying principles, whereas novices tend to use superficial meanings of words and diagrams for purposes of classification. The finding of Chi and her colleagues suggests that experts in physics possess knowledge that connects their knowledge of physics principles to the empirical meanings of words and diagrams that appear in problems and generates abstract problem representations. In particular, experts and novices may not process diagrams in the same way: Experts usually are able to interpret diagrams according to implicit physics principles, whereas novices are likely to "read" directly the concrete objects such as blocks, pulleys, and tables shown in diagrams.

The expert–novice differences in physics can also be seen in procedural knowledge for problem solving. For instance, Simon and Simon (1978) found evidence that physics experts solve problems in a "forward" way from the given data to the goal, whereas novices try to solve problems in a "backward" way from the goal by searching for appropriate data to satisfy each subgoal.

For instance, suppose that a block of weight W is in equilibrium on an inclined plane with a slope of θ degrees, being pushed against by a constant force of magnitude F parallel to the slope. In this situation, our problem is to find the value of the friction coefficient μ for the friction between the block and the slope. (This problem will be discussed again in the next section in a more concrete format.) We can easily solve this problem by first substituting F, W, and θ, all given in the problem, into the equation $f + W \sin \theta - F = 0$, to find f, where f is the friction force parallel to the slope, then substituting W and θ into $N - W \cos \theta = 0$, to find N, where N is the normal force perpendicular to the slope, and finally substituting f and N into the formula $f = \mu N$, to obtain the value of μ. (Variables and their specific values will be identified later.) This is the *working-forward strategy* for problem solving, so named because it starts to solve a problem by applying the data available in the problem and working forward to attain the goal.

On the other hand, we are also able to solve the same problem by starting from the goal, that is, first by finding the equation, $f = \mu N$, that includes the goal variable, μ, and identifying "free" variables, here f and N, then by finding, for each of these variables, an equation that contains the variable, and so forth. The data given in the problem, W, F, and θ, in our case, are substituted into retrieved equations whenever they are included in those equations. The solution process terminates when no "free" variables remain in retrieved equations. Because this problem-solving strategy works backward by starting from the goal variable and retrieving equations that contain relevant variables, it is called the *working-backward strategy*. Thus, the finding of Simon and Simon suggests that physics experts and novices tend to take the working-forward and working-backward strategies, respectively.

This line of work was elaborated further by Larkin, McDermott, Simon, and Simon (1980). They showed that experts are able to start inference from the information directly available in the problem, but novices generally infer backward from the expected final solution. The working-forward strategy often is learned as domain-specific procedures that are applicable to limit problems, whereas the working-backward strategy can be a general method encompassing different problem domains. Thus, the foregoing results suggest that physics experts possess proceduralized knowledge tailored to solve problems efficiently in particular domains, but novices' problem-solving procedures often are weak and general.

In summary, the studies on expert–novice differences, including those mentioned earlier, generally suggest that physics experts possess well-organized abstract knowledge for constructing abstract problem representations from the viewpoint of underlying principles, as well as specific knowledge for solving problems in domain-dependent and procedurally efficient ways. On the other hand, novices tend to generate naive problem representations based on commonsense knowledge and try to solve problems using relatively domain-independent weak methods. Those characteristics of novices' knowledge often lead to both misconceptions and inefficient problem-solving search.

Cognitive representations and their shifts

As implied earlier, one of the important issues related to physics expertise is how physics problems are represented cognitively. Some studies have examined this problem of representations more directly. For instance, Larkin (1982) found that experts and novices tend to use qualitatively different spatial representations for solving elementary hydraulics problems: Physics experts tend to solve problems by interpreting the attached diagrams to compare the initial and final problem states, and by trying to reduce the differences between those states in some particular, spatial ways. In contrast, novices may try to solve those problems by attending to local features in the diagrams and formulating equations based on the perceived local features.

Most of the proposed cognitive models for physics expertise are represented in sentential forms. Our introspection, however, tells us that physics expertise is supported not only by sentential representations but also by imagerial or diagrammatic representations. By "imagerial representations" we mean internal representations that often take "visual" forms. Diagrammatic representations are external representations that take the form of diagrams, as used in Larkin's hydraulics problems. Although imagerial representations for physics expertise are still far from the reach of cognitive research, the structure and use of diagrammatic representations are beginning to be studied in some detail. Pioneering work in that direction has been done by Larkin and Simon (1987). They presented production-system models for drawing inferences from physics diagrams and suggested that it is the two-dimensional spatial structure of diagrams that allows a *computationally efficient* (Larkin & Simon, 1987) search for information relevant to solving problems.

For example, suppose that two blocks, A and B, are hung at the two ends of a string S that is wound round a pulley P attached to a ceiling. Then we can draw a spatial diagram in which A, one end of S, P, the other end of S, and B are connected in this order and infer the acceleration of block A by relating objects and forces directly from the diagram. It may be a computationally efficient way of inference, as compared with inference using simply a set of sentences represented by lists of symbols or other symbolic structures. Although this example is much simpler than those given by Larkin and Simon (1987), diagrams are likely to include structures that allow computationally more efficient inference than sentential forms can, as Larkin and Simon suggested.

Not only problem representations themselves but also their shifts are important in identifying physics expertise. Among the relatively scarce reports on empirical results for shifts in cognitive representations, one by Anzai and Yokoyama (1984) provided evidence that experts tend not to shift internal representations so often, whereas novices' internal representations are relatively unstable. Novices are apt to change internal representations more often than experts are and seem not to be able to decide which representation is the best for solving a problem.

For example, let us consider the yo-yo problem mentioned earlier. If one can generate a problem representation composed of the fulcrum and momentum, it is not difficult to apply the lever principle to find that the yo-yo will move in the same direction as the hand pulling the string. Actually, when a cue relevant to the momentum at the contact point between one of the yo-yo's disks and the table surface is given with the problem, as shown in Figure 3.2(a), then some novices find it easy to change the representation to one involving abstract momentum terms (Anzai & Yokoyama, 1984).

An interesting problem to test whether such an abstract physics representation is available in the mind is the variant of the yo-yo problem in which the radius of the yo-yo's axle is larger than the radius of the disks, as shown in Figure 3.2(b). Examples of abstract diagrams for the original and the variant yo-yo problems are shown in Figures 3.2(c) and 3.2(d), respectively. Using Figure 3.2(d) it is easy to find, by applying the lever principle, that the yo-yo in the variant problem will roll in the direction *opposite* to the hand pulling the string. These examples suggest not only the adequacy of abstract representations for solving a physics problem that often leads to naive misconceptions but also the powerful role of diagrams as external aids in the use of abstract representations.

Also, Anzai and Yokoyama reported that particular kinds of internal representations are sensitive to external cues relevant to problems. They suggested that the sensitivity of represensational shifts is affected by at least three information sources: (1) a given problem, (2) the student's knowledge, and (3) hints relevant to the problem. For instance, the external cue consisting of the set comprising momentum and fulcrum is apt to produce a change in representation to one that can lead to the correct solution, but the cue of the set comprising momentum, fulcrum, center of gravity, friction force, and a note on friction force is likely to lead to the false solution "will not move." This result suggests that the generation of abstract representations appropriate for solving a problem requires some organization of abstract terms, not mere independent collections of possibly relevant pieces of knowledge.

The process of constructing and shifting cognitive representations for physics problems has also been advanced by means of computer modeling. For example, McDermott and Larkin (1978) presented a computer model of representational shifts in physics problem solving that started with a crude representation based on superficial meanings in physics word problems and, using some procedural knowledge, constructs intermediate and then final representations that are based on more formal knowledge of physics. Novak (1977) built a computer system that could read physics word problems, draw corresponding two-dimensional diagrams, and solve the problems using internal representations of those diagrams. In addition, de Kleer (1977) constructed a computer model of multiple representations and their use for mechanics problems, and Anzai (1987) implemented a computer system that could solve physics problems by making representational shifts based on various heuristics for causal and spatial inferences. Such studies use computer models to suggest that (1) physics experts may represent physics problems cognitively in

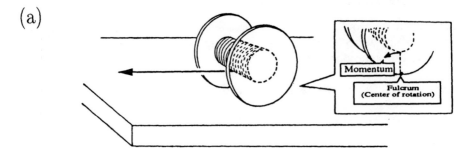

(a)

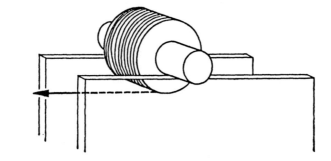

(b)

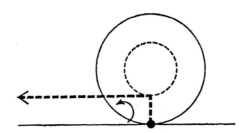

(c)

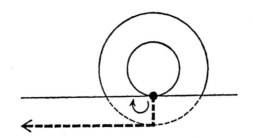

(d)

Figure 3.2. (a) Cues given for the yo-yo problem. (b) A variant of the yo-yo problem. (c) An abstract diagram for the original yo-yo problem. (d) An abstract diagram for the variant yo-yo problem.

more than one way, (2) experts in physics possess the procedural knowledge for effective use of those multiple representations, and (3) more abstract or simpler representations can be structured from less abstract or more complex ones in some algorithmic ways. This line of work has been more sharply focused, from the structural viewpoint, by Reif and Heller (1982; Heller & Reif, 1984; Reif, 1987) in their models of representations in physics.

Such computer programs tend to model the transition from one representation to another as in the preceding item 3. Even among experts, however, problem solving may not proceed in a unidirectional sequence but may opportunistically switch between commonsense knowledge and abstract knowledge. For example, Roschelle and Greeno (1987), working on verbal-protocol data, contrasted that relational framework with the transitional framework presented by McDermott and Larkin (1978). In their relational framework, Roschelle and Greeno emphasized experts' use of preexisting mental models, contrasting with the transitional framework in which experts tend to exploit abstract models. As they noted, this contrast is relative, and actually both frameworks are embodied in experts' problem solving.

To sum up, the work on cognitive representations has begun to establish inferential functions, representational shifts and their stability, and other essential properties of representations for physics problem solving, encompassing a range from sentential to diagrammatic forms.

General problem-solving knowledge and self-monitoring

Problem-solving strategies can be divided into those with weak methods and those with strong methods. Weak methods are general methods independent of domain-specific knowledge and include generate-and-test procedures, trial-and-error search, means–ends analysis, and problem reduction. Strong methods involve various strategies to exploit domain-specific knowledge to find an efficient solution. Because virtually no one possesses the full range of domain-specific knowledge in physics, even an expert physicist should use weak methods when strong methods cannot be applied. Actually, Larkin (1977) found such behavior empirically. She had several physicists solve problems that were novel to them, and she found that most of the physicists used general, weak methods to find adequate initial representations of given problems.

General problem-solving knowledge not only serves as a "front end" for activating relevant domain-specific knowledge but also encompasses many different levels of knowledge. For example, knowledge for solving problems concerning the pressures of liquids, centers of masses, and electric circuits has similar structures at various levels of generality. Thus, if a system has general problem-solving knowledge for each level of generality, and also knowledge for connecting it with knowledge specific to each domain of mechanics and electricity, then the system may solve problems in both domains. Such a system was actually implemented by Larkin, Reif, Carbonell, and Gugliotta

(1988). Their model was an instance of a physics problem-solving system that attempted to overcome domain specificity through general problem-solving knowledge.

Another line of research on the use of general problem-solving knowledge for physics includes the work of Langley, Simon, Bradshaw, and Zytkow (1987) on descriptive models of discovery. They assumed that scientific discoveries in physics, such as those by Kepler and Black, occur through a process of problem solving, and they proposed computational models of discovery based on general problem-solving knowledge for comparing and manipulating data and symbols.

Recent developments in cognitive problem solving have aroused some interest in metacognitive processes such as self-monitoring. In the area of physics expertise, Chi, Bassok, Lewis, Reimann, and Glaser (1987) used an elaborative verbal-protocol method to find that students who demonstrated good performance in solving physics problems tended to possess greater ability for elaborative explanations of their own solution processes than did those who achieved lower scores. They discovered that good students tended to generate self-explanations and self-monitoring statements more frequently than did poor students. Also, most of the self-explanations by the former group referred to justifications that elaborated conditions, actions, or goals for problem solving and gave meaning to quantitative expressions. Although the functions of self-explanation and self-monitoring in physics expertise have yet to be fully examined, and such metaprocesses are not easy to define rigorously, the results of Chi and associates suggest that learning in physics is not based solely on induction from working on many examples but also involves elaboration of the problem-solving process based on what learners believe they do not know about physics.

Other issues

This has been a brief overview of the recent results of cognitive studies of physics problem solving and expertise. A review of cognitive work on physics expertise up to the early 1980s is available (Chi, Glaser, & Rees, 1982). Our overview suggests that the structures and functions of cognitive representations for physics expertise are now much better understood than they were in the middle 1970s, thanks to intensive work during more than ten years. Note, in particular, that this work is now being extended not only to representations in sentential forms but also to qualitatively different forms, such as diagrams.

Also, the studies on cognitive representations suggest that the knowledge for physics expertise is well organized, extending to a large realm of declarative and procedural memories. Particularly, new discoveries by physics experts will necessitate large and effectively indexed knowledge bases in physics and other related fields.

On the other hand, it should be noted that most of the recent cognitive research on physics has been limited to "routine" problem solving by experts and novices. That is, the primary concern has been with the simple problems often seen in high school or college textbooks. Although such routine problems are the real problems with which engineers deal, experts at the frontiers of physics are trying to discover the unknown principles of the physical world and to construct *new* types of representations that will help explain it in scientific terms. Only those who succeeded in generating novel representations will be long remembered in the history of physics: Copernicus, Newton, Galileo, Maxwell, Faraday, Planck, Einstein, and Yukawa, just to name a few.

Thus, although many of the essential aspects of physics expertise have begun to be attacked from a cognitive viewpoint, there are many research issues still waiting to be addressed. As mentioned earlier, topics to be addressed in the future include the functions of imagerial and diagrammatic representations; the organization, development, and retrieval of large knowledge bases; and the processes of discovery of the research frontiers of theoretical and experimental physics. Note also that in reference to the issue of knowledge bases, metaknowledge for restructuring them may be a key issue from the cognitive viewpoint. Although these topics have already been treated to some extent, as described in this section, further cognitive work in these areas will shed new light on the science of cognition in physics.

DIAGRAMS AND PHYSICS EXPERTISE

Experts in physics are all proficient at drawing physics diagrams and at making inferences from those diagrams. Novices are not. Although these points are intuitively obvious, little research has been reported on the function of diagrammatic representations in physics problem solving. In this section, we discuss various functions of diagrams in physics, referring to an excerpt from an experiment on learning how to draw and use physics diagrams.

Functions of diagrams of physics

Diagrams are ubiquitous in various subdomains of physics. One of the most important functions of physics diagrams is to *generalize* various relations between abstract entities. By schematizing the generalized relations of physics entities in diagrams, physicists may be able to infer relations that hold for many different problems. The Feynman diagram used by expert physicists is a typical example. Another kind of function for diagrams in physics is to represent *specific* problems for some specific goals. By representing a particular problem with a set of diagrams, physicists not only can recognize the underlying structure of the problem but also can organize computationally efficient inference procedures for solving it. Note that these two functions may be applied to the same physics diagram. The second function refers to one specific problem, whereas the first generally involves more than one problem. For instance, vector diagrams for elementary mechanics can be applied to both generalized and specific representations. The functional distinction is sometimes useful when we discuss particular issues related to one of the functions. We are concerned here particularly with the second function of diagrammatic representations.

The problem-representing function of physics diagrams has two aspects: (1) representing a problem and (2) drawing inferences toward a solution. That is, when a physics problem, at any level of difficulty, is to be solved, it tends to be represented by a set of diagrams, and those diagrams often are used for inferring various relations. The invention and use of diagrams can be at the heart of physics expertise because diagrams often can connect representation and inference efficiently.

Among the cognitive processes that use diagrams in physics, the inference process has been modeled by Larkin and Simon (1987). Their model sets up a spatially represented diagram and tries to make inferences from the diagram, using spatially coded production rules. On the other hand, we are concerned here with the empirical question of the process whereby the novice learns how to produce computationally efficient diagrammatic representations.

An experiment on learning to draw diagrams and make inferences

One method of conducting a detailed investigation of learning via the diagramming process is to ask a novice student to try to solve the same problems repeatedly, and then to compare the resulting spontaneously drawn diagrams. Typically, a novice tries to understand problem sentences by means of common sense and tends to construct naive representations that can lead to false solutions. We expect that a novice's diagrams will reflect this empirical modeling. On the other hand, when one has accumulated more knowledge about solving physics problems, one's constructed representations tend no longer to be superficial but, rather, to be results of abstract scientific thinking regarding physics entities. Diagrams drawn by students at this level tend to be abstract and easily adapted to new problems. The following experiment was designed to determine whether results to support that expectation would be observed. Some of the results were reported earlier (Anzai, 1982).

Method. The subject, a graduate from a liberal-arts college, had not taken any physics courses while in college. She was given a university-level physics textbook (Sears & Zemansky, 1970) and asked to study it, beginning with the first chapter. She was allowed to read explanatory passages in chapters; to ask the experimenter any questions; to use a notebook to draw diagrams, write equations, and perform computations; and to consult the tables of trigonometric functions in the textbook. No feedback regarding correct solutions was given for the exercise problems throughout the experiment.

The first chapter, "Composition and Resolution of Vectors," taught graphic representation of vectors in the x–y plane and simple vector-calculation algorithms such as rectangular decomposition. The subject began by studying the text, and then solved all 16 problems in the exercise section within about 2.5 hours. The subject was asked to think aloud during the exercise sessions, and the verbal-protocol data were tape-recorded.

Next, the subject proceeded to the second chapter, "Equilibrium of a Particle," which concerned the elementary mechanics of mass particles, including Newton's first and third laws. The subject read and studied the text and then worked on 25 problems in the exercise section. After solving the last problem, she returned to the first problem, and again solved 23 of the 25 problems. She then solved 24 of the 25 problems (all except Problem 2-1). Let us call those three rounds R1, R2, and R3. The rounds do not include the time spent studying the text. The subject was asked to think aloud during all of the exercise sessions, and the protocol data were tape-recorded for subsequent analysis.

The whole experiment took roughly twenty hours, including the study sessions with the text and the three rounds of exercises. It was not continuous, of course, but was self-paced during a period of twenty-eight days.

Results and discussion. The subject took roughly 500, 275, and 200 minutes for rounds R1, R2, and R3, respectively. Qualitatively, there is an effect of repetitive problem solving. Solution time and accuracy, though not reported here, were much better for R3 than for R1. Performance during R2 was between those for R1 and R3. Here, we select one problem (Problem 2-22) as an example and present the results in some detail. Problem 2-22 is as follows:

> *2-22(a)* If a force of 86 lb parallel to the surface of a 20° inclined plane will push a 120-lb block up the plane at constant speed, what force parallel to the plane will push it down at constant speed? *(b)* What is the coefficient of sliding friction?

Actually, Problem 2-22 is an instance of one of the problems discussed earlier. To solve it, the subject took 9 minutes 44 seconds for R1, 5 minutes 55 seconds for R2, and 3 minutes 56 seconds for R3. Four days after the sessions were over, she was asked to solve Problem 2-22 again. Let us call that fourth round R4. R4 took 3 minutes 50 seconds.

If we take a detailed look into the think-aloud protocols, the diagrams drawn, and the equations written in R1–R4, we see some important differences. The data on those differences derive from the sequence of the subject's actions obtained from the think-aloud protocols and the experimenter's observations. In particular, in each round, the subject usually drew a diagram first and then moved to make inferences for problem solving. The results for those two phases, the diagramming phase and the inference phase, are discussed next.

The diagramming phase. Figure 3.3 shows the four diagrams drawn during R1–R4. The diagram drawn for Problem 2-22 during R1 obviously is different

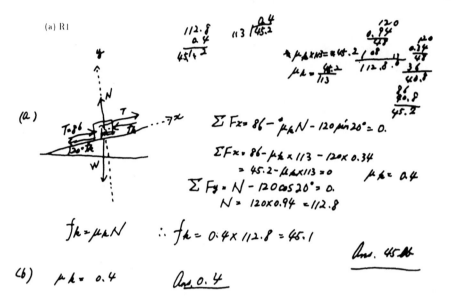

Action sequence

1. Drawing the inclined plane of 20°.
2. Drawing the block of 120lb.
3. Drawing the arrow of $T = 86$ at left.
4. Drawing the arrow of f_k at right.
5. Drawing T at right.
6. Drawing f_k at left.
7. Drawing the normal force N.
8. Drawing the arrow of W.
9. Drawing the y-axis.
10. Drawing the x-axis.
11. Writing $\sum F_x = 0$ (variables: N, μ_k).
12. Writing $\sum F_y = 0$ (variables: N), and computing N.
13. Substituting N of 12. into 11., and computing μ_k.
14. Writing $f_k = \mu_k N$, substituting μ_k and N into it, and computing f_k.
15. Writing the answer μ_k.

Figure 3.3 (continues on next three pages). Diagrams drawn and equations written for Problem 2-22 in (a) R1, (b) R2, (c) R3, and (d) R4 of the experiment.

from those generated during R2–R4. In R1, the arrows representing the pushing force of 86 lb and the frictional force f_k were drawn initially in a way that did not apply directly to inference procedures, although it did correspond to the problem statement. Also, the x and y axes were drawn explicitly. In R2, the arrow for 86 lb was again drawn first as the "pushing force" at the left side of the block, and also the y axis was drawn. The diagrams drawn during R3

(b) R2

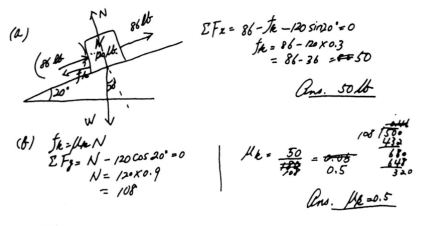

Action sequence

1. Drawing the inclined plane of 20°.
2. Drawing the block of 120lb.
3. Drawing the arrow of 86lb at left.
4. Drawing the arrow of f_k.
5. Drawing the arrow of 86lb at right.
6. Drawing the normal force N.
7. Drawing the arrow of W.
8. Drawing the angle of 20° for W, and also the y-axis.
9. Writing $\sum F_x = 0$ (variables: f_k), and computing f_k.
10. Writing $f_k = \mu_k N$ (variables: μ_k, N).
11. Writing $\sum F_y = 0$ (variables: N), and computing N.
12. Substituting f_k of 9. and N of 11. into 10., and computing μ_k.

Figure 3.3 (*cont.*).

and R4 are similar, but both differ from those generated during R1 and R2. First, no redundant arrow like the pushing force was drawn, and the corresponding force of 86 lb was drawn directly as the force emanating from the right side of the block.

Second, all of the arrows radiate out from a single point, which corresponds to the point of mass that represents the block.

The foregoing process of diagramming can be regarded primarily as the process of transforming a cognitive representation to another that is more appropriate for achieving the goal of solving problems. Figure 3.4 illustrates a possible process for generating diagrammatic representations from this transformational point of view. First, we can assume that a set of procedures S_1 generates from the problem description, M_0, the problem's initial representation, M_1, in a list form, as shown at the top of Figure 3.4. Next, making some inference by using physics knowledge, M_1 can be updated to M_2. The set of procedures S_2 that maps M_1 to M_2 includes heuristic knowledge for assuming

(c) R3

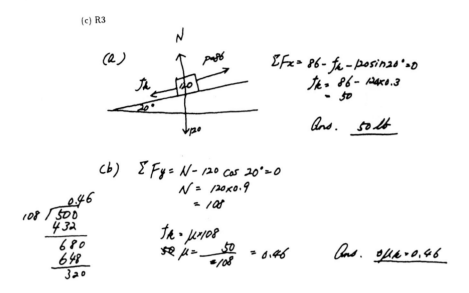

$\sum F_x = 86 - f_k - \rho o \sin 20° = 0$

$f_k = 86 - 120 \times 0.3$

$= 50$

(Ans.) $\underline{50 \, lb}$

(b) $\sum F_y = N - 120 \cos 20° = 0$

$N = 120 \times 0.9$

$= 108$

$f_k = \mu \times 108$

$50 \quad \mu = \dfrac{50}{108} = 0.46$

(Ans.) $\underline{of \mu_k = 0.46}$

Action sequence

1. Drawing the inclined plane of 20°.
2. Drawing the block of 120lb.
3. Drawing the arrow of $P = 86$.
4. Drawing the arrow of f_k.
5. Drawing the normal force N.
6. Drawing the arrow of 120lb.
7. Writing $\sum F_x = 0$ (variables: f_k), and computing f_k.
8. Writing $\sum F_y = 0$ (variables: N), and computing N.
9. Writing $f_k = \mu_k \times 108$, substituting f_k of 7. and N of 8. into it., and computing μ_k.

Figure 3.3 (*cont.*).

that a block is box-shaped as a default and for finding entities that cause the sliding friction. Note that M_1 and M_2 are represented in sentential or list structure. On the other hand, M_2 can be transformed by some set of procedures S_3 into the representation M_3 in Figure 3.4 that contains *spatial* forms, where each point i ($i = 1, \ldots, 12$) refers to the appropriate location of the point in the x–y plane. S_3 includes spatial heuristics for locating the origin and destination of each force vector, as well as the block's and plane's vertices in the x–y plane. Also, note that M_3 extracts from M_1 and M_2 "commonsense" terms such as *push-up* and *push-down*. M_3 reflects the subject's partially empirical representation, which is shown clearly in the diagram drawn in R1. A diagram corresponding to M_3 is illustrated in Figure 3.4.

Continuing our elaborations of representations, we obtain the final representation M_n. A diagram corresponding to M_n is shown in Figure 3.4. M_n partially corresponds to the diagrams drawn in R3 and R4 and contains various abstract terms for the forces. Note that, in M_n, point 5 is shared by the

(d) R4

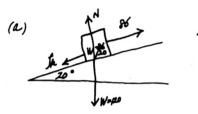

(a)

$$\Sigma F_x = 86 - f_k - 120 \sin 20° = 0$$
$$f_k = 86 - 120 \times 0.3$$
$$= 86 - 36$$
$$= 50$$

Ans. 50 lb

(b) $$\Sigma F_y = N - \#\ 120 \cdot \cos 20° = 0$$
$$N = 120 \times 0.9$$
$$= 108$$

$$\emptyset \ \mu_k \times 108 = 50$$
$$\mu_k = \frac{50}{108}$$
$$= 0.46$$

Ans 0.846

Action sequence

1. Drawing the inclined plane of 20°.
2. Drawing the block of 120.
3. Drawing the arrow of 86.
4. Drawing the arrow of f_k.
5. Drawing the normal force N.
6. Drawing the arrow of $W = 120$.
7. Writing $\Sigma F_x = 0$ (variables: f_k), and computing f_k.
8. Writing $\Sigma F_y = 0$ (variables: N), and computing N.
9. Writing $\mu_k \times 108 = 50$, and computing μ_k.

Figure 3.3 (*cont.*).

point of mass for block 1 and the origins of the four force vectors. This implies that the force vectors in the corresponding spatial diagram take a form adequate for computing the equilibrium by the vector-decomposition method.

The inference phase. The equations written by the subject during R1–R4 are shown in Figure 3.3. In the inference phase of R1, the subject first wrote down the two formulas $\Sigma F_x = 0$ and $\Sigma F_y = 0$ (where F_x and F_y are the magnitudes of the x and y components of a force vector, F, respectively), without thinking much about what quantity was being sought. She first solved $\Sigma F_x = 0$ to find μ_k, then used ΣF_y to get N, and then solved $f_k = \mu_k N$ to obtain f_k, where f_k is the magnitude of the force pushing the block down, μ_k is the coefficient of kinetic friction, and N is the magnitude of the normal force exerted on the block. Although the subject ultimately solved the problem, her initial choice of equations was by trial and error, rather than systematized. In the inferencing phase of R2, the strategy was partially the same as in R1. That is, although f_k was computed by using only $\Sigma F_x = 0$, which is the proper solution method, the subject next wrote down the formula $f_k = \mu_k N$, and then

M_1 {*(force force1 86lb (parallel-to plane1) (push-up block1)) (plane plane1 (inclined 20°)) (block block1 120lb move-constant-speed Shape?) (force force2 Magnitude? (parallel-to plane1) (push-down force2 block1)) (Sliding-friction? between Object1? Object2?)*}.

M_2 $M_1 \cup${*(block block1 120lb move-constant-speed box-shaped) (Sliding-friction? between block1 plane1)*} - {*(block block1 120lb move-constant-speed Shape?) (Sliding-friction? between Object1? Object2?)*}.

M_3 $M_2 \cup${*(point-from force1 point1) (point-to force1 point2) (point-from force2 point3) (point-to force2 point4) (locate block1 point5) (shape block1 (point6 point7 point8 point9)) (locate plane1 point10) (shape plane1 (point11 point10 point12))*}.

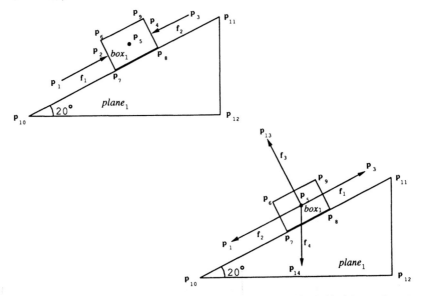

M_n {*(force force1 86lb (parallel-to plane1) (external-force block1)) (plane plane1 (inclined 20°)) (block block1 120lb move-constant-speed center-of-mass) (force force2 Magnitude? (parallel-to plane1) (frictional-force block1 plane1)) (Sliding-friction? between block1 plane1) (force force3 (normal-force block1 plane1)) (force force4 (gravity-force block1 plane1)) (point-from force1 point5) (point-to force1 point3) (point-from force2 point5) (point-to force2 point1) (locate block1 point5) (shape block1 (point6 point7 point8 point9)) (locate plane1 point10) (shape plane1 (point11 point10 point12)) (point-from force3 point5) (point-to force3 point13) (point-from force4 point5) (point-to force4 point14)*}.

Figure 3.4. Process of generating diagrammatic representations.

wrote $\Sigma F_y = 0$. That process was similar to the working-backward strategy (defined earlier in this chapter) employed by novice subjects in the experiments of Larkin et al. (1980). On the other hand, the inference strategy used in R3 and R4 was completely working forward (in the same sense as defined earlier). That is, values for f_k and N were computed first from $\Sigma F_x = 0$ and $\Sigma F_y = 0$, respectively, and then those values were substituted into $f_k = \mu_k N$ to obtain the value of μ_k.

In summary, the subject learned inference strategies, starting from trial-and-error search for adequate equations, moving to the working-backward strategy for seeking the value of μ_k, and then moving to the working-forward strategy to pick up appropriate equations consecutively to find the values of variables. Our results provide empirical evidence of one student's consecutive acquisition of inference procedures at various levels of expertise, where the procedures were similar to those undertaken in a comparative analysis by Larkin et al. (1980). Also, note that the strategy-acquisition process, from trial and error to working backward and then to working forward, was similar to those observed in puzzle problem solving (Anzai & Simon, 1979) and a simulated ship-steering task (Anzai, 1984). That suggests that our result may be extendable to domains other than elementary physics.

Suggestions from the experimental analysis. The foregoing results from the experiment suggest that repetition in solving exercise problems may have helped the subject to learn to draw diagrams and make inferences in an increasingly sophisticated manner. In particular, it seems clear that the subject acquired during the twenty hours of the experiment some relatively general procedural knowledge for (1) transforming verbal problem statements into sketchy diagrammatic representations and then to abstract free-body diagrams and (2) making inferences more efficiently in a working-forward fashion.

The data for the other twenty-two problems in the same experiment generally support this conclusion (Anzai, 1982). Furthermore, the results from a transfer experiment conducted four days after this experiment suggest that the knowledge acquired by the subject was general enough to be adapted to new problems.

RELATION BETWEEN DIAGRAMMING AND MAKING INFERENCES

The foregoing results and analysis suggest that there may be some cognitive relation between the learning of diagramming procedures and the learning of inference strategies. Here, let us consider such a possible relation between the learning of the two processes. Although the following argument is not yet supported sufficiently by empirical data, I believe that the hypothesis to be presented is highly plausible. The argument in this section was partly suggested by Katz (Katz & Anzai, 1991).

First, note that the force vectors drawn in the diagram in R1 do not share an origin at the point of mass for the block. Indeed, the force vectors were drawn as a direct translation of the problem statement. Also, in R1, the subject activated the formulas $\Sigma F_x = 0$ and $\Sigma F_y = 0$ spontaneously, with no reference to specific variables. Those choices suggest that our novice learner applied initial diagram drawing, inference making, and the vector-decomposition method essentially independently.

Next, notice that the frictional force f_k can easily be discovered and computed if the x–y coordinate system is taken to be parallel to the inclined plane, with the center of the block as the origin, because it then becomes easier to infer that computing f_k is reduced simply to summing the lengths of the x components of the force vectors. The argument applies similarly to the normal force N and the y components of the forces. This selection of an effective coordinate system could be triggered by application of the vector-decomposition method. These investigations suggest that the subject's construction of M_n would help evoke the working-forward strategy, because its utility would be highly increased by the separate attention to the specific forces f_k and N. Actually, as seen in R3 and R4, the subject took the working-forward strategy whenever she drew diagrams that corresponded to M_n. On the other hand, it should be noted that the working-forward strategy is not easily learned unless variables are forwardly related in some specific order of retrieving equations. To accomplish this, there must be an intermediate stage of organizing relations among appropriate variables, in between the two extrema of the trial-and-error process and the working-forward strategy (see Lesgold, 1984, for related points). In our experiment, this stage may correspond to the working-backward strategy apparently used in R2. This argument leads to a hypothesis that at first the initial empirical diagramming and trial-and-error inferences lead to a more abstract and efficient type of diagramming, and a working-backward inference strategy. The vector-decomposition method, one of the procedural principles in elementary mechanics, can therefore by applied effectively, and then the more abstract diagrams acquired in that way will evoke a sophisticated working-forward inference strategy. Figure 3.5 illustrates this possible strategy-acquisition process. The figure involves a recognition process, which is included for completing the relation between the diagramming and inference-making processes.

In more general terms, the initial choices of procedures for drawing empirical figures and a naive strategy for inference equations seem to be essentially independent. After those procedures and strategy are activated, the vector-decomposition principle should evoke procedures for drawing diagrams with all force vectors emanating from the point of mass. Next, that evocation will lead to a working-backward inference strategy with a more appropriate arrangement of problem-solving equations. Then, that strategy will be transformed to a working-forward strategy via relating variables forward. At that point, refined diagrams can help one infer the directions of force vectors and extract and relate adequate variables. In brief, the two processes, diagramming and inference making, seem to be guided by the methodological

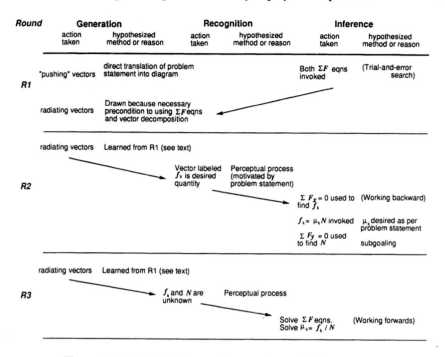

Figure 3.5. Relation between diagramming and inference processes.

principle of vector decomposition to intertwine themselves in the process of learning to understand and solve physics problems.

To summarize, I suggest that the process of learning to draw diagrams and make inferences in physics problem solving involves a *principle-guided boot-strapping* of two initially independent processes, as shown by the meandering sequence of arrows in Figure 3.5. Although the analysis was made with longi-tudinal data from one subject, and the idea of bootstrapping still awaits full examination, this may provide a new explanation of how one can learn to draw sophisticated diagrams while learning advanced inference strategies, and vice versa.

EXPERTISE IN PHYSICS AND OTHER DOMAINS

A person who is working on physics problems must *recognize* the underlying structures of the problems, *generate* representations appropriate for discovering solutions, and make *inferences* on the generated representa-tions. Recognition, generation, and inference are three main components of the processes in physics problem solving and expertise, and a large body of literature has accumulated around these topics, as described in the first part of this chapter. Particularly for physics experts, recognition involves theoretical knowledge of physics, generation often is accompanied by abstract diagrams, and inference is made by efficient strategies like working forward, as noted earlier. In physics, the three components can be integrated in the learning process in some bootstrapping fashion, as suggested in the second part of this chapter.

These process components of expertise are not unique to physics. Rather, they seem to be the chief components in many different problem domains. In particular, chess and medical diagnosis are domains that have been well investigated in terms of recognition and inference (Charness, chapter 2, this volume; Patel & Groen, chapter 4, this volume). In this section, we provide some comparisons between expertise in physics and expertise in other domains, particularly chess and clinical diagnosis, and try to squeeze out some generalities from the domain-specific results. Although most of the following discussion is still speculative, I believe it indicates important topics worthy of investigation. Also, it should be noted that chess and medical diagnosis are discussed next simply as example domains for comparison. It would be beyond the scope of this chapter to discuss whether this argument is applicable to other domains, such as mathematics, music, sports, repairing machines, reading, writing, memory, perception, and even social skills.

Inference making and constraints

In spite of the generality of the inference component in expertise, it seems that the methods of inference making are different in physics, chess, and medical diagnosis. Here, let me clarify those differences and argue that one of the principal sources of differences derives from the structures of tasks and the knowledge available for problem solving. Specifically, I believe that the formation of inference strategies in a domain can be affected by the structures of the tasks and by the knowledge of the problem-solvers.

First, consider interaction with the outside world. Physics is an endeavor essentially of one particular person, whereas chess players and diagnosticians usually interact with opponents and patients, respectively, although certainly there are some exceptions to those situations. In any case, if a task is interactive, it may be more difficult to automatize inference processes by working-forward strategies, because those strategies generally involve domain-specific procedures that tend to become disordered when there is an interruption. In chess, for instance, the working-forward strategy corresponds to planning by searching forward from a specific problem state. In this sense, a chess player is generally able to work forward without the opponent's interruption, but that process of working forward can sometimes be upset by an unexpected move from the opponent.

On the other hand, it may be easier to implement working-backward inferencing strategies when interaction occurs. That is because subgoals may be hierarchically stored in memory when those strategies are applied: Inference can restart, at some appropriate subgoals, toward ends that were not searched for, even if the process is interrupted, although such strategies may put a heavier burden on short-term memory (Anzai & Uesato, 1982; Lesgold, 1984). Working-backward strategies seem to be comparatively robust against uncertainty caused by opponents' or patients' sudden changes in behavior. Thus, qualitative differences in experts' inference strategies in various domains could be attributed not merely to individuals but also to the interactive nature of the task.

Second, I suggest that inference strategies are influenced by the structure of domain-specific knowledge. Knowledge for inference in chess seems to consist largely of a set of search and planning heuristics that apply to different situations. Clinical medicine seems relatively similar to chess because of its reliance on empirical heuristics, though some part of it can be supported by modern medical sciences. In both domains, the essential process of problem solving may lie in the recognition of relevant features, and then the use of heuristic inference based on what is found. Early work on clinical problem solving, for instance, suggests that medical doctors tend to generate a few hypotheses on the basis of recognized relevant information, and then try to gather data to support those hypotheses (Elstein, Shulman, & Sprafka, 1978).

In this respect, physics is somewhat different from chess and clinical medicine. Physicists have developed general theories encompassing many different problems; therefore, once problems are transformed into representations that are well supported by a relevant theory, inferences can be made by using methodologies related to the theory. These knowledge-based differences in inference making sometimes can be matters of degree (e.g., the early part of a chess game often involves fairly general concepts called "opening theory"). But note that the goals of knowledge in physics, chess, and clinical diagnosis differ: The goal of physics knowledge is to discover general and compact theories, chess knowledge concerns how to win, and knowledge for clinical diagnosis is aimed at curing each patient. These differences in goals can lead to differences in the structures of knowledge and thus in inference strategies.

One caveat for the foregoing kind of comparative analysis is that data can come from tasks of different levels. Physicists have been working mainly on routine problem-solving tasks that can be qualitatively different from the tasks treated in research on chess and clinical medicine. If professional physicists are confronted with novel and difficult problems, for example, they may revert to using weak general methods of problem solving, rather than pursue working-forward procedures (Larkin, 1977). On the other hand, the use of working-forward strategies may be specific not just to physics experts but to any task in which the relations of relevant variables are well understood. Also, working-backward strategies could be relevant to any task whose hierarchical goal structure is relatively easy to represent and keep in memory.

Thus, the structures of tasks, goals, and knowledge encompassing various domains may provide general characteristics of inference strategies that seemingly differ across domains.

Coordination of recognition and inference

Experts in some problem domains, such as physics, chess, or medical diagnosis, can be regarded as problem-solvers trying to achieve goals under constraints. Much literature on cognitive problem solving suggests that, in such circumstances, recognition and inference are two principal factors that dominate experts' performance (Greeno & Simon, 1988). Those two factors are not independent, however. Pruning search trees for efficient inference making requires swift recognition. Retrieval of relevant knowledge for encoding appropriate representations necessitates effective inference. Here, we take the domains of chess, physics, and medical diagnosis to consider the relations between recognition and inference in expertise.

Let us consider chess first. Recognition memory for chess experts may actually involve some selective inference (Charness, chapter 2, this volume). Chess experts usually are far superior to novices at recognizing and memorizing meaningful chessboard patterns (Chase & Simon, 1973), and their eyes may track relevant positions in highly efficient ways (Tikhomirov & Poznyanskaya, 1966). Expertise in chess is, at least for the first approximation, some amalgamation of recognition and inference based on a variety of heuristic knowledge (Charness, chapter 2, this volume).

The same conclusion applies to physics. A physicist looking into a problem, perceives its relevant parts but may search systematically for other relationships. For instance, physics diagrams can be used not only to recall adequate information from memory but also to make computationally efficient inferences (Larkin & Simon, 1987). The results of the experiment described earlier in this chapter suggest that learning to be an expert may involve complex coordination between inference and recognition. Also, although experts in physics usually are quick to recognize and categorize problems on the basis of knowledge of underlying principles (Chi et al., 1981), as well as being efficient in searching for solutions by working forward (Larkin et al., 1980), the cases in between those two extremes may be more common in practice.

In medical diagnosis, too, recognition and inference are essential components of expertise, but in a somewhat different manner. In the usual clinical cases, before the diagnoses of medical doctors are completed they may rely on backward inference rather than working forward, and on search for solutions of open problems in a generic fashion (Patel & Groen, chapter 4, this volume). Also, an expert diagnostician may learn to recognize particular features in data and to look for other features based on what has been discovered (Lesgold, 1984). In actual situations, doctors may be compelled by the pressure of time to coordinate their processes of recognition and inference making to achieve a proper diagnosis.

In summary, I suggest that one of the dominant process factors for expertise is coordination between recognition and inference, at least if we restrict our attention to problem-solving domains such as chess, physics, and medical diagnosis.

Functional similarity in recognition and generation of diagrams

As argued earlier in this chapter, people can learn to draw physics diagrams that will be relevant for making effective inferences. Diagrams, however, are not always self-generated; in some cases they are given directly to the problem-solver. It should be interesting to see if these two modes of cognitive processing of diagrams have similar functions in achieving problem solutions. Because such functional relations are still largely unknown, let us undertake some preliminary discussion characterizing the relations between the recognition and generation of diagrams.

First, consider the recognition of diagrams in problem solving. There have been many studies of the cognitive relations between texts and diagrams. For example, diagrams have been suggested to function by encoding problem schemas and retrieval cues for recognition (Gick & Holyoak, 1983). Also, diagrams may provide good spatial cues for efficient inference making (Larkin & Simon, 1987). That view seems to have been supported by an eye-movement analysis in which experts in mechanical skills attended to diagrams much longer than did novices when juxtaposed texts were short (Hegarty & Just, 1989). That long duration of attention may be attributable to the sub-jects' efforts to encode relevant schemas or to find appropriate retrieval cues.

But most of those studies on relations between texts and diagrams were concerned with diagrams provided to subjects, rather than self-generated diagrams as discussed in this chapter. In this respect, the following experimental results have come from the few studies that have sought to clarify the functional relations between diagram recognition and generation.

In one of our experiments we asked subjects to solve a problem analogous to, but easier than, Duncker's radiation problem, and then to solve a problem similar to the radiation problem itself (Anzai & Kinoe, 1984). The analogy problem asked subjects how to extinguish fire in a house that had windows in its walls, using streams of water. Although the analogical transfer with that problem was not easy for our subjects, as found by Gick and Holyoak (1983), the subjects who were shown two-dimensional figures produced much better results than did those who were shown three-dimensional projections. That result suggested that a two-dimensional figure was better suited for finding a solution to the target problem. This hypothesis was supported by our second experiment (Anzai & Kinoe, 1984). In the second experiment, the same experimental conditions were kept, except that subjects were not given pre-pared figures but were allowed to draw figures of their spontaneously gener-ated visual images. The results were clear: The subjects who drew two-dimensional figures were much better at analogical transfer than those who drew three-dimensional figures. These results suggest that there are cases in which recognition and generation of figures will have similar functional effects for solving problems.

This hypothesis of functional similarity may be a good starting point for analyzing the relations between recognition and generation of diagrams. In particular, if the functional-similarity hypothesis holds, then the results reported for experts' recognition abilities might be extended to the generation of diagrams.

In physics, experts are able to recognize the structures of physics problems and diagrams by using their knowledge of underlying principles, as discussed in the first part of this chapter. A counterpart of this ability can be seen in diagrams drawn by experts: Such diagrams tend to be principle-oriented abstractions of physical objects and their relations that are quite different from realistic drawings. In both the recognition and generation processes, the recognized and generated representations may be physics diagrams that include appropriate information for solving problems, and, as argued earlier in this chapter, the abilities to recognize and generate physics diagrams may be acquired through the process of learning by doing. The end result of this learning process should be the acquisition of knowledge that can support the functionally similar abilities of diagram recognition and generation.

Note that this possible correspondence between diagram recognition and diagram generation in analogical problem solving and physics is largely correlative rather than causal or logical. Also, we have not yet reached a point at which we can say much about functional similarities in other domains, such as chess and clinical diagnosis. Probably one exception is that chess experts are known to be adept not only at recognizing meaningful chessboard patterns but also at generating relevant arrangements of chess pieces from memory (Chase & Simon, 1973). Generation of patterns from memory in chess may also be a good starting point in the quest of functional relations between recognition and generation.

Learning processes

As noted earlier, the strategy-acquisition process – proceeding from trial and error to working backward and then to working forward – proposed in this chapter can be observed in other circumstances such as the Tower of Hanoi puzzle (Anzai & Simon, 1979) and the steering of simulated ships (Anzai, 1984). Note that all of these results were investigated in the same kinds of experiments, namely, longitudinal experiments involving one subject and repetitive trials. One reason few process theories like ours have been presented may be that most experiments on expertise have used comparative analyses of subjects at different levels of expertise. We take another direction: nurturing a layperson to be an expert, and observing the microstructure of the learning process. We need to wait and see if this approach can be taken in other disciplines, although one notable example of exceptional memory has been reported: Chase and Ericsson (1982) had a subject learn long digit sequences, and they presented a microscopic account of how such memory processes worked.

Also, Patel and Groen (chapter 4, this volume) suggest, in relevance to clinical problem solving, that the development of expertise can be understood by the three-stage process of learning (1) adequate knowledge representations, (2) ways of distinguishing between relevant and irrelevant information, and (3) how to use relevant information in an efficient manner. This proposed learning process matches well with our theory of strategy acquisition. As noted earlier, however, medical diagnosis is a much more complex and open domain than physics, and hence the acquisition of medical generic expertise through this learning process could be more complicated.

SUMMARY

The first part of this chapter presented an overview of recent cognitive work on physics expertise and noted the importance of cognitive representations. Mere emphasis on cognitive representations in general, however, may not differentiate between expertise in physics and expertise in other domains. Rather, we should attend particularly to the structure and function of the knowledge to which physics experts owe their expertise.

Toward that end, the second part of this chapter provided a cognitive analysis of the process of learning to make and use diagrams in physics problem solving. Although the hypothesis (principle-guided bootstrapping) proposed in this chapter to explain the intertwined process of learning to draw diagrams and solve problems needs a more elaborate analysis, the hypothesis may explicate at least some part of the knowledge underlying physics expertise.

Furthermore, we discussed the relations between expertise in physics and other domains, such as chess and medical diagnosis, and performed a comparative analysis of domain-specific results. That analysis suggested that the apparent domain specificity of expertise may involve some generalities. Notably, I argued that task-constrained inference strategies; the cooperative use of recognition, generation, and inference; and the process of learning inference strategies in different domains could be explained in a domain-general fashion if we took the structures of tasks and the structures of underlying theories and knowledge as explanatory dimensions.

In particular, much cognitive representation by physics experts should be constrained by the structural characteristics of physics theories and tasks. Those representations are also constrained by the cognitive information-processing mechanisms of the experts themselves. These two constraints on representations are not independent. Especially, the cognitive economy demanded by human information-processing mechanisms may be responsible, at least in part, for the requirements of generality, simplicity, and consistency in physics theories. As a result, an important goal of cognitive work on physics expertise is to understand how expertise emerges from these constraints. Our endeavors toward that end, together with research efforts on expertise in other disciplines, are now progressing in an effort to find scientific explanations for expertise in general, beyond comparative analyses of expert–novice differences and domain-specific issues.

ACKNOWLEDGMENTS

I thank Neil Charness, Anders Ericsson, and Irvin Katz for their comments on various versions of this chapter.

REFERENCES

Anzai, Y. (1982). *Role of problem-solving knowledge in understanding problems* (C.I.P. Paper No. 440). Pittsburgh: Carnegie-Mellon University, Department of Psychology.

Anzai, Y. (1984). Cognitive control of real-time event-driven systems. *Cognitive Science, 8,* 221–254.

Anzai, Y. (1985). *The psychology of problem solving.* Tokyo: Chuokouronsha.

Anzai, Y. (1987). *Architecture for problem understanding in physics problem solving.* Paper presented at the 3rd International Conference on Artificial Intelligence and Education, Learning Research and Development Center, University of Pittsburgh.

Anzai, Y., & Kinoe, Y. (1984). Effects of figures in analogical problem solving. In *Proceedings of the First Annual Conference of the Japanese Cognitive Science Society* (pp. 52–53). Kyoto.

Anzai, Y., & Simon, H. A. (1979). The theory of learning by doing. *Psychological Review, 86,* 124–140.

Anzai, Y., & Uesato, Y. (1982). Learning recursive procedures by middleschool children. In *Proceedings of the 4th Annual Conference of the Cognitive Science Society* (pp. 100–102). Ann Arbor: Cognitive Science Society.

Anzai, Y., & Yokoyama, T. (1984). Internal models in physics problem solving. *Cognition and Instruction, 1,* 397–450.

Chase, W. G., & Ericsson, K. A. (1982). Skill and working memory. In G. H. Bower (Ed.), *The psychology of learning and motivation* (Vol. 16, pp. 1–58). New York: Academic Press.

Chase, W. G., & Simon, H. A. (1973). Perception in chess. *Cognitive Psychology, 4,* 55–81.

Chi, M. T. H., Bassok, M., Lewis, M. W., Reimann, P., & Glaser, R. (1987). Self-explanations: How students study and use examples in learning to solve problems. *Cognitive Science, 13,* 145–182.

Chi, M. T. H., Feltovich, P. J., & Glaser, R. (1981). Categorization and representation of physics problems by experts and novices. *Cognitive Science, 5,* 121–152.

Chi, M. T. H., Glaser, R., & Rees, E. (1982). Expertise in problem solving. In R. Sternberg (Ed.), *Advances in the psychology of human intelligence* (Vol. 1, pp. 7–75). Hillsdale, NJ: Erlbaum.

Clement, J. (1982). Students' preconceptions in introductory mechanics. *American Journal of Physics, 50,* 66–71.

de Kleer, J. (1977). Multiple representations of knowledge in a mechanics problem solver. In *Proceedings of the 5th International Joint Conference on Artificial Intelligence* (pp. 299–304). Cambridge, MA.

diSessa, A. (1982). Unlearning Aristotelian physics: A study of knowledge-based learning. *Cognitive Science, 6,* 37–75.

Elstein, A. S., Shulman, L. S., & Sprafka, S. A. (1978). *Medical problem solving: An analysis of clinical reasoning.* Cambridge, MA: Harvard University Press.

Gick, M. L. (1989). Two functions of diagrams in problem solving by analogy. In H. Mandl & J. R. Levin (Eds.), *Knowledge acquisition from text and pictures* (pp. 215–230). Amsterdam: Elsevier.

Gick, M. L., & Holyoak, K. J. (1983). Schema induction and analogical transfer. *Cognitive Psychology, 15,* 1–38.

Greeno, J. G., & Simon, H. A. (1988). Problem solving and reasoning. In R. C. Atkinson, R. J. Herrnstein, G. Lindzey, & R. D. Luce (Eds.), *Stevens' handbook of experimental psychology. Vol. 2: Learning and cognition* (pp. 589–672). New York: Wiley.

Hegarty, M., & Just, M. A. (1989). Understanding machines from text and diagrams. In H. Mandl & J. R. Levin (Eds.), *Knowledge acquisition from text and pictures* (pp. 171–194). Amsterdam: Elsevier.

Heller, J. I., & Reif, F. (1984). Prescribing effective human problem-solving processes: Problem description in physics. *Cognition and Instruction, 1,* 177–216.

Katz, I. R., & Anzai, Y. (1991). The construction and use of diagrams for problem solving. In. R. Lewis & S. Otsuki (Eds.), *Advanced research on computers in education* (pp. 27–36). Amsterdam: Elsevier.

Langley, P. W., Simon, H. A., Bradshaw, G. L., & Zytkow, J. M. (1987). *Scientific discovery: Computational explorations of the creative processes.* Cambridge, MA: MIT Press.

Larkin, J. H. (1977). *Problem solving in physics.* Technical report, Group in Science and Mathematics Education, University of California, Berkeley.

Larkin, J. H. (1982). *Spatial reasoning in solving physics problems* (C.I.P. Paper No. 434). Pittsburgh: Carnegie-Mellon University, Department of Psychology.

Larkin, J. H., McDermott, J., Simon, D. P., & Simon, H. A. (1980). Models of competence in solving physics problems. *Cognitive Science, 4,* 317–345.

Larkin, J. H., Reif, F., Carbonell, J., & Gugliotta, A. (1988). FERMI: A flexible expert reasoner with multi-domain inferencing. *Cognitive Science, 12,* 101–138.

Larkin, J. H., & Simon, H. A. (1987). Why a diagram is (sometimes) worth ten thousand words. *Cognitive Science, 11,* 65–99.

Lesgold, A. M. (1984). Acquiring expertise. In J. R. Anderson & S. M. Kosslyn (Eds.), *Tutorials in learning and memory* (pp. 31–60). San Francisco: Freeman.

McClosky, M., Caramazza, A., & Green, B. (1980). Curvilinear motion in the absence of external forces: Naive beliefs about the motion of objects. *Science, 210,* 1139–1141.

McCloskey, M., & Kohl, D. (1983) Naive physics: The curvilinear impetus principles and its role in interactions with moving objects. *Journal of Experimental Psychology: Learning, Memory, and Cognition, 9,* 146–156.

McDermott, J., & Larkin, J. H. (1978). Representing textbook physics problems. In *Proceedings of the 2nd National Conference of the Canadian Society for Computational Studies of Intelligence* (pp. 156–164). Toronto.

Novak, G. (1977). Representation of knowledge in a program for solving physics problems. In *Proceedings of the 5th International Joint Conference on Artificial Intelligence* (pp. 286–291). Cambridge, MA.

Reif, F. (1987). Interpretation of scientific or mathematical concepts: Cognitive issues and instructional implications. *Cognitive Science, 11,* 395–416.

Reif, F., & Heller, J. I. (1982). Knowledge structure and problem solving in physics. *Educational Psychologist, 17,* 102–127.

Roschelle, J., & Greeno, J. G. (1987). *Mental models in expert physics reasoning* (Report No. GK-2). Berkeley: University of California.

Sears, F. W., & Zemansky, M. W. (1970). *University physics* (4th ed.). Reading, MA: Addison-Wesley.

Simon, D. P., & Simon, H. A. (1978). Individual differences in solving physics problems. In R. S. Seigler (Ed.), *Children's thinking: What develops?* (pp. 325–348). Hillsdale, NJ: Erlbaum.

Simon, H. A. (1973). The structure of ill-structured problems. *Artificial Intelligence, 4,* 181–201.

Tikhomirov, O. K., & Poznyanskaya, E. D. (1966). An investigation of visual search as a means of analyzing heuristics. *Soviet Psychology, 5,* 2–15.

Trowbridge, D. E., & McDermott, L. C. (1980). Investigation of student understanding of the concept of velocity in one dimension. *American Journal of Physics, 48,* 1020–1028.

Trowbridge, D. E., & McDermott, L. C. (1981). Investigation of student understanding of the concept of acceleration in one dimension. *American Journal of Physics, 49,* 242–253.

Viennot, L. (1979). Spontaneous reasoning in elementary dynamics. *European Journal of Science Education, 1,* 205–221.

White, B. Y. (1983). Sources of difficulty in understanding Newtonian dynamics. *Cognitive Science, 7,* 41–65.

White, B. Y. (1984). Designing computer games to help physics students understand Newton's laws of motion. *Cognition and Instruction, 1,* 69–108.

4 The general and specific nature of medical expertise: a critical look

VIMLA L. PATEL AND GUY J. GROEN

1. INTRODUCTION

In the literature on cognitive psychology there are cognitive theories that claim a certain amount of generality. The validity or plausibility of large-scale cognitive theories of expertise cannot be directly established by a few experiments or even by empirical evidence alone. Rather, it depends on convergent evidence from a number of sources. Much of the support for these theories comes from their widespread use in cognitive psychology, as a means of describing problem-solving processes, and their adoption in research on artificial intelligence, as the basic methodology for the development of expert systems. But most theories in this field are based on belief in the existence of empirical regularities that are characteristic of experts. The absence of such regularities casts serious doubt on a particular theory's plausibility.

Two fundamental empirical findings in research on expert–novice comparisons have been the phenomena of *enhanced recall* and *forward reasoning*. The first refers to the fact that experts have superior memory skills in recognizing patterns in their domains of expertise. This is extensively reviewed by Ericsson and Smith (chapter 1, this volume). The second pertains to the finding that in solving routine problems in their domains, expert problem-solvers tend to work "forward" from the given information to the unknown. With the exception of Anzai's study (chapter 3, this volume), this is not so extensively treated in this volume, but it has been discussed at length in a recent article by Hunt (1989), to which the reader is referred for a review of both the empirical evidence and the conceptual background.

"Forward" reasoning usually is contrasted with backward reasoning, in which the problem-solver works from a hypothesis regarding the unknown back to the given information. It might be noted that the distinction is frequently made, perhaps more generally, in terms of goal-based (backward) versus knowledge-based (forward) heuristic search (e.g., Hunt, 1989). We phrase the distinction in terms of data and hypotheses because it relates more clearly to the types of empirical paradigms in which we are most interested. It is less theoretical and closer to the level of what one might expect to see in actual data.

The distinction between forward and backward reasoning is closely related to another distinction between strong problem-solving methods, which are highly constrained by the problem-solving environment, and weak methods, which are only minimally constrained. As Hunt pointed out, the two distinctions are logically independent. Forward reasoning, however, is highly error-prone in the absence of adequate domain knowledge because there are no built-in checks in the legitimacy of the inferences. Therefore, success in using forward reasoning is constrained by the environment because a great deal of relevant knowledge is necessary. Hence, it is a strong method for all practical purposes. In contrast, backward reasoning is slower and may make heavy demands on working memory (because one has to keep track of such things as goals and hypotheses). It is, therefore, most likely to be used when domain knowledge is inadequate, in which case there is a need for a method of reasoning that is minimally hampered by this lack of knowledge. Hence, backward reasoning usually is a symptom of a weak method. It is important to note that the term "weak" is being used in the technical sense of "weak constraints" as opposed to "strong constraints." This does not imply that it is a weak way of solving a problem! In fact, a weak method is preferable when (as is likely to be the case with anyone but an expert) relevant prior knowledge is lacking.

The extent to which the phenomena of enhanced recall and forward reasoning are related is important because a considerable amount of the earlier research on expert–novice differences was based on the assumption that there is a close relation between the pattern of recall of a problem-solving situation and the processes used in reasoning about the problem. The fact that the free-recall paradigm is also far more straightforward, from a practical point of view, than most paradigms designed to examine problem-solving processes led to an emphasis on the recall phenomenon and relative neglect of direct characterization of either expert or novice reasoning. The purposes of this chapter are to reevaluate that assumption in the light of our own empirical results and to rephrase it in a more realistic fashion. That will provide a context for evaluating the current state of the art and suggesting some promising areas for future research. Although our focus is on the relations between recall and reasoning, it will be seen that this leads to the consideration of a considerably more general set of issues.

Our research was originally motivated by observations of certain apparent anomalies between medicine and other domains in regard to the results of expert–novice comparisons. Specifically, Elstein, Shulman, and Sprafka (1978) found no evidence of forward reasoning in clinical diagnosis. They emphasized the role of backward reasoning and the use of hypotheticodeductive approaches. Furthermore, they found no differences between experts and novices except in the extent of the knowledge base. Also, a number of experiments (Norman, Jacoby, Feightner, & Campbell, 1979; Muzzin et al., 1982) indicated no differences between experts and novices in overall recall of clinical cases (although, paradoxically, there were differences in "chunking"). As a result, an important segment of our research came to be concerned with exploring the generality of forward reasoning and enhanced recall phenomena and the extent to which they are related both to each other and to what might superficially be thought of as an obvious fact of expertise: the attainment of an accurate or complete solution to a well-defined problem in the expert's knowledge domain.

Our interest in these phenomena stemmed from the fact that in the domain of medicine, behavior typical of expertise in other domains appeared to become stable only at high levels of specialization. We found, however, that many of the highly trained specialists we were studying made incomplete diagnoses of clinical cases in their areas of specialization (Patel, Groen, & Arocha, 1990). That led to a shift in our orientation away from expert–novice comparisons and toward an emphasis on the factors determining accurate performance and the robustness of the recall and forward-reasoning phenomena under variations of these factors. In this chapter, we begin by showing that the results of our research along these lines imply that these phenomena are not as closely related as was implied by what Ericsson and Smith (chapter 1, this volume) refer to as the original theory. Specifically, there appears to be a ceiling effect associated with the recall of clinical cases. Beyond that level, however, there continues to be a strong relation between diagnostic accuracy and the use of forward reasoning.

In light of those findings, we argue that it might be useful to make a distinction between two types of expertise: a general kind, which is correlated with performance on free-recall tasks, and a specific kind, which is correlated with diagnostic accuracy and the forward-reasoning phenomenon. We also consider the possibility of a third kind of expertise, associated with the effective use of weak methods or backward reasoning. We conclude by considering the implications of our results for understanding the performance of novices and intermediates in highly domain-specific tasks. In particular, we suggest that the development from novice to expert can best be understood as a three-stage process. The first involves the development of adequate knowledge-structure representations. The second involves the development of ways of distinguishing between relevant and irrelevant information in a problem. The third involves learning how to use these relevant representations in an efficient fashion.

To obtain some kind of context for this argument, it is necessary to begin by attempting to provide somewhat finer demarcations in the continuum between experts and novices than are usually given. In order to do this, it is necessary to begin by considering the criteria by which expertise is defined. The most precise are external criteria, where some method of independent classification exists. This may take the form of either a simple linear ordering or a nonlinear hierarchy that can be pictured as a tree with its root at the bottom. An example of the former is the official rating system, from class C to grand master, used in chess. An example of the latter is the system of certification, in terms of specialties and subspecialties, used in medicine. It seems reasonable to argue that this is a more realistic depiction of expertise, because the linear system, even though it is by far the most frequently used, is almost always in approximation to a hierarchical ordering, or possibly to something even more complex. This is apparent in every academic discipline. Even in chess, masters specialize in different opening variations. In computer programming, systems programmers are a different breed from applications programmers.

One advantage of the hierarchical ordering is that it is possible to consider much finer gradations of expertise. In particular, it is possible to distinguish between specific expertise (e.g., cardiology) and generic expertise (e.g., medicine). An individual may possess both, or only the generic expertise. A disadvantage is that it does not extend all the way down the expert–novice continuum because, at some point prior to the acquisition of generic expertise, it collapses into a simple linear ordering. Moreover, this does not correspond in a neat fashion to the hierarchical ordering. Thus, a medical resident may be developing skills in both cardiology and general medicine at the same time. This suggests that it is desirable to consider three kinds of developmental sequences. The first is a straightforward linear ordering from novice to generic expert. The second is a nonlinear hierarchy beginning at the point where specialized knowledge begins to branch off from generic knowledge. The third is the result of combining the two others and collapsing the result into a simple linear ordering. Whereas the first two are more fundamental, the third is more convenient for expository purposes and also has the advantage of reflecting the normal practice of researchers in the area. We begin by using it to define some terms in a fashion that will be used consistently throughout this chapter:

Layperson: An individual who has only commonsense or everyday knowledge of the domain.

Beginner: An individual who has the prerequisite knowledge assumed by the domain.

Novice: A layperson or a beginner.

Intermediate: By default, we define this as anyone who is above the beginner level but below the subexpert level.

Subexpert: An individual with generic knowledge, but inadequate specialized knowledge, of the domain.

Expert: An individual with specialized knowledge of the domain.

A number of things should be noted about these definitions. First, it is assumed that the domain is sufficiently well defined that it is possible to distinguish between generic and specific knowledge. Second, the notion of "intermediate" is not well defined at all; we shall clarify this notion later. Finally, we make a distinction between two kinds of novices, because many technical domains require prior knowledge for even minimal comprehension. For example, in chess, a beginner is one who knows the rules of chess, whereas a layperson does not.

Having made these distinctions, we now turn to a review of the extent to which our experimental results indicate relations among diagnostic accuracy, recall, and directionality of reasoning. We begin by considering experts and subexperts, and we show that there exists a systematic relation between accuracy and directionality of reasoning, but no differences in recall. We then consider intermediates and novices, and we show that whereas there is a relation between accuracy and recall, it is considerably more complex than has been suggested elsewhere.

2. METHODS OF ANALYSIS

In a standard, basic experimental procedure, subjects were shown a written description of a clinical case. Each subject was asked to read that text for a specific period of time, after which it was removed. The subjects were asked to write down as much of the text as they could remember and then to describe the underlying pathophysiology of the case without reference to either the text or the previous recall response. Finally, the subjects were asked to provide a diagnosis. Variants of this paradigm for our various experiments included (1) free recall only, (2) free recall and diagnosis, and (3) free recall and diagnostic explanation.

For analysis of the data, the diagnoses were coded as accurate, partially accurate, or inaccurate. A diagnosis was characterized as accurate when it was completely correct (i.e., with all its components included), as partially accurate when some components of the diagnosis were included, and as inaccurate when no diagnostic components were included.

2.1. Analysis of comprehension

In general, our research in comprehension has been based on the working hypothesis that free-recall experiments fail to yield coherent results because of methodological inadequacies in defining the basic units of recall. We have found, in a series of studies, that the use of propositional techniques leads to the isolation of systematic differences between experts and novices.

By means of the techniques of propositional analysis, based on the work of Kintsch (1974) and Frederiksen (1975), the clinical texts and the response protocols were analyzed. Details of the methods of analysis can be found elsewhere (Patel & Groen, 1986). The protocols were scored for recalls against the stimulus texts according to the method described by Patel, Groen, and Frederiksen (1986). In summary, the stimulus texts were initially segmented into clauses and then propositionally represented. Next, the subjects' protocols were segmented and matched against the original text propositions. The scoring involved marking every item in the subjects' protocols that corresponded to the literal semantic content of the original text. These were termed *recalls*. Transformations made by the subjects on propositions in the text were scored as *inferences*. The propositions in the clinical cases were classified as *disease-relevant* or *disease-irrelevant,* based on experts' classification.

2.2. Identifying forward reasoning

When attempting to identify the directionality of reasoning of the subjects, we found that we were unable to use the straightforward problem-solving paradigm because standard think-aloud techniques yielded extremely sparse protocols. As a result, we used a paradigm that we called *diagnostic explanation*, in which subjects were requested to explain the pathophysiology, or causal patterns, underlying the clinical case.

For each pathophysiological-explanation protocol, a semantic-network representation of the causal and conditional rules was obtained, using the method described by Patel and Groen (1986). Our basic approach in analyzing these data was to begin by representing the propositional structure of a protocol as a semantic network. Within this structure, the propositions that describe attribute information are called *nodes,* and those that describe relational information are called *links.* The attributes in the subjects' protocols could be characterized as facts originating from the stimulus text or attributes that were inferred or hypothesized. The causal and conditional relationships that form a major part of the semantic network arising from our data closely resemble the rules in an expert system such as NEOMYCIN (Clancey, 1988). This system consists of hypothesis-directed rules and data-directed rules, which can be viewed as equivalent to forward and backward reasoning. It can be shown that there is an isomorphism between this semantic network and a set of related production rules (Patel & Groen, 1986).

In order to be more precise about our analysis, some notions from graph theory (Sowa, 1984) are used to represent the semantic network in terms of components. These have been described in considerable detail (Groen & Patel, 1988). In summary, a graph is defined as a nonempty set of nodes and a set of arcs leading from node N to a node N'. A graph is "connected" if there exists a path, directed or undirected, between any two nodes. In a directed path, every node has a source and a target connecting it to its immediate successor. If the graph is not connected, then it breaks down into disjoint components.

In terms of these notions, a semantic network is formed by nodes and connecting paths. Nodes may represent either clinical findings or hypotheses, whereas the paths represent directed connections between nodes. Forward reasoning corresponds to an oriented path from a fact to a hypothesis. Thus, forward-directed rules are identified whenever a physician attempts to generate a hypothesis from the findings in a case. Backward-directed rules correspond to an oriented path from a hypothesis to a fact. Pure forward reasoning refers to a network in which all paths are oriented from fact to hypothesis. Pure backward reasoning refers to a network in which all paths are oriented from hypothesis to fact.

In order to determine the extent to which all the subjects used similar processes, it was convenient for us to consider the canonical knowledge that was being used, that is, the knowledge that exists in textbooks or, more informally, in the common knowledge base of expert subjects, as described in many of our studies (Joseph & Patel, 1990; Patel, Evans, & Kaufman, 1989c; Patel & Groen, 1986). In summary, we asked experts who were not subjects in the experiment to describe the basic causal mechanisms underlying the case that led to the correct diagnosis and some possible alternative diagnoses. The knowledge embodied in the semantic network, or the production-rules formalism necessary to generate the diagnosis, was represented as causal rules in a semantic reference model. Those causal rules could be transformed into production rules. The rules generated from the subjects' protocols could then be compared with the rules in the reference model.

3. EMPIRICAL RESULTS

As pointed out earlier, the empirical results are discussed in relation to three phenomena: recall, diagnostic accuracy, and forward reasoning.

3.1. Experts and subexperts

The main reason for the classification of subjects was to distinguish between two basic categories of recall phenomena. The first concerned the experts and subexperts, and the second involved novices and intermediates. In this latter category, quite marked recall phenomena were found; they will be discussed in the next section. In this section, we concentrate on showing that there were no differences between experts and subexperts in terms of recall, despite distinct differences in other aspects of performance.

As might be expected, one such difference concerned diagnostic accuracy. In general, accuracy decreased as a transition was made from the level of expert to that of subexpert. Our primary evidence came from two sets of data: The first investigation compared the performance of subjects from three subspecialties – cardiology, surgery, and psychiatry – in explaining a clinical problem in the domain of cardiology (Patel et al., 1990). The problem we posed was infectious endocarditis with aortic insufficiency: The patient had contracted an infection from a contaminated needle, possibly from intravenous drug use. The aortic heart valve had been affected, and the patient displayed signs of acute infection, which indicated a serious case of endocarditis. In fact, the data from the cardiologists were taken from this experiment. Five of seven cardiologists made completely accurate diagnoses, whereas the other two cardiologists gave partially correct diagnoses. One of the six surgeons was able to provide a completely accurate diagnosis; the rest of the surgeons were only partially correct. Psychiatrists, by contrast, provided either partially correct or incorrect diagnoses. All but one psychiatrist identified the general aspect of the diagnosis: infection. These results are summarized in Figure 4.1.

The second study involved within-subject comparisons rather than between-subject comparisons (Patel et al., 1990). The subjects were endocrinologists

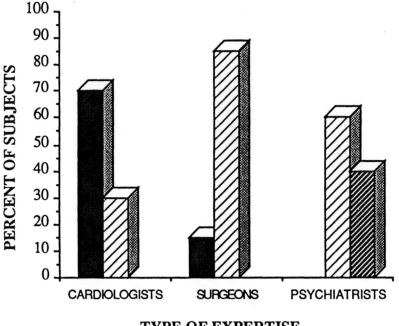

 Completely Accurate Diagnosis

 Partially Accurate Diagnosis

Inaccurate Diagnosis

Figure 4.1. Diagnostic accuracy as a function of type of expertise on the cardiology problem.

and cardiologists. Each subject was given a case in endocrinology and a case in cardiology. One further variable was introduced: The subjects in each discipline were divided into practitioners and researchers. The practitioners, who had M.D. degrees, spent 70 percent or more of their time seeing patients, with little or no research activity. The researchers, who had both M.D. and Ph.D. degrees, spent 70 percent or more of their time in biomedical research.

The clinical text on the endocrinology problem was structured, and it described the case of a 63-year-old woman who suffered from an advanced state of autoimmune thyroid disorder (Hashimoto's thyroiditis). The clinical text on the cardiology problem was ill-structured, and it described the case of a 62-year-old man suffering from cardiac tamponade with pleural effusions.

Table 4.1. *Percentages of cues (propositions) recalled and diagnostic accuracy by experts and subexperts on clinical cases*

Cues recalled	Diagnosis		
	Accurate	Partially accurate	Inaccurate
Case 1			
Relevant propositions	64	61	65
Irrelevant propositions	36	39	35
Case 2			
Relevant propositions	60	66	55
Irrelevant propositions	40	34	45

Three of four endocrinology practitioners and all four endocrinology researchers made completely accurate diagnoses of the clinical problem in endocrinology. All the endocrinologists, however, made inaccurate diagnoses in the cardiology case. The diagnoses in the endocrinology case were precise, with no alternative diagnoses given. That was in contrast to the cardiology case, where many alternative diagnoses were generated by the subjects.

Three of four cardiologist practitioners and two of four cardiologist researchers provided completely accurate diagnoses of the clinical problem in cardiology. In contrast to the endocrinologists, however, the cardiologists provided other alternatives besides the correct diagnosis. Seven of eight cardiologists provided incomplete diagnoses of the clinical problem in endocrinology, with only the most general aspects of the problem being identified. There were no alternatives provided. One cardiologist practitioner made a completely accurate diagnosis.

Despite the pronounced link between diagnostic accuracy and the relevant expertise, there were no differences in recall of the clinical cases. Table 4.1 gives a summary of the patterns of recall of the cardiologists, surgeons, and psychiatrists in case 1 (cardiology case) and the cardiologists and endocrinologists in case 2 (endocrinology case) as a function of diagnostic accuracy. There clearly were no differences in recall of relevant or irrelevant propositions as a function of diagnostic accuracy in either of the clinical cases.

Similar results were obtained in our second experiment, in which all subjects were able to recall the information in the text, irrespective of their specific areas of expertise. Both the cardiologists and the endocrinologists were able to select the relevant propositions and provide a summary of the most important features of the text, even if an inaccurate diagnosis was ultimately given. It is clear from these results that our experts and subexperts were identical with respect to recall, even though they differed drastically with respect to diagnostic accuracy. In other words, *it is the level of expertise, rather than the degree of recall, that is strongly predictive of diagnostic accuracy.*

The presence or absence of forward reasoning does, however, appear to be strongly related to diagnostic accuracy. Patel and Groen (1986) found that all subjects who made completely accurate diagnoses showed the use of pure forward reasoning, whereas none of the subjects who made inaccurate diagnoses showed this phenomenon. Similarly, the one surgeon who made a completely accurate diagnosis on the same clinical case showed the use of pure forward reasoning, whereas none of the other surgeons or the psychiatrists showed it (Patel et al., 1990).

The results of the experiment involving experts within and outside their domains of expertise are more complicated to describe, because more difficult problems were employed. In general, no subject who made an inaccurate and incomplete diagnosis showed evidence of pure forward reasoning. The pattern of results for subjects who made complete and accurate diagnoses always consisted of two components. The main component was an explanation of the disease that included the diagnosis. This was always generated by pure forward reasoning. The second component essentially consisted of tying up the loose ends, the information that was irrelevant to the main diagnosis. This did not involve the use of pure forward reasoning.

This is illustrated with an example from a pathophysiological explanation by an expert endocrinologist researcher working on the endocrine problem. Figure 4.2 shows the semantic-network representation of the protocol, generated by the method described earlier. The explanation was constructed to justify the diagnosis and to explain the biomedical cues in the problem. The order of reasoning was completely forward, except at the very end of the protocol, where "fluid retention" and "dry skin" were explained in terms of "ineffective diuresis" and "decreased T3 and T4," respectively. There was one large component with forward chaining leading to a diagnosis, and two small components that tied up loose ends with backward reasoning to explain cues not related to the main diagnosis.

The cardiology case contained cues that strongly indicated an alternative diagnosis. The protocols began with a set of components that consisted of ruling out alternative diagnoses by the expert practitioners, using pure forward reasoning. That was followed by the component containing the principal diagnosis. In contrast to the first experiment, all the components were generated by pure forward reasoning by subjects with accurate and complete diagnoses.

The cardiologists and endocrinologists solving the problems that were out of their domains of expertise did not provide complete diagnoses, and their protocols showed the use of a mixture of forward and backward reasoning. This is illustrated with an example from an explanation of the cardiology problem provided by an endocrinology researcher. Figure 4.3 shows the semantic-network representation of the protocol. The expert ruled out the alternative diagnoses of cirrhosis and nephrotic syndrome before attempting to represent the diagnosis of primary cardiac failure, all using reasoning in a

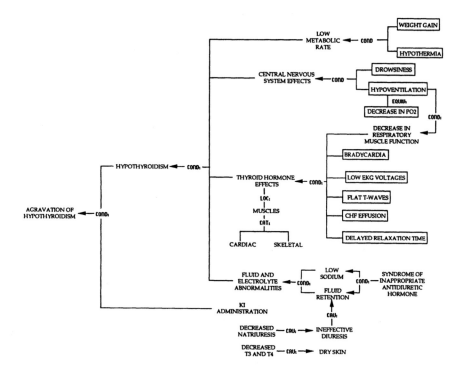

Figure 4.2. Semantic-network representation of the explanation of the endocrinology problem by an endocrinologist researcher.

forward direction. That was followed by the use of both forward and backward reasoning to explain the diagnosis.

The tasks used in the foregoing studies were explanation-based, since the subjects read the complete text before explaining the problem. Some additional insights have been gained by investigating the effects of a sequential task on diagnosis. In such tasks, the subjects are asked to make diagnoses, and those diagnoses are modified or refined on the basis of further input information. In one such study (Joseph & Patel, 1990) the subjects were given a clinical case (Hashimoto's thyroiditis) presented one segment at a time on a microcomputer. They were prompted to think aloud after presentation of each segment of the case. The subjects in the study were domain experts, endocrinologists, and cardiologists. The results showed no significant differences between the groups in terms of selection of relevant and critical cues from the case. The experts generated accurate diagnostic hypotheses early in the problem encounter and spent the rest of the time evaluating in order to confirm and refine the diagnosis by explaining the patient cues. The sub-experts also generated accurate diagnostic hypotheses, but at a later point, after many more cues had been presented. Those subjects had difficulty in evaluating the hypotheses against the given information, which resulted in

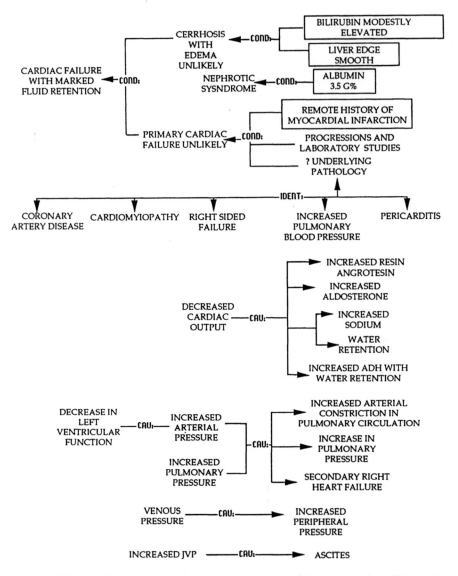

Figure 4.3. Semantic-network representation of the explanation of the cardiology problem by an endocrinologist researcher.

inability to discriminate between and eliminate alternative diagnoses. These studies are consistent with other findings that if an expert makes an initial accurate diagnosis, subsequent evaluation of that diagnosis always confirms it rather than generates alternative possibilities (Patel et al., 1989c). This is equivalent to generating an accurate diagnosis using pure forward reasoning when all the information is given at one time. If, however, the diagnosis is not accurate, then at the evaluation phase of the problem solving, alternative diagnoses may be generated, or some additional patient cues will have to be explained. This will result in backward reasoning.

3.2. Doctor–patient interactions

In order to explore the nature of expertise in a more interactive natural task, a study was carried out on expertise in doctor–patient interaction during a clinical interview (Kaufman & Patel, 1988). The study evaluated the differences between subjects at three levels of expertise in acquiring and using information obtained from a patient during the clinical interview. Endocrinologists, residents, and senior medical students interviewed a volunteer endocrine outpatient and provided a list of differential diagnoses.

The patient interviewed was a 22-year-old Asian male who presented with two episodes of severe muscle weakness and other manifestations. The patient's problem was diagnosed as hypokalemic periodic paralysis associated with hyperthyroidism. This is an uncommon disorder of the thyroid gland, involving episodes of paralysis associated with a marked decrease in serum potassium concentration.

In order to characterize the performances of experts during the clinical interview, an epistemological framework to identify appropriate units of knowledge, together with a formal method of discourse analysis to code the doctor–patient interaction, was necessary. A complete description of the framework has been given (Patel et al., 1989c). Within this epistemological framework, clinical knowledge is hierarchically organized from observations → findings → facets (diagnostic components) → diagnosis. *Observations* are units of information that are recognized as potentially relevant in the problem-solving context. *Findings* are composed of sets of observations that are relevant in a diagnostic context. *Facets* are clusters of findings that are suggestive of diagnostic components. Specific combinations of facets lead to a diagnosis.

The methods used to characterize the doctor–patient dialogue were derived from linguistic pragmatics. The analysis was designed to capture the pragmatic features of data acquisition and the management of data flow by the clinician. Our interest was in how a clinician identifies problem-specific cues, concludes findings, and derives meaning from higher-order relations in the data. The coded doctor–patient dialogue was limited to aspects of the discourse that revealed the context in which clinical inferences were made and the problem representation was formulated.

The transcribed dialogue was segmented into units of doctor–patient exchanges. An exchange is simply a physician-question–patient-response pairing that forms the basis of any interview. An exchange is characterized by any pair of utterances on the part of both participants, not necessarily a completed question or response. The analysis focuses principally on the questions and assertions advanced by the physician. Only the contents of the observations that the patient reported were evaluated.

Specific strategies used by the experts and novices can be identified within this context. Data-gathering strategies can be guided by the goal of deriving findings and meaningful relations among findings in the patient's history. This process is principally a bottom-up approach, generating facets and differential diagnoses from the elements in a problem space. This is referred to as *diagnostic reasoning* or data-driven reasoning. Once the problem representation is sufficiently elaborated and expectations are built up, the inquiry is directed toward eliciting specific findings that correspond to the physician's diagnostic hypotheses. This top-down process is referred to as *reasoning predictively*. It is expected that physicians initially adopt a data-driven strategy and later shift to a predictive reasoning strategy when they have a working hypothesis (facet or diagnosis). Under this interactive condition, the directionality of reasoning is likely to be in the forward direction until some loose ends are generated, at which time the reasoning may shift to the backward direction to account for the unexplained data.

The results show that selective acquisition and use of information were related to expertise. That selective use could be viewed as a hierarchical structure beginning with observations, findings, facets, and diagnoses, each contributing successively to a more nearly complete clinical context. Such organization facilitated evaluation of generated hypotheses or diagnoses by selective use of predictive reasoning. Experts arrived at accurate diagnoses because their initial hypotheses were generally accurate, which resulted in accurate prediction of subsequent findings. The general pattern of results found from the analysis of expert–patient dialogue is illustrated in Figure 4.4 by an example from a dialogue between an expert and a patient. The expert used a few initial cues to generate a useful diagnosis. Based on that diagnosis, certain predictions were made, and subsequent questions were asked of the patient to confirm those predictions, using reasoning in the predictive direction. The interaction resulted in findings (responses) that agreed with the hypothesis. The negative findings were generated to eliminate the alternative hypothesis. Few loose ends were generated.

Residents were unable to discriminate between various diagnostic subcategories because their initial hypotheses were inaccurate. The general pattern of results found from analysis of the resident–patient dialogue is illustrated by an example from a dialogue between a resident and the patient in Figure 4.5. Initially, few cues were used to arrive at a diagnostic component, which was not a useful or accurate diagnosis. The reasoning was in a forward direction. The accurate diagnosis resulted in predictions that generated negative findings (responses) during subsequent questioning and thus interfered with any resolution of the diagnosis. The negative findings led to further exploration, which resulted in further inaccurate diagnoses, and the cycle repeated itself. That finally resulted in a collection of alternative possible diagnoses, none of which could be ruled out. The general use of explanatory strategies and the inability to discriminate between various alternative diagnoses were quite characteristic of residents' behavior. That may have been reflective of their intermediate

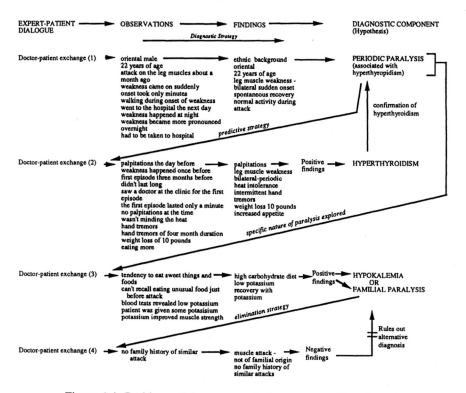

Figure 4.4. Problem-solving process during expert–patient interview.

stages of knowledge, because there was a collection of loose ends for which they could not account.

Findings from this study show the use of predictive reasoning to evaluate and refine a diagnosis after it had been generated. It also appears that experts did not use detailed scientific biomedical information during diagnostic reasoning (forward reasoning). Such information is important during predictive reasoning (Patel, Evans, & Groen, 1989a). Biomedical information provides the "glue" to hold various pieces of information together in a coherent fashion. Physicians do not use this information in their everyday practice, but they do appear to have it when probed for a biomedical explanation of a problem.

3.3. Novices and intermediates

Thus far we have been discussing the differences between subjects at a quite high level of general expertise, because they were mostly qualified physicians with extensive clinical experience. Below that level, distinct differences in recall emerged. To some extent, those differences were similar to what has been observed elsewhere in the literature. We have shown, in a number of experiments, that experts recall significantly more relevant proposi-

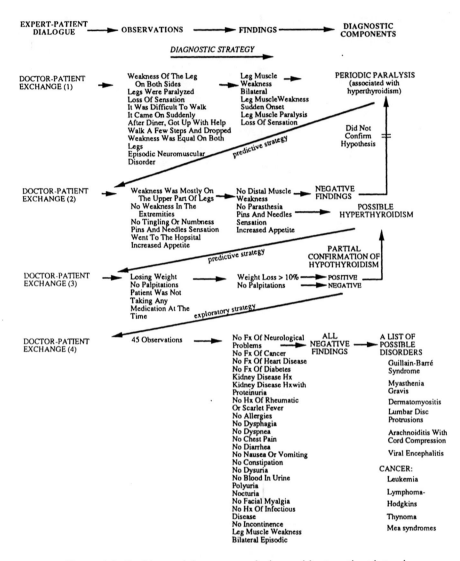

Figure 4.5. Problem-solving process during resident–patient interview.

tions than do novices (Coughlin & Patel, 1987; Patel & Ericsson, 1990; Patel et al., 1986). Needless to say, this is related to differences in diagnostic accuracy. The pattern of performance by intermediates, however, was not quite what might have been expected on the basis of those results. The results of a number of experiments we conducted indicate that recall and other variables have nonmonotonic relations to the degree of expertise.

We conducted a series of experiments using three groups of subjects: novices, intermediates, and experts. A summary of each experiment, its subjects, and its task is given in Table 4.2. The novices, intermediates, and experts were

Table 4.2. *Summary of subjects and tasks on comprehension studies*

Experiment	Novices	Intermediates	Experts	Tasks
I	First-year college students entering premedical program	Students in the 1-year premedical program before entering medical school	Students with undergraduate science degrees before entering medical school	Comprehension of patient-problem texts
II	First-year medical students	Second-year students	Internists	Comprehension of clinical-science texts
III	Second-year medical students	Fourth-year students	Internists	Comprehension of patient-problem texts

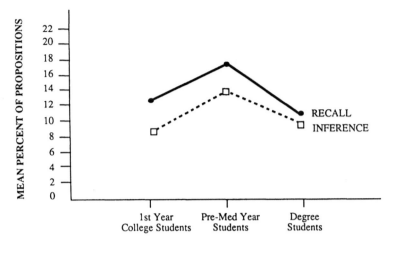

Figure 4.6. Mean percentages of propositions by group and response type for medical students entering medical school.

classified according to our earlier definitions. The tasks varied from comprehension of clinical-science material to comprehension of texts describing patients' clinical problems. In these experiments, clinical-science texts containing descriptions of scientific topics related to clinical practice (e.g., fever and cancer), as well as clinical-problem texts containing descriptions of patients' problems (infectious endocarditis), were presented in written form to the subjects. They were asked to read text and then recall the information in them. The protocols were analyzed propositionally, and the propositions were scored as recalls and inferences against the original texts.

Experiment I, which was part of V. Medley-Mark's master's study (Medley-Mark, 1986), included three groups of subjects with differing premedical backgrounds. The students were characterized as belonging to novice, intermediate, or expert categories, based on years of premedical training. Novices and expert students recalled and inferred significantly fewer items of information than did intermediate students. Figure 4.6 shows the mean percentages of propositions recalled and inferred by the three groups of subjects. This pattern of results also holds for the recall of total relevant and nonrelevant information, as shown in Figure 4.7, which gives the mean percentages of relevant and nonrelevant information recalled by the three groups of medical students. None of the subjects provided a completely accurate diagnosis.

In experiment II, first-year medical students and internists recalled and inferred significantly less information from the general clinical texts on fever and cancer than did the second-year students [$F(2, 21) = 6.304, p < .005$] (Patel & Ericsson, 1990). A further analysis of these results shows that physi-

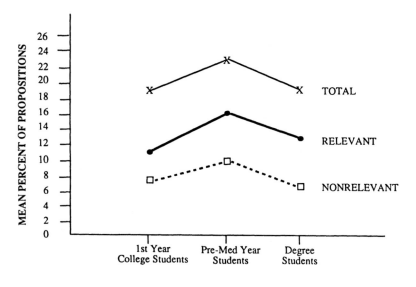

Figure 4.7. Mean percentages of propositions by group and relevance of information for medical students entering medical school.

cians operated more on the highly relevant information by making selective inferences. The intermediates operated on both high- and low-relevance information, showing their inability to discriminate between relevant and nonrelevant information.

In experiment III, fourth-year medical students recalled and inferred significantly more information than did either second-year students or internists on the comprehension of two clinical-problem texts: infectious endocarditis and gastrointestinal cancer. The patterns of recall of relevant propositions were the same after the propositions were separated into relevant and nonrelevant propositions (Patel, 1986). Figure 4.8 shows the mean percentages of propositions recalled and inferred on the basis of relevance and experience. The results indicate rather reliably that recall was nonmonotonically related to the length of the training period or the level of expertise. This implies that outcome measures emphasizing recall are not accurate indices of underlying knowledge and do not measure the effective use of knowledge. It might be noted that, once again, we see that recall phenomena were independent of diagnostic accuracy, because intermediates were more accurate than novices but less accurate than experts, as shown in Figure 4.9. All the physicians made completely accurate diagnoses; 70 percent of the third-year students made completely accurate diagnoses, and 30 percent made partially accurate diagnoses. Forty percent of the second-year students correctly identified some components of the diagnosis, and 60 percent made partially accurate diagnoses.

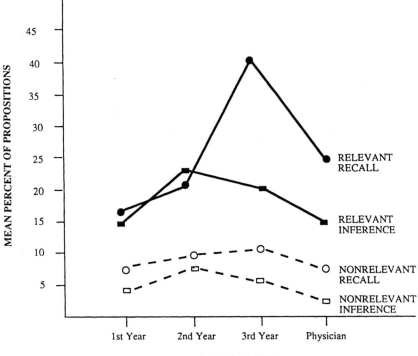

Figure 4.8. Mean percentages of propositions recalled and inferred by relevance and experience level on two clinical-problem texts.

Twenty percent of the first-year students made partially accurate diagnoses, and 55 percent made completely inaccurate diagnoses. The rest of the first-year students did not provide a diagnosis.

In other words, diagnostic accuracy is typically developmentally monotonic, whereas recall is nonmonotonic. Similar results were obtained by Schmidt, Boshuizen, and Hobus (1988). They showed that the intermediate peak could be manipulated by varying the time of exposure to the texts. Thus, with an extremely short exposure time (30 seconds), the peak disappeared. In general, with shorter exposure times there were corresponding decrements in performance. Those decrements occurred for the novices and the intermediates but not for the experts. That may imply that the U-shaped curve may reflect more motivational phenomena that result from a trade-off between speed and accuracy.

On the other hand, an alternative possibility is that the nonmonotonicity reflects differences in problem representations. Some support for that position comes from Lesgold et al. (1988), who suggested that their results indicated that the development of expertise sometimes reaches points of impasse

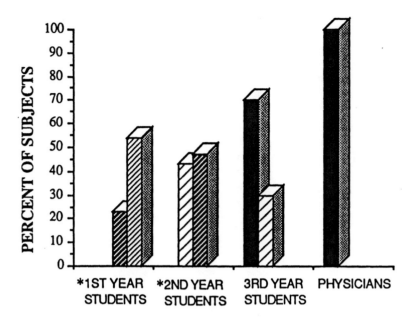

LEVEL OF EXPERTISE

 Completely Accurate Diagnosis

Partially Accurate Diagnosis

 Component Diagnosis Only

Inaccurate Diagnosis

*The numbers do not add up to 100% because
some subjects did not provide a diagnosis

Figure 4.9. Diagnostic accuracy as a function of expertise.

where superficial and deep methods conflict. These impasses mirror the
U-shaped curves found in our studies.

Before ending this section, we shall describe a recall experiment in which a
somewhat unexpected result was found when the clinical case was scrambled
(Coughlin & Patel, 1987): Two clinical cases in two structural forms (typical

and random) were presented to family physicians and second-year medical students. The results show that the physicians recalled significantly more critical cues than the students. When the case had a temporally ordered, underlying disease process, however, the random structure of the text disrupted the physicians' ability to recall critical cues, as well as the accuracy of their diagnosis. The students were unaffected by the problem type or structure form.

Thus, when working on a normally structured problem, experts did significantly better than novices; when the problem structure was disrupted, novices were unaffected, but experts' performance deteriorated to the level of novice performance. This finding is similar to those for chess (Chase & Simon, 1973). For the clinical case in which there were initially no specific relations among the cues, however, the physicians' processing of the information was not greatly affected by subsequent disruption of the structure.

4. IMPLICATIONS

4.1. Generality of results

To summarize, we have two sets of results. The first set concerns experts and subexperts and can be viewed as reflecting the development of specific expertise. It shows that recall measures have no relevance to this issue, at least once the generic expertise is developed, because there is a ceiling effect on the recall of relevant information. In contrast, forward reasoning appears to be closely related to diagnostic accuracy. The second set of results concerns intermediates and novices and reveals the development of generic expertise. Here, there are strong recall effects, but the most significant finding is that recall is nonmonotonic, as a function of diagnostic accuracy, with intermediates recalling more than experts or novices do.

It seems reasonable to assert that these results have some generality outside the domain of medicine. The results concerning forward reasoning are consistent with the empirical findings in other domains. Although the ceiling effect on recall may be task-specific, it is not necessarily domain-specific. Thus, both Ericsson and Charness discuss evidence suggesting that the correlation between skill and recall is not as high as the original Chase-Simon theory predicted. This suggests that ceiling effects may occur rather generally with tasks such as those we used, where specific expertise was necessary for solving the problem but only generic expertise was necessary for comprehending the problem. The issue of the generality of the results regarding nonmonotonicity is less clear. They could simply have resulted from the peculiarities of the standard medical curriculum. On the other hand, phenomena of this kind are well known in the developmental literature, although the tasks studied usually have not involved recall. More strictly in relation to the differences among experts, intermediates, and novices, Saariluoma (1990) found a nonmonotonic effect with respect to depth of search by chess players. This suggests that a major problem in assessing the generality of these results may lie in their theoretical interpretation, because most of the results from other domains have involved processes other than recall.

The most obvious conclusion to be drawn from our results is that most of the simpler notions regarding the development of expertise were inadequate. That is because they depended on the assumption that there actually existed high correlations among our three phenomena: recall, diagnostic accuracy, and forward reasoning. Thus, a theory that simply assumes that the development of expertise is related to the development of better and better representations cannot be true. Rather, the development of representations follows a somewhat jagged course. But those fluctuations are not reflected in the accuracy of performance. In other words, we are essentially attempting to explain a relationship involving three variables: *accuracy of performance, recall,* and *directionality of reasoning.* The first is monotonically related to expertise, and the second is nonmonotonically related to expertise. The third seems to be an all-or-none phenomenon that may be related not to the developmental pattern at all but, rather, to the two extremes of the expert–novice continuum.

These findings seem sufficient to reject two kinds of theories. The first is based on the notion that expert diagnosis is simply a process of pattern recognition. Although this theory is not espoused by many psychologists, it is still prevalent among medical educators and some physicians. The second is what might be called a theory of expertise based on a flat set of production rules (i.e., rules that cannot be structured in some kind of natural hierarchy). Again, this probably is no longer taken seriously by most psychologists but may still be prevalent among some knowledge engineers working on the development of expert systems. Both of these theories posit a close relationship between chunk size in working memory and performance in problem-solving tasks. Hence, they predict a monotonically increasing relationship between recall and diagnostic accuracy, which as we have seen, does not hold. These findings also tend to refute notions of the development of expertise that are based on overlay theories, which predict the development from novice to expert via acquisition by the novice of expert production rules. It should be noted that there is ample evidence from other areas, especially "intelligent tutoring systems," that this approach does not work (Wenger, 1987).

To account for these phenomena in a more satisfactory manner, it is necessary to consider more sophisticated approaches. But many of these are dependent on architectural considerations (in the sense of accepting a specific set of assumptions regarding the nature of the underlying processing assumptions). One candidate might be some kind of connectionist theory. But a fundamental issue in developing an account along such lines is the fact that connectionist models have been developed primarily from recognition data. Hence, the issue of whether such a model can be developed to account for free-recall and diagnostic-explanation data is difficult to resolve at this time.

An architectural approach that must be considered in more detail is the SOAR model of Laird, Rosenbloom, and Newell (1985). This is of interest for two reasons. First, in a sense, SOAR represents a prototype for expert systems of the future because it goes far beyond current "flat" systems by positing a nontrivial chunking mechanism, a learning mechanism, and methods for making transitions between forward and backward reasoning. Second, it is germane to our results, in two ways: The first is that a mechanism in SOAR that switches between different problem spaces in response to "impasses" in reasoning may account for our findings regarding the presence or absence of forward reasoning. The second regards an intriguing anomaly in current versions of SOAR. Newell (personal communication) has found that after extensive learning, SOAR tends to form what he calls "extensive chunks," in the sense of extremely large chunks that tend to slow down the reasoning capabilities of the system. Whereas he views this as reflecting a fundamental inconsistency between SOAR and realistic empirical data (to the extent that he is currently rewriting his entire chunking mechanism to remove the phenomenon), it may be that it is more realistic than he believes, because a version of an extensive-chunking hypothesis could explain our results with intermediate subjects. Inherent in the extensive-chunking notion is the idea that large, unmanageable chunks are being generated that result in unmanageable production systems. It seems possible that a similar phenomenon accounted for the nonmonotonicity we found with our intermediate subjects.

There is one other theory that appears promising. Groen and Patel (1988) suggested an approach based on the van Dijk and Kintsch (1983) theory of comprehension and its extension into problem solving by Kintsch and Greeno (1985). This divides the process of problem solving into two parts, one that involves developing a representation of a text and another that focuses on creating interactions between elements of this representation and a situation model based on prior knowledge of the domain. Essentially, the elements of the text base will activate general schemata, which in turn will activate more specific subschemata until the final diagnosis is obtained. The advantage of such a mechanism is that its diagnostic accuracy is determined not by the content of the text base alone but by the properties of preexisting schemata, based on situations. This would explain how two different schemata might be activated by the same text base. The notions of van Dijk and Kintsch can also explain the phenomenon of the intermediate "hump." Experts can be assumed to use a macrostructure to filter out unnecessary information. If intermediates lack that macrostructure, they may be expected to remember information in a raw form. In fact, we have found that the intermediate hump effect vanishes when comparisons are made on the basis of relevant macrostructure inferences (Patel & Ericsson, 1990).

4.2. Three kinds of expertise

Generic expertise. Rather than dwell on the adequacies or inadequacies of these theories, it is better to develop a more global approach. Basically, we distinguish between two developmental sequences that we claim have different properties. The first concerns the development of generic expertise. It is primarily concerned with the acquisition of adequate representations. Both experts and subexperts possess generic expertise, as is evidenced by the fact that there is a ceiling effect in their free recall. As we suggested earlier, this implies the existence of some schema or macrostructure representation that is based on their experience in practical problems and guarantees the retention of crucial facts in a clinical case.

A description of the development of generic expertise demands an explanation of the nonmonotonic nature of intermediate recall. This is a rather complex issue, because nonmonotonicity occurs not just in recall but in an extremely wide variety of other tasks. Further, the phenomenon is not restricted to subjects who had recently learned a new domain. It also occurs with individuals who have many years of experience, an extreme example being the chess masters studied by Saariluoma (1990), who might well be viewed as experts were it not for the fact that they were being compared with grand masters. In our own research we found that medical residents made far more differential diagnoses than did students or experts (Patel et al., 1989c). In another study, medical residents requested significantly more laboratory tests for a patient than did either experts or final-year medical students (Trottier & Patel, 1987). Similar results were reported by Lesgold et al. (1988), who found that residents identified more features in X-ray films as relevant to the interpretation of a clinical problem and also offered a greater variety of differential diagnoses.

As we mentioned, analogous results can be found in the developmental literature. Lesgold et al. (1988) summarized those results and attempted to integrate them with findings coming from the expert–novice tradition. They suggested that one explanation that is consistent with the developmental results is a transition from perceptual to cognitive processing. This they viewed as consisting in the building of increasingly refined versions of schemata developing through a "cognitively deep" form of generalization and discrimination. Their contention was that this process will inevitably involve periods in which deeper processing does not produce a better outcome. It is during those periods that the nonmonotonic effects take place.

This explanation assumes that deep processing is characteristic of experts and that, given enough experience, it will yield results superior to those achieved by the intermediates. However, the studies reviewed by Charness indicate that deep analysis is not in fact the hallmark of expert reasoning in chess. More generally, the forward reasoning that appears to be most characteristic of accurate performance by experts in their own domains is a rather superficial process. In fact, it seems almost designed by nature to restrict deep processing. An alternative explanation is that experts have developed schemata that filter out irrelevant material, because if such a mechanism is not present, then forward reasoning will be prone to failure. If this material is not filtered out, attempts will be made to process it. The normal result will be some kind of unnecessary search. This notion of extraneous search obviously explains

Saariluoma's results in chess. We can postulate a reasonable mechanism to account for the identification of unnecessary features and the excessive generation of diagnoses and laboratory tests found in the medical experiments. The nonmonotonicity of recall may indicate one reason for this extraneous search because it may be initiated by the accessing of irrelevant prior knowledge activated by the irrelevant information in working memory. On the other hand, the recall itself may be partly generated by extraneous search. On the assumption that intermediates under time pressure will not indulge in extraneous search, this would explain the puzzling finding by Schmidt and Boshuizen that the intermediate nonmonotonicity can be made to disappear by using short exposure times.

Specific expertise. The second sequence concerns the development of specific expertise. Here, the basic issue is not the development of new representations. In fact, it seems possible to assume that the representations of a clinical situation are quite stable. What is missing in a subexpert are certain crucial components of necessary knowledge.

Two crucial and related phenomena do appear to require explanation. The first question is why some experts are accurate in their diagnoses although others are not. The second is why inaccuracy is always associated with a transition from forward reasoning to backward reasoning. Our plausible explanation is that such a transition is caused by feelings of uncertainty regarding one's conclusions. An explanation along these lines is consistent with the technique used by most expert systems for medical diagnosis, which is to attach a certainty factor to each decision that is made. However, such an explanation results in problems because it can be shown that such certainty factors do not satisfy the axioms of probability theory (Adams, 1984).

It is possible, however, to explain most of our data without invoking the assumption of uncertainty. It can be assumed that rules that are present in an individual's knowledge will be fired by data and that a forward-reasoning process will take place. However, if a diagnosis is inaccurate, then a number of rules will remain that are not linked to the main diagnosis. Facts in the text base that fire these rules essentially serve as loose ends. We already discussed the results indicating that even subjects with accurate results appear to be aware of such unresolved components of the text base, and they frequently explain them by a process of backward reasoning.

It seems reasonable to assume that in some cases experts may not be aware that their knowledge is leading to an inaccurate diagnosis but are simply aware of the existence of the nonsalient cues that cannot be linked to the main diagnosis. In other words, the only difference between accurate and inaccurate diagnosis is the presence of loose ends. A diagnosis might be viewed as a theory about a clinical case. The loose ends are essentially anomalies. Much as anomalies are highly correlated with an inaccurate theory, so loose ends are correlated with an inaccurate diagnosis. It is usually when they are faced with anomalies that scientists resort to the classical hypotheticodeductive method (e.g., Groen & Patel, 1985), which is a form of backward reasoning. It should be noted, however, that scientific theories persist despite anomalies, and inaccurate diagnoses may persist in an analogous fashion.

It is well known that anomalies do not necessarily result in a change in theory. Thus, the transition from forward to backward reasoning sometimes may be motivated by the desire to "patch up" a diagnosis by reinterpreting data that are inconsistent with it. but it may also result in the further development of specific expertise. Such development might occur when an expert attempts to explain the loose ends constructively, rather than simply to justify an existing hypothesis. Such a constructive explanation might be related to the kind of dialectical process described by Scardamalia and Bereiter (chapter 7, this volume).

Domain-independent expertise. There remains the possibility of a more general kind of expertise that is domain-independent. There is a well-known distinction in the problem-solving literature between weak and strong methods. This is expertise in the heuristics needed to explore ill-structured domains. Such heuristics, which usually are called weak methods (Newell, 1988), come into play when the knowledge base is inadequate and it is necessary to search for information. In contrast, strong methods are more akin to decision making than to search and are highly dependent on an adequate knowledge base. It is important to note that weak methods are not necessarily naive or unsophisticated. For example, the more general aspects of the scientific method are heuristics of this type. Hence, it is important to consider the possibility that they may play a role even in the kind of knowledge-based expertise we have discussed in this chapter.

Because weak methods tend to make use of some form of backward reasoning, evidence that they are in fact being used comes from the points in our protocols where forward reasoning breaks down. This seems to be associated with two kinds of developments: One is an incomplete or inaccurate diagnosis; the other is the existence of loose ends. As we pointed out, these may be related because incomplete diagnostic explanations have loose ends. Thus, it seems reasonable to argue that loose ends give rise to weak methods. This has some significance because it may give some insight as to how expertise evolves. Perkins and Salomon (1989) have suggested that explanation may be an important mechanism for nontrivial learning. One way this might occur is through a SOAR-like mechanism. The goal of our experts is to give a coherent, consistent explanation. Loose ends are essentially gaps in the coherence (using, for example, the notion of van Dijk and Kintsch that coherence involves propositions linked into a connected component). It therefore becomes important to establish consistency between disconnected components. In SOAR, learning begins with the recognition of an impasse, of which an inconsistency would be a clear sign. Thus, the breakdown of forward reasoning may reflect a search to account for anomalous data that would cast doubt on the diagnosis.

5. GENERALITY AND COMMONALITY WITH OTHER DOMAINS

We suggested that our research may be generalizable to other areas, but this suggestion needs to be examined closely. The issue is one of whether medicine is a somewhat peculiar domain, different from others studied by investigators of expert–novice differences. Medicine does, in fact, have certain distinguishing traits. One is that it consists of two kinds of knowledge: academic knowledge of basic sciences, which usually is taught first, and situational knowledge, which is learned in the clinical setting. It is this latter kind of knowledge in which medical specialists are experts. The issue of how basic science knowledge fits into this expertise is highly controversial (Patel, Evans, & Groen, 1989b). It is clear that whereas basic scientific knowledge is necessary for expertise, a physician normally is not an expert in basic science. It might be argued, therefore, that our results are artifacts of this rather peculiar combination of these two areas. The intermediate phenomenon may reflect the nature of basic scientific knowledge in contrast to clinical knowledge. The reasoning of experts may reflect the fact that physicians become accustomed to reasoning differently in situations where they are under a great deal of pressure. It can be argued against this position, however, that most of the phenomena normally studied in research on expert–novice differences have similar properties, even though they may occur in medicine in a pronounced form. For example, chess involves the learning of a large amount of book knowledge, as Charness (chapter 2, this volume) points out. Any chess master will have learned that at some early stage of development. But a chess master develops expertise by playing many tournament games. It can be argued that such games are highly situational and are analogous to the situations in which physicians learn clinical medicine.

Physics does bear a certain resemblance to the academic side of medicine. It is the area in which the most solid evidence exists for the use of forward reasoning on routine problems, and of weak methods in nonroutine situations (Anzai, chapter 3, this volume). There are, however, two major differences. The first is that whereas physics problems are stated verbally, physicists make extensive use of visual representations, as discussed by Anzai (chapter 3, this volume). Although visual representations are extremely important in areas of medicine such as radiology and dermatology, they appear to play no role in the domains we have been considering. The second difference is that in physics there is no close correspondence to the clinical situation. Although the physicist may be forced into situations (as when teaching) requiring rapid problem solving under stressful circumstances, no person-to-person interaction is embedded in the physics problem, as Anzai (chapter 3, this volume) points out. Chess has more of the real-time interpersonal flavor of medicine. Hence, in many respects, medicine lies between chess and physics, and the kinds of issues raised by Charness (chapter 2, this volume) are as pertinent as those raised by Anzai (chapter 3, this volume). We have elaborated elsewhere

(Patel et al., 1989a) on a distinction made by Schaffner (1986) between domains that are learned as integrated deductive systems and those that are learned through exemplars. Physics and the biological sciences underlying medicine fall in the former category. On the other hand, chess and clinical medicine would seem to belong to the latter category.

6. GENERAL DISCUSSION

In this chapter, we have attempted to consider both those aspects of expertise that are highly specific to a domain and those that are more generic, in the sense that they seem to generalize across related domains. Our results concerning domain specificity are no different from what most other investigators in the area have observed. Thus, experts make use of their specialized domain knowledge to solve problems using forward reasoning. But the extremely strong connection between forward reasoning and accuracy of performance may go somewhat beyond the findings of other investigators (without being inconsistent with them). Also, we are able to be more systematic in stating what induces backward reasoning. This is important because backward reasoning usually is associated with the use of weak methods. In the case of the performances of experts in explaining cases with loose ends, backward reasoning appears to be utilized as a strong method. It is tempting to generalize and speculate that even with subexperts, backward reasoning frequently reflects the application of a powerful knowledge base. This is because what is characteristic of our experts and subexperts is an absence of the type of behavior that is not directly relevant to the solution of a problem. In other words, a distinguishing trait of experts, even outside their domains of specialization, is knowledge of what not to do. This may be what lies behind what we have termed "generic expertise." Because forward reasoning is notoriously unreliable in the presence of irrelevant information, it is reasonable to conclude that this generic expertise is a necessary condition for accurate problem solving when this method is used.

In contrast, intermediates do not seem to be able to screen out irrelevant information. They might be characterized as not knowing what not to do. Even if they possess adequate prior knowledge, they are likely to be distracted by irrelevant cues, to formulate unnecessary goals, and to access extraneous parts of their knowledge base. Thus, generic expertise seems to yield a demarcation between experts and intermediates.

We have suggested elsewhere (Groen & Patel, 1990) that the transition from novice to intermediate to expert has a flavor akin to a theory of developmental stages (nonmonotonicity is also an issue in developmental research). It is therefore tempting to speculate that a satisfactory explanation of results such as ours might be found in something analogous to a developmental-stage theory. An example is to be found in the suggestion by Lesgold et al. (1988) that the acquisition of expertise in radiology consists of a period of perceptual learning followed by a period of cognitive learning. Schmidt, Norman, and Boshuizen (1990) recently suggested a complex sequence of stages to explain most of the results that we have mentioned in this chapter.

We believe, however, that our results do not readily lend themselves to stagelike interpretations (Patel & Groen, in press). There are two ways in which the notion of a stage can be used (Groen & Kieran, 1983). The first is a way of organizing data in a developmental order. The second is to develop an underlying theory that explains why this developmental order is somehow necessary. If we wish to adopt an information-processing approach (as opposed to more classical developmental approaches such as that of Piaget), this carries with it the presupposition that some kind of developmental mechanism exists that is responsible for transitions between stages. The task of specifying such transition mechanisms is extremely difficult. In particular, it is more difficult than developing a theory of learning, because in the latter case one is not concerned with explaining why one kind of behavior must always occur later than another.

Because of this, it is extremely important to have an extensive data base of empirical phenomena and to be certain that the stages are invariant before attempting to develop a stage theory. For example, it might be tempting to speculate that generic expertise precedes specific expertise in a stagelike fashion. But all our data in support of generic expertise came from subjects who had already acquired specific expertise. Hence, we are delineating two aspects of expertise rather than two stages. It is quite possible that generic expertise may be achieved only through the acquisition of a large amount of specific expertise.

There are more solid arguments for the stagelike nature of the distinctions among intermediates, experts, and novices; but the distinctions are based on a process that is quite simple to describe without having to appeal to transition mechanisms. Intermediates conduct irrelevant searches, whereas experts do not. Novices do not conduct irrelevant searches simply because they do not have a knowledge base to search. What seems to be needed is some kind of cognitive-learning theory that can explain how a developing knowledge base can give rise to irrelevant search and how, as a result of extensive experience in a narrow domain, it can give rise to the ability to filter out irrelevant information and suppress the irrelevant search.

Of course, this issue is easy to state, but it is not likely to be easy to resolve. It is important to resolve it, however, because although we have a performance theory of expertise, we have no adequate description of the learning mechanism. It seems clear that theories based purely on knowledge expansion or on the development of better and better representations are inadequate. Recent formulation of learning mechanisms provided by Holland, Holyoak, Nisbett, and Thagard (1986) and Scardamalia and Bereiter (chapter 7, this volume), as well as Holyoak's suggestions on the development of a symbolic connectionist learning model (chapter 12, this volume), are examples of promising candidate theories worthy of further investigation.

ACKNOWLEDGMENTS

The work reported in this chapter was supported in part by a grant from the Medical Research Council of Canada (MH004) to Vimla L. Patel. We would like to thank Keith Holyoak, Anders Ericsson, Neil Charness, David Kaufman, and José Arocha for their insightful comments and discussions of issues reported in this chapter.

REFERENCES

Adams, J. B. (1984). Probabilistic reasoning and certainty factors. In B. G. Buchanan & E. H. Shortliffe (Eds.), *Rule-based expert systems: The MYCIN experiments of the Stanford Heuristic Programming Project* (pp. 263–271). Reading, MA: Addison-Wesley.

Chase, W. G., & Simon, H. A. (1973). Perception in chess. *Cognitive Psychology, 1,* 55–81.

Clancey, W. (1988). Acquiring, representing, and evaluating a competence model of diagnosis. In M. Chi, R. Glaser, & M. J. Farr (Eds.), *The nature of expertise* (pp. 343–418). Hillsdale, NJ: Erlbaum.

Coughlin, L. D., & Patel, V. L. (1987). Processing of critical information by physicians and medical students. *Journal of Medical Education, 62,* 818–828.

Elstein, A. S., Shulman, L. S., & Sprafka, S. A. (1978). *Medical problem solving: An analysis of clinical reasoning.* Cambridge, MA: Harvard University Press.

Frederiksen, C. H. (1975). Representing the logical and semantic structure of knowledge acquired from discourse. *Cognitive Science, 7,* 371–458.

Groen, G. J., & Kieran, C. (1983). In search of Piagetian mathematics. In H. Ginsburg (Ed.), *The development of mathematical thinking* (pp. 351–374). New York: Academic Press.

Groen, G. J., & Patel, V. L. (1985). Medical problem-solving: Some questionable assumptions. *Medical Education, 19,* 95–100.

Groen, G. J., & Patel, V. L. (1988). The relationship between comprehension and reasoning in medical expertise. In M. Chi, R. Glaser, & M. J. Farr (Eds.), *The nature of expertise* (pp. 287–310). Hillsdale, NJ: Erlbaum.

Groen, G. J., & Patel, V. L. (1990). Professional and novice expertise in medicine. In M. Smith (Ed.), *Toward a unified theory of problem solving: Views from content domains* (pp. 35–44). Hillsdale, NJ: Erlbaum.

Holland, J. H., Holyoak, K. J., Nisbett, R. E., & Thagard, P. R. (1986). *Induction: Processes of inference, learning, and discovery.* Cambridge, MA: MIT Press.

Hunt, E. (1989). Cognitive science: Definition, status, and questions. *Annual Review of Psychology, 40,* 603–629.

Joseph, G.-M., & Patel, V. L. (1990). Domain knowledge and hypothesis generation in diagnostic reasoning. *Journal of Medical Decision Making, 10,* 31–46.

Kaufman, D. R., & Patel, V. L. (1988). The nature of expertise in the clinical interview: Interactive medical problem solving. In *Proceedings of the Tenth Annual Conference of the Cognitive Science Society* (pp. 461–467). Hillsdale, NJ: Erlbaum.

Kintsch, W. (1974). *The representation of meaning in memory.* Hillsdale, NJ: Erlbaum.

Kintsch, W., & Greeno, J. G. (1985). Understanding and solving word arithmetic problems. *Psychological Review, 92,* 109–129.

Laird, J. E., Rosenbloom, P. S., & Newell, A. (1985). *Chunking in SOAR: The anatomy of a general learning mechanism* (technical report). Pittsburgh: Carnegie-Mellon University, Department of Computer Science.

Lesgold, A. (1989). Context-specific requirements for models of expertise. In D. Evans & V. Patel (Eds.), *Cognitive science in medicine: Biomedical modeling* (pp. 373–400). Cambridge, MA: MIT Press.

Lesgold, A., Rubinson, H., Feltovich, P., Glaser, R., Klopfer, D., & Wang, Y. (1988). Expertise in a complex skill: Diagnosing x-ray pictures. In M. Chi, R. Glaser, & M. J. Farr (Eds.), *The nature of expertise* (pp. 311–342). Hillsdale, NJ: Erlbaum.

Medley-Mark, V. (1986). *The relationship between premedical background and processing of medical information by novices.* Unpublished master's thesis, Centre for Medical Education, McGill University, Montreal, Canada.

Muzzin, L. J., Norman, G. R., Jacoby, L. L., Feightner, J. W., Tugwell, P., & Guyatt, G. H. (1982). Manifestations of expertise in recall of clinical protocols. In *Proceedings of the 21st Annual Conference on Research in Medical Education* (pp. 163–168). Washington, DC: American Association of Medical Colleges.

Newell, A. (1988, August). *Unified theory of problem solving.* Paper presented at the Tenth Annual Conference of the Cognitive Science Society, Montreal, Canada.

Norman, G. R., Jacoby, L. L., Feightner, J. W., & Campbell, G. J. M. (1979). Clinical experience and the structure of memory. In *Proceedings of the 18th Annual Conference on Research in Medical Education* (pp. 214–218). Washington, DC: American Association of Medical Colleges.

Patel, V. L. (1986). *Relationship between representation of textual information and underlying problem representation in medicine* (Technical Report CME86-CS1). Montreal: Centre for Medical Education, McGill University.

Patel, V. [L.], & Ericsson, A. (1990). *Expert–novice differences in clinical text understanding* (Technical Report CME90-CS13). Montreal: Centre for Medical Education, McGill University.

Patel, V. L., Evans, D. A., & Groen, G. J. (1989a). Biomedical knowledge and clinical reasoning. In D. Evans & V. Patel (Eds.), *Cognitive science in medicine: Biomedical modeling* (pp. 49–108). Cambridge, MA: MIT Press.

Patel, V. L., Evans, D. A., & Groen, G. J. (1989b). On reconciling basic science and clinical reasoning. *Teaching & Learning in Medicine: An International Journal,* *1*(3), 116–121.

Patel, V. L., Evans, D. A., & Kaufman, D. R. (1989c). Cognitive framework for doctor–patient interaction. In D. Evans & V. Patel (Eds.), *Cognitive science in medicine: Biomedical modeling* (pp. 253–308). Cambridge, MA: MIT Press.

Patel, V. L., & Groen, G. J. (1986). Knowledge-based solution strategies in medical reasoning. *Cognitive Science, 10,* 91–116.

Patel, V. L., & Groen, G. J. (in press). Developmental accounts of the transition from student to physician: Some problems and suggestions. *Academic Medicine.*

Patel, V. L., Groen, G. J., & Arocha, J. F. (1990). Medical expertise as a function of task difficulty. *Memory & Cognition, 18*(4), 394–406.

Patel, V. L., Groen, G. J., & Frederiksen, C. H. (1986). Differences between students and physicians in memory for clinical cases. *Medical Education, 20,* 3–9.

Perkins, D. N., & Salomon, G. (1989). Are cognitive skills context-bound? *Educational Researcher, 18*(1), 16–25.

Saariluoma, P. (1990). Apperception and restructuring in chess players' problem solving. In K. Gilhooly, M. T. G. Keane, R. H. Logie, & G. Erdos (Eds.), *Lines of thinking: Reflections of the psychology of thought* (Vol. 2, pp. 41–57). London: Wiley.

Salomon, G., & Perkins, D. N. (1989). Rocky roads to transfer: Rethinking mechanism of a neglected phenomenon. *Educational Psychologist, 24*(2), 113–143.

Schaffner, K. F. (1986). Exemplar reasoning about biological models and diseases: A relation between the philosophy of medicine and philosophy of science. *Journal of Medicine & Philosophy, 11,* 63–80.

Schmidt, H., Boshuizen, H. P. A., & Hobus, P. P. M. (1988). Transitory stages in the development of medical expertise: The "intermediate effect" in clinical case representation studies. In *Proceedings of the Tenth Annual Conference of the Cognitive Science Society* (pp. 139–145). Hillsdale, NJ: Erlbaum.

Schmidt, H., Norman, G., & Boshuizen, H. P. A. (1990). A cognitive perspective on medical expertise: Theory and implications. *Academic Medicine, 65*(10), 611–621.

Sowa, J. F. (1984). *Conceptual structures.* Reading, MA: Addison-Wesley.

Trottier, M., & Patel, V. L. (1987). Medical expertise and reasoning about laboratory tests. *Professions Education Researcher, 20,* 3–9.

van Dijk, T. A., & Kintsch, W. (1983). *Strategies of discourse comprehension.* New York: Academic Press.

Wenger, E. (1987) *Artificial intelligence and tutoring systems: Computational and cognitive approaches to the communication of knowledge.* Los Altos, CA: Morgan Kaufmann Publishers.

5   Motor-skill experts in sports, dance, and other domains

FRAN ALLARD AND JANET L. STARKES

Skilled motor performance encompasses an enormous range of human activities, including industrial tasks, sport skills, recreational opportunities, entertainment extravaganzas, and the actions of everyday life. In this chapter we consider skill in sport, broadly defining sport as situations in which individuals or teams compete against one another through the medium of physical action, with one of the competitors being declared a winner. We also venture into the domain of dance, both ballet and modern, in our analysis of the talents displayed by highly skilled movement experts. And a microsurgeon or two will make special guest appearances. We wish to consider motor skills in terms of two components. Clearly, sport experts are better able to execute the motor skills of their particular domains than are less skilled performers; sport experts excel in performing appropriate actions. In addition, we argue that sport experts have greater cognitive skills in their particular areas than do other performers; sport experts have superior knowledge of the domain. A critical question for understanding motor expertise concerns the linking of the knowledge to the performance: How are knowing and doing related?

Sports differ greatly in the balance between knowing and doing; a weight lifter or a sprinter needs to have knowledge about the techniques of movement essential for success. This knowledge about movement seems different from the cognitive, tactical skill required of the basketball point guard or the squash player. We begin by dividing sport skills into domains of action, into skill categories that capture common features that cut across particular sport environments.

A common distinction found in the motor-skill literature concerns the differences between "closed" and "open" skills. Closed skills are defined as skills that are displayed by performance in a consistent, typically stationary, environment (Poulton, 1957), whereas open skills are displayed by performance in a moving, dynamic environment. In order to appreciate cognitive differences in motor skills, it is necessary to look at the differences in open and closed skills in more detail.

Open and closed skills differ in two respects. The first difference concerns the environment in which the skill is displayed. In addition to being exercised in a changing environment, most open skills are exercised with an opponent

126

present in the environment throughout the competition; in fact, in sports such as boxing, the opponent is the single most important aspect of the environment. For closed skills, competitors do not act at the same time, typically taking turns in performing.

The second difference between open and closed skills involves the role of a particular motor pattern. For closed skills, motor patterns *are* the skills; it is critical that the performer be able to reproduce consistently and reliably a defined, standard movement pattern. For open skills, it is the effectiveness of a motor pattern in producing a particular environmental outcome that constitutes the skill. As Gentile (1972) has pointed out, it is possible for an open-skill performer to have a consistent motor pattern that simply does not work to produce the desired environmental consequence.

Open and closed skills may be further categorized according to the dimension of motor performance (speed, accuracy) emphasized by the sport. Table 5.1 shows such a taxonomy of skills, with the left column representing "pure" open and closed skills as they are typically described in the literature. We have broken sport skills down into smaller categories characterized by the demand for accuracy or consistency in performance, for speed of performance, for strength, and for endurance. For all but true closed skills, which place great demands on the technical skill of the performer, the other skill categories require movements that are within the capacities of most of us, at least some of the time. Virtually anyone can throw a dart at a target with some chance of success, but the need to hit the "triple 20" consistently restricts the careers of many. Similarly, most of us can run and lift and have some measure of endurance, but not to the point where we are ready for top-flight competition. True open skills are difficult because of the complexity of the environment and the need to select the most appropriate action for the occasion.

All sports in the taxonomy require that the performer be able to carry out the requisite motor tasks. We now consider the cognitive skills necessary for the various constituents of the skill taxonomy. Closed speed skills, open and closed strength skills, and endurance skills require tactical and strategic knowledge on the part of performers, in that athletes must understand their own capabilities and perform accordingly. The importance of "on-line" cognition to guide performance is most readily seen for true open skills, true closed skills, and speeded open skills. We now turn to a closer examination of the specific aspects of cognition important for the targeted categories of sport skills.

COGNITION AND CLOSED SKILL: THE ROLE OF SKILLED MEMORY

For technique motor skills such as dance, diving, or figure skating, memory is critical in two different ways. First, for performing the individual movement elements, each skill must be carried out with reference to a defined technical standard or widely accepted ideal "form." Very often, performances

Table 5.1. *Skill taxonomy*

Skill	True open/closed	Emphasis on accuracy/consistency	Emphasis on speed	Emphasis on strength	Emphasis on endurance
Closed skills: a skill performed (a) in an invariant environment and (b) having the production of a particular motor pattern as its goal	Technique skills: Ballet Gymnastics Figure skating Diving Synchronized swimming	Note simplicity of movement elements: Darts Bowling Shooting Archery (Note that an exception to the simplicity rule occurs for golf)	Note simplicity of movement elements: Sprints (track) Cycling Swimming (But note that an environmental event, finishing fastest, is the goal)	Note simplicity of movement elements: Weight lifting Field events (shot put, discus) (Again, an environmental event is the goal)	Note simplicity of movement elements: Marathon Triathalon (Yet again, an environmental event is the goal)
Open skills: a skill performed (a) in a dynamic environment, often including an opponent, and (b) having the production of a particular environmental event as its goal	True open skills Basketball Hockey Soccer Field hockey Football Combatives	Simplicity of movement, but difficulty of sport magnified by opponent: Pool Curling Horseshoes Shuffleboard Lawn bowling	Volleyball Racquet sports	Football lineman Tug-of-war	

of technique skills are judged according to how closely the performance matches the ideal form. The role of memory in the initial acquisition of technique skills is to establish a template or standard for proper form, allowing on-line comparison between the actual and the ideal during performance.

Many technique skills also involve the learning and performance of long sequences of movement elements. A second role for memory is recall of the sequences that constitute a performance, as in figure skating, gymnastics, and some forms of dance. In each of these activities, performers must recall movement routines that can last from three minutes to several hours. To date, the expertise literature has revealed the importance of skilled memory for a variety of domains, most notably digit span (Chase & Ericsson, 1981), dinner orders (Ericsson & Polson, 1988), and mental calculation (Staszewski, 1988). This section examines the role of skilled memory in technique skills.

Skilled-memory theory has five established principles (Ericsson & Polson, 1988):

1. Experts encode information using existing semantic-memory patterns.
2. The use of retrieval structures at encoding guarantees the accessibility of information at the time of recall.
3. Encoded information is stored in long-term memory (LTM) and can be retrieved over surprisingly long intervals.
4. The speed of encoding increases with practice.
5. Memory skill is domain-specific and does not transfer to different situations.

Studies of skilled ballet dancers and figure skaters have shown that skilled memory is an important aspect of skill in their domains. Starkes, Deakin, Lindley, and Crisp (1987) conducted a study to examine the roles of choreographic structure and motor performance in the recall of ballet sequences. In Experiment 1, two groups of 11-year-old dancers were tested, one expert group from the National Ballet School of Canada and a novice group of equal experience from local ballet schools. The stimuli for the study were videotaped sequences of eight ballet steps. No music accompanied the steps. For the structured trials, the order of the elements was selected by an experienced choreographer; for the unstructured trials, the elements were randomly selected from the same set of elements used to construct the choreographed sequences. In each trial, the subjects viewed a videotaped model performing the sequence twice, and they immediately attempted to recall the sequence either by performing the steps or by naming the sequence of steps. The results of the study (Figure 5.1) show an interaction between skill level and structure for ballet recall. Choreographed stimuli led to enhanced recall of ballet sequences for the young experts.

Serial-position accuracy for ballet steps is not at all like serial-position recall for verbal material. Success in the typical verbal-recall task shows both primacy and recency effects, whereas success in the recall of ballet steps shows only a primacy effect. The absence of a recency effect in these data may in part be due to the way in which subjects recall; it does not make sense in

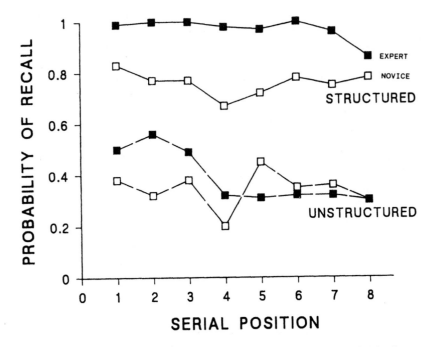

Figure 5.1. Probabilities of recall across serial positions for both young expert and novice ballet dancers.

recalling a dance sequence to report the last few elements first, as is often done in verbal free-recall studies. Once a subject forgets one item in a sequence, the tendency is for recall of all following items to be doomed, quite unlike the situation for a subject in a verbal memory study, who can simply say "blank" and continue to report any remaining items.

Experiment 2 addressed the nature of the primacy effect observed among young expert dancers and attempted to determine if there was any cuing effect for the music presented with the dance steps. Choreographed sequences from Experiment 1 were presented to a second group of young expert dancers. The subjects viewed the eight step sequences accompanied by music, then recalled the steps by performance either with or without music. As shown in Figure 5.2, music enhanced their recall of the dance steps, but again, typical verbal-memory serial-position recall accuracy was not observed.

Deakin (1987) demonstrated similar effects for expert and novice figure skaters recalling free-skating elements. In a situation similar to the motor recall of ballet steps, strong primacy effects, but no recency effects, were found among expert and novice figure skaters. Thus, the recall of elements for the technique skills of dance and figure skating seems to involve memory techniques quite different from those seen with verbal recall; although each element in a sequence has a name, subjects do not seem to perform on the

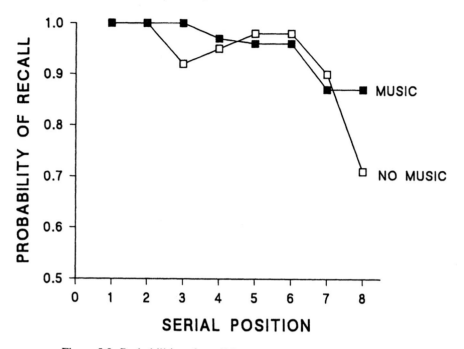

Figure 5.2. Probabilities of recall for young expert ballet dancers across serial positions with and without music during recall.

basis of learned names. It can be argued that lack of a recency effect for recall of dance and skating sequences is due to output interference, such that the performance of early elements interferes with the storage of later items in short-term memory (STM). If that is so, the mode of output – verbal or performance – should interact with serial-position accuracy. That was not observed for either figure skating or ballet recall.

In terms of strategies of recall, there appear to be clear differences between expert and novice dancers. After viewing the movement sequences, novices tended to rush to perform the recall before memory had faded, much like someone rushing to telephone for a pizza while simultaneously holding in working memory eleven topping items plus the telephone number. Ballet experts can be observed making hand movements while watching ballet sequences, a strategy known as "marking," in which dancers substitute hand positions for foot (or whole-body) positions. At recall, experts often take their time and retrieve parts of the sequence by repeating the hand positions used during the original presentation of the sequence. Expert dancers develop both a sensitivity to choreography and unique memory techniques to encode sequences of movements.

During these studies, an incidental observation revealed just how effectively dancers are able to encode steps. While conducting the ballet studies just described, we had the opportunity to observe an adult principal dancer with the National Ballet company performing a new piece for the first time. After one demonstration, accompanied by verbal labeling of the steps executed by the choreographer, the dancer was able to perform a 96-step sequence. In that "routine" learning session, the dancer employed both hand movements and verbal labels to mark steps and combinations of steps.

The need for ballet dancers and figure skaters to recall long sequences of movements results in superior memory for these experts, but is this the same sort of "skilled memory" observed in other areas of expertise? As far as we can tell, yes, it is. The memory skills of dancers and skaters described to date seem to fit with the principles of skilled memory outlined by Ericsson and Polson (1988). Experts in technique skills do encode information using existing semantic-memory structures; in fact, a large component to learning the skill elements in these domains is learning the vocabulary. As we have described for ballet dancers, a common encoding strategy is to mark movement sequences, to encode foot positions rapidly with hand movements. For both skating and dance, retrieval structures in the form of music are routinely used in performance. Deakin (1987) has shown that memory for free-skating elements among expert figure skaters is not influenced by tasks interpolated between presentation of the sequence and recall, at least a suggestion that the memory used by skilled skaters is LTM. We have not looked at any learning studies for technique-skill performers and can say nothing about the speed with which they encode. The skill-by-structure interaction observed among dancers and skaters recalling choreographed and random elements illustrates that the memory skill used was specific to the combinations of elements they typically encounter.

Differences in dance choreography present another example of the sensitivity of the dancer to the structure found within the domain. Dance can be divided into ballet and modern dance, both of which are choreographed, but in different ways, using different movement patterns. Occasionally, given the creative bent of the modern-dance choreographer, dancers are required to perform pieces that are notable for their random movements and lack of choreographic structure. In creative modern dance, the movements do not have established names as in ballet; there is, however, a notation system for defining the constituent movements. Laban (1956) first described the elements of structure in modern dance and developed a complex notation system for the representation of movement. By definition, an unstructured series of movements in modern dance goes against Laban's principles of movement quality, direction, and relationship to gravity. Does this mean the creative modern dancer must develop the ability to recall any and all movement sequences?

We sought to test the recall of structured and unstructured creative modern-dance sequences by expert and novice modern dancers. The experts were dancers from a performing company; the novices were students who had taken twenty-four hours of introductory classes in modern dance. The structured sequences reflected Laban's movement criteria; the unstructured se-

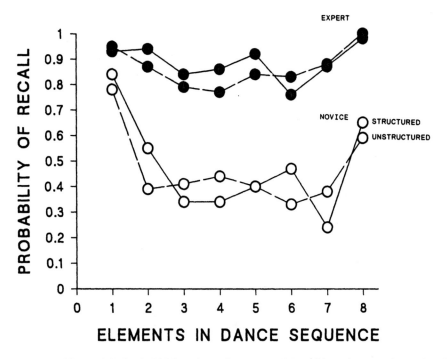

Figure 5.3. Probabilities of recall across serial positions for experienced and inexperienced creative modern dancers with dance sequences either structured or unstructured.

quences were purposely random. Figure 5.3 shows that experts were much more accurate than novices at sequence recall and that structure does not aid recall for experienced modern dancers. For creative modern dancers, then, memory skill must encompass the ability to encode movement sequences literally picked at random.

TRUE OPEN SKILLS AND COGNITION

We next consider the cognitive skill shown by athletes practicing true open skills. Because most true open skills feature the same sort of tactical knowledge important for the game of chess, it is not surprising that many of the techniques for investigating the nature of chess skill have been used to investigate open sport skills. In particular, the five-second recall task has proved particularly effective in the study of open sport skills.

Allard, Graham, and Paarsalu (1980) showed slides made during basketball games to varsity and intramural basketball players. Half of the slides showed structured plays during a game, depicting scenes such as a point guard about to initiate a play from the top of the "key." The other slides showed unstructured game situations, such as a turnover or a scramble for the loose ball.

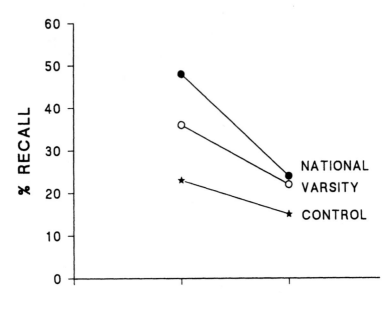

Figure 5.4. Percentage recall for each group of structured and unstructured game information.

After a four-second period, the subjects recalled the positions of as many players as possible by placing magnets on a metal board with a basketball court drawn to scale on its surface. Varsity players recalled more player positions correctly than did intramural players, but only for structured game situations.

Starkes and Deakin (1985) reported similar findings for a recall task presented to field-hockey players of varying abilities. The expert group was composed of members of the Canadian national women's field-hockey team, ranked second in the world at the time of testing. An intermediate-ability group of university varsity players and a novice group of physical-education majors were also tested. As in the basketball study, the subjects looked at slides showing structured and unstructured game situations, and their recall involved placing magnets on a magnetic board depicting a hockey pitch. The viewing time was somewhat longer in this study (eight seconds) because of the greater number of player positions to be recalled; field hockey has 11 players per side, whereas basketball has 5 players. As Figure 5.4 illustrates, the national-team players were superior to varsity and novice players with structured game situations only. In keeping with the correlation between skill and structure typically found in the five-second recall task, varsity players were better than novices with structured game situations.

Thus, the five-second recall task used so successfully to demonstrate expertise in many cognitive domains has proved itself in sport-skill domains as well. As we shall describe shortly, the skill-by-structure interaction characteristic of five-second recall performance by experts has not been found in all sport domains we have investigated – those domains emphasizing speed seem to require a different mode of dealing with the environment. To illustrate further the sensitivity of athletes to information from their particular skill domains, we reveal here (with great relief) the results of a class project that followed a discussion of domain-specific patterns and skill. "Do you mean to say," challenged a student, "that a hockey player is unable to recall a schematic basketball play but can recall a hockey play?" "And vice versa?" he added to emphasize his point. The instructor boldly affirmed that such was the case and invited the student to test the hypothesis.

The student tested five varsity hockey players and six varsity basketball players for their ability to recall five-second presentations of three basketball plays and three hockey plays. The plays were presented on paper in a schematic X-and-O manner, and players subsequently drew representations of all the positions and actions they could recall. Happily, hockey players recalled 73% of the hockey plays and 60% of the basketball plays, whereas basketball players recalled 54% of the hockey plays and 70% of the basketball plays. The interaction between the player and the nature of the play recalled was significant [$F(1, 19) = 7.98, p = .019$], even with such a small number of subjects. The study is particularly interesting because the two sports share many features: the numbers of players in action at any one time, similar playing arenas divided into offensive and defensive zones, similar tactics to free individuals for shots, and the X-and-O method used by coaches to represent plays schematically.

We have also used a second empirical approach taken from the study of cognitive skill to demonstrate the importance of semantic memory for sport expertise: the sorting procedure used by Chi, Feltovich, and Glaser (1981) in their investigations of physics expertise. Allard and Burnett (1985) had basketball players and fans sort photographs of basketball concepts and skills into categories that made sense to them. Cluster analysis showed the players' sorts to be like a textbook, breaking hierarchically from major defensive and offensive clusters into categories for individual and team defense within the defensive cluster, and into individual-shooting and team-offense concepts within the offensive cluster. The sorting by the fans indicated that the photos had been grouped according to how many players were shown in them. Thus, all photos showing ten players were placed in the same category, even though the photos illustrated such different concepts as zone defense, trapping pressure defenses, high-post offenses, and double-stack offenses.

In a recent master's thesis, Parker (1989) had 15 hockey fans, 14 experienced hockey players, and 8 hockey coaches sort photographs from hockey games into categories "using whatever rules or principles that seem sensible to you." Parker's fans were required to have had a minimum of 2 years, but fewer than 5 years, as amateur players in order to be included in the study.

The fans proved to be true Canadians, watching, on average, 1.4 hockey games per week. His players had 17.8 years of playing experience, on average, with their highest playing levels ranging from the National Hockey League (NHL) to Canadian Major Junior. The coaches had both extensive playing experience (17.9 years) and extensive coaching experience (10.4 years, in leagues ranging from the NHL to Canadian Major Junior). The photos sorted by Parker's subjects were of actual game play, whereas those sorted by Allard and Burnett's subjects had been examples of basketball concepts selected from textbooks.

Parker's findings will be discussed in detail in a subsequent publication. Here, we should like to show how the sorting differed among the groups, and also to contrast hockey categories and basketball categories. Consider first the categories produced by the sortings of the three groups of subjects, ignoring the strength of agreement within each group (the variability of sorting was naturally higher for the fans). As shown in Table 5.2, each group sorted the photos into five major categories representing the fundamentals of hockey: breakouts (moving the puck out of one's own end of the ice and into the opponent's end), face-offs, fore-checking (attacking the advancing puck carrier), power plays (one team having a player off the ice serving a penalty), and scoring chances. Although the five categories were used by each group, the individual photos placed within a given category varied as a function of the subject group.

The fans tended to misclassify photos when they could not identify the action they were seeing. Fans classified one fore-checking photo as a scoring chance because they were unable to determine which team was in possession of the puck. Similarly, uncontested breakouts, an uncontested drive for the net, and power-play opportunities were all placed in the same category by fans. That was sensible in that in each case one team was in control of the puck, but it showed little understanding of the situations. Players and coaches showed good agreement in assigning photos to major categories, with one exception. Players and coaches showed figure–ground reversal with three of the photos, with the coaches seeing the situations as scoring threats and the players seeing the situations as fore-checking. The coaches saw the offensive potential in the situations, whereas the players were seeing from the perspective of the defense.

Although there was good agreement among the groups in terms of the major concepts being shown, the hierarchical structures within the categories were quite different for the three groups. The fans tended to see no consistent structure other than the major categories, whereas the coaches made fine discriminations within categories.

Finally, it is interesting to compare the categorizations of basketball and hockey experts. We found that our basketball experts sorted photos into two major clusters corresponding to offensive and defensive skills. The hockey coaches sorted all photos according to the degree of offensive threat depicted; with the exception of the fore-checking category, none of the hockey groups

Table 5.2. *Hockey sorting categories*

Category	Fans (N = 15)	Players (N = 14)	Coaches (N = 8)
Face-offs	4/5 correctly classified	5/5 correctly classified	5/5 correctly classified
Breakouts	7 photos selected	10 photos selected (7/10 same as those of fans)	9 photos selected (7/9 same as those of fans)
Power plays	5 photos selected (2 same as those for players and coaches, but fans included 3 irrelevant photos)	2/2 correctly classified	2/2 correctly classified
Fore-checking	4 photos selected (1 in agreement with players and coaches)	5 photos selected (1 in agreement with fans and coaches; includes 3 photos categorized by coaches as scoring chances)	5 photos selected (1 in agreement with players, and 4 in agreement with fans)
Scoring chances	10 photos selected (5 in agreement with players and coaches, but fans included misidentified photos of face-off and fore-checking)	8 photos selected (5 in agreement with fans and coaches; little differentiation within category)	9 photos selected (5 in agreement with fans and players; category differentiated into 4 subcategories)

Note: Agreement over all groups occurred for 19 of 30 photos (63%).

used a defensive category in their sorting. There are two possible reasons for such different categories emerging from basketball and hockey sorting performances. Ability to recognize as well as to execute multiple defensive tactics is a vital aspect of success in basketball, but less so in hockey. Hockey features attacks that develop in an instant, making the ability to be on the offense a vital aspect of hockey success.

Clearly, then, open sports seem to require cognitive skills more often associated with "pure" cognitive skills such as chess or physics. Why should that be so? What is it about open sports, particularly team sports, that requires cognition? First, anticipation is essential for high-level performance in sports, and anticipation comes from recognizing what is taking place on the field. Second, symbolic representations of team offensive and defensive structures are vital for communication between players and coaches, and among players. Third, a player cannot function without understanding his or her role in the structure of the team. As Bartlett described it, "The skilled performer must know more *what* to do rather than *how* to do it" (Knapp, 1963, p. 66).

COGNITION AND OPEN SKILLS WITH SPEED STRESS

Given the differences described for basketball and hockey, it should not be surprising to find cognitive differences among the skills in the different categories of the skill taxonomy shown in Table 5.1. Consider the category of open skills with speed stress; getting even more specific, consider the sport of volleyball. Volleyball is one of the most popular sports in the world, played on beaches, in backyards, and in playgrounds, as well as in the Olympic Games. One of the reasons for its popularity is its simplicity; there are five fundamental skills in volleyball – bump, set spike, dig, and serve – all simple to execute when the ball is lofted high over the net. Things get more difficult as the speed of the game increases at more advanced levels of competition.

Early in our work we were surprised by the performance of volleyball players in a five-second recall task. Because basketball and volleyball have plays and patterns, we expected that experienced volleyball players would show the standard skill-by-structure interaction observed among our basketball players. That proved not to be the case: In one study, skilled players were superior to unskilled (intramural) players at recall of both structured and unstructured schematic plays, and in a second study the skilled and unskilled players showed no differences in accuracy of recall.

Considering the speed at which volleyball is played, we asked our volleyball players to perform a speeded ball-detection task (Allard & Starkes, 1980). Players at different skill levels were given brief glimpses (16 milliseconds) of slides of volleyball game and nongame situations (time-outs, warm-ups). In half of the slides, a ball was present. Players were required to indicate with a vocal response whether or not the ball was present. Experienced volleyball players were faster, though no more accurate, than less skilled players at the ball-detection task. The detection-speed advantage for ball spotting was found to be independent of context – game or nongame background made little difference. But the detection-speed advantage was found only when the ball was the target; when we asked our skilled subjects to search for another volleyball-court target – a referee – they were no faster than less skilled players. From these data we have argued that in speeded sports, such as volleyball, focusing on the offensive pattern of the opposition would be detrimental to defensive play. In fact, volleyball offensive plays often are designed to disguise the point of attack until the last fraction of a second. It would be a far sounder strategy to focus on an aspect of the environment that cannot be used to deceive – the ball.

Borgeaud and Abernethy (1987) reported a skill-by-structure interaction for the recall of dynamic volleyball sequences. In fact, the interaction observed in their study was caused by the performance of the novice subjects.

Among novice players, recall is poorer for structured sequences than for unstructured performance, whereas better players show no recall differences for structured or unstructured plays. This is quite different from the typical finding on five-second recall that the performance of novices does not change as a function of the nature of the stimuli whereas experts improve with structure. There is nothing in the Borgeaud and Abernethy data to make us change our view that performers in speeded open sports must become skilled searchers, rather than skilled pattern recognizers. Comparison of volleyball players, basketball players, and closed-skill athletes suggests that the requirements of the skill environment determine the cognitive strategy adopted by the athlete: search for volleyball, patterns for basketball, and skilled memory for closed motor skills.

KNOWING AND DOING

The case we have been developing is that real-world motor skill comprises both knowing and doing. By "knowing" we do not mean knowledge about how to perform motor skills; we do not mean knowing about doing. Rather, the "knowing" component of interest here is what is essential to direct the intake of environmental information in an appropriate way and to store sport-specific patterns, tactics, and retrieval structures. The "doing" component is essential for the execution of actions, sport techniques, and motor-control programs. The balance between knowing and doing varies within different categories of skills. In some categories, primarily the closed skills, action dominates. In other categories, mainly open skills, knowing is very important for expert performance.

The terms "knowing" and "doing" sound similar to the condition → action terminology used in production-system models of skills (Anderson, 1982). In such models, skill is developed as condition–action links are formed, compiled, strengthened, tuned, and generalized. In production systems, the action called for by a condition often is an additional cognitive operation performed on the data in working memory, rather than an actual motor response. It is essential for accurate and rapid performance of cognitive skills, such as adding numbers or solving geometry problems, that specific environmental conditions call for appropriate actions in a particular order, that a series of productions become compiled into "superproductions." For motor skills, we do not believe that condition → action links are the fundamental building blocks of skill; the worst thing that can happen to an open-skill athlete is to become predictable or stereotyped in particular situations – the pressure is to be flexible in performance, rather than automatic. We shall argue that knowing and doing are quite different aspects of motor skill and shall reveal our initial attempts to fracture the knowing and the doing for a variety of motor-skill domains.

Examples of the independence of knowing and doing in regard to motor skills are common in daily life. Sports fans, coaches, umpires and judges, and sportscasters all have rich semantic memories for facts important for their particular roles, generally along with little ability to perform the physical skills required in the domain. On the other hand, it is quite possible to acquire motor-skill techniques to a high level of consistency and still be unable to play a particular sport well. "Practice players" are well known in many open-skill sports; these are players who excel during practice but are unable to perform well in a real game. Many tennis and squash beginners have discovered that bouncing a ball back to oneself off a wall is poor preparation for playing an actual opponent. Thus, knowing and doing seem to be separable components of motor skill, from a commonsense perspective. We have been attempting the same sort of separation between knowing and doing in an experimental context, focusing on the role of the knowing–doing link. Should the two components be found to be linked as skill develops, should skill be found to reside in the linkages, then changing the nature of the action required by a particular condition should degrade performance.

Our attempts at splitting knowing and doing took three forms. First, skilled individuals were required to perform different movements in the domains of their skills, essentially leaving knowing alone while changing the doing. Second, we provided the knowing side with augmented information while holding the demands on the doing side constant in order to determine if additional information in one of the units would facilitate performance. Third, we attempted to construct a new skill from old parts that already existed on both the knowing and doing sides, although the parts had never previously been linked.

Leave knowing alone; change doing

Videogames. Videogames are wonderful tools for studying the development of psychomotor skill, and they are particularly useful for distinguishing the knowing and doing components. Because most game units intended for home use (e.g., Colecovision, Nintendo) are designed to be used with a variety of game controllers, it is a simple matter to change the actions needed by a skilled player to play a given game. The movements required to control videogames are straightforward and simple to learn, although the games can be highly complex.

Consider what might be the result of changing the controller for a highly skilled videogame player. The first possibility is that the knowing component of the game is most important, whereas the actual movements performed are so simple as to be trivial. If that is the case, the performance of a skilled player should not change with the controller. It is, however, possible that the doing component is most important; at least for some fast-action games, one must be able to make lightning-fast moves to save one's screen life. If that is the case, then changing the controller should have a devastating influence on game play. Finally, there is the possibility that the link between knowing and doing is most important. In that case, the performance decrement produced by changing the game controller should be directly related to the strength of the link; the stronger (or the more automatic) the link, the greater the decline in performance.

Baba (1986), in one of her experiments to investigate the nature of videogame skill, tested subjects who were either experts or novices at the Colecovision game "Lady Bug." This is a fast-action maze-type game wherein the player, in order to score points, uses a joystick to control a Lady Bug running through the maze on the screen and eating items that suddenly appear. At the same time, the Lady Bug must avoid predatory insects that jump from a bug box at the center of the screen, with menace in their hearts for the Lady Bug. Unlike similar games such as Pacman, the Lady Bug maze has movable turnstiles, making it possible to trap bugs, leaving Lady Bug free to collect her goodies unmolested. Baba's expert subjects were nine individuals, each of whom had 200–350 hours of experience playing the game. The poorest expert was able to score 80,000 points consistently, and the best player could score 500,000 points per game. The novice subjects tested had little or no experience with Lady Bug.

The controllers used in play consisted of the standard Colecovision controller and an Atari joystick. Both controllers are spring-centered, with four switches corresponding to the directions the Lady Bug is able to move. The controllers are quite different in terms of "feel" (see Baba, 1986, Appendix E, for exact technical descriptions of the two controllers). The Coleco controller is a short, fat, mushroom-shaped device, with a great deal of play before switch closure. The Atari joystick is much larger and must be held with two hands; it feels much stiffer than the Coleco controller because less movement is required to close the switch.

In addition to playing Lady Bug with the two controllers, Baba's subjects played a game that was new to both the experts and novices – Ms. Pacman – with the same two controllers. Thus, in regard to the knowing and doing possibilities, if knowing was dominant, then Lady Bug experts should have been better than novices at playing the Lady Bug game, regardless of the controller used, and little difference in game scores should have been seen as a function of controller. The experts and novices should not have differed in playing the new game. If doing was dominant, the experts should always have done best when performing with the Coleco controller, regardless of which game was being played. Finally, if the link between the knowing and the doing was vital, the performance of the experts should have been best with the Lady Bug game played with the Coleco controller.

Baba had each of her subjects play Lady Bug and Ms. Pacman for twenty minutes with each of the controllers (Coleco and Atari). The results were identical for the four dependent variables analyzed (total game score, mean game score, mean screen score, number of screens played per game). Main effects were found for skill and condition, and there was a skill-by-condition interaction. Simple effects analysis of the skill-by-condition interaction showed that the performance of expert Lady Bug players playing the Lady Bug game was significantly poorer when using the Atari controller (approximately 80 percent of Coleco-controller score), but the controller made no difference in the performance of experts in playing the Ms. Pacman game. The controller being used by novice subjects had no impact on their performance. In addition, the expert players were better at Lady Bug than the novices were, with either controller. Finally, Ms. Pacman scores showed no differences due to skill or controller.

These data show that doing did not dominate, as the type of controller used had no impact on performance in a new game. As would have been predicted for knowing's being dominant, Lady Bug experts were better at their game than novices were, when using either controller, and the performance of experts and novices did not differ in the new game. But the significant decrease in performance by experts using the Atari controller with Lady Bug seems to provide clear support for the overriding importance of the link between the knowing and the doing; the videogame player needs to know both the game and the consequences of controller actions on the game – the more automated the link, the better the play.

If automatization of the knowing–doing link is the most important aspect for performance, then the stronger the link, the greater the drop in performance that should be observed when the nature of the link is modified. In a recent investigation, Anderson, Brown, Cooke, Flegel, and Schneider (1988) practiced the Nintendo game "Super Mario" for a total of 24 hours, about 10 percent of the practice time logged by Baba's experts. After the practice trials, the subjects played for a half hour using a second controller. Super Mario is another fast-action game, but it differs from Lady Bug in that it is not a maze-clearing game. As all videogame fans will know, Super Mario is a member of the "Donkey Kong" series of games. In this particular game, Mario scrolls to the right at a speed controlled by the player, who is able to make Mario run, jump, duck, punch, swim, and throw fireballs in order to defeat all enemies (which include hostile turtles, Mario-eating plants, flying fish) and eventually (32 screens later) rescue a lost princess.

The Nintendo system was used in their study because it allowed more radical changes in the actions used to control the game than the Coleco system did. The Nintendo game uses a control pad: a small, flat device containing two round buttons used to cause jumping and running, two oblong buttons used to start and select the game, and a cross that is depressed to control the directions of Mario's movements. It is also possible to control the game by using a conventional joystick with buttons mounted on the base. The various hand movements needed to control the game are quite different: individual finger movements for the Nintendo controller as opposed to wrist (direction) and finger (action) movements for the joystick.

After 24 hours of practice with Super Mario, the scores of five subjects were blocked into the log means of five trials. Linear regression of trial blocks on log-mean scores showed excellent fit in four of five cases (R^2 values .97, .974,

.96, .93, .69). The effect of changing the controller was dramatic, reducing game scores to an average of 36 percent of the scores obtained on the preceding block of practice trials. Linear regression equations showed that subjects with the second controller were performing at a level attained halfway through the practice trials.

The Super Mario data are puzzling. It would be expected that the performance losses observed after 24 hours of practice would be less than the losses observed after 200 hours of practice, owing to decreased automaticity. In fact, Baba's subjects were able to perform at 80 percent of their normal level, whereas the subjects of Anderson and associates performed at 36 percent of the normal level. Because the two studies differed in many dimensions other than level of expertise (different games played, different scoring systems, the greater difference between controllers for Super Mario), a third controller-shift study was performed.

Anderson (1989) had six subjects practice for 1.5 hours with Super Mario, using one controller (three subjects practiced with the Nintendo controller, and three with the joystick); then the subjects switched controllers for a final half-hour session. Three additional subjects alternated controllers every half hour. Because different subjects completed different numbers of games during a given half-hour period, the practice trials were blocked into four quarters for each subject for analysis. Significant learning was seen over the 1.5-hour practice period [$F(3, 15) = 8.37$, $p = .001$] for log game scores. The effects of changing controllers were evaluated by dividing the switched trials into two blocks, corresponding to initial and final switched trials. In the first switched trials, subjects' scores were not significantly different from scores in the initial practice trials. Scores in the last half of the switched trials, however, were almost identical with those in final practice trials – 31,634 points for last practice trials, 31,997 for last switched-controller trials. Thus, with 1.5 hours of practice, switching the doing component resulted in performance equal to that in the initial learning trials, but that performance rapidly returned to the level the individual was achieving before the switch. The group alternating between controllers showed no significant learning, although all three subjects improved their performance over the first three practice sessions, only to drop for the final session. The need for the alternating group to learn two different sets of actions may have been responsible for the lack of significant learning seen in this group.

It is legitimate to compare the results of switching controllers in the two Super Mario studies. The data show that the less the practice with a particular controller (presumably a situation involving the least automaticity), the greater the drop in game score with a controller change, but the faster the recovery. Including Baba's experts in the analysis, the greater the skill level of the performers, the less the performance decrement when the doing side of performance must be modified – clearly not what would be predicted on the basis of skill's being a function of a knowing–doing link. It seems simpler to suggest that knowing and doing a skill may be two independent sources of information for a performer; when faced with a controller change, the performer must simply learn a new set of actions rather than break old links.

Knowing and doing and learning microsurgery. A second instance of the dissociation of knowing and doing was investigated by Starkes (1990). She described the case of a surgeon trained to work in a normal "macroscopic" operating environment who then had to learn microsurgery. The surgeon understood what had to be done in a procedure, how many sutures should be used and how to tie them, how to avoid thrombosis, how to test patency of a vessel, and so forth. Initially, none of that information was of use, because the motor demands and techniques of microsurgery are entirely different from those of normal surgery. Under the microscope, all gross and fine movements must be scaled down, tremor must be controlled, and unfamiliar microscopic instruments must be mastered. In addition, the surgeon must learn to control the focus and magnification of the microscope with foot pedals. Clearly, this is a situation in which the knowing, as we have characterized it in this chapter, is in place but the doing side is dramatically different for the performer.

Starkes's subject, M, was a practicing oral surgeon observed while first learning microsurgery. The basic motor skill learned by M in microsurgery training was the conventional interrupted suturing technique. It is the most frequently used technique for microscopic anastomoses, although it requires more maneuvers and takes longer than other suturing techniques. Speed is never a factor in the practice of this task; atraumatic handling of the blood vessel and accuracy of needle and suture placement are vital. Whereas the surgeon moves as slowly as is necessary to perform the task, it is obvious that one measure of skill and movement efficiency is the time required per suture.

Figure 5.5 shows M's learning curve over a 5-day course in microsurgery. In addition, recall data are shown for Day 10. Data were collected by monitoring performance through a second eyepiece on the microscope. To pass the course, a surgeon must accomplish an end-to-end anastomosis of a femoral artery and vein in a rat. This means that the blood vessel must be clamped in two locations, a small piece of the vessel must be removed from between the clamps, and the two open ends of the vessel must be sutured back together. Afterward, the vessel must withstand patency tests, and normal blood flow must be restored. For the purposes of this study, the dependent measures assessed were the number of sutures actually accomplished in comparison with the number required, the time to insert the needle in both sides of the blood vessel and finish tying the suture, and, finally, whether the completed anastomosis passed a functional patency test. While the measure remained the same, the nature of the course dictated that task difficulty would change across days. On Day 1, the subject learned to suture surgical-glove material. The period from Day 2 to noon on Day 5 was spent learning to perform end-to-end anastomoses of femoral arteries in sedated rats. The last half of Day 5 and all of Day 10 were spent perfecting the technique on the femoral vein.

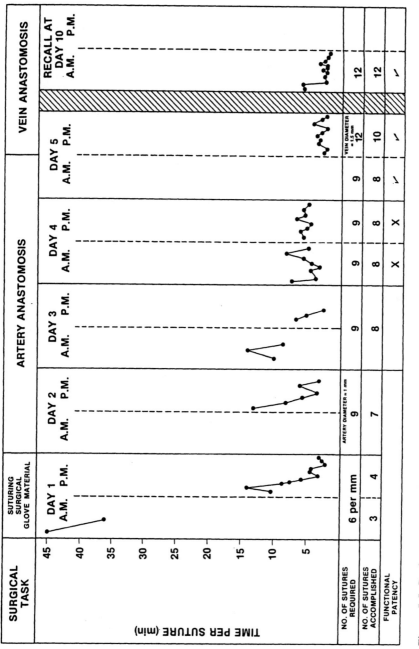

Figure 5.5. Performance learning curve for a novice microsurgeon (M) over 5 days and again at Day 10 recall. Reproduced from J. L. Starkes, Eye-hand coordination in experts: From athletes to microsurgeons, in C. Bard, M. Fleury and L. Hay (eds.), *Development of eye-hand coordination across the life span*, 1990, with the permission of University of South Carolina

Each transition involved increasing task difficulty; the vein was more difficult to handle than the artery and required that 12 sutures be placed around a 1.5 millimeter–diameter vessel. In using the microscope, M had to learn to inhibit movements in his forearms, hands, and fingers, to work foot pedals simultaneously to control focus and magnification levels, and to adjust working technique within a range of 9× to 40×. What may be an acceptable amount of movement at 9×, where the depth of field is 2 centimeters, often looks like an earthquake at 40×, where the depth of field is only 2 millimeters.

As the learning curve demonstrates, Day 1 can be particularly difficult for macrosurgeons. They are forced to abandon heretofore successful movement techniques. Microsurgical instruments are supported with different parts of the fingers than are regular instruments, and all wrist movement must be inhibited. From Day 2 to Day 4, M's suturing became more accurate, less variable, and less traumatic to the vessel. Functional patency was finally achieved on Day 5. Even though patency had been achieved, M was not able to perform the required number of sutures until Day 10. By the end of Day 10, he was performing quite well, although his average time per suture was 209 ± 87 seconds.

At that point, Starkes attempted to determine just how skilled M's performance was, relative to those of an intermediate-level microsurgeon (IP) with 3 years of surgical experience and a world-renowned microsurgeon (A) with many years of experience. For a series of 12 sutures, M required 209 ± 87 seconds per suture, IP required 72 ± 24 seconds, and A required only 38 ± 12 seconds. Whereas the skills for doing microsurgery can be acquired in a few days, they become refined only after years of practice.

One surprising aspect of microsurgery is that movements can be learned that could never be perceived by the naked eye. Current theoretical ideas regarding direct perception would argue for a link between the acuities of the perceptual system and the controlled system. In microsurgery, visual capability is magnified fortyfold, and the motor system can learn to work within this environment. Thus, the motor system clearly is capable of using sensory information that falls outside the range of normal self-produced movement, speaking against any innate sensorimotor integration and for the power of strategy in motor-skill learning.

Starkes's observations on M's education in microsurgery are consistent with the findings in the videogame studies reported earlier: Learning occurs for both knowing and doing. If M had had to learn to break old condition–action links learned as a macrosurgeon, he might still be enrolled in the microsurgery course. His old "automatisms" gave him trouble only during the initial day of practice.

Splitting knowing and doing by augmenting knowing

Our second approach to splitting knowing and doing was to provide the knowing side with augmented information on the task to be performed and then to determine whether such information could aid performance. The task investigated was hitting a baseball. The subjects were experienced hitters playing in one of the best leagues in southern Ontario. Ranton (1989) had eight batters attempt to hit 10 balls under each of three conditions. A control condition consisted of 10 pitches in the strike zone, with the pitches being a mixture of dropping and rising balls. For the pitch condition, the batter was informed before each pitch whether the ball would drop or rise. For the location condition, the batter was informed before each pitch whether the ball would be a high strike or a low strike. For all three conditions, the pitchers varied the pitch speed as they saw fit, and were in fact trying to strike out the batters. The same pitcher was used for all three conditions for a single batter, and the conditions were presented in a counterbalanced order.

Consider how prior information about the pitch or its location might affect the hitter. Because he has no information about the speed of the pitch, he is unable to make any sort of preparatory adjustment to his swing on the basis of what he has been told. He may be able to pick up information on the trajectory of the ball sooner. We would argue that the doing part of hitting is the same for all conditions, in that the hitter must execute a smooth, well-timed swing. Obviously, the knowledge provided to the batter has been augmented, but what about the knowing–doing link? An "automatic" notion of the nature of the link between knowing and doing would suggest that the appearance of the ball in a particular place at a particular time (the condition) would call forth particular swing parameters (the action), with the most experienced hitters having the strongest and most automatic links. In fact, anecdotal baseball lore would favor such a relationship. The most difficult pitches to hit are the pitches that all start out looking alike (e.g., fastballs, change-ups, split-finger fastballs), exactly what would be predicted if there were an automatic link between seeing and swinging. Thus, a "skill in the link" idea would seem to predict little performance change with prior information about pitch or location.

In fact, Ranton found that advance information did aid hitting. Defining a "hit" as a ball falling into the playing area (no fielders were present, and obviously not all of these batted balls would be hits in a real game), he found an average of 4.25 contacts for control trials, 6.125 contacts when the pitch (drop or rise) was known, and 5.5 contacts when the location (high or low) was known. The difference between control and pitch conditions was significant [$F(2, 14) = 4.49, p = .03$], whereas the control–location difference was marginal ($p = .09$). In fastball, pitches that drop or rise are the most difficult to hit, because the up or down movement of the ball occurs at about the time the ball reaches the plate, with little warning from trajectory cues as to what the pitch will actually do. Providing advance information about the type of pitch to experienced hitters will allow them to adjust their swings, to modify the link between what is seen and what is done.

The construction of a skill

The picture of the relationship between knowing and doing that is emerging is one of independent data bases for knowing and doing, with skilled individuals having the ability to forge new links between knowing and doing as required by the situation. If that is the case, it should be possible to construct skilled performance from currently existing elements, even when the elements have never been practiced together. To investigate that possibility, we returned to the domain of microsurgery. We recruited our intermediate-level surgeon, IP, for the cause and asked her to perform a task well known to her in real space – handwriting – under various levels of magnification. Knowledge of how to write the words we asked IP to write, her name and several low-frequency words ("gentry," "dactyl," "ingot," "ironic"), clearly was in her repertoire. But IP had never attempted to write under a microscope. In fact, she had to adapt tools for the task, "writing" with microsurgical forceps on carbon paper. The microwriting was attempted at magnifications of 16×, 25×, and 40×, and then the words were photographed and compared with her normal handwriting.

Figure 5.6 illustrates IP's normal writing and her writing at the various levels of magnification. It seems evident that even at 40× magnification, the movements were distinctively those of IP. At 40× magnification, technical problems arose: IP had to adjust her pressure on the carbon paper so as not to get entangled with the individual paper fibers. Thus, any difficulties seen at high magnification seem to be attributable to problems with writing materials, not to IP's ability to perform the task. It should be noted that whereas IP had never before written microscopically, she had no doubt that she could do so. This shows how a new skill, microwriting, can be constructed from existing elements of knowing and doing.

COGNITIVE SKILL AND MOTOR SKILL

We have been attempting to show that skill in knowing and skill in doing are essential components of human motor skill. We do not see knowing and doing as being linked by the likes of condition → action relationships; rather, we argue that knowing and doing can develop and be influenced independently. For the expert, the knowing and doing elements that already exist can be combined as required.

This position leads to the view that motor skills and cognitive skills are quite different aspects of human performance. For many fundamental mental operations, such as recognizing letters or words, performing mathematical calculations, or understanding speech, a person needs to deal with the environment consistently by performing a specific set of mental operations. For many cognitive skills, the "action" side of the production frequently is another cognitive operation, such as creating a mnemonic code for a series of digits or dinner orders, or calculating subproducts in mental arithmetic. The cognitive operation performed is highly effective for the particular task, but typically does not generalize to other situations; mnemonic codes that work for digit span are not effective for letter recall. For cognitive skill, then, many different instances of the same type of material are dealt with by being fed through the

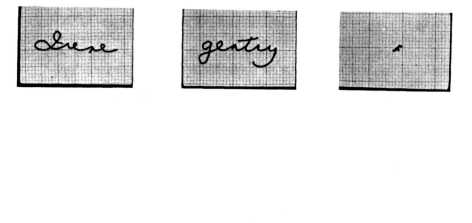

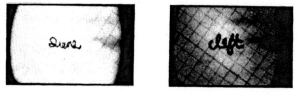

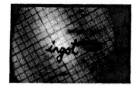

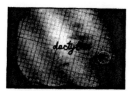

Figure 5.6. Microwriting of high- and low-frequency words by an intermediate microsurgeon (IP) at magnifications of 16×, 25×, and 40×. Top three are actual size (two normal followed by one at 40×). Magnification of top pair below them is 40×; that of next lower pair is 25×; that of bottom pair is 16×. The illustration itself has been reduced to 89 percent of its original size for this book.

same set of cognitive operations. It is not reasonable that the motor system would become tied to conditions as does the cognitive system. The motor system must remain a "general-purpose" system, capable of generating the variety of actions that get us through daily life; the motor system must be generative enough to allow us to hold objects with our fingers, hands, or teeth, or under our chin, depending on the circumstances. The more ways in which basketball players can score, the better players they are. In fact, it seems to be difficult for the motor system to perform actions consistently; many of the closed motor skills described earlier in this chapter are difficult simply because they require invariant performance. It seems to be easier for the motor system to produce a consistent environmental outcome, such as holding an object, than to reproduce or even repeat actions consistently, such as duplicating one's drive off the preceding tee.

The clear implication of the independence between knowing and doing is that the appropriate linking of doing to the current state of knowing is critical for motor skill. It is flexibility in linking, rather than the establishment of stable links, that is vital for successful motor performance.

Others have made similar proposals concerning the independence of verbal and action systems. In particular, Annett (1981, 1985, 1986) has shown how skill in a motor task, such as doing the breast stroke or tying shoes, has no relation to the ability of the individual to describe what he or she is doing. The neuropsychological evidence for independent procedural and declarative memories (e.g., Squire & Zola-Morgan, 1988) seems similar to what we are suggesting here. In the first half of this chapter we described the knowing part of sport skill, a skill component that is similar to the semantic-memory component described for many other skills. The doing part of sport skill has also been under investigation for years by motor-skill experimenters (e.g., Schmidt, 1988). These experimenters have asked questions about the units of doing and have considered such contenders as motor programs (precompiled sets of motor commands thought to be capable of running performance without feedback) and motor schemata (more flexible general routines, requiring operator input to run). Many of the general questions posed by these investigators have led to unsatisfactory conclusions or no conclusions, with the result that many experimenters have turned to the study of how the motor system controls the most fundamental movements. It might be that the doing system must be investigated along with an operating knowing system to be truly understood.

REFERENCES

Allard, F., & Burnett, N. (1985). Skill in sport. *Canadian Journal of Psychology, 39,* 294–312.
Allard, F., Graham, S., & Paarsalu, M. E. (1980). Perception in sport: Basketball. *Journal of Sport Psychology, 2,* 14–21.

Allard, F., & Starkes, J. L. (1980). Perception in sport: Volleyball. *Journal of Sport Psychology, 2,* 22–33.

Anderson, D. (1989). *The effects of transferring from one controller to another when playing a computer videogame.* Unpublished honors thesis, Department of Kinesiology, University of Waterloo.

Anderson, D., Brown, S., Cooke, L., Flegel, J., & Schneider, T. (1988). *Acquisition of videogame skill.* Unpublished manuscript, University of Waterloo.

Anderson, J. R. (1982). Acquisition of cognitive skill. *Psychological Review, 89,* 369–406.

Annett, J. (1981, September). *Action, language and imagination.* Paper presented to the Cognitive Section of the British Psychological Society.

Annett, J. (1985). Motor learning: A review. In H. Heuer, V. Kleinbeck, & K.-H. Schmidt (Eds.), *Motor behavior: Programming, control and acquisition* (pp. 189–212). Berlin: Springer-Verlag.

Annett, J. (1986). On knowing how to do things. In H. Heuer & C. Fromm (Eds.), *Generation and modulation of action patterns* (pp. 187–200). Berlin: Springer-Verlag.

Baba, D. M. (1986). *Determinants of videogame performance.* Unpublished Ph.D. thesis, University of Waterloo.

Bourgeaud, P., & Abernethy, B. (1987). Skilled perception in volleyball defense. *Journal of Sport Psychology, 9,* 400–406.

Chase, W. G., & Ericsson, K. A. (1981). Skilled memory. In J. R. Anderson (Ed.), *Cognitive skills and their acquisition.* Hillsdale, NJ: Erlbaum.

Chi, M. T. H., Feltovich, P. J., & Glaser R. (1981). Categorization and representation of physics problems by experts and novices. *Cognitive Science, 5,* 121–152.

Deakin, J. M. (1987). *Cognitive components of skill in figure skating.* Unpublished Ph.D. thesis, University of Waterloo.

Ericsson, K. A., & Polson, D. G. (1988). A cognitive analysis of exceptional memory for restaurant orders. In M. T. H. Chi, R. Glaser, & M. J. Farr (Eds.), *The nature of expertise* (pp. 23–70). Hillsdale, NJ: Erlbaum.

Gentile, A. M. (1972). A working model of skill acquisition with application of teaching. *Quest, 17,* 3–23.

Knapp, B. (1963). *Skill in sport.* London: Routledge & Kegan Paul.

Laban, R. (1956). *Principles of dance and movement notation.* London: Macdonald E. Evans.

Parker, S. G. (1989). *Organization of knowledge in ice hockey experts.* Unpublished master's thesis, University of New Brunswick.

Poulton, E. C. (1957). On prediction in skilled movements. *Psychological Bulletin, 54,* 467–478.

Ranton, D. (1989). *Information used by skilled fastball players when batting.* Unpublished honors thesis, Department of Kinesiology, University of Waterloo.

Schmidt R. A. (1988). *Motor control and learning: A behavioral emphasis* (2nd ed.). Champaign, IL: Human Kinetics.

Squire, L. R., & Zola-Morgan, S. (1988). Memory: Brain systems and behavior. *Trends in Neurosciences, 11,* 170–175.

Starkes, J. L. (1990). Eye–hand coordination in experts: From athletes to microsurgeons. In C. Bard, M. Fleury, & L. Hay (Eds.), *Development of eye–hand coordination across the lifespan* (pp. 309–326). Columbia: University of South Carolina Press.

Starkes, J. L., & Deakin, J. M. (1985). Perception in sport: A cognitive approach to skilled performance. In W. F. Straub & J. M. Williams (Eds.), *Cognitive sport psychology*. Lansing, NY: Sport Science Associates.

Starkes, J. L., Deakin, J. M., Lindley, S., & Crisp, F. (1987). Motor versus verbal recall of ballet sequences by young expert dancers. *Journal of Sport Psychology, 9,* 222–230.

Staszewski, J. J. (1988). Skilled memory and expert mental calculation. In M. T. H. Chi, R. Glaser, & M. J. Farr (Eds.), *The nature of expertise* (pp. 71–128). Hillsdale, NJ: Erlbaum.

6   *Musical expertise*

JOHN SLOBODA

This chapter treats six connected issues having to do with musical expertise. Section 1 examines the difficulties associated with characterizing expertise in a way that offers a genuine foothold for cognitive psychology, and I suggest that expertise may not, in fact, be "special" in any cognitively interesting sense. Section 2 goes on to review some experimental studies of music, which suggest that most members of a culture possess tacit musical expertise, expressed in their ability to use high-level structural information in carrying out a variety of perceptual tasks. This expertise seems to be acquired through casual exposure to the musical forms and activities of the culture. Section 3 provides two detailed examples of exceptional musical expertise (a musical savant and a jazz musician) that apparently developed in the absence of formal instruction, suggesting that normal and "exceptional" expertise may be parts of a single continuum. The evidence presented in section 4 suggests that a major difference between musical expertise and many other forms of expertise is that musical expertise requires an apprehension of a structure–emotion mapping. Without this, the ability to perform with "expression" cannot be acquired. Section 5 outlines some evidence to suggest that these structure–emotion links become firmly established during middle childhood, under certain conditions, and that these conditions are predictive of future development of musical expertise. Finally, section 6 reviews some research efforts that are attempts to clarify the precise nature of the structure–emotion link and are showing that definite types of structures seem to mediate distinct emotions.

1. WHAT IS EXPERTISE?

In beginning to think about how a psychologist who deals with music could contribute in a specific way to a volume on expertise, it became clear to me that most of the recently published work on musical competence has made little attempt to define or characterize musical expertise. What we have, instead, is a varied collection of empirical studies on single aspects of what some musicians do. The topics of such studies range from pitch memory (Ward & Burns, 1982), through synchronization in performance (Rasch, 1988), to planning a composition (Davidson & Welsh, 1988), and it is not

153

immediately clear that such accomplishments have anything in common other than the fact that they are different aspects of handling the organized sounds our various societies label as music.

That observation led back to a logically prior question: Is there anything that all examples of expertise *in general* should or might have in common? More precisely, is there anything about the *internal* psychological structures of certain accomplishments that marks them out as examples of expertise? It is important to remember that when someone is declared an expert, that is a social act that may or may not correspond to an intrinsic characteristic of the person so designated.

One possible definition of an expert is "someone who performs a task significantly better (by some specified criterion) than the majority of people." According to this definition, Chase and Ericsson's (1981) digit memorizer SF is an expert. If, however, digit-span recall became a popular hobby, then he might well be overtaken by sufficient numbers of people so that he would cease to be considered an expert. Such a relativistic attribution of expertise clearly would preclude the possibility of any *cognitive* account of expertise, because the cognitive apparatus that earned SF expert status would remain precisely the same after SF was no longer labeled an expert. It does, however, seem to me that exactly such a relativistic conception underlies much common talk of expertise, and to a certain extent determines the agendas of "expertise" research.

For cognitive psychology to have an authentic foothold, we have to find a characterization of expertise that will allow any number of people (up to and including all) to be expert in a particular area. For instance, many would, I think, agree that the vast majority of people are expert speakers of their native languages. I shall later suggest that the majority of our population possess particular types of musical expertise. A possible definition with this outcome might relate to the reliable attainment of specific goals within a specific domain. So, for instance, one is an expert diner if one can get a wide variety of foodstuffs from plate to mouth without spilling anything.

An apparent problem with this definition, however, is that there is no lower limit to the simplicity or specificity of the task to which one can appply it. For instance, this definition would allow each of us to be expert at pronouncing his or her own name or at folding his or her arms. It may seem that we need more than goal attainment to attribute expertise. For instance, one may want to say that an expert is someone who can make an appropriate response to a situation that contains a degree of unpredictability. So the expert bridge player is one who can work out the play most likely to win with a hand that the player has never seen before; the expert doctor is one who can provide an appropriate diagnosis when faced with a configuration of symptoms never before encountered. In this way we might be able to carve out precisely the set of activities in which the contributors to this book have been interested.

On further examination, however, it is not as easy to apply this distinction as it might first appear. Pronouncing one's own name can also be seen as an act requiring the handling of unpredictability. It is an act that is occasioned by cues (external or internal) that can vary. One must be able to retrieve and execute the required motor program regardless of the immediate mental context. The complexity of these apparently simple acts is soon revealed when one attempts to construct machines that can do the same tasks, as the discipline of artificial intelligence has amply documented (e.g., visual recognition [Marr, 1982]).

It is difficult for me to escape the conclusion that we should abandon the idea that expertise is something special and rare (from a cognitive or biological point of view) and move toward the view that the human organism is in its essence expert. The neonatal brain is already an expert system. "Becoming expert" in socially defined ways is the process of connecting "intrinsic" expertise to the outside world so that it becomes manifest in particular types of behaviors in particular types of situations. I believe that Fodor (1975), from another point of view, was articulating a similar proposal: To broadly paraphrase Fodor, "You can't learn anything you don't already know."

To look at expertise in this way may require reversal of some of our perspectives on familiar situations. For instance, when considering Chase and Ericsson's (1981) study of SF, it is easy to allow one's focus of attention to fall on the two hundred hours of practice that moved him from average to the world's best, implicitly equating the acquisition of the expertise with the work that went on in the practice period under observation. The perspective to which I am increasingly drawn suggests that we focus our attention instead on what SF brought to the experimental situation. SF's intimate knowledge of running times was, from this perspective, the principal manifestation of expertise that "bootstrapped" the digit-span task, and it seems to me that the most interesting psychological considerations are how and why that knowledge came to be applied to the task in hand when it did. What determined that it would be applied after about fifteen hours of practice rather than instantaneously or not at all? A plausible answer to that question may well be "chance" (e.g., a particular sequence of numbers that strongly reminded SF of a well-known running time).

In other words, the broad answer to the question of how SF became expert at the digit-span task is that he was able to increment his expertise by approximately 0.01 percent in a situation in which he was already expert at a number of things, including running times, that supplied the other 99.99 percent of what was needed. And each of those preceding areas of expertise was likewise resting on other forms of expertise in the same relationship in a constant, unbroken sequence back to birth and beyond. What made SF "exceptional" in conventional terms was no more than a unique set of life experiences. In the sections that follow, I pursue some implications of this way of looking at expertise as applied to music.

2. ACQUIRING MUSICAL SKILL

One of the principal reasons for studying expertise is practical. Given that it would be socially desirable for certain manifestations of expertise to be more widespread than they are, we want to know what we can do to assist people to acquire them. The issue becomes acute in relation to formal education, where the general perception is that we set up environments that are supposed to encourage expertise, but that many individuals still do not achieve levels that we know to be possible (whether it be learning a foreign language, a musical instrument, or physics skill). We want to be able to tell teachers that there are principled things that they can do to increase the frequency of those 0.01 percent increments in learning.

Music is no exception to this, and music teachers are continually inquiring of psychologists how psychological insights can inform their work. It is their perception that musical expertise is taught and acquired with great difficulty. They speak of "tone-deaf" children (usually children unable to sing in tune); they speak of the difficulty of teaching sight reading, of teaching rhythm, of teaching good intonation on a string instrument, and so on.

My early research on the skill of sight reading has been summarized elsewhere (Sloboda, 1984). That research was carried out under the influence of the previously published work of Chase and Simon (1973) on chess perception. Their research showed that, like playing chess, reading of music depended on an ability to pick up various sorts of patterns in the stimulus. For instance, good sight readers were found to be much more prone than poor sight readers to a sort of "proofreader's error" (Sloboda, 1976a) whereby notational mistakes out of character with the genre were automatically corrected back to what the genre would have predicted. Their ability to use music structure to "chunk" notes could account for their superior short-term memory for notation (Halpern & Bower, 1982; Sloboda, 1976b).

Encouraging as it was to find results for music that so clearly paralleled Chase's findings, I became progressively more disheartened as I talked about those results to groups of teachers. The question they all asked was of what prescriptions I would draw from my results for the teaching of sight reading, and after some hand waving I really had to admit that there were no prescriptions that I could draw at that time. I did not know how one could teach children to "see" structures.

Since then I have come to realize that in order to "see" musically significant structures, one first must be able to "hear" those structures, and I have learned from reading some excellent recent research that the process of coming to "hear" musical structure is a process that occurs quite naturally for the majority of children as a function of normal enculturation. For instance, Zenatti (1969) showed that children at age 7 show a distinct memory advantage for sequences conforming to rules of normal tonal progression, as compared with atonal sequences. This advantage is not shared by children of age 5. Similar results were obtained from studying children's songs (Dowling,

1982, 1988; Gardner, Davidson, & McKernon, 1981). There is a definite age progression from tonal inconsistency and instability toward conformity to the norms of the tonal culture.

An experiment I conducted earlier (Sloboda, 1985a) showed that the progressing of the ability to discriminate between "legal" and "illegal" sequences did not seem to depend on children's receiving any sort of formal music instruction. Almost no children at age 5 made meaningful discriminations, whereas almost all 11-year-olds made discriminations in accordance with those of adults (and music harmony textbooks). The children who were receiving formal music lessons did not fare better than other children.

Although many experiments with adults have shown cognitive differences between musicians and nonmusicians, some studies have shown little difference. For instance, Deliege and El Ahmahdi (1990) showed that musicians and nonmusicians were remarkably similar in the segmentations they suggested for an atonal piece. That may have been partly attributable to the relative unfamiliarity of the genre to both groups. More strikingly, Bigand (1990) showed that nonmusicians had an ability similar to that of musicians to classify superficially different conventional tonal melodies into groups containing underlying structural similarities. Studies of memory recall for melodies (Sloboda & Parker, 1985) have shown that musicians and nonmusicians have similar abilities to preserve higher-order structure at the expense of note-to-note detail.

The research literature, therefore, leads to the conclusion that human beings pick up quite high-level implicit (or tacit) knowledge about some major structural features of the music of their culture. They gradually improve their ability to do this over the first ten or more years of life and preserve this ability into adulthood. We may presume that this is achieved through informal engagement in the everyday musical activities that abound in almost all human cultures (e.g., nursery rhymes, hymns, dances, popular songs, playground games). In our own culture these forms are, of course, massively reinforced through the broadcast media.

In this way, almost every member of a culture is a musical expert, but the expertise is usually hidden and tacit. It may not exhibit itself in abilities to sing or play. It is, however, manifested in a variety of perceptual and memory tasks. Nearly all of us can identify some kinds of "wrong notes" when we hear them, even though we cannot always say why the notes are "wrong."

Tacit expertise depends, in part, on being in a culture in which one is exposed to products in the specified domain without the necessity for active engagement. This allows the dissociation between receptive expertise and productive expertise. Such a dissociation would not normally occur in chess, or bridge, or physics, because the only way one normally gets exposure to the relevant structures is by *doing* the activity.

It is not the purpose of this essay to give an account of the various developments in understanding what it is that people know when they know about music structure. Suffice it to say that it seems necessary to postulate mechanisms for representing music that are multidimensional and hierarchical. This means that music can be characterized by points of greater or lesser prominence or distance from one another and that various dimensions may be in synchrony or in opposition. This gives rise to complex patterns of tension and resolution at different hierarchical levels. Some of the most influential characterizations of musical representation have been offered by Lerdahl and Jackendoff (1983), Krumhansl (1990), and Meyer (1973).

More pertinent for our current purposes is the observation that at least some of these structures seem capable of being represented in a connectionist network (Bharucha, 1987). A connectionist model of the brain shows one way in which it might be possible for knowledge of complex structures to be built up simply as a result of frequent exposure to relevant examples. Such an activity seems to be an essential requirement of any mechanism that acquires expertise from environments that are not engineered to be instructional (i.e., most environments).

3.   ACQUISITION OF MUSICAL EXPERTISE IN NONINSTRUCTIONAL SETTINGS

Musical expertise, in the foregoing sense, is possessed by the majority of untutored members of any culture. This is not, however, what most people mean when they refer to musical expertise; they mean overt skills of performance or composition. Surely these cannot be acquired other than through formal instruction. It is certain that such skills are acquired mainly through instruction, at least in our culture, but there is some evidence that such instruction is not necessary. Several cases of overt expertise have apparently arisen without any formal tuition or intervention by other experts. An examination of these cases is particularly important if we are to isolate the general conditions for the acquisition of expertise.

3.1. Musical prodigies and savants

There have been several documented cases of children who showed exceptional precocity at various musical skills. Some of them, such as Mozart, went on to become exceptional adults. Others did not sustain their exceptionality into adult life (see Bamberger, 1986, for a cognitive account of adolescent "burnout" among musical prodigies). One of the fullest accounts of a child musical prodigy was given by Revesz (1925), who made an intensive study of the young Hungarian prodigy Erwin Nyherigazy (EN). Although EN had a great deal of formal tuition and support from professional musicians from an early age, he soon surpassed his teachers in his ability to commit tonal piano music to memory on one or two exposures.

There is another group of prodigies who, by and large, do not receive formal instruction: the so-called idiots savants (see Treffert, 1988, for a recent review). The savant is a person of generally low IQ, usually male, and often autistic, who has developed a skill in one defined area to a level quite exceptional compared with the general population. Although such cases have been reported in the literature for many years, the reports have mostly been only anecdotal and impressionistic contributions to the psychiatric literature. Only in the past decade have systematic investigations of musical savants been reported in the cognitive literature (e.g., Miller, 1987).

One of these studies concerned the autistic savant NP (Sloboda, Hermelin, & O'Connor, 1985). At the time of detailed study, NP was in his early twenties, and we were able to document his ability to recall a tonal piano movement almost perfectly twelve minutes after first hearing it. Two features of the study were particularly noteworthy: (1) His ability did not extend to a simple atonal piece, and (2) the few errors in his recall of the tonal piece were largely in conformity with the rules of the genre. We concluded that NP's recall ability was predicated on his ability to code and store tonal music in terms of its structural features. In that respect, NP's ability was every bit as "intelligent" as the memory performance of chess masters. Other studies of musical savants (Hermelin, O'Connor, & Lee, 1987; Miller, 1987; Treffert, 1988) have confirmed the importance of structural knowledge in supporting their skills.

Because NP was still relatively young when studied, it was possible to talk to people who knew him at different points in his life and observed his ability develop. It seems that NP's early life was one of considerable cultural deprivation. As far as we know, he had few, if any, opportunities to interact with musical instruments and was not encouraged to sing or to engage with music. His precocity was first noticed at about the age of 6 years, when he spontaneously reproduced at the piano a song that a staff member at his day-care center had just played. From the point on, he was given many opportunities and encouragements to interact with music and musical instruments, although nothing approaching "instruction" was ever possible with this profoundly nonverbal individual. Even now his "lessons" consist of a pianist playing pieces that NP then reproduces. A tape recording of his accomplishments at the age of 8 years shows memory and performance skills that were impressive for an autistic child, though by no means as polished and outstanding as his current performances.

How did NP's skill compare with "normal" skill at the various stages of his life? At age 6 or 7, it was not clear that his memorization abilities were abnormally good. Most untutored children of that age are capable of memorizing short songs, and many can succeed in picking them out on a piano by a process of trial and error. What distinguished NP at that age was his ability to map his internal knowledge of songs directly and without error onto the piano keyboard and to choose appropriate fingering patterns. His performances of tonal music have always been characterized by an absence of hesitation or experimentation, no doubt assisted by his possession of absolute pitch. We have no information that would help us to explain how NP acquired his knowledge without having had any known opportunity to practice before the age of 6.

For the period of his early twenties, the comparison with normals showed a somewhat different pattern. His technical accomplishments were then not unusual. Many reasonably proficient pianists can choose appropriate fingerings for musical passages immediately and automatically. What made NP quite unusual was the *length* of the musical material he could commit to accurate memory after a single hearing. This is a skill shared by few adults at any level of musical expertise, although there are adult musicians of my acquaintance who claim that they could do what NP does when they were age 12 or 13. They no longer can do it, because it has not seemed interesting or worthwhile for them to practice and maintain that particular skill.

We may ask what conditions seem to be associated with the acquisition of the expertise of NP and other savants. The first common factor seems to be a high degree of intrinsic motivation for engagement with a single activity sustained over many years. Such motivation usually has a strong obsessional component, in that given freedom, the savant will spend all available time on the activity, without ever tiring of it.

The second factor is an environment that provides frequent opportunities for the practice of the skill in question. In the case of a musical savant, this may include the provision of regular access to instruments, broadcast media, and musical events. It is possible to suppose that whatever level of cultural deprivation NP suffered during his earliest years, he at least would have been exposed to music through the broadcast media.

The third factor is, of course, the exceptional amount of time spent in cognitive engagement with the materials and activities relevant to the skill in question (practice). It is difficult to estimate the amount of time NP spent thinking about music when not playing or listening to it, but obvious external involvement probably amounted to four to five hours per day.

The fourth factor, therefore, is the availability of the time and opportunity to "indulge" the obsession. It may be because fewer societal demands are made on people with low IQs that they are "allowed," even encouraged, to devote their attentions in this way.

The fifth factor is the complete absence of negative external reinforcement related to attainment or lack of it. There is, therefore, little possibility of a savant's developing self-doubt, fear of failure, or any of the other blocks that inhibit and sometimes prevent normal or exceptional accomplishment.

3.2. Jazz musicians

It is probable that many of the world's musical cultures, particularly the informal, nonliterate "folk" cultures, have been breeding grounds for expertise. Some anthropological work (e.g., Blacking, 1976) suggests that this is true of indigenous Third World cultures. The jazz culture of New Orleans in the early part of this century may not have been greatly different from those other cultures in many respects. Its advantage for us is that jazz rapidly spread from New Orleans to become part of mass culture and contributed an entirely new facet to the face of Western culture. Its leaders became cult heroes, and jazz itself became a subject for intensive academic scrutiny. For these reasons, we have far more detailed biographical information about jazz musicians than about the musicians from all of the world's other nonliterate cultures put together.

It appears that most of the early jazz players were self-taught. Among the self-taught players who became international names were Bix Beiderbecke, Roy Eldridge, and Louis Armstrong. Collier's (1983) study of Armstrong is particularly detailed, and it allows us to look at Armstrong's musical development in some detail as a "prototype" of untutored expertise.

Armstrong spent most of his early years in a neighborhood known as "Black Storeyville," an area designated for black prostitution. One of the features of that neighborhood was the continual live music, performed by dance bands and "tonk" bands, which often would play on the street to attract custom. Having little knowledge of the world outside, Armstrong had little more than pimps and musicians as male role models. His father had abandoned his mother before he was born. His childhood was one of extreme poverty and deprivation, and from the age of 7 years he had to work, steal, and hustle to make money for his mother and himself. At the age of 8 or 9 years he formed a vocal quartet with some other boys in order to pick up pennies on street corners. The group lasted two or three years and probably practiced and performed in public two or three times per week. That provided several hundred hours of improvised part singing, which as Collier observed, "would have constituted a substantial course in ear training – far more than most conservatory instrumentalists get today."

At the age of 13 or 14 years, Armstrong was involved in an incident with a gun and was, as a result, sent to the Colored Waif's Home (known as the Jones Home). There the boys were taught reading, writing, and arithmetic, with gardening as a sideline. The home had a band that played once a week around the city. After six months in the home, Armstrong was allowed to join the band, first playing tambourine, then drums, then alto horn. It is clear from contemporary accounts that many of the bands playing in the streets of New Orleans were fairly informal groups with an "anything goes" attitude. It was quite easy for a novice to join in the general noise, just playing the notes he knew, and his mistakes and split notes would pass without comment. Armstrong quickly learned how to get sounds out of the horn, and his vocal experience made it easy for him to work out appropriate parts to the songs the band played. His talent was noticed, and he was promoted to bugle player. He gradually improved to become the band's leader, but he left the home and the band after two years, at age 16. Nothing he experienced in the home would merit the term "formal teaching."

Armstrong found casual work driving a coal cart, which occupied his days, but during the evenings he began playing jazz in the blues bands of the tonks. He did not at that stage own a cornet, and so it was impossible for him to practice. He simply went around to the various bands asking cornetists to let him sit in for a few numbers. Blues music provided a good vehicle for gaining jazz expertise. Blues songs featured slow tempos in two or three of the easiest keys. The set melodies were of the simplest sort; in many cases there was no set melody at all, and the cornetist would string phrases together from a small repertoire of stock figures.

At age 17, Armstrong acquired his first cornet and began to practice and work regularly at one of the tonks. The work paid little, and so he kept his coal job during the day. At some point in that period Armstrong met Joe Oliver, acknowledged as the best cornetist in New Orleans. Armstrong began hanging around the places where Oliver played, running errands, carrying his case, and eventually sitting in for him. Oliver became Armstrong's sponsor and to some extent his teacher. According to Collier, however, Oliver did not influence Armstrong's style and probably did little more than show Armstrong some new tunes and possibly a few alternative fingerings.

By age 19, Armstrong was finding employment on local riverboat excursions. Then, for three summers running, he made long trips, playing every day. For the first time in his life music had become his predominant activity. The band played seven nights per week, doing fourteen numbers and encores each night. They rehearsed two afternoons per week, and the repertoire changed every two weeks. It was only after joining the riverboats that Armstrong learned how to read music and had to acquire the discipline of playing what was written rather than what he felt like playing. When he left the riverboats at age 23, he was an established professional musician.

If Armstrong's early life was a prototype for untutored acquisition of expertise, which of its features might we highlight for future corroboration? One obvious feature was the casual immersion in a rich musical environment with many opportunities to listen and observe. A second feature was the early systematic exploration of a performance medium (in his case, voice). Third, as far as we can judge, his early experiences allowed a great deal of freedom to explore and experiment without negative consequences. A fourth feature was a lack of distinction between "practice" and "performance." The learning took place on the job. A fifth feature was an enduring motivation to engage in music – in Armstrong's case, a complex mix of internal and external motivations, but arguably with internal motivations dominating. A sixth feature was a graded series of opportunities and challenges available or sought out as the expertise developed.

In many ways, this list of features fits the case of a savant such as NP. The principal differences in the two examples cited here relate to motivation and challenge. NP's motivation did not have a significant external component, and partly for that reason it is not clear that his challenges either arose or were grasped with the same frequency as those of Armstrong. It is easy to imagine NP remaining on a performance plateau. Armstrong went on growing and changing throughout his life.

What these case studies show is that high levels of expertise are achievable without instruction. This does not, of course, mean that instruction is useless. By providing a structured progression of information and challenges for a learner, geared precisely to the learner's capacities at a given time, a teacher may be able to accelerate a learner's progress. Not every person has the opportunity to extract the relevant experiences from the "natural" environment that Armstrong had. A formal instructional environment can engineer the conditions for such extraction. The danger of all such environments is that goals and standards are imposed on the learner, rather than being chosen. The consequence can be to inhibit intrinsic motivation and originality (Amabile, 1983). If external constraints are extreme, it may even be that the ability to enjoy music will be destroyed.

In this connection, one other difference between NP and Armstrong has not been brought out thus far. One of the most striking aspects of NP's musical life was its lack of affect. All pieces in his repertoire were played in a "wooden," unexpressive manner. Although his immediate reproduction showed some of the expressive features of the model, within twenty-four hours all expressive variation was "washed out," leaving a rigid metronomical husk. It was as if NP had no means of understanding (and thus relating to the structure of) the small variations in timing, loudness, and timbre that are the lifeblood of musical performances. From the earliest recording we have of Armstrong's music, in contrast, we find a richly expressive, flexible performance that bends tone and time in ways that have strong impact on many listeners. Armstrong is not hailed as the king of jazz for his technique, impressive as it was. There are others who match or surpass him in technique. He is revered for the life he could breathe into the simplest material.

NP was one of a rather small number of people who appear to gain complete satisfaction from relating to music as pure structure or syntax. What brings the vast majority of us to music, and keeps us with it, is something additional: its power to mediate a vast range of emotionally toned states, ranging from the subtle to the overwhelming. Because modern systematic studies of music have approached it with the tools of cognitive science and linguistics, the emotional aspect of music has been virtually overlooked, and naive readers of modern research studies might be forgiven for thinking that music is simply another kind of complex structure to be apprehended, like chess or physics.

I know that those who are expert in chess or physics say that there is beauty and emotion in those activities too, but there is a sense in which such things are not central to the skill. One can write a perfectly effective computer program for chess that will not need any information about how particular chess positions or games will affect the emotions of certain human players. I think there is a strong case for saying that a computer could never adequately simulate Louis Armstrong without some implementation of a theory of the emotions.

4. EXPRESSION AND EMOTION AS FOUNDATIONAL ASPECTS OF MUSICAL EXPERTISE

Those approaching music with the prejudices and preoccupations of experimental psychology have been wary of examining the emotional aspect, for methodological and conceptual reasons. Rather than examine these reasons in detail, I should like to point to some recent investigations that seem to have "opened doors" into this area.

The advent of the microcomputer and microtechnology has, for the first time, made possible easy and accurate transfer of detailed performance information into computers for sophisticated analysis. The past decade has seen a number of studies (Clarke, 1985; Gabrielsson, 1983; Shaffer, 1981; Sloboda, 1983; Sundberg, 1988; Todd, 1985) that have measured minute expressive variations in performance loudness and timing. These studies have shown several things: (1) A given player can consistently repeat given variations on successive performances; (2) these perturbations are not random but, rather, are intentional, and performers can alter them to a greater or lesser extent at will; (3) many of these perturbations are rule-governed and relate to the formal structure of the music in systematic ways.

My own studies (Sloboda, 1983, 1985b), for instance, have shown that timing deformations are organized around the strong metrical beats of tonal melodies in a way that makes the metrical structure clearer for listeners than it is when such deformations are not present. Although we do not yet have the evidence, this line of research suggests that all effective expression may be systematic and rule-governed in this way, helping to highlight musical structures in a way that makes their emotion-bearing content more manifest to listeners.

The other line of contemporary thinking that converges with the experimental work on expression is the music-theory work of such writers as Leonard Meyer (Meyer, 1956, 1973) and Fred Lerdahl (1988a, 1988b; Lerdahl & Jackendoff, 1983). Meyer has convincingly argued that emotion in music arises out of the complex, often subliminal web of expectations and violations of expectations that musical structures unfold over time (Narmour, 1977). Lerdahl (1988b) takes this a step farther by suggesting that only structures that have certain formal properties (such as discreteness and hierarchical organization) can be directly detected by listeners (Balzano, 1980; Shepard, 1982). Only such structures will be effective in creating the types of tensions and resolutions that can support the emotional activities and responses peculiar to music. Lerdahl has particularly enraged certain sections of the avant-garde music community by claiming that traditional tonal music satisfies his criteria, whereas such forms as serial music do not. This could be used as an explanation of why tonality has been able to resist all attempts to oust it from center stage in music and why many avant-garde genres have but limited appeal. The general thrust of all this thinking about music gets independent support from cognitive theorists (e.g., Ortony, Clore, & Collins, 1988) who characterize the cognitive substrate of all emotion in terms of the violations of various classes of expectations.

These strands of work lead toward the following set of working hypotheses about the vast central bulk of the world's music:

1. One major function of music is to suggest or mediate a range of emotional responses.
2. Common musical structures have particular perceptible properties that support the patterns of expectation underlying such emotions.
3. Expression in musical performance has the effect of making these structural features more prominent, and thus of heightening the emotional response.

5. THE ROOTS OF MUSICAL EXPERTISE

At the beginning of this chapter, I asked whether all aspects of musical expertise have anything in common. By a rather circuitous route I now come to a proposed answer, which is that they involve apprehension and use of the structure–emotion link. At whatever level, and for whatever activity, what makes the behavior *musically,* as opposed to technically or perceptually, expert is its manifestation of this link. I take it as axiomatic that emotions do not have to be learned (although they may be refined and differentiated through experience). They are part of the "expert system" with which we are born. So what must be learned is how to apprehend those features of musical structures that can be mapped onto and therefore evoke our existing emotions.

Hevner's (1936) pioneering work showed that adult members of a culture generally agree on the emotional characterization of a passaage of music, in that they tend to select similar adjectives to describe it (e.g., majestic, gloomy, playful). Gardner (1973) has shown that this ability develops through childhood, with younger children able to use only rather crude descriptions (such as "loud" or "jumpy"). It is, of course, possible that particular kinds of music have come to acquire conventional meanings by routes that do not involve the listener's own emotions. Laboratory studies of people's abilities to *describe* music do not show how these abilities were acquired.

Direct observational studies of children's emotional responses to music have been rare. Moog's (1976) studies showed that preverbal infants could demonstrate quite strong expressions of delight or fear on hearing music. The available evidence suggests that tone quality is the aspect of music that elicits the strongest early reactions. Smooth, treble-register sounds seem to elicit the strongest reactions of attention and pleasure. Most children below the age of 5 years seem not to be particularly interested in unpitched rhythms and seem not to differentiate emotionally between music played in conventional harmony and that played dissonantly.

As children grow older, it is less easy to record emotional responses by direct observation. Socialization leads to significant suppression of direct emotional expression. An alternative approach that I have been pursuing (Sloboda, 1989) is to ask adults to recall musical experiences from the first ten years of life. The literature on autobiographical memory (Brown & Kulik, 1977; Rubin & Kozin, 1984) suggests that experiences connected with significant emotion may be particularly retrievable. The method also has the advantage of tapping musical experience in a range of naturalistic contexts, rather than in restricted experimental contexts. In addition to asking these adults for information about childhood events and their contexts, I also ask them if those experiences had any particular significance for them. Information about the involvement of music in their lives, including formal music tuition, is also collected.

The findings from these studies indicate that most subjects seem to be capable of producing at least one memory. Some people readily recalled as many as ten different events. No event was recalled from an age earlier than 3 years, but from 4 to 10 years the age spread was fairly even. Analysis of the words used by adults to describe the character of their experiences (both of the music itself and of their reaction to it) showed an interesting age progression. Memories from around age 5 tended to characterize music in rather neutral descriptive terms (e.g., "fast," "loud," "simple"), and the responses to it in terms of general positive enjoyment (e.g., "love," "like," "enjoy," "excited," "happy"). Looking back to age 8, subjects characterized music in terms of its affective or sensual characteristics (e.g., "beautiful," "liquid," "funny"), and the responses to it were recalled in terms of wonder or surprise (e.g., "enthralled," "incredulous," "astounded," "overwhelmed," "awe-struck"). Finally, harking back to around age 9, some memories contained strong feelings of sadness (e.g., "melancholy," "sad," "apprehensive").

It is of particular significance that the ability to respond to music in terms of wonder arises at about the age when children can be shown to distinguish reliably between tonal and atonal music. This strongly suggests that the particular violations of expectations that mediate some of the more "advanced" emotional responses to music require the ability to represent music in terms of the structural categories of tonal music. It is also significant that the progression of responsivity seems to owe nothing to explicit formal instruction. The majority of the experiences reported *preceded* the onset of formal musical training, and in several cases such an experience spurred the child to seek instruction. Learning the structure–emotion link seems to proceed in the absence of formal instruction.

Some of the memories reported clearly had the status of what some people call "peak experiences" – unusual and deeply rewarding experiences of a complex emotional/intellectual character. The research showed that people who have had such peak experiences were more likely than others to pursue involvement with music for the rest of their life. The experiences provided a strong source of internal motivation to engage with music in a systematic way (arguably in part to increase the likelihood of replicating the experiences). Educators wishing to raise the general level of musical skill might well be advised to consider how they can help increase the frequency of such experiences in the population, because it is clear that not every child has them.

The memory research provided some interesting clues on this latter point as well. It was discovered that almost none of those peak experiences had occurred in situations of external constraint or anxiety. The most likely environment for a peak experience was at home, on one's own or with friends and family, and while listening to music. The least promising environment was at school, with teachers, while performing. The individual stories graphically revealed the kinds of anxieties and humiliations many children were made to suffer in relation to music by insensitive adults or through insensitive educational practices. These acted as strong disincentives to further engagement with music and seemed to block the possibility of making links between emotions and the intrinsic characteristics of music.

A similar lesson emerges from a recent study of leading American concert pianists by Sosniak (1989). None of those in her sample showed exceptional promise as a child, but in every case their early lessons were associated with fun and exploration, rather than with practical achievement. It seems that, at least for the crucial early stages of musical development, there is no special strategy we should recommend to educators, other than to stop worrying about particular apparent skill deficiencies and concentrate on not getting in the way of children's enjoyment and exploration of music. In such contexts, children become natural experts who spontaneously seek what they require to bring their expertise to bear on particular practical accomplishments.

6. MUSICAL STRUCTURE AND EMOTION

The final question I wish to raise in this chapter concerns the precise nature of the structure–emotion link: What structures elicit what emotions, and why? Although musicologists have long debated this point (e.g., Cooke, 1959; Meyer, 1956), there have been remarkably few attempts to collect empirical data on it. A few physiological studies (e.g., Goldstein, 1980; Nakamura, 1984) have shown that reliable changes in such indices as heart rate and skin conductance can be shown as people listen to specific pieces of music. But such studies generally have not involved subjecting the music itself to detailed structural analysis. A particular characteristic of emotional responses to music is that they often change in nature and intensity over the duration of a piece and are linked to specific events (rather than being a general "wash" of a particular mood). In this respect, they are similar in nature to emotional responses to drama or fiction. To my knowledge, no published studies provide data on the specific points in musical compositions at which intense or peak emotional experiences take place. One problem is that it is difficult to get intersubjective agreement on how to characterize these experiences. Some of my own recent research entails an attempt to circumvent this problem by asking people to report (retrospectively, at this stage) on the locations in musical compositions at which they reliably experience direct physical manifestations of emotion (e.g., tears, shivers). A significant minority of subjects have been willing and able to do this and have provided a corpus of some 165 "moments" of reliable emotional response. Full details of this study are reported in Sloboda (1991). An analysis of the subset comprising classical instrumental excerpts has revealed three clusters of structural features associated with three different types of responses. These are summarized in Table 6.1.

Table 6.1. *Emotion and musical structure*

Emotional response	Associated structural features
Tears or lump in throat	Descending circle of 5ths in harmony Melodic appoggiatura Melodic or harmonic sequence Harmonic or melodic acceleration to cadence
Shivers down spine or goose pimples	Enharmonic change Delay of final cadence New or unprepared harmony Sudden dynamic or textural change
Racing heart and "pit of stomach" sensations	Harmonic or melodic acceleration Sudden dynamic or textural change Repeated syncopation Prominent event arriving earlier than expected

This pattern requires confirmation with other types of music and also by direct observation in experimental situations. If confirmed, it will show that many of the emotional responses to music require that the listener, at some level, represent high-level structure. For instance, one cannot define "melodic appoggiatura" apart from a description of music in terms of strong and weak beats within a metrical structure and of discord and resolution within a tonal framework. This is one reason we find it difficult to respond emotionally to the music of other cultures as do the members of those cultures. We have not yet assimilated the means of representing their musical structures that would allow the appropriate structure–emotion links to be activated.

We have many interesting and important questions to explore, such as why these particular structures mediate these particular emotions in the way that they do. Research, however, has begun to clarify a major strand in musical expertise that distinguishes it starkly from the other forms of expertise represented in this volume. It suggests that the central conditions for acquisition of musical expertise are as follows:

1. Existence in a musical culture of forms that have perceptible structures of certain kinds (as specified by Lerdahl and others)
2. Frequent informal exposure to examples of these forms over a lifetime
3. Existence of a normal range of human emotional responses
4. Opportunity to experience these emotions mediated through perceived musical structures, which in itself requires
5. Opportunity to experience music in contexts free of externally imposed constraints or negative reinforcements

If we can ensure these conditions, then the problems associated with bringing individuals to levels of achievement we would currently regard as exceptional may turn out to be trivial.

REFERENCES

Amabile, T. M. (1983). *The social psychology of creativity.* New York: Springer-Verlag.
Balzano, G. J. (1980). The group-theoretic description of twelvefold and microtonal pitch systems. *Computer Music Journal, 4,* 66–84.
Bamberger, J. (1986). Cognitive issues in the development of musically gifted children. In R. J. Sternberg & J. E. Davidson (Eds.), *Conceptions of giftedness* (pp. 388–416). Cambridge University Press.
Bharucha, J. J. (1987). Music cognition and perceptual facilitation: A connectionist framework. *Music Perception, 5,* 1–30.
Bigand, E. (1990). Abstraction of two forms of underlying structure in a tonal melody. *Psychology of Music, 19,* 45–59.
Blacking, J. (1976). *How musical is man?* London: Faber.
Brown, R., & Kulik, J. (1977). Flashbulb memories. *Cognition, 5,* 73–99.
Chase, W. G., & Ericsson, K. A. (1981). Skilled memory. In J. R. Anderson (Ed.), *Cognitive skills and their acquisition* (pp. 141–189). Hillsdale, NJ: Erlbaum.
Chase, W. G., & Simon, H. A. (1973). The mind's eye in chess. In W. G. Chase (Ed.), *Visual information processing* (pp. 215–281). New York: Academic Press.
Clarke, E. F. (1985). Structure and expression in rhythmic performance. In P. Howell, I. Cross, & R. West (Eds.), *Musical structure and cognition* (pp. 209–236). London: Academic Press.
Collier, J. L. (1983). *Louis Armstrong: An American genius.* New York: Oxford University Press.
Cooke, D. (1959). *The language of music.* London: Oxford University Press.
Davidson, L., & Welsh, P. (1988). From collections to structure: The developmental path of tonal thinking. In J. A. Sloboda (Ed.), *Generative processes in music: The psychology of performance, improvisation and composition* (pp. 260–285). London: Oxford University Press.
Deliege, I., & El Ahmahdi, A. (1990). Mechanisms of cue extraction in musical groupings: A study of perception, on *Sequenza VI* for viola solo by Luciano Berio. *Psychology of Music, 19,* 18–44.
Dowling, W. J. (1982). Melodic information processing and its development. In D. Deutsch (Ed.), *The psychology of music* (pp. 413–430). New York: Academic Press.
Dowling, W. J. (1988). Tonal structure and children's early learning of music. In J. A. Sloboda (Ed.), *Generative processes in music: The psychology of performance, improvisation and composition* (pp. 113–128). London: Oxford University Press.
Foder, J. A. (1975). *The language of thought.* Hassocks, Sussex: Harvester Press.
Gabrielsson, A. (1988). Timing in music performance and its relation to music experience. In J. A. Sloboda (Ed.), *Generative processes in music: The psychology of performance, improvisation and composition* (pp. 27–51). London: Oxford University Press.
Gardner, H. (1973). Children's sensitivity to musical styles. *Merrill-Palmer Quarterly of Behavioral Development, 19,* 67–77.

Gardner, H., Davidson, L., & McKernon, P. (1981). The acquisition of song: A developmental approach. In *Documentary report of the Ann Arbor Symposium*. Music Educators' National Conference, Reston, VA.

Goldstein, A. (1980). Thrills in response to music and other stimuli. *Physiological Psychology, 8*, 126–129.

Halpern, A. R., & Bower, G. H. (1982). Musical expertise and melodic structure in memory for musical notation. *American Journal of Psychology, 95*, 31–50.

Hermelin, B., O'Connor, N., & Lee, S. (1987). Musical inventiveness of five idiots-savants. *Psychological Medicine, 17*, 79–90.

Hevner, K. (1936). Experimental studies of the elements of expression in music. *American Journal of Psychology, 48*, 246–268.

Krumhansl, C. (1990). *Tonal structures and music cognition*. New York: Oxford University Press.

Lerdahl, F. (1988a). Tonal pitch space. *Music Perception, 5*, 315–350.

Lerdahl, F. (1988b). Cognitive constraints on compositional systems. In J. A. Sloboda (Ed.), *Generative processes in music: The psychology of performance, improvisation and composition* (pp. 231–259). London: Oxford University Press.

Lerdahl, F., & Jackendoff, R. (1983). *A generative theory of tonal music*. Cambridge, MA: MIT Press.

Marr, D. A. (1982). *Vision*. San Francisco: Freeman.

Meyer, L. B. (1956). *Emotion and meaning in music*. Chicago: University of Chicago Press.

Meyer, L. B. (1973). *Explaining music*. Berkeley: University of California Press.

Miller, L. K. (1987). Sensitivity to tonal structure in a developmentally disabled musical savant. *Psychology of Music, 15*, 76–89.

Moog, H. (1976). *The musical experience of the preschool child* (C. Clarke, Trans.). London: Schott.

Nakamura, H. (1984). Effects of musical emotionality upon GSR and respiration rate: The relationship between verbal reports and physiological responses. *Japanese Journal of Psychology, 55*, 47–50.

Narmour, E. (1977). *Beyond Schenkerism: The need for alternatives in music analysis*. Chicago: University of Chicago Press.

Ortony, A., Clore, G. L., & Collins, A. (1988). *The cognitive structure of the emotions*. Cambridge: Cambridge University Press.

Rasch, R. A. (1988). Timing and synchronization in ensemble performance. In J. A. Sloboda (Ed.), *Generative processes in music: The psychology of performance, improvisation and composition* (pp. 70–90). London: Oxford University Press.

Revesz, G. (1925). *The psychology of a musical prodigy*. London: Kegan Paul, Trench, & Trubner.

Rubin, D. C., & Kozin, M. (1984). Vivid memories. *Cognition, 16*, 81–95.

Shaffer, L. H. (1981). Performance of Chopin, Bach, and Bartok: Studies in motor programming. *Cognitive Psychology, 13*, 326–376.

Shepard, R. N. (1982). Structural representations of musical pitch. In D. Deutsch (Ed.), *The psychology of music* (pp. 344–390). New York: Academic Press.

Sloboda. J. A. (1976a). The effect of item position on the likelihood of identification by inference in prose reading and music reading. *Canadian Journal of Psychology, 30*, 228–236.

Sloboda, J. A. (1976b). Phrase units as determinants of visual processing in music reading. *British Journal of Psychology, 68*, 117–124.

Sloboda, J. A. (1983). The communication of musical metre in piano performance. *Quarterly Journal of Experimental Psychology, A35,* 377–396.

Sloboda, J. A. (1984). Experimental studies of music reading: A review. *Music Perception, 2,* 222–236.

Sloboda, J. A. (1985a). *The musical mind: The cognitive psychology of music.* London: Oxford University Press.

Sloboda, J. A. (1985b). Expressive skill in two pianists: Style and effectiveness in music performance. *Canadian Journal of Psychology, 39,* 273–293.

Sloboda, J. A. (1989). Music as a language. In F. Wilson & F. Roehmann (Eds.), *Music and child development: Proceedings of the 1987 Biology of Music Making Conference* (pp. 28–43). St. Louis: MMB Music.

Sloboda, J. A. (1991). Music structure and emotional response: Some empirical findings. *Psychology of Music, 19* (2).

Sloboda, J. A., Hermelin, B., & O'Connor, N. (1985). An exceptional musical memory. *Music Perception, 3,* 155–170.

Sloboda, J. A., & Parker, D. H. H. (1985). Immediate recall of melodies. In P. Howell, I. Cross, & R. West (Eds.), *Musical structure and cognition* (pp. 143–167). London: Academic Press.

Sosniak, L. (1989). From tyro to virtuoso: A long-term commitment to learning. In F. Wilson & F. Roehmann (Eds.), *Music and child development: Proceedings of the 1987 Biology of Music Making Conference* (pp. 274–290). St. Louis: MMB Music.

Sundberg, J. (1988). Computer synthesis of musical performance. In J. A. Sloboda (Ed.), *Generative processes in music: The psychology of performance, improvisation and composition* (pp. 52–59). London: Oxford University Press.

Todd, N. (1985). A model of expressive timing in tonal music. *Music Perception, 3,* 33–58.

Treffert, D. A. (1988). The idiot savant: A review of the syndrome. *American Journal of Psychiatry, 145,* 563–572.

Ward, W. D., & Burns, E. M. (1982). Absolute pitch. In D. Deutsch (Ed.), *The psychology of music* (pp. 431–452). New York: Academic Press.

Zenatti, A. (1969). *Le développement génétique de la perception musicale.* Monographies Français Psychologique No. 17.

7 Literate expertise

MARLENE SCARDAMALIA AND CARL BEREITER

The commonsense notion of expertise treats it as a state – almost a state of grace – in which abundant knowledge and skill make it possible to accomplish with ease things that the nonexpert can do, if at all, only with difficulty. This commonsense notion has been elaborated by Dreyfus and Dreyfus (1986) and supported by a host of expert–novice comparisons in various fields.

A notable exception to this "on top of it all" picture of expertise comes from the study of writing. Expert writers generally are found to work harder at the same assigned tasks than nonexperts, engaging in more planning and problem solving, more revision of goals and methods, and in general more agonizing over the task (Bereiter & Scardamalia, 1987; Flower & Hayes, 1980; Scardamalia & Bereiter, 1987). Previous literature has characterized experts by their precise recall of complex, task-specific patterns and by the ease with which they gain acccess to just the right information (Ericsson & Staszewski, 1989; Larkin, McDermott, Simon, & Simon, 1980; Patel & Groen, 1986). In contrast, expert writers have been found to take more time than novices just to start writing the first sentence of a simple narrative (Zbrodoff, 1984), and far longer to complete a one- to two-page essay (Paris, 1986). It is the novice, not the expert, whose rate of text production is fast enough to match handwriting speed. When it comes to memory for text, more advanced writers have been found to have less ready access to the contents of texts they have written. When they produce texts, they bring to mind a great deal of information that they later toss out. Meanwhile, their novice counterparts can recall with greater speed and equal accuracy the texts they have written, and the thoughts that first come to mind are the ones novices tend to use when producing their texts – few, if any, dead ends (Bereiter & Scardamalia, 1987; Scardamalia & Paris, 1985). So, more wrong turns, more revisions, more time, more effort, and more recall problems as one gets "better."

These observations might suggest that expertise in writing is radically different from expertise in most other fields. We do not see it that way. There is one activity in which experts in a variety of fields have been found to invest more effort than have novices. It is the activity of constructing a problem representation – identifying and elaborating constraints, goals, relevant principles, and analogues (Glaser & Chi, 1988). This is also the major respect in which the composing processes of expert writers are found to differ from those of novices (Flower & Hayes, 1980). Where task domains differ is in the consequences of this problem-representing activity. In the case of the physicist solving a textbook physics problem, the usual consequence is that the problem comes to be recognized as of a familiar type that the expert can solve in a straightforward manner, thus achieving net savings in time and effort over the novice, who must proceed in a more groping manner (Chi, Glaser, & Rees, 1982). In the case of writing, however, the likely effect of elaborating constraints is to produce a more complex and novel task. Task execution, instead of being simplified, comes to require simultaneous attention to so many constraints that the writer runs the risk of information-processing overload (Beaugrande, 1984). Instead of being able to execute a plan in a straightforward manner, the skilled writer has to keep returning to planning; writing is interrupted by pauses during which the writer consults top-level goals or global constraints before making local decisions (Flower & Hayes, 1981).

None of this seems peculiar to writing, however. Rather, it would seem to be characteristic of any task in which people are trying to extend themselves or to achieve a novel or superior result. It happens that with writing, this situation is easy to achieve experimentally, whereas it is not in many other fields. The kind of physics problem that a novice can tackle is unlikely to be elaborated by the expert into a significant intellectual challenge, whereas even the most mundane writing tasks, made deliberately simple so as to be accessible to novice writers, seem to elicit creative effort from experts.

Studies of readers at different levels of skill show parallels between reading and writing expertise. Again, more work for the more accomplished. It takes the form of more backtracking in the text to pick up missed information, reading more slowly at points of difficulty, and putting in more effort to summarize the text (Bereiter & Bird, 1985; Johnston & Afflerbach, 1985). As with writing, the apparent anomaly can be explained by the fact that better readers set more difficult tasks for themselves – in this case, tasks of fuller or deeper comprehension and integration of old and new information. This becomes evident in studies of comprehension monitoring, where texts are doctored to contain inconsistencies or insufficiently explained statements. Better readers recognize and try to solve the comprehension problems, whereas poorer readers glide past without noticing them (Baker, 1985; Garner, 1980; Scardamalia & Bereiter, 1984).

We shall have more to say about expert approaches to reading and writing later. For the present, however, the point we want to make is that studies of reading and writing bring out an aspect of expertise that is typical of expertise as it is practiced in the real world and that tends to be hidden in most expert–novice research. Expert physicists do not spend their days solving textbook problems. They spend their days, or at least the high points of their days, working on problems that are hard for them. That is how they make advances in their fields, and it is also how they advance their own competence. Experts acquire their vast knowledge resources not by doing what falls comfortably within their competence but by working on real problems that force them to extend their knowledge and competence. That is not only how they become experts, we suggest, but also how they remain experts and avoid falling into the ruts worn by repeated execution of familiar routines.

This growing edge of expertise is our main concern in this chapter, for it is the place where reading and writing interact most importantly with other activities.

THE INTERACTION BETWEEN LITERATE EXPERTISE AND OTHER FORMS OF EXPERTISE

In most modern domains of expertise it is necessary to read and write, even to read and write well. But not terribly well – not so well that a bacteriologist, for instance, must take time away from doing research in order to perfect the skills of reading and writing about bacteria. Except within the literary world itself, the world where literature is produced and processed, reading and writing are generally regarded merely as what educationists refer to as *tool skills*. They are useful, but – here is the crucial point as far as our current topic is concerned – one is not required to be expert at them. This view, however, reflects an unfortunately limited conception of how the knowledge-enhancing components of literate expertise work.

Every kind of expertise involves subordinate skills, but these skills vary in terms of how integrally they are involved. For many scientists, mathematics is so intimately connected with their work that it would be difficult to tell where expertise in science leaves off and expertise in mathematics begins. One might say the same for scientists' use of reading and writing. Scientific expertise and literate expertise may be so fused that it would be difficult to disentangle them. At the opposite extreme, a sales representative may need to drive a car when working, but there is no problem in distinguishing between expertise in selling and expertise in driving. Furthermore, it is clear that expertise in selling is not significantly enhanced by expertise in driving. Both may contribute to total sales, but in quite separate ways. Reading and writing would seem to be to the athlete what the car is to the sales representative – not an integral part of competence, perhaps not even as necessary as the car, but having the potential to contribute. Contributions for the athlete may come in the form of expert written advice, helpful record-keeping activity, inspirational biographies, and so forth.

To ask whether the roles of reading and writing are more like that of mathematics in the physical sciences or more like that of automobile driving to the traveling salesman is to ask how these abilities interact. Even in cases where reading and writing are both judged important, many modern psychologists would rate their contributions differently. They would see writing as quite separable from expertise in the field. Reading, however, they would see as inseparable. Reading researchers have stunningly demonstrated that how well one will understand a written text will depend preeminently on the extent of one's knowledge of the field discussed in the text (Bransford & Johnson, 1972). According to the resulting knowledge-based or "schema-theoretic" view, there is no general expertise in reading. Beyond a few basic skills, one's expertise in reading in a particular area is coextensive with one's knowledge of the area.

We believe this view is somewhat mistaken with regard to both writing and reading. Writing is more intimately involved with expertise in learned domains than it would seem on the surface, and reading expertise, though intimately connected with expert knowledge, is sufficiently distinct to interact with it in an important way. Both reading and writing, we claim, *can* interact significantly with other kinds of expertise, but they do not necessarily do so.

Note that this issue is separate from the issue of the importance of reading or writing to performance in a domain. Charness (chapter 2, this volume) indicates that reading plays a significant role in chess expertise. To claim that reading interacts with chess skill would be to claim something beyond this. Reading could be as important as Charness indicates and yet be no more than a tool skill. It could be, for instance, that the chess literature makes only modest demands on literate skills and that, beyond this, one's ability to comprehend and profit from the chess literature is wholly dependent on one's knowledge of chess. In that case, it would make no sense to talk about expertise in reading chess literature. But if there are chess experts who can be distinguished from their peers by an extraordinary ability to derive benefit from reading chess literature, and this ability appears to enhance or give a different character to their chess expertise, then it would be profitable to hypothesize and study literate expertise in the domain of chess. In general, according to our accounts, *being an expert reader and writer within some domain means reading and writing in ways that maximize the productive interaction between these activities and others going on at the growing edge of expertise.*

DIALECTICAL PROCESSES IN EXPERT FUNCTIONING

We shall first sketch in very general terms a conception of what it means for reading and writing to interact with domain-specific competencies in the advancement of expertise. After that we shall describe reading and writing expertise in ways that relate to this general conception.

What goes on at the most general level in expert functioning is an interaction between domain knowledge and immediate cases, as suggested in Figure 7.1. Domain knowledge is used to interpret or deal with the immediate case. In turn, the immediate case yields information that may be used to modify domain knowledge, sometimes in a major way. We call the process "dialectical" because of this two-way influence. Note that the process may go through a number of cycles. One may do something with the immediate case that leads to reformulating the domain knowledge, which in turn results in a different idea about what to do with the immediate case, and so forth.

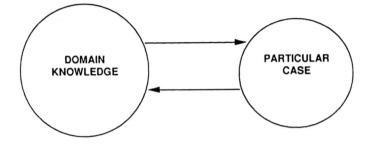

Figure 7.1. The dialectical process in expertise.

We are arguing that this dialectical process is part of what it means to be an expert. It is not an epiphenomenon or sideline activity. Nonexperts are liable to fall short in this dialectical process, for several reasons. Most familiar is failure of the left-to-right process. Domain knowledge may not be appropriately applied to the immediate case, either because critical elements are lacking (Heller & Reif, 1984) or because the knowledge is not represented in a functional way (Anzai & Yokoyama, 1984). More interesting, however, is failure of the right-to-left process. Nonexperts may solve a problem, but fail to learn from it. Sweller (1988) has obtained a variety of experimental evidence that this occurs in solving school mathematics and science problems. More expertlike students, on the other hand, are observed to pause after solving a problem, seemingly to extract generalizable knowledge from the experience (Davis & McNight, 1979). Nonexperts may also fail at the level of executive procedures. Mathematics novices are notorious for failing to check results against prior knowledge to see if they make sense, and this may be partly due to lack of knowledge of checking procedures (Riley, Greeno, & Heller, 1983). Revision of writing is similarly rare among novices, especially the kind of revision that would suggest changes in the knowledge base (Nold, 1981). The fact that students can carry out revisions when given various forms of external support (Scardamalia & Bereiter, 1983) implies that they are capable of both left-to-right and right-to-left processes, but lack the executive structure or self-regulatory skills needed to sustain them. In general, nonexperts seem inclined toward a unidirectional process of "do it and be done with it."

Dialectical processes in reading and writing are subtypes of the general process we have sketched. Figure 7.2 represents the process in reading, where the immediate case is a text to be understood. In this context we adopt the terms of van Dijk and Kintsch (1983), who described two kinds of mental representations formed during text comprehension. Their *situation model* refers to that portion of domain knowledge to which a particular text is relevant. Their *textbase* refers to a mental representation specific to the particular text – a representation of the text's propositional content. In the dialectical process the situation model is used as the basis for inferences necessary in constructing

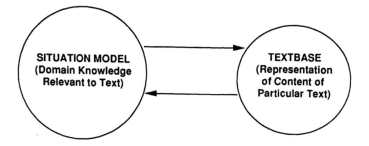

Figure 7.2. The dialectical process in expert text comprehension.

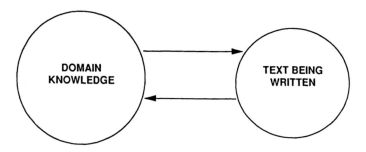

Figure 7.3. The dialectical process in expert text composition.

the textbase, and the comprehension of text propositions in turn modifies the situation model. The desired result is coherent understanding of what the text says and appropriate modifications of domain knowledge in response to text information. Failures may occur in not bringing relevant knowledge to bear on comprehending the text (Bransford & Johnson, 1972), in not reconsidering prior knowledge in the light of text information, and in halting the dialectical process when only a superficial level of understanding has been achieved.

The sketch for writing processes (Figure 7.3) is based on the knowledge-transforming model for written composition that we have presented elsewhere (Bereiter & Scardamalia, 1987; Scardamalia & Bereiter, 1987). The part of the process everyone is aware of is the left-to-right process of using domain knowledge to produce a text. Numerous expert writers have testified to the importance of the right-to-left process, however – to the effect that writing can have on their knowledge (Wason, 1980). Nonexpert writers, on the other hand, show little of this reverse process, as a result of which their domain knowledge is little influenced in the course of writing about it (Bereiter & Scardamalia, 1987).

The unifying idea in all these models is an interaction between the general and the particular. On the left, in each, we have the person's knowledge as it is brought forward by some particular event, act, or text. On the right we have the representation of a particular problem. For a doctor this may be a particular patient's case; for the writer it is the text being written; for the reader it is the text being read; for the architect it is a particular building project; and so forth.

Research typically identifies expert–nonexpert differences in the left-hand circle, in domain knowledge (which we take to include skills as well as declarative knowledge). While in no way discounting this well-documented finding, we point out that differences may also be found in the back-and-forth *process* that goes on between domain knowledge and particular cases. Expertise is characterized by high levels of such activity, whereas nonexpert behavior is characterized by an attenuated or unidirectional passage of information. The result is that experts keep enhancing their competence through encounters with particular cases, whereas this is less true of nonexperts – another version of the rich getting richer while the poor get poorer. But there is nothing paradoxical about it. The dialectical process by which domain knowledge enhances responses to particular cases and responses to particular cases enhance domain knowledge may go some distance toward explaining how experts got to be experts in the first place.

KNOWLEDGE-TRANSFORMING VERSUS KNOWLEDGE-TELLING APPROACHES TO WRITING

The synergistic relation between literate expertise and other forms of expertise is easiest to see in the case of writing. In the typical study of writing expertise, writers at differing levels of accomplishment are assigned topics on which everyone might be assumed to have sufficient knowledge for a short composition – describing one's own job, for instance, or discussing some popular issue, such as the banning of handguns. Despite the ordinariness of the topics, it invariably turns out that the documents produced by the more expert writers are not only better expressed but also far richer in content. Although this result is not surprising, its explanation is far from obvious. Three possibilities are (1) that good writers generally know more, (2) that they do not actually know more but have better access to their knowledge when writing, and (3) that they neither know more nor have easier access to their knowledge, but, through striving to produce a good composition, they persist until they have mined their knowledge resources more thoroughly. As noted previously, there is support from protocol analyses to support the third hypothesis. The second hypothesis is supported by findings that show novice writers to have difficulty in retrieving content from memory and to be helped by contentless prompts (Scardamalia, Bereiter, & Goelman, 1982). The first hypothesis is plausible, given that expert writers usually are older. Suppose, then, that there is truth in all three – that good writers know more to begin with, have easier access to what they know when writing, and persist longer in trying to retrieve relevant content. The idea of interaction is that these factors are not independent but support one another: Trying harder to retrieve good content for writing builds easier access routes and results in discovering previously unrecognized connections among items of knowledge; greater connectedness facilitates the comprehension and retention of new information; knowing more permits the formulation of more ambitious goals in writing, which results in more challenging tasks of knowledge retrieval; and so on.

Professional writers often testify to the value of writing in developing their own knowledge and understanding. Writing is described as a process of discovery, of creating order out of chaos, or of coming to understand what one means. Sartre went so far as to say that when, because of blindness, he could no longer write, he could no longer think either. Voss, Blais, Means, Greene, and Ahwesh (1989) found that in the social sciences, solving a problem and building an argument in defense of the solution advance hand in hand. At the same time that people generate proposed solutions, they generate arguments in defense of them. This is not mere self-protection, Voss claims, but a way of directing thought when there are no empirical or mathematical checks, as there often are in the harder sciences. But Voss conjectures that physical scientists rely on argument too, in the early stages of developing their ideas, as evidenced by much of the content of their scientific journals. The pervasiveness of journal keeping itself, of course, testifies to a value in writing that extends well beyond mere record keeping. Journals of scientists often read like someone thinking by means of writing, rather than merely writing down thoughts already formed in the mind.

All of this indicates that writing has benefits beyond the obvious ones of communicating and keeping records. It has epistemic benefits. These epistemic benefits tend to go unheralded, because they involve not the acquisition of new information but, rather, the *transformation* of knowledge already in the mind. If we look more deeply into how this knowledge-transforming effect is achieved, we shall see in fairly explicit form what it means for writing expertise and subject-matter expertise to interact synergistically. We shall do this through the use of contrastive models.

The nonexpert approach to writing can be identified with a *knowledge-telling* model, which minimizes many of the problems of text production but as a result misses out on the cognitive benefits of writing. The expert approach is identified with a *knowledge-transforming* model, which solves rhetorical and knowledge-related problems interactively, thus simultaneously enhancing writing expertise and subject-matter understanding.

The knowledge-telling process

From both their writings and their thinking aloud while composing, it is evident that inexpert writers tend to transfer information from memory to paper with a minimum of transformation. Their texts tend to reflect the order in which they thought of things, rather than an order imposed on the content as a result of planning (Flower, 1979; Scardamalia & Bereiter, 1987). Their thinking-aloud protocols are relatively barren of thoughts about goals or main ideas. Instead, they read like first drafts of a text (Bereiter, Burtis, & Scardamalia, 1988; Burtis, Bereiter, Scardamalia, & Tetroe, 1983; Scardamalia & Paris, 1985). Particularly lacking in their protocols are signs of reflection – of reconsidering previous ideas or decisions (Bereiter et al., 1988; Scardamalia, Bereiter, & Steinbach, 1984).

As a result, the composing process contributes little to the development of understanding. It may even have a degrading effect, because of the tendency to say what is easiest to say. This knowledge-telling process (Bereiter & Scardamalia, 1987; Scardamalia & Bereiter, 1987) is an efficient way to generate texts that conform to the requirements of topic and genre, which are the main requirements of school writing assignments. It is possible to become skillful at knowledge telling. But we would not apply the term *expertise* to such skill, because it lacks the dialectical character that we discussed earlier. It is skill in the execution of routines, and it lacks the progressive character found in prototypical instances of expertise.

The knowledge-telling process generates text content in a straight-ahead fashion by using memory probes drawn from the topic assignment, from mental models of text structure, and from text already generated. For present purposes, the important thing about the model is that it contains no loops by which the results of the writing process get fed back into the domain knowledge base. If one's knowledge of a topic is rich and coherently organized, then one probably will generate a good text using the knowledge-telling process. But generating such a text will not have improved one's knowledge.

The knowledge-transforming process

The kind of writing process that does improve knowledge is represented in Figure 7.4. The model illustrated is an elaboration of the one presented in Figure 7.3. Its central feature is the existence of two interconnected problem spaces, one concerned with problems of domain knowledge (the "content space") and the other (the "rhetorical space") concerned with problems having to do with the text being written. Generally, results from the content space are transferred to the rhetorical space as goals. For instance, the decision, arrived at in the content space, that it is morally wrong for animals to be kept in zoos becomes translated into the rhetorical goal of persuading readers to adopt this position. Results from the rhetorical space are passed to the content space in the form of problems or questions. These can influence domain knowledge in a variety of ways. The following are some examples (additional examples have been developed elsewhere – Scardamalia & Bereiter, 1985):

1. Rhetorical problems in defending a position, when converted into a search through the content space for supporting information, may result in discovering the relevance of previously ignored facts or, on the other hand, realizing that the belief one has been upholding is unwarranted.
2. The need to shorten a text may lead to more critical analysis of the importance of related items of knowledge.

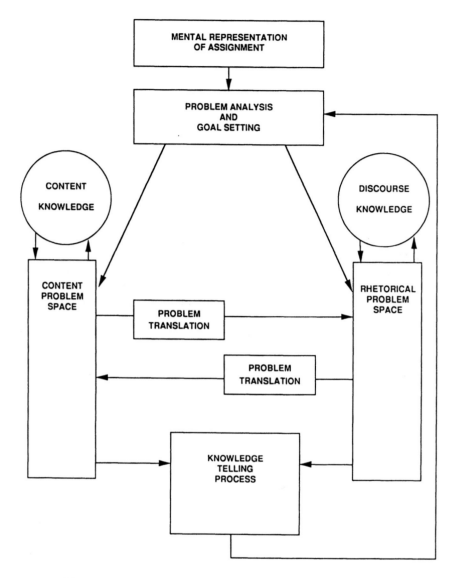

Figure 7.4. Structure of the knowledge-transforming model.

3. The rhetorical need for a transitional statement bridging subtopics may lead to discovery of a previously unrecognized relationship.

4. The rhetorical need to make a text more interesting may lead to questioning, within the content space, of what is interesting about various items of information, and this may bring new insights to light.

5. Problems of word choice and of definition may lead to deeper analysis of distinctions and to clearer conceptualization within the content space.

The back-and-forth process of solving rhetorical and knowledge-related problems interactively accounts for the much greater quantity of mental activity exhibited in experts' thinking-aloud protocols, as compared with those of inexpert writers. Implicit in this process is a synergistic relation between literary expertise and expertise in the subject matter of the discourse. The more sophisticated one's rhetorical knowledge, and the more effort one puts into solving rhetorical problems, the more challenging should be the problems that will be fed back into the content space. Solving those problems is likely to generate more complex and subtly qualified knowledge, thus presenting greater rhetorical challenges when it comes to trying to communicate it in writing. Meeting those challenges will enhance rhetorical sophistication, and so on in a spiral of increasing competence on both sides.

We are only hypothesizing this spiral effect. Studies of writing development have not been carried out over sufficiently long periods to have documented such an effect. Still, it seems a reasonable inference from what can be discerned over short periods of time as experts think aloud while composing. There probably are exceptions. We suspect that there are writers who become so skillful rhetorically that they are able to solve almost all problems within the rhetorical space, without having to resort to further problem solving in the content space. They are able to "write around their ignorance," which, as one prize-winning journalist told us, is what all good columnists do. There probably are also experts who do little knowledge transforming in the course of writing, whose approach to writing is that of the fluent knowledge-teller, but who rely on conversations with colleagues to provide the necessary knowledge-transforming dialectic. We know one person who exploits conversation so shamelessly in this way that sometimes in conversing with him we have the feeling that we are engaged in a thinking-aloud rehearsal of his next book. Finally, there are experts who evidently rely on other representational media, such as diagrams or mathematical notation, but who carry out a knowledge-transforming process functionally equivalent to the one we describe for writing (cf. John-Steiner, 1987). Thus, there are alternative ways to carry on the knowledge-transforming dialectic. But writing must surely hold a privileged position because of its wide applicability, its power to encode such a wide range of information, its constant availability, and its record-preserving advantages.

EXPERTISE IN READING

Writing expertise is well recognized, whereas reading expertise sounds a bit odd. Because reading produces no distinct product, and because its effects are always joined with those of domain knowledge, it has a more ambiguous status. We believe, however, that there is a great deal to be gained by distinguishing expert and inexpert approaches to reading.

There is an enormous body of research comparing variously defined groups of good and poor readers. Most of this research, however, compares readers who are grossly deficient in reading ability with readers who are not. Although such research offers insights worthy of consideration, it does not provide a good starting point for inquiry into the nature of reading expertise.

As indicated earlier, our conception of expertise in reading draws on the van Dijk and Kintsch (1983) theory, which posits two mental representations that are constructed during text comprehension. One, called the *textbase*, is a propositional representation of what the text says – something that for present purposes we may equate with a summary. The other is a *situation model*, which in the case of nonfiction will be a mental representation of some aspect or portion of the real world, as suggested by text information. The two representations are to some extent independent. People who lack sufficient knowledge of the subject matter may be unable to construct a situation model, but they may nevertheless be able to construct a textbase that is sufficient for summarizing, answering questions about, and making inferential connections among statements in the text. One may remember the situation model but forget the text model – that is, assimilate the new information but forget where one heard it, or retain a conclusion while forgetting the argument that led up to it.

Construction of both the textbase and the situation model depends on a reader's knowledge of the domain, but there is also a process involved, analogous to the knowledge-transforming process in writing. This becomes apparent when skilled readers are asked to think aloud as they attempt to comprehend texts on topics that are unfamiliar or difficult for them. In these cases, the meaning of the text is treated as problematic, and they employ a variety of strategies to solve the problem (Bereiter & Bird, 1985; Johnston & Afflerbach, 1985). Accomplished readers make deliberate use of linguistic information, such as lexical repetition, relational terms, and features of text organization. They monitor their comprehension and set up "watchers" for needed information. When difficulties are encountered, they employ tactics such as the following, observed by Johnston and Afflerbach (1985, p. 223):

> Consolidation or reviewing to "firm it up."
> Skimming to "put it together."
> Scanning to find the source of difficulty.
> Re-reading.
> Reading more slowly.
> Listing to "cram it all in."
> Pressing on in the hope of later resolution.
> Refocusing on a different level of text.
> Resetting goals at a different level of understanding.

That there is an element of learned skill involved is indicated by the fact that even academically successful teenagers show little evidence of such problem-solving strategies, and their reading comprehension improves when the strategies are taught to them (Bereiter & Bird, 1985).

Inexpert readers, in their thinking-aloud protocols, reveal a process similar to knowledge telling (Scardamalia & Bereiter, 1984). It is a straight-ahead process in which each text statement is interpreted immediately and not reconsidered in the light of subsequent information. On a summarization task, it appears as the "copy-delete" strategy identified by Brown, Day, and Jones (1983). As text statements are processed one at a time, the reader judges each statement in isolation as to whether it is important enough to retain ("copy") or whether it is to be ignored. Surprisingly, this strategy works reasonably well. Superficial clues enable students to make importance judgments that agree fairly well with those of experts; thus, they are able to restrict their attention to the kinds of information likely to be required for test taking or answering teachers' questions. The organization of these informational fragments under topical headings proves to be an efficient memorizing procedure (Shimmerlik, 1978), more effective for recall than for trying to interpret the text as a propositional structure. But as for advancing one's knowledge through reading, the inexpert process falls short with respect to both kinds of text representation. The textbase tends to be superficial, missing the implicit propositions that require inference (Bransford, Stein, Shelton, & Owings, 1981), and inexpert readers tend to overlook anomalous information in texts, that is, information inconsistent with their prior knowledge or situation models (Baker, 1985; Markman, 1981).

Expert reading strategies, like those listed from Johnston and Afflerbach (1985), are focused on construction of the textbase. Operations involving the situation model have received less attention. We have, however done studies in which students have been asked to think aloud in response to texts that convey new information, some of it in conflict with prior knowledge (Bereiter & Scardamalia, 1989). For instance, one text segment was as follows:

> Harmful germs are not trying to be bad when they settle down in your body. They just want to live quietly, eat, and make more germs.

This passage contradicts the whole popular image of germs, which we have seen vividly dramatized in television commercials and children's cartoons, where disease germs are invariably depicted as aggressors. Some students accurately paraphrased the text, indicating construction of an adequate textbase, and yet showed no sign of recognizing its implications for their understanding of germs:

> That means they don't want to really hurt you, but they just want to live quietly and eat the food you digest and all the things that could go in your stomach and they just want to get more bacteria.

By contrast, there were students who recognized that there was a problem about what to do with the new information. For example:

> That's hard to believe. Let's see. Then I always thought [of] germs moving around or fighting us. I didn't think that they would just settle down and raise a family. That's not exactly my idea of a germ.

Finally, there were a very small number who not only recognized a problem but set about trying to solve it with their available knowledge:

> Well, they don't really know that they're bad, but they're just living their normal way but everybody else thinks they're bad.

Or another:

> Well, I guess they don't know they are hurting you. . . . Well, I'm not sure. They are killed by other cells in your body. I wonder what they think, if they knew that they were doing something so they could prevent it or something, or if scientists could find a way that bacteria or viruses could live in your body without hurting you.

Really expert reading, observed only rarely in school-age readers, would involve cycles of attention to textbase and situation model, modifying each in response to problems arising from the other, much as we observe in expert writers. Thus, the same dialectical process is involved as in writing, with the same kind of knowledge-transforming result, except that in reading there is the added benefit of new information.

These ideas can be directly connected to our earlier discussion. The textbase is a case model; that is, it is a representation of the text as a particular case. The situation model, on the other hand, is a part of domain knowledge – a part to which the text at hand happens to be relevant.[1] In acquiring expertise in a domain, constructing situation models is obviously what counts most. Our hypothesis is that, indeed, it counts for so much that people striving to attain expert knowledge in a domain will be inclined to concentrate their efforts on building and tuning their situation models and accordingly will put as little effort as they can into constructing textbases. Such neglect of the textbase maximizes immediate gains in new knowledge at the expense of possibly significant revisions or even major transformations of existing knowledge.

The proposal that people invest too much effort in the situation model and not enough in the textbase may seem improbable, given that the emphasis in formal education seems to be entirely in the opposite direction. Examinations, assignments, and teachers' questions all tend to demand accurate representation of what the text says, whereas the implications of text information for knowledge of the world may be discussed, but they are seldom the focus of task demands. The notorious weaknesses of students in applying textbook information to real-world situations could be taken as a consequence of this textbase emphasis, and this is a problem not limited to low-achieving young-

---

[1] This is true only of expository texts, but they are the main concern of this discussion. In reading fiction, one constructs a situation model that bears much or little relation to the real world, depending on the genre, but that in any case represents an imaginary world with reference to which the text is to be interpreted. The situation model may nevertheless have an existence separate from the textbase. One may, for instance, recall quite a bit of the adventures of Tom Sawyer and Huckleberry Finn without necessarily remembering which adventures occurred in which book.

sters. Voss et al. (1989) found that college-educated people who had studied economics were little better than those who had not when it came to thinking through real-world problems having to do with prices, interest rates, and the federal budget deficit.

Such findings, however, do not establish that students are successful in constructing textbase representations and fail only in constructing situation models. The National Assessment of Educational Progress (1981) included a task in which students were to read an essay, advance a proposition about the essay, and defend it with evidence drawn from the essay itself – hence, a task that focused on the textbase rather than on external knowledge. Performance of 17-year-olds was for the most part abysmal. They were no better able to operate on information residing in the text in front of them than they were, in studies like that of Voss et al. (1989), to operate on their world knowledge. A perennial complaint of English teachers, reinforced by the National Assessment findings, is that students cannot be induced to pay attention to the text as such. They persist in treating *Macbeth* as a series of real-world happenings and discussing it in those terms (Was Macbeth or Lady Macbeth more to blame? Is there any substance to witchcraft?), rather than trying to grasp more fully what is actually said in the play.

It has been said of one leading intellectual, by one of his assistants, that he does not actually read books; he raids them. That is, he always knows what he is looking for in a book, and he does not let the rest of the text stand in the way as he goes after what he is seeking. This is an extreme case of dominance of the situation model over the textbase; nothing is constructed in the textbase that is not immediately relevant to the situation model. Although this represents an efficient way of getting information from a text (similar to the way one normally gets information from a telephone directory or dictionary), the efficiency is gained by sacrificing opportunities for the text to produce significant modifications of one's understanding.

Let us consider, however, at the opposite extreme, the literary critic, for whom the textbase should be dominant. For the critic, that is, the dominant process should be creating a rich and sophisticated representation of the text and what it says. Although the critic may at the same time learn from the text, such personal gains in knowledge are incidental. Critics who could find in a text only what they were looking for or what was personally relevant to them would not be considered expert, any more than physicians who find in their patients only the symptoms they are anticipating. Indeed, the literary critic's task is much like that of the physician. It is to bring domain knowledge to bear in such a way as to deal expertly with the individual case.

But what about experts in other disciplines, whose concern is both with their own knowledge and with the knowledge extant in their discipline and often represented in texts written by others? Is reading for them a matter of finding information to incorporate into their situation models, as it is for our rapacious intellectual? Or is it a variety of case expertise, as it is for the literary critic? Ideally, it should be both. There is a question of balance, however, that has to be worked out in both epistemological and practical terms.

Scientists and other seekers of principles aim to build knowledge of maximum generality, and so their interest in particular cases is instrumental. There is hardly any reason why scientists should invest effort in knowing what particular texts say except insofar as it contributes to their knowledge of a domain. But particular cases can be extremely important if they exhibit anomalies that challenge current knowledge. The bacterial culture that refuses to behave according to rule becomes suddenly of great interest to the biologist, who will study it and try to understand it in exquisite detail, until the implications of its strange behavior can be known. Biologists would consider it an essential part of their expertise to be good at dealing with such particular cases. But texts that refuse to behave according to rule are also in need of special attention, and some biologists may be ill-prepared to carry out the analyses such texts require. Our point is that something of the expertise of the literary specialist needs to accompany the expertise of specialists in other disciplines.

Subject-matter experts as inexpert readers

Bazerman (1985) interviewed seven physicists about their journal-reading behavior and observed four of them as they searched and scanned journals in a library. Bazerman found the physicists' reading to be dominated by the specific purposes of their research:

> All through the reading process the physicists interviewed carefully selected what they pay attention to and retain based on the needs of their own research. The continuation of their own research projects forms the purpose for the reading and, thus, determines what they want to get from reading. (Bazerman, 1985, pp. 5–6)

Thus, for these scientists, the situation model seemed to prevail over the textbase to an extreme degree. They were highly selective both in what articles they read and in what they attended to within an article. "Theoreticians, for example, may go right to the results of experimental articles to see what kind of data is obtained and must be accounted for by their theory; they are likely to skip over methodological sections as uninteresting and theoretical sections as familiar" (Bazerman, 1985, p. 11).

Is this expert reading or not? Certainly it represents a skill adapted to the information needs and time constraints of research careers. But the way Bazerman's subjects went about choosing which articles to read and which to skip is highly reminiscent of the copy-delete strategy of immature readers – the strategy of making instant judgments of the importance of individual text statements on the basis of surface indicators. Bazerman found his physicists making judgments about which articles to read mainly on the basis of key words in titles and recognition of authors. Reading abstracts or scanning the actual article was used mainly to eliminate articles that had misleadingly passed the first tests – for instance, articles whose titles indicated the use of a technique relevant to the physicist's own research but, as it would turn out, in an unrelated context. Like the copy-delete strategy, this is a time-efficient strategy that probably has fairly good validity. What it will miss is material whose relevance cannot be detected by simple association, because it depends on inference.

Although the scientists interviewed by Bazerman expressed a desire to watch for articles that might have radical implications, redefining an area or causing a major change in schema, the way they went about reading did not seem likely to uncover such material. When an article did not accord with the reader's perception of a problem, the reader tended to ignore the differences and attend only to what could be assimilated. "This selective evaluation," Bazerman (1985, p. 17) noted, "is strong evidence for the priority of one's individual schema in evaluating results over an absolute, textually based standard."

It could well be that this highly selective, schema-driven approach to "keeping up with the literature" is optimal for scientists in a fast-moving field. If it is, this would indicate that literate expertise of the kind required of literary specialists is irrelevant and might even be counterproductive in such fields. Bazerman did not attempt to evaluate the physicists as readers. He did, however, note one subject, BP2, who stood out from the rest. BP2 read more widely than the others and more critically, and he scribbled many marginal comments as he read.

> BP2, . . . as head of a laboratory, has wide reading responsibilities and a critical function, but he also reports that ever since childhood he has read broadly and critically. Whether he became a lab head because of these habits or developed these habits as part of his rise and then reinterpreted his childhood to fit his new self-conception, there is role-appropriate behavior. (Bazerman, 1985, p. 20)

This passage suggests that for BP2, reading was more than a tool skill, that it was integrally involved in his scientific expertise. Literate expertise may have interacted with scientific expertise, influencing the kind of scientific career that BP2 constructed and in turn being influenced by it – an example of the synergism that we have claimed can take place between literate expertise and domain expertise.

Would it be going too far to suggest that BP2 may have been the only expert reader in Bazerman's sample and that for the other scientists their reading was simply a highly practiced tool skill that met their needs? We suspect that many subject-matter experts are in fact poor readers in an important sense. They may be skillful at picking up new information that elaborates or validates their existing schemata, but they are insensitive to text information that has knowledge-transforming implications, that calls for altering or abandoning existing schemata or for subordinating them to some more inclusive schema. When they encounter such information, their tendency is to overlook it or to misinterpret it as saying something familiar, something they can either accept as already believed or else reject as having already been discredited.

Such inexpert readers may nevertheless continue to grow as experts in their disciplines, thanks to the fact that there are other sources of knowledge-transforming information besides reading. Paramount among these alternative sources are discussion and other kinds of face-to-face information exchange. It is interesting that even computer scientists, accustomed to disseminating their daily thoughts over computer networks, feel they must get together several times a year to listen to one another make speeches and to argue about what is said, thus falling back on the information technology that has characterized academia since before the invention of the printing press. We suspect that many experts depend on such personal media to initiate major changes in their thinking, after which they can go home and use reading to provide substance for the new schemata. Reading thus plays an important role, but the main knowledge-transforming processes go on elsewhere.

That experts might have deficiencies when it comes to reading the literature in their own fields is, if not unthinkable, seemingly unthought. Peters and Ceci (1982) made cosmetic changes to 12 published research articles and resubmitted them to the psychological journals that had previously published them. Only 3 of the 12 were recognized as resubmissions; of the remaining 9 articles, 8 were rejected, most often for methodological flaws. The Peters and Ceci (1982) article provoked many responses from journal editors and others who attempted to explain the results (56 responses were published along with the original article). Biases of various sorts, irresponsibility, and scientific incompetence on the part of reviewers were all treated as serious possibilities. Never mentioned, so far as we could detect, was the possibility that expertise in psychology may not be a sufficient qualification for the kind of reading a journal editor or reviewer is supposed to do. It seems that when educated people misread something, deficient reading ability is never advanced as a hypothesis. Rather, the misreading is attributed to carelessness, ignorance, or some general intellectual deficit.

Coughlin and Patel (1986) found that the accuracy of diagnoses by experienced medical specialists declined dramatically when the description of an easy case was scrambled so that a critical piece of information that normally would have appeared early in the description came toward the end. (The critical information was that the symptoms were of very recent origin, a fact that ruled out otherwise plausible diagnoses.) It would appear that the specialists quickly formed a diagnosis using what they assumed to be the key facts, and then overlooked the information that should have cast a whole different light on the case. Presumably this would not have happened in real life, because the critical information would have been obtained early and thus would have prevented the misdiagnosis.

With a more difficult case, however, scrambling the order in which facts were presented had no effect. Indeed, with the scrambled order, experts did significantly better on the difficult case than they did on the easy case. Thus, it is not that the physicians were incapable of constructing an accurate situation model from nonstandard text information; it is simply that under normal circumstances such processes are not brought into play.

The journal *Behavioral and Brain Sciences* provides a way to look at the role of misreadings in scholarly controversy. Each main article is accompanied by invited commentaries from qualified scholars, and then the author or authors of the original article respond to these commentaries. Main articles cover a wide range, from neuroscience to social sciences and philosophy. We examined the authors' responses for twenty articles published in the years 1981 and 1982.[2] The mean number of allegations of misreading per author response was close to three, the range being from zero to eight. The commonest allegations were simple oversight and attributing to the author statements that either were not made or were contradicted by statements in the target text.

What do these findings demonstrate? They could be taken to suggest that some experts in the behavioral and brain sciences are poor readers. But the data are hardly definitive on that point. Possibly it was not the commentators who misread the target articles, but the authors of the target articles who misread the commentaries. Or in many cases there may have been defensible differences in interpretation, so that no real failings in reading are indicated. What the findings do show, however, is that reading can be problematic even for people who are experts on the topic in question. This suggests a role for reading expertise that is distinguishable from the role of subject-matter expertise, which is the main point we are trying to make.

TRADE-OFFS BETWEEN DOMAIN EXPERTISE AND LITERATE EXPERTISE

Our argument has been that literate expertise involves a dialectical process that serves to advance domain knowledge. Experts may limit their own development by adopting a facile, knowledge-telling approach to writing that although it may serve immediate purposes, deprives them of the knowledge-transforming benefits of a more expert approach to writing. Similarly, they may limit their development by concentrating too much on extracting targeted information from texts and not engaging in the dialectical process whereby a fuller and deeper representation of what the text says can have a transforming effect on existing knowledge.

It must also be recognized, however, that expert reading and writing, as we have described them, are effortful problem-solving processes that compete for time and mental resources with other activities involved in expert careers. There is, therefore, a trade-off. One could put so much effort into knowledge-transformative writing and deep reading that one would lose ground in pursuing the main goals of the work. "There are those who read books, and there

---

[2] These were all of the "target" articles published in *Behavioral and Brain Sciences* during that period, omitting special issues and book commentaries, where the focus was not on the particular document published but on a larger topic or work.

are those who write books," said a friend of ours, pointing out one painful trade-off with which academic people must deal. He might have added that "there are also those who achieve things worth writing books about." Somehow, experts in learned fields must contrive to do all three – read, write, and do something to write about. Finding the best balance is, of course, an individual matter, and can never be wholly satisfactory. It should help, however, to be aware of the synergistic possibilities of carrying out all three activities in ways that extend the limits of one's expertise, thus making it possible for all three to move to higher levels.

CONCLUSION

In this chapter we have not been concerned with reading and writing expertise in their own right, so much as with how they interact with other forms of expertise. Of the many skills that play supporting roles in expertise, reading and writing are of particular interest, not only because of their generality – they are significant in almost all modern occupations – but more especially because they function at the *growing edge* of expert competence. The least understood aspect of expertise is how it is acquired and perfected. Vague notions of "experience" and "practice" obscure what is undoubtedly the socially most significant issue in the study of expertise, the issue of why there are such great differences in competence among people with equivalent amounts of experience and practice. No one is disturbed by the fact that experienced physicians are better at diagnosis than interns. We are all disturbed by the possibility that our health may fall into the hands of physicians whose diagnostic expertise has not kept pace with their years of experience. We would like to believe that our doctor, among other things, reads medical journals, and not only reads them but understands them in ways that may deepen understanding and alter mistaken beliefs. We would also like to believe that our doctor thinks seriously about our problems and those of other patients and builds up an increasingly sophisticated body of case knowledge. Would it not be reassuring to know that our doctor even goes so far as to put some of that emerging awareness down in writing, the better to think about it?

ACKNOWLEDGMENTS

This chapter draws on research supported by the Ontario Ministry of Education, under its block transfer grant to the Ontario Institute for Studies in Education, and by the Social Sciences and Humanities Research Council of Canada.

REFERENCES

Anzai, Y., & Yokoyama, T. (1984). Internal models in physics problem solving. *Cognition and Instruction, 1*(4), 397–450.

Baker, L. (1985). How do we know when we don't understand? Standards for evaluating text comprehension. In D. L. Forrest-Pressley, G. E. MacKinnon, & T. G. Waller (Eds.), *Metacognition, cognition and human performance: Vol. 1. Theoretical perspectives* (pp. 155–205). Orlando, FL: Academic Press.

Bazerman, C. (1985). Physicists reading physics: Schema-laden purposes and purpose-laden schema. *Written Communication, 2*(1), 3–23.

Beaugrande, R. de. (1984). *Text production: Toward a science of composition.* Norwood, NJ: Ablex.

Bereiter, C., & Bird, M. (1985). Use of thinking aloud in identification and teaching of reading comprehension strategies. *Cognition and Instruction, 2*(2), 131–156.

Bereiter, C., Burtis, P. J., & Scardamalia, M. (1988). Cognitive operations in constructing main points in written composition. *Journal of Memory and Language, 27*(3), 261–278.

Bereiter, C., & Scardamalia, M. (1987). *The psychology of written composition.* Hillsdale, NJ: Erlbaum.

Bereiter, C., & Scardamalia, M. (1989). Intentional learning as a goal of instruction. In L. B. Resnick (Ed.), *Knowing, learning, and instruction: Essays in honor of Robert Glaser* (pp. 361–392). Hillsdale, NJ: Erlbaum.

Bransford, J. D., & Johnson, M. K. (1972). Contextual prerequisites for understanding: Some investigations of comprehension and recall. *Journal of Verbal Learning and Verbal Behavior, 11*(6), 717–726.

Bransford, J. D., Stein, B. S., Shelton, T. S., & Owings, R. A. (1981). Cognition and adaptation: The importance of learning to learn. In J. Harvey (Ed.), *Cognition, social behavior, and the environment* (pp. 93–110). Hillsdale, NJ: Erlbaum.

Brown, A. L., Day, J. D., & Jones, R. S. (1983). The development of plans for summarizing texts. *Child Development, 54*(4), 968–979.

Burtis, P. J., Bereiter, C., Scardamalia, M., & Tetroe, J. (1983). The development of planning in writing. In G. Wells & B. M. Kroll (Eds.), *Explorations in the development of writing* (pp. 153–174). New York: Wiley.

Chi, M. T. H., Glaser, R., & Rees, E. (1982). Expertise in problem solving. In R. Sternberg (Ed.), *Advances in the psychology of human intelligence* (Vol. 1, pp. 17–76). Hillsdale, NJ: Erlbaum.

Coughlin, L. D., & Patel, V. L. (1986, April). *Text comprehension and clinical expertise.* Paper presented at a meeting of the American Educational Research Association, San Francisco.

Davis, R. B., & McNight, C. C. (1979). Modelling the processes of mathematical thinking. *Journal of Children's Mathematical Behavior, 2*(2), 91–113.

Dreyfus, H. L., & Dreyfus, S. E. (1986). *Mind over machine.* New York: Free Press.

Ericsson, K. A., & Staszewski, J. J. (1989). Skilled memory and expertise: Mechanisms of exceptional performance. In D. Klahr & K. Kotovsky (Eds.), *Complex information processing: The impact of Herbert A. Simon* (pp. 235–267). Hillsdale, NJ: Erlbaum.

Flower, L. S. (1979). Writer-based prose: A cognitive basis for problems in writing. *College English, 41*(1), 19–37.

Flower, L. S., & Hayes, J. R. (1980). The cognition of discovery: Defining a rhetorical problem. *College Composition and Communication, 31*(1), 21–32.

Flower, L. S., & Hayes, J. R. (1981). The pregnant pause: An inquiry into the nature of planning. *Research in the Teaching of English, 15*(3), 229–243.

Garner, R. (1980). Monitoring of understanding: An investigation of good and poor readers' awareness of induced miscomprehension of text. *Journal of Reading Behavior, 12*(1), 55–63.

Glaser, R., & Chi, M. T. H. (1988). Overview. In M. T. H. Chi, R. Glaser, & M. J. Farr (Eds.), *The nature of expertise* (pp. xv–xxvii). Hillsdale, NJ: Erlbaum.

Heller, J. I., & Reif, F. (1984). Prescribing effective human problem-solving processes: Problem description in physics. *Cognition and Instruction, 1*(2), 177–216.

John-Steiner, V. (1987). *Notebooks of the mind.* New York: Harper & Row.

Johnston, P., & Afflerbach, P. (1985). The process of constructing main ideas from text. *Cognition and Instruction, 2*(3–4), 207–232.

Larkin, J. H., McDermott, J., Simon, D. P., & Simon, H. A. (1980). Models of competence in solving physics problems. *Cognitive Science, 4*(4), 317–345.

Markman, E. M. (1981). Comprehensive monitoring. In W. P. Dixon (Ed.), *Children's oral communication skills* (pp. 61–84). New York: Academic Press.

National Assessment of Educational Progress. (1981). *Reading, writing, thinking.* Denver: National Assessment of Educational Progress.

Nold, E. W. (1981). Revising. In C. H. Frederiksen & J. F. Dominic (Eds.), *Writing: The nature, development and teaching of written communication* (pp. 67–79). Hillsdale, NJ: Erlbaum.

Paris, P. L. (1986). *Goals and problem solving in written composition.* Unpublished doctoral dissertation, York University, Toronto.

Patel, V., & Groen, G. (1986). Knowledge based solution strategies in medical reasoning. *Cognitive Science, 10*(1), 91–116.

Peters, D. P., & Ceci, S. J. (1982). Peer-review practices of psychological journals: The fate of published articles, submitted again. *Behavioral and Brain Sciences, 5*(2), 187–255.

Riley, M. S., Greeno, J. G., & Heller, J. I. (1983). Development of children's problem-solving ability in arithmetic. In H. P. Ginsburg (Ed.), *The development of mathematical thinking* (pp. 153–196). New York: Academic Press.

Scardamalia, M., & Bereiter, C. (1983). The development of evaluative, diagnostic, and remedial capabilities in children's composing. In M. Martlew (Ed.), *The psychology of written language: Developmental and educational perspectives* (pp. 67–95). New York: Wiley.

Scardamalia, M., & Bereiter, C. (1984). Development of strategies in text processing. In H. Mandl, N. Stein, & T. Trabasso (Eds.), *Learning and comprehension of text* (pp. 379–406). Hillsdale, NJ: Erlbaum.

Scardamalia, M., & Bereiter, C. (1985). Development of dialectical processes in composition. In D. R. Olson, N. Torrance, & A. Hildyard (Eds.), *Literacy, language, and learning: The nature and consequences of reading and writing* (pp. 307–329). Cambridge: Cambridge University Press.

Scardamalia, M., & Bereiter, C. (1987). Knowledge telling and knowledge transforming in written composition. In S. Rosenberg (Ed.), *Advances in applied psycholinguistics: Vol. 2. Reading, writing, and language learning* (pp. 142–175). Cambridge: Cambridge University Press.

Scardamalia, M., Bereiter, C., & Goelman, H. (1982). The role of production factors in writing ability. In M. Nystrand (Ed.), *What writers know: The language, process, and structure of written discourse* (pp. 173–210). New York: Academic Press.

Scardamalia, M., Bereiter, C., & Steinbach, R. (1984). Teachability of reflective processes in written composition. *Cognitive Science, 8*(2), 173–190.

Scardamalia, M., & Paris, P. (1985). The function of explicit discourse knowledge in the development of text representations and composing strategies. *Cognition and Instruction, 2*(1), 1–39.

Shimmerlik, S. M. (1978). Organization theory and memory for prose: A review of the literature. *Review of Educational Research, 48*(1), 103–120.

Sweller, J. (1988). Cognitive load during problem solving: Effects on learning. *Cognitive Science, 12*(2), 257–285.

Sweller, J., Mawer, R. F., & Ward, M. R. (1983). Development of expertise in mathematical problem solving. *Journal of Experimental Psychology: General, 112*(4), 639–661.

van Dijk, T. A., & Kintsch, W. (1983). *Strategies of discourse comprehension.* New York: Academic Press.

Voss, J. F., Blais, J., Means, M. L., Greene, T. R., & Ahwesh, E. (1989). Informal reasoning and subject matter knowledge in the solving of economics problems by naive and novice individuals. In L. B. Resnick (Ed.), *Knowing, learning, and instruction: Essays in honor of Robert Glaser* (pp. 217–249). Hillsdale, NJ: Erlbaum.

Wason, P. C. (Ed.). (1980). Dynamics of writing [special issue]. *Visible Language, 14*(4).

Zbrodoff, N. J. (1984). *Writing stories under time and length constraints.* Unpublished doctoral dissertation, University of Toronto.

8 The process–performance paradox in expert judgment

How can experts know so much and predict so badly?

COLIN F. CAMERER AND ERIC J. JOHNSON

1. INTRODUCTION

A mysterious fatal disease strikes a large minority of the population. The disease is incurable, but an expensive drug can keep victims alive. Congress decides that the drug should be given to those whose lives can be extended longest, which only a few specialists can predict. The experts work around the clock searching for a cure; allocating the drug is a new chore they would rather avoid.

In research on decision making there are two views about such experts. The views suggest different technologies for modeling experts' decisions so that they can do productive research rather than make predictions. One view, which emerges from behavioral research on decision making, is skeptical about the experts. Data suggest that a wide range of experts like our hypothetical specialists are not much better predictors than less expert physicians, or interns. Furthermore, this view suggests a simple technology for replacing experts – a simple linear regression model (perhaps using medical judgments as inputs). The regression does not mimic the thought process of an expert, but it probably makes *more* accurate predictions than an expert does.

The second view, stemming from research in cognitive science, suggests that expertise is a rare skill that develops only after much instruction, practice, and experience. The cognition of experts is more sophisticated than that of novices; this sophistication is presumed to produce better predictions. This view suggests a model that strives to mimic the decision policies of experts – an "expert (or knowledge-based) system" containing lists of rules experts use in judging longevity. An expert system tries to match, not exceed, the performance of the expert it represents.

In this chapter we describe and integrate these two perspectives. Integration comes from realizing that the behavioral and cognitive science approaches have different goals: Whereas behavioral decision theory emphasizes the *performance* of experts, cognitive science usually emphasizes differences in experts' *processes* (E. Johnson, 1988).

A few caveats are appropriate. Our review is selective; it is meant to emphasize the differences between expert performance and process. The generic

195

decision-making task we describe usually consists of repeated predictions, based on the same set of observable variables, about a complicated outcome – graduate school success, financial performance, health – that is rather unpredictable. For the sake of brevity, we shall not discuss other important tasks such as probability estimation or revision, inference, categorization, or trade-offs among attributes, costs, and benefits.

The literature we review is indirectly related to the well-known "heuristics and biases" approach (e.g., Kahneman, Slovic, & Tversky, 1982). Our theme is that experts know a lot but predict poorly. Perhaps their knowledge is biased, if it comes from judgment heuristics or they use heuristics in applying it. We can only speculate about this possibility (as we do later, in a few places) until further research draws the connection more clearly.

For our purposes, an expert is a person who is experienced at making predictions in a domain and has some professional or social credentials. The experts described here are no slouches: They are psychologists, doctors, academics, accountants, gamblers, and parole officers who are intelligent, well paid, and often proud. We draw no special distinction between them and extraordinary experts, or experts acclaimed by peers (cf. Shanteau, 1988). We suspect that our general conclusions would apply to more elite populations of experts,[1] but clearly there have been too few studies of these populations.

The chapter is organized as follows: In section 2 we review what we currently know about how well experts perform decision tasks, then in section 3 we review recent work on expert decision processes. Section 4 integrates the views described in sections 2 and 3. Then we examine the implications of this work for decision research and for the study of expertise in general.

2. PERFORMANCE OF EXPERTS

Most of the research in the behavioral decision-making approach to expertise has been organized around performance of experts. A natural measure of expert performance is predictive accuracy; later, we discuss other aspects. Modern research on expert accuracy emanates from Sarbin (1944), who drew an analogy between clinical reasoning and statistical (or "actuarial") judgment. His data, and the influential book by Meehl (1954), established that in many clinical prediction tasks experts were *less* accurate than simple formulas based on observable variables. As Dawes and Corrigan (1974, p. 97) wrote, "the statistical analysis was thought to provide a floor to which the judgment of the experienced clinician could be compared. The floor turned out to be a ceiling."

---

[1] While presenting a research seminar discussing the application of linear models, Robyn Dawes reported Einhorn's (1972) classic finding that three experts' judgments of Hodgkin's disease severity were uncorrelated with actual severity (measured by how long patients lived). One seminar participant asked Dawes what would happen if a certain famous physician were studied. The questioner was sure that Dr. So-and-so makes accurate judgments. Dawes called Einhorn; the famous doctor turned out to be subject 2.

2.1. A language for quantitative studies of performance

In many studies, linear regression techniques are used to construct statistical models of expert judgments (and to improve those judgments) and distinguish components of judgment accuracy and error.[2] These techniques are worth reviewing briefly because they provide a useful language for discussing accuracy and its components.

A subject's judgment (denoted Y_s) depends on a set of informational cues (denoted $X_1, \ldots, X_n$). The cues could be measured objectively (college grades) or subjectively by experts (evaluating letters of recommendation). The actual environmental outcome (or "criterion") (denoted Y_e) is also assumed to be a function of the same cues.

In the comparisons to be described, several kinds of regressions are commonly used. One such regression, the "actuarial" model, predicts outcomes Y_e based on observable cues X_i. The model naturally separates Y_e into a predictable component $\hat{Y}_e$, a linear combination[3] of cues weighted by regression coefficients $b_{i,e}$, and an unpredictable error component Z_e. That is,

$$Y_e = \sum b_{i,e} X_i + z_e \qquad \text{(actuarial model)} \qquad (1)$$
$$= \hat{Y}_e + z_e$$

Figure 8.1 illustrates these relationships, as well as others that we shall discuss subsequently.

2.2. Experts versus actuarial models

The initial studies compared expert judgments with those of actuarial models. That is, the correlation between the expert judgment Y_s and the outcome Y_e (often denoted r_a, for "achievement") was compared with the correlation between the model's predicted outcome $\hat{Y}_e$ and the actual outcome Y_e (denoted R_e).[4]

Meehl (1954) reviewed about two dozen studies. Cross-validated actuarial models outpredicted clinical judgment (i.e., R_e was greater than r_a) in all but one study. Now there have been about a hundred studies; experts did better in only a handful of them (mostly medical tasks in which well-developed theory outpredicted limited statistical experience; see Dawes, Faust, & Meehl,

---

[2] Many regression studies use the general "lens model" proposed by Egon Brunswik (1952) and extended by Hammond (1955) and others. The lens model shows the interconnection between two systems: an ecology or environment, and a person making judgments. The notation in the text is mostly lens-model terminology.

[3] Although the functions relating cues to the judgment and the outcome can be of any form, linear relationships are most often used, because they explain judgments and outcomes surprisingly well, even when outcomes are known to be nonlinear functions of the cues (Dawes & Corrigan, 1974).

[4] The correlation between the actuarial-model prediction and the outcome Y_e is the square root of the regression R^2, and is denoted R_e. A more practical measure of actuarial-model accuracy is the "cross-validated" correlation, when regression weights derived on one sample are used to predict a new sample of Y_e values.

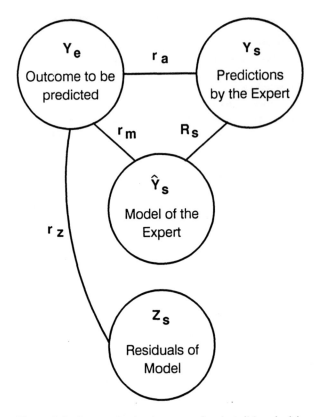

Figure 8.1. A quantitative language for describing decision performance.

1989). The studies have covered many different tasks – university admissions, recidivism or violence of criminals, clinical pathology, medical diagnosis, financial investment, sports, weather forecasting. Thirty years after his book was published, Meehl (1986, p. 373) suggested that "there is no controversy in social science that shows such a large body of qualitatively diverse studies coming out so uniformly in the same direction."

2.3. Experts versus improper models

Despite their superiority to clinical judgment, actuarial models are difficult to use because the outcome Y_e must be measured, to provide the raw data for deriving regression weights. It can be costly or time-consuming to measure outcomes (for recidivism or medical diagnosis), or definitions of outcomes can be ambiguous (What is "success" for a Ph.D.?). And past outcomes must be used to fit cross-validated regression weights to predict current outcomes, which makes models vulnerable to changes in true coefficients over time. Therefore, "improper"[5] models – which derive regression weights without using Y_e – might be more useful and nearly as accurate as proper actuarial models.

In one improper method, regression weights are derived from the Y_s judgments themselves; then cues are weighted by the derived weights and summed. This procedure amounts to separating the overall expert judgment Y_s into two components, a modeled component $\hat{Y}_s$ and a residual component z_s, and using only the modeled component $\hat{Y}_s$ as a prediction.[6] That is,

$$Y_s = \Sigma b_{is} X_i + z_s$$
$$= \hat{Y}_s + z_s \qquad (2)$$

If the discarded residual z_s is mostly random error, the modeled component $\hat{Y}_s$ will correlate more highly with the outcome than will the overall judgment, Y_s. (In standard terminology, the correlation between $\hat{Y}_s$ and Y_e, denoted r_m, will be higher than r_a.)

This method is called "bootstrapping" because it can improve judgments without any outcome information: It pulls experts up by their bootstraps. Bowman (1963) first showed that bootstrapping improved judgments in production scheduling; similar improvements were found by Goldberg (1970) in clinical predictions based on MMPI scores[7] and by Dawes (1971) in graduate admissions. A cross-study comparison showed that bootstrapping works very generally, but usually adds only a small increment to predictive accuracy (Camerer, 1981a). Table 8.1 shows some of those results. Accuracy can be usefully dissected with the lens-model equation, an identity relating several interesting correlations. Einhorn's (1974) version of the equation states

$$r_a = r_m R_s + r_z (1 - R_s^2)^{1/2} \qquad (3)$$

where R_s^2 is the bootstrapping model R^2 (how closely the judge resembles the linear model), and r_z is the correlation between bootstrapping-model residuals z_s and outcomes Y_e (the "residual validity"). If the residuals z_s represent only random error in weighing and combining the cues, r_z will be close to zero. In this case, r_m will certainly be larger than r_a, and because $R_s \leq 1$, bootstrapping will improve judgments. But even if r_z is greater than zero (presumably because residuals contain some information that is correlated with outcomes), bootstrapping works unless

---

[5] By contrast, actuarial models often are called "optimal linear models," because by definition no linear combination of the cues can predict Y_e more accurately.

[6] Of course, such an explanation is "paramorphic" (Hoffman, 1960): It describes judgments in a purely statistical way, *as if* experts were weighing and combining cues in their heads; the process they use might be quite different. However, Einhorn, Kleinmuntz, and Kleinmuntz (1979) argued persuasively that the paramorphic regression approach might capture process indirectly.

[7] Because suggested Minnesota Multiphasic Personality Inventory (MMPI) cutoffs were originally created by statistical analysis, it may seem unsurprising that a statistical model beats a judge who tries to mimic it. But the model combines scores *linearly*, whereas judges typically use various scores in configural nonlinear combinations.

$$r_z \geq r_m \left(\frac{1 - R_s}{1 + R_s} \right)^{\frac{1}{2}} \tag{4}$$

For $R_s = .6$ (a reasonable value; see Table 8.1), residual validity r_z must be about half as large as model accuracy for experts to outperform their own bootstrapping models. This rarely occurs.

When there are not many judgments, compared with the number of variables, the regression weights in a bootstrapping model cannot be estimated reliably. Then one can simply weight the cues equally[8] and add them up. Dawes and Corrigan (1974) showed that equal weights worked remarkably well in several empirical comparisons (the accuracies of some of these are shown in the column r_{ew}, in Table 8.1). Simulations show that equal weighting generally works as well as least squares estimation of weights unless there are twenty times as many observations as predictors (Einhorn & Hogarth, 1975). As Dawes and Corrigan (1974) put it, "the whole trick is to decide what variables to look at and then to know how to add" (p. 105).

2.4. Training and experience: experts versus novices

Studies have shown that expert judgments are less accurate than those of statistical models of varying sophistication. Two other useful comparisons are those between experts and novices and between experienced and inexperienced experts.

Garb (1989) reviewed more than fifty comparisons of judgments by clinical psychologists and novices. The comparisons suggest that (academic) training helps but additional experience does not. Trained clinicians and graduate students were more accurate than novices (typically untrained students, or secretaries) in using the MMPI to judge personality disorders. Students did better and better with each year of graduate training. The effect of training was not large (novices might classify 28% correctly, and experts 40%), but it existed in many studies. Training, however, generally did *not* help in interpreting projective tests (drawings, Rorschach inkblots, and sentence-completion tests); using such tests, clinical psychologists probably are no more accurate than auto mechanics or insurance salesmen.

Training has some effects on accuracy, but experience has almost none. In judging personality and neurophysiological disorders, for example, clinicians do no better than advanced graduate students. Among experts with varying amounts of experience, the correlations between amount of clinical experience and accuracy are roughly zero. Libby and Frederick (1989) found that experience improved the accuracy of auditors' explanations of audit errors only slightly (although even inexperienced auditors were better than students).

In medical judgments too, training helps, but experience does not. Gustaf-

---

[8] Of course, variables must be standardized by dividing them by their sample standard deviations. Otherwise, a variable with a wide range would account for more than its share of the variation in the equally weighted sum.

Table 8.1. *Examples of regression-study results*

Study	Prediction task	Mean accuracy of:					
		Model fit, R_s	Judge, r_a	Bootstrapping model, r_m	Bootstrapping residuals, r_z	Equal-weight model, r_{ew}	Actuarial model,[a] R_e
Goldberg (1970)	Psychosis vs. neurosis	.77	.28	.31	.07	.34	.45
Dawes (1971)	Ph.D. admissions	.78	.19	.25	.01	.48	.38
Einhorn (1972)	Disease severity	.41	.01	.13	.06	n.a.	.35
Libby (1976)[b]	Bankruptcy	.79	.50	.53	.13	n.a.	.67
Wiggens & Kohen (1971)	Grades	.85	.33	.50	.01	.60	.57

[a]All are cross-validated R_e except Einhorn (1972) and Libby (1976).
[b]Figures cited are recalculations by Goldberg (1976).
Source: Adapted from Camerer (1981a) and Dawes & Corrigan (1974).

son (1963) found no difference between residents and surgeons in predicting the length of hospital stay after surgery. Kundel and LaFollette (1972) reported that novices and first-year medical students were unable to detect lesions from radiographs of abnormal lungs, but fourth-year students (who had had some training in radiography) were as good as full-time radiologists.

These tasks usually have a rather low performance ceiling. Graduate training may provide all the experience one requires to approach the ceiling. But the myth that additional experience helps is persistent. One of the psychology professors who recently revised the MMPI said that "anybody who can count can score it [the MMPI], but it takes expertise to interpret it." (*Philadelphia Inquirer*, 1989). Yet Goldberg's (1970) data suggest that the only expertise required is the ability to add scores with a hand calculator or paper and pencil.

If a small amount of training can make a person as accurate as an experienced clinical psychologist or doctor, as the data imply, then lightly trained paraprofessionals could replace heavily trained experts for many routine kinds of diagnoses. Citing Shortliffe, Buchanan, and Feigenbaum (1979), Garb (1989) suggested that "intelligent high school graduates, selected in large part because of poise and warmth of personality, can provide competent medical care for a limited range of problems when guided by protocols after only 4 to 8 weeks of training."

It is conceivable that outstanding experts are more accurate than models and graduate students in some tasks. For instance, in Goldberg's (1959) study of organic brain damage diagnoses, a well-known expert (who worked very slowly) was right 83% of the time, whereas other Ph.D. clinical psychologists got 65% right. Whether such extraordinary expertise is a reliable phenomenon or a statistical fluke is a matter for further research.

2.5. Expert calibration

Whereas experts may predict less accurately than models, and only slightly more accurately than novices, they seem to have better self-insight about the accuracy of their predictions. Such self-insight is called "calibration." Most people are poorly calibrated, offering erroneous reports of the quality of their predictions, and these reports systematically err in the direction of overconfidence: When they say a class of events are 80% likely, those events occur less than 80% of the time (Lichtenstein, Fischhoff, & Phillips, 1977). There is some evidence that experts are less overconfident than novices. For instance, Levenberg (1975) had subjects look at "kinetic family drawings" to detect whether the children who drew them were normal. The results were, typically, a small victory for training: Psychologists and secretaries got 66% and 61% right, respectively (a coinflip would get half right). Of these cases about which subjects were "positively certain," the psychologists and secretaries got 76% and 59% right, respectively. The psychologists were better calibrated than novices – they used the phrase "positively certain" more cautiously (and appropriately) – but they were still overconfident.

Better calibration of experts has also been found in some other studies (Garb, 1989). Expert calibration is better than novice calibration in bridge (Keren, in press), but not in blackjack (Wagenaar & Keren, 1985). Doctors' judgments of pneumonia and skull fracture are badly calibrated (Christensen-Szalanski & Bushyhead, 1981; DeSmet, Fryback, & Thornbury, 1979). Weather forecasters are extremely well calibrated (Murphy & Winkler, 1977). Experiments with novices showed that training improved calibration, reducing extreme overconfidence in estimating probabilities and numerical quantities (Lichtenstein et al., 1977)

2.6. Summary: expert performance

The depressing conclusion from these studies is that expert judgments in most clinical and medical domains are no more accurate than those of lightly trained novices. (We know of no comparable reviews of other domains, but we suspect that experts are equally unimpressive in most aesthetic, commercial, and physical judgments.) And expert judgments have been worse than those of the simplest statistical models in virtually all domains that have been studied. Experts are sometimes less overconfident than novices, but not always.

3. EXPERT DECISION PROCESSES

The picture of expert performance painted by behavioral decision theorists is unflattering. Why are experts predicting so badly? We know that many experts have special cognitive and memory skills (Chase & Simon, 1973; Ericsson & Polson, 1988; Larkin, McDermott, Simon, & Simon, 1980). Do expert *decision-makers* have similar strategies and skill? If so, why don't they perform better? Three kinds of evidence help answer these questions: process analyses of expert judgments, indirect analyses using regression models, and laboratory studies in which subjects become "artificial experts" in a simple domain.

3.1. Direct evidence: process analyses of experts

The rules and cues experts use can be discovered by using process tracing techniques – protocol analysis and monitoring of information acquisition. Such studies have yielded consistent conclusions across a diverse set of domains.

Search is contingent. If people think like a regression model, weighting cues and adding them, then cue search will be simple – the same variables will be examined, in the same sequence, in every case. Novices behave that way. But experts have a more active pattern of contingent search: Subsets of variables are considered in each case, in different sequences. Differences between novice and expert searches have been found in studies of financial analysts

(Bouman, 1980; E. Johnson, 1988), auditors (Bedard & Mock, 1989), graduate admissions (E. Johnson, 1980), neurologists (Kleinmuntz, 1968), and physicians (Elstein, Shulman, & Sprafka, 1978; P. Johnson, Hassebrock, Duran, & Moller, 1982).

Experts search less. A common finding in studies of expert cognition is that information processing is less costly for experts than for novices. For example, expert waiters (Ericsson & Chase, 1981) and chess players (Chase & Simon, 1973) have exceptional memory skills. Their memory allows more efficient encoding of task-specific information; if they wanted to, experts could search and sit cheaply through more information. But empirical studies show that experts use *less* information than novices, rather than more, in auditing (Bedard, 1989; Bedard & Mock, 1989), financial analysis (Bouman, 1980; E. Johnson, 1988), and product choice (Bettman & Park, 1980; Brucks, 1985; E. Johnson & Russo, 1984).

Experts use more knowledge. Experts often search contingently, for limited sets of variables, because they know a great deal about their domains (Bouman, 1980; Elstein et al., 1978; Libby & Frederick, 1989). Experts perform a kind of diagnostic reasoning, matching the cues in a specific case to prototypes in a casual brand of hypothesis testing. Search is contingent because different sets of cues are required for each hypothesis test. Search is limited because only a small set of cues are relevant to a particular hypothesis.

3.2. Indirect evidence: dissecting residuals

The linear regression models described in section 2 provide a simple way to partition expert judgment into components. The bootstrapped judgment is a linear combination of observed cues; the residual is everything else. By dissecting the residual statistically, we can learn how the decision process experts use deviates from the simple linear combination of cues. It deviates in three ways.

Experts often use configural choice rules. In configural rules, the impact of one variable depends on the values of other variables. An example is found in clinical lore on interpretation of the MMPI. Both formal instruction and verbal protocols of experienced clinicians give rules that note the state of more than one variable. A nice example is given by an early rule-based system constructed by Kleinmuntz (1968) using clinicians' verbal protocols. Many of the rules in the system reflect such configural reasoning: "Call maladjusted if $P_a \geq 70$ unless $M_t \leq 6$, and $K \geq 65$." Because linear regression models weight each cue independently, configural rules will not be captured by the linear form, and the effects of configural judgment will be reflected in the regression residual.

Experts use "broken-leg cues." Cues that are rare but highly diagnostic often are called broken-leg cues, from an example cited by Meehl (1954; pp. 24–

25): A clinician is trying to predict whether or not Professor A will go to the movies on a given night. A regression model predicts that the professor will go, but the clinician knows that the professor recently broke his leg. The cue "broken leg" probably will get no weight in a regression model of past cases, because broken legs are rare.[9] But the clinician can confidently predict that the professor will not go to the movies. The clinician's recognition of the broken-leg cue, which is missing from the regression model, will be captured by the residual. Note that while the frequency of any one broken-leg cue is rare, in "the mass of cases, there may be *many (different) rare kinds of factors*" (Meehl, 1954, p. 25).

Note how the use of configural rules and broken-leg cues is consistent with the process data described in section 3. To use configural rules, experts must search for different sets of cues in different sequences. Experts also can use their knowledge about cue diagnosticity to focus on a limited number of highly diagnostic broken-leg cues. For example, in E. Johnson's (1988) study of financial analysts, experts were much more accurate than novices because they could interpret the impact of news events similar to broken-leg cues.

Experts weight cues inconsistently and make errors in combining them. When experts do combine cues linearly, any inconsistencies in weighting cues, and errors in adding them, will be reflected in the regression residual. Thus, if experts use configural rules and broken-leg cues, their effects will be contained in the residuals of a linear bootstrapping model. The residuals also contain inconsistencies and error. By comparing residual variance and test–retest reliability, Camerer (1981b) estimated that only about 40% of the variance in residuals was error,[10] and 60% was systematic use of configural rules and broken-leg cues. (Those fractions were remarkably consistent across different studies.) The empirical correlation between residuals and outcomes, r_z, however, averaged only about .05 (Camerer, 1981a) over a wider range of studies. Experts are using configural rules and broken-leg cues systematically, but they are not highly correlated with outcomes. Of course, there may be some domains in which residuals are more valid.[11]

3.3. Artificial experts

A final kind of process evidence comes from "artificial experts," subjects who spend much time in an experimental environment trying to induce accurate judgmental rules. A lot of this research belongs to the tradition

---

[9] Unless a broken leg has occurred in the sample used to derive regression weights, the cue "broken leg" will not vary and will get no regression weight.
[10] These data correct the presumption in the early bootstrapping literature (e.g., Dawes, 1971; Goldberg, 1970) that residuals were entirely human error.
[11] A recent study with sales forecasters showed a higher r_z, around .2 (Blattberg & Hoch, 1990). Even though their residuals were quite accurate, the best forecasters only did about as well as the linear model. In a choice between models and experts, models will win, but a mechanical combination of the two is better still: Adding bootstrapping residuals to an actuarial model increased predictive accuracy by about 10%.

of multiple-cue probability learning (MCPL) experiments that stretches back decades, with the pessimistic conclusion that rule induction is difficult, particularly when outcomes have random error. We shall give three more recent examples that combine process analysis with a rule induction task.

Several studies have used protocol analysis to determine *what* it is that artificial experts have learned. Perhaps the most ambitious attempts to study extended learning in complex environments were Klayman's studies of cue discovery (Klayman, 1988; Klayman & Ha, 1985): Subjects looked at a complex computer display consisting of geometric shapes that affected the distance traveled by ray traces from one point on the display to another. The true rule for travel distance was determined by a complex linear model consisting of seven factors that varied in salience in the display. None of Klayman's subjects induced the correct rule over 14 half-hour sessions, but their performances improved steadily. Some improvement came from discovering correct cues (subjects correctly identified only 2.83 of 7 cues, on average). Subjects who systematically experimented, by varying one cue and holding others fixed, learned faster and better than others. Because the cues varied greatly in how much they affected distance, it was important to weight them differently, but more than four-fifths of the rules stated by subjects did not contain any numerical elements (such as weights) at all. In sum, cue discovery played a clear role in developing expertise in this task, but learning about the relative importance of cues did not.

In a study by Meyer (1987), subjects learned which attributes of a hypothetical metal alloy led to increases in its hardness. As in Klayman's study, subjects continued to learn rules over a long period of time. The true rule for hardness (which was controlled by the experimenter) was linear, but most subjects induced configural rules. Subjects made only fairly accurate predictions, because the true linear rule could be mimicked by nonlinear rules. Learning (better performance) consisted of adding more elaborate and baroque configural rules, rather than inducing the true linear relationships.

In a study by Camerer (1981b), subjects tried to predict simulated wheat-price changes that depended on two variables and a large interaction between them (i.e., the true rule was configural). Subjects did learn to use the interaction in their judgments, but with so much error that a linear bootstrapping model that omitted the interaction was more accurate. Similarly, in E. Johnson's (1988) financial-analyst study, even though expert analysts used highly diagnostic news events, their judgments were inferior to those of a simple linear model.

3.4. Summary: expert decision processes

Studies of decision processes indicate that expert decision makers are like experts in other domains: They know more and use their knowledge to guide search for small subsets of information, which differ with each case. Residuals from bootstrapping models and learning experiments also show that experts use configural rules and cues not captured by linear models (but these are not always predictive). The process evidence indicates that experts know more, but what they know does not enable them to outpredict simple statistical rules. Why not?

4. RECONCILING THE PERFORMANCE AND PROCESS VIEWS OF EXPERTISE

One explanation for the process–performance paradox is that prediction is only one task that experts must perform; they may do better on other tasks. Later we shall consider this explanation further. Another explanation is that experts are quick to develop configural rules that often are inaccurate, but they keep these rules or switch to equally poor ones. (The same may be true of broken-leg cues.) This argument raises three questions, which we address in turn: Why do experts develop configural rules? Why are configural rules often inaccurate? Why do inaccurate configural rules persist?

4.1. Why do experts develop configural rules?

Configural rules are easier. Consider two common classes of configural rules, conjunctive (hire Hope for the faculty if she has glowing letters of recommendation, good grades, *and* an interesting thesis) and disjunctive (draft Michael for the basketball team if he can play guard *or* forward *or* center extremely well). Configural rules are easy because they bypass the need to trade off different cues (Are recommendations better predictors than grades?), avoiding the cumbersome weighting and combination of information. Therefore, configural rules take much less effort than optimal rules and can yield nearly optimal choices (E. Johnson & Payne, 1985).[12]

Besides avoiding difficult trade-offs, configural rules require only a simple categorization of cue values. With conjunctive and disjunctive rules, one need only know whether or not a cue is above a cutoff; attention can be allocated economically to categorize the values of many cues crudely, rather than categorizing only one or two cues precisely.

Prior theory often suggests configural rules. In his study of wheat prices, Camerer (1981b) found that subjects could learn of the existence of a large configural interaction only when cue labels suggested the interaction a priori. Similarly, cue labels may cause subjects to learn configural rules where they are inappropriate, as in Meyer's (1987) study of alloy hardness. These prior beliefs about cue–outcome correlations often will be influenced by the "representativeness" (Tversky & Kahneman, 1982) of cues to outcomes; the representativeness heuristic will sometimes cause errors.

---

[12] Configural rules are especially useful for narrowing a large set of choices to a subset of candidates for further consideration.

Besides their cognitive ease and prior suggestion, complex configural rules are easy to learn because it is easy to weave a causal narrative around a configural theory. These coherent narratives cement a dependence between variables that is easy to express but may overweight these "causal" cues, at the cost of ignoring others. Linear combinations yield no such coherence. Meehl (1954) provides the following example from clinicial psychology, describing the case of a woman who was ambivalent toward her husband. One night the woman came home from a movie alone. Then:

> Entering the bedroom, she was terrified to see, for a fraction of a second, a large black bird ("a raven, I guess") perched on her pillow next to her husband's head. . . . She recalls "vaguely, some poem we read in high school." (p. 39)

Meehl hypothesized that the woman's vision was a fantasy, based on the poem "The Raven" by Edgar Allen Poe: "The [woman's] fantasy is that like Poe's Lenore, she will die or at least go away and leave him [the husband] alone." Meehl was using a configural rule that gave more weight to the raven vision because the woman knew the Poe poem. A linear rule, simply weighting the dummy variables "raven" and "knowledge of Poe," yields a narrative that is much clumsier than Meehl's compelling analysis. Yet such a model might well pay attention to other factors, such as the woman's age, education, and so forth, which might also help explain her ambivalence.

Configural rules can emerge naturally from trying to explain past cases. People learn by trying to fit increasingly sophisticated general rules to previous cases (Brehmer, 1980; Meyer, 1987). Complicated configural rules offer plenty of explanatory flexibility. For example, a 6-variable model permits 15 two-way interactions, and a 10-variable model allows 45 interactions.[13] In sports, for instance, statistics are so plentiful and refined that it is easy to construct subtle "configuralities" when global rules fail. Bucky Dent was an average New York Yankee infielder, except in the World Series, where he played "above his head," hitting much better than predicted by his overall average. (The variable "Dent" was not highly predictive of success, but adding the interaction "Dent" × "Series" was.)[14] Because people are reluctant to accept the possibility of random error (Einhorn, 1986), increasingly complicated configural explanations are born.

Inventing special cases is an important mechanism for learning in more

---

[13] A linear model with k cues has only k degrees of freedom, but the k variables offer $k(k - 1)/2$ multiplicative two-variable interactions (and lots of higher-order interactions).

[14] We cannot determine whether Dent was truly better in the World Series or just lucky in a limited number of Series appearances. Yet his success in "big games" obviously influenced the Yankees' owner, George Steinbrenner (who has not otherwise distinguished himself as an expert decision-maker). He named Dent manager of the Yankees shortly after this conference was held, citing his ability as a player "to come through when it mattered." Dent was later fired 49 games into the season (18 wins, 31 losses), and the Yankees had the worst record in Major League baseball at the time.

deterministic environments, where it can be quite effective. The tendency of decision-makers to build special-case rules mirrors more adaptive processes of induction (e.g., Holland, Holyoak, Nisbett, & Thagard, 1986, chapter 3, esp. pp. 88–89) that can lead to increased accuracy. As Holland and associates pointed out, however, the validity of these mechanisms rests on the ability to check each specialization on many cases. In noisy domains like the ones we are discussing, there are few replications. It was unlikely, for example, that Dent would appear in many World Series, and even if he did, other "unique" circumstances (opposing pitching, injuries, etc.) could always yield further "explanatory" factors.

In sum, configural rules are appealing because they are easy to use, have plausible causal explanations, and offer many degrees of freedom to fit data. Despite these advantages, configural rules may have a downfall, as detailed in the next section.

4.2. Why are configural rules often inaccurate?

One reason configural rules may be inaccurate is that whereas they are induced under specific and often rare conditions, they may well be applied to a larger set of cases. Often, people induce such rules from observation, they will be overgeneralizing from a small sample (expecting the sample to be more "representative" of a population that it is – Tversky & Kahneman, 1982). This is illustrated by a verbal protocol recorded by a physician who was chair of a hospital's admissions committee for house staff, interns, and residents. Seeing an applicant from Wayne State who had very high board scores, the doctor recalled a promising applicant from the same school who had perfect board scores. Unfortunately, after being admitted, the prior aspirant had done poorly and left the program. The physician recalled this case and applied it to the new one: "We have to be quite careful with people from Wayne State with very high board scores. . . . We have had problems in the past."

Configural rules may also be wrong because the implicit theories that underlie them are wrong. A large literature on "illusory correlation" contains many examples of variables that are thought to be correlated with outcomes (because they are similar) but are not. For example, most clinicians and novices think that people who see male features or androgynous figures in Rorschach ink-blots are more likely to be homosexual. They are not (Chapman & Chapman, 1967, 1969). A successful portfolio manager we know refused to buy stock in firms run by overweight CEOs, believing that control of one's weight and control of a firm are correlated. Because variables that are only illusorily correlated with outcomes are likely to be used by both novices and experts, the small novice–expert difference suggests that illusory correlations may be common.

Configural rules are also likely to be unrobust to small errors, or "brittle."[15]

---

[15] Although the robustness of linear models is well established, we know of no analogous work on the *un*robustness of configural rules.

Linear models are extremely robust; they fit nonlinear data remarkably well (Yntema & Torgerson, 1961). That is why omitting a configural interaction from a bootstrapping model does not greatly reduce the accuracy of the model.[16] In contrast, we suspect that small errors in measurement may have great impacts on configural rules. For example, the conjunctive rule "require good grades *and* test scores" will lead to mistakes if a test score is not a predictor of success or if the cutoff for "good grades" is wrong; the linear rule that weights grades and scores and combines them is less vulnerable to either error.

4.3. Why do inaccurate configural rules persist?

One of the main lessons of decision research is that feedback is crucial for learning. Inaccurate configural rules may persist because experts who get slow, infrequent, or unclear feedback will not learn that their rules are wrong. When feedback must be sought, inaccurate rules may persist because people tend to search instinctively for evidence that will confirm prior theories (Klayman & Ha, 1985). Even when feedback is naturally provided, rather than sought, confirming evidence is more retrievable or "available" than disconfirming evidence (Tversky & Kahneman, 1973). The disproportionate search and recall of confirming instances will sustain experts' faith in inaccurate configural rules. Even when evidence does disconfirm a particular rule, we suspect that the natural tendencies to construct such rules (catalogued earlier) will cause experts to refine their rules rather than discard them.

4.4. Nonpredictive functions of expertise

The thinking of experts is rich with subtle distinctions, novel categories, and complicated configural rules for making predictions. We have given several reasons why such categories and rules might arise, and persist even if they are inaccurate. Our arguments provide one possible explanation why knowledgeable experts, paradoxically, are no better at making predictions than novices and simple models.

Another explanation is that the knowledge that experts acquire as they learn may not be useful for making better predictions about important long-range outcomes, but it may be useful for other purposes. Experts are indispensable for measuring variables (Sawyer, 1966) and discovering new ones (E. Johnson, 1988).

Furthermore, as experts learn, they may be able to make more kinds of predictions, even if they are no more accurate; we speculate that they mistake their increasing fertility for increasing accuracy. Taxi drivers know lots of alternative routes when they see traffic on the Schuylkill Expressway (cf.

---

[16] Linear models are robust to nonlinearities provided the relationship between each predictor and outcome has the same direction for any values of the other predictors (although the relationship's magnitude will vary). This property is sometimes called "conditional monotonicity."

Chase, 1983), and they probably can predict their speeds on those alternative routes better than a novice can. But can the experts predict whether there will be heavy traffic on the expressway better than a statistical model can (using time of day, day of week, and weather, for example)? We doubt it.

There are also many social benefits of expertise that people can provide better than models can. Models can make occasional large mistakes that experts, having common sense, would know to avoid (Shanteau, 1988).[17] Experts can explain themselves better, and people usually feel that an expert's intuitive judgments are fairer than those of a model (cf. Dawes, 1971).

Some of these attitudes toward experts stem from the myth that experts are accurate predictors, or the hope that an expert will never err.[18] Many of these social benefits should disappear with time, if people learn that models are better; until then, experts have an advantage. (Large corporations have learned: They use models in scoring credit risks, adjusting insurance claims, and other activities where decisions are routine and cost savings are large. Consumers do think that such rules are unfair, but the cost savings overwhelm their objections.)

5. IMPLICATIONS FOR UNDERSTANDING EXPERT DECISION MAKING

Our review produces a consistent, if depressing, picture of expert decision-makers. They are successful at generating hypotheses and inducing complex decision rules. The result is a more efficient search of the available information directed by goals and aided by the experts' superior store of knowledge. Unfortunately, their knowledge and rules have little impact on experts' performance. Sometimes experts are more accurate than novices (though not always), but they are rarely better than simple statistical models.

An inescapable conclusion of this research is that experts do some things well and others poorly. Sawyer (1966) found that expert measurement of cues, and statistical combination of them, worked better than expert combination or statistical measurement. Techniques that combine experts' judgments about configural and broken-leg cues with actuarial models might improve performance especially well (Blattberg & Hoch, 1990; E. Johnson, 1988).

Of course, expert performance relative to models depends critically on the

---

[17] This possibility has been stressed by Ken Hammond in discussions of analytical versus intuitive judgment (e.g., Hammond, Hamm, Grassia, & Pearson, 1987). For example, most of the unorthodox moves generated by the leading backgammon computer program (which beat a world champion in 1979) are stupid mistakes an expert would catch; a few are brilliant moves that might not occur to an expert.

[18] A model necessarily errs, by fixing regression coefficients and ignoring many variables. It "accepts error to make less error" (Einhorn, 1986). An expert, by changing regression coefficients and selecting variables, conceivably could be right every time. This difference is made dramatic by a medical example. A statistician developed a simple linear model to make routine diagnoses. Its features were printed on a card doctors could carry around; the card showed several cues and how to add them. Doctors wouldn't use it because they couldn't defend it in the inevitable lawsuits that would result after the model would have made a mistake.

task and the importance of configural and broken-leg cues. There may be tasks in which experts beat models, but it is hard to think of examples. In pricing antiques, classic cars, or unusual real estate (e.g., houses over $5 million), there may be many broken-leg cues that give experts an advantage, but a model including the expert-rated cue "special features" may also do well.

Tasks involving pattern recognition, like judging the prospective taste of gourmet recipes or the beauty of faces or paintings, seem to involve many configural rules that favor experts. But if one adds expert-rated cues like "consistency" (in recipes) or "symmetry" (in faces) to linear models, the experts' configural edge may disappear.

Another class of highly configural tasks includes those in which variable weights change across subsamples or stages. For instance, one should play the beginning and end of a backgammon or chess game differently. A model that picks moves by evaluating position features, weighting them with fixed weights, and combining them linearly will lose to an expert who implicitly changes weights. But a model that could shift weights during the game could possibly beat an expert, and one did: Berliner's (1980) backgammon program beat the 1979 world champion.

There is an important need to provide clearer boundaries for this dismal picture of expert judgment. To what extent, we ask ourselves, does the picture provided by this review apply to the other domains discussed in this volume? Providing a crisp answer to this question is difficult, because few of these domains provide explicit comparisons between experts and linear models. Without such a set of comparisons, identifying domains in which experts will do well is speculation.

We have already suggested that some domains are inherently richer in broken-leg and configural cues. The presence of these cues provides the opportunity for better performance but does not necessarily guarantee it. In addition, the presence of feedback and the lack of noise have been suggested as important variables in determining the performances of both experts and expert systems (Carroll, 1987). Finally, Shanteau (1988) has suggested that "good" experts are those in whom the underlying body of knowledge is more developed, providing examples such as soil and livestock judgment.

6. IMPLICATIONS FOR THE STUDY OF EXPERTISE

Expertise should be identified by comparison to some standard of performance. Random and novice performances make for natural comparisons. The linear-model literature suggests that simple statistical models provide another, demanding comparison.

The results from studies of expert decision making have had surprisingly little effect on the study of expertise, even in related tasks. For instance, simple linear models do quite well in medical-judgment tasks such as the hypothetical task discussed at the beginning of this chapter. Yet most of the work in aiding diagnosis has been aimed at developing expert systems that can mimic human expert performance, not exceed or improve upon it.

Expert systems may predict less accurately than simple models because the systems are *too much* like experts. The main lesson from the regression-model literature is that large numbers of configural rules, which knowledge engineers take as evidence of expertise, do not necessarily make good predictions; simple linear combinations of variables (measured by experts) are better in many tasks.

A somewhat ironic contrast between rule-based systems and linear models has occurred in recent developments in connectionist models. Whereas these models generally represent a relatively low level of cognitive activity, there are some marked similarities to the noncognitive "paramorphic" regression models we have discussed. In many realizations, a connectionist network is a set of units with associated weights that specify constraints on how the units combine the input received. The network generates weights that will maximize the goodness of fit of the system to the outcomes it observes in training (Rumelhart, McClelland, & PDP Research Group, 1986).

In a single-layer system, each unit receives its input directly from the environment. Thus, these systems appear almost isomorphic to simple regressions, producing a model that takes environmental cues and combines them, in a linear fashion, to provide the best fit to the outcomes. Much like regressions, we would expect simple, single-layer networks to make surprisingly good predictions under uncertainty (Jordan, 1986; Rumelhart et al., 1986).

More complex, multilayer systems allow for the incorporation of patterns of cues, which resemble the configural cues reported by experts. Like human experts, we suspect that such hidden units in these more complex systems will not add much to predictive validity in many of the domains we have discussed. The parallel between regression models and connectionist networks is provocative and represents an opportunity for bringing together two quite divergent paradigms.

Finally, we note that this chapter stands in strong contrast to the chapters that surround it: Our experts, while sharing many signs of superior expert processing demonstrated in other domains, do not show superior performance. The contrast suggests some closing notes. First, the history of the study of expert decision making raises concerns about how experts are to be identified. Being revered as an expert practitioner is not enough. Care should be given to assessing actual performance. Second, the case study of decision making may say something about the development of expertise in general and the degree to which task characteristics promote or prevent the development of superior performance. Experts fail when their cognitive abilities are badly matched to environmental demands.

In this chapter we have tried to isolate the characteristics of decision tasks that (1) generate such poor performance, (2) allow experts to believe that they are doing well, and (3) allow us to believe in them. We hope that the contrast between these conditions and those provided by other domains may contribute to a broader, more informed view of expertise, accounting for experts' failures as well as their successes.

ACKNOWLEDGMENTS

The authors contributed equally; the order of authors' name is purely alphabetical. We thank Helmut Jungermann, as well as Anders Ericsson, Jaqui Smith, and the other participants at the Study of Expertise conference in Berlin, 25–28 June 1989, at the Max Planck Institute for Human Development and Education, for many helpful comments. Preparation of this chapter was supported by a grant from the Office of Naval Research and by NSF grant SES 88-09299.

REFERENCES

Bedard, J. (1989). Expertise in auditing: Myth or reality? *Accounting, Organizations and Society, 14*, 113–131.

Bedard, J., & Mock, T. J. (1989). *Expert and novice problem-solving behavior in audit planning: An experimental study.* Unpublished paper, University of Southern California.

Berliner, H. J. (1980). Backgammon computer program beats world champion. *Artificial Intelligence, 14*, 205–220.

Bettman, J. B., & Park C. W. (1980). Effects of prior knowledge, exposure and phrase of choice process on consumer decision processes. *Journal of Consumer Research, 17*, 234–248.

Blattberg, R. C., & Hoch, S. J. (1990). Database models and managerial intuition: 50% database + 50% manager. *Management Science, 36*, 887–899.

Bouman, M. J. (1980). Application of information-processing and decision-making research, I. In G. R. Ungson & D. N. Braunstein (Eds.), *Decision making: An interdisciplinary inquiry* (pp. 129–167). Boston: Kent Publishing.

Bowman, E. H. (1963). Consistency and optimality in management decision making. *Management Science, 10*, 310–321.

Brehmer, B. (1980). In one word: Not from experience. *Acta Psychologica, 45*, 223–241.

Brucks, M. (1985). The effects of product class knowledge on information search behavior. *Journal of Consumer Research, 12*, 1–16.

Brunswik, E. (1952). *The conceptual framework of psychology.* University of Chicago Press.

Camerer, C. F. (1981a). The validity and utility of expert judgment. Unpublished Ph.D. dissertation, Center for Decision Research, University of Chicago Graduate School of Business.

Camerer, C. F. (1981b). General conditions for the success of bootstrapping models. *Organizational Behavior and Human Performance, 27*, 411–422.

Carroll, B. (1987). Expert systems for clinical diagnosis: Are they worth the effort? *Behavioral Science, 32*, 274–292.

Chapman, L. J., & Chapman, J. P. (1967). Genesis of popular but erroneous psychodiagnostic observations. *Journal of Abnormal Psychology, 73*, 193–204.

Chapman, L. J., & Chapman, J. P. (1969). Illusory correlation as an otstacle to the use of valid psychodiagnostic signs. *Journal of Abnormal Psychology, 46,* 271–280.

Chase, W. G. (1983). Spatial representations of taxi drivers. In D. R. Rogers & J. H Sloboda (Eds.), *Acquisition of symbolic skills* (pp. 391–405). New York: Plenum.

Chase, W. G., & Simon, H. A. (1973). Perception in chess. *Cognitive Psychology, 4,* 55–81.

Christensen-Szalanski, J. J. J., & Bushyhead, J. B. (1981). Physicians' use of probabilistic information in a real clinical setting. *Journal of Experimental Psychology: Human Perception and Performance, 7,* 928–935.

Dawes, R. M. (1971). A case study of graduate admissions: Application of three principles of human decision making. *American Psychologist, 26,* 180–188.

Dawes, R. M., & Corrigan, B. (1974). Linear models in decision making. *Psychological Bulletin, 81,* 97.

Dawes, R. M., Faust, D., & Meehl, P. E. (1989). Clinical versus actuarial judgment. *Science, 243,* 1668–1674.

DeSmet, A. A., Fryback, D. G., & Thornbury, J. R. (1979). A second look at the utility of radiographic skull examination for trauma. *American Journal of Radiology, 132,* 95–99.

Einhorn, H. E. (1974). Expert judgment: Some necessary conditions and an example. *Journal of Applied Psychology, 59,* 562–571.

Einhorn, H. J. (1972). Expert measurement and mechanical combination. *Organization Behavior and Human Performance, 7,* 86–106.

Einhorn, H. J. (1986). Accepting error to make less error. *Journal of Personality Assessment, 50,* 387–395.

Einhorn, H. J., & Hogarth, R. M. (1975). Unit weighting schemas for decision making. *Organization Behavior and Human Performance, 13,* 171–192.

Einhorn, H. J., Kleinmuntz, D. N., & Kleinmuntz, B. (1979). Linear regression and process tracing models of judgment. *Psychological Review, 86,* 465–485.

Elstein, A. S., Shulman, A. S., & Sprafka, S. A. (1978). *Medical problem solving: An analysis of clinical reasoning.* Cambridge, MA: Harvard University Press.

Ericsson, K. A., & Chase, W. G. (1981). Exceptional memory. *American Scientist, 70*(6), 607–615.

Ericsson, K. A., & Polson, P. G. (1988). An experimental analysis of the mechanisms of a memory skill. *Journal of Experimental Psychology: Learning, Memory, and Cognition, 14,* 305–316.

Ericsson, K. A., & Simon, H. A. (1987). Verbal reports as data. *Psychological Review, 87,* 215–251.

Garb, H. N. (1989). Clinical judgment, clinical training, and professional experience. *Psychological Bulletin, 105,* 387–396.

Goldberg, L. R. (1959). The effectiveness of clinicians' judgments: The diagnosis of organic brain damage from the Bender-Gestalt test. *Journal of Consulting Psychology, 23,* 25–33.

Goldberg, L. R. (1968). Simple models or simple processes? *American Psychologist, 23,* 483–496.

Goldberg, L. R. (1970). Man versus model of man: A rationale, plus some evidence, for a method of improving on clinical inferences. *Psychological Bulletin, 73,* 422–432.

Gustafson, J. E. (1963). The computer for use in private practice. In *Proceedings of Fifth IBM Medical Symposium,* pp. 101–111. White Plains, NY: IBM Technical Publication Division.

Hammond, K. R. (1955). Probabilistic functioning and the clinical method. *Psychological Review, 62,* 255–262.

Hammond, K. R. (1987). Toward a unified approach to the study of expert judgment. In J. Mumpower, L. Phillips, O. Renn, & V. R. R. Uppuluri (Eds.), *NATO ASI Series F: Computer & Systems Sciences: Vol. 35, Expert judgment and expert systems* (pp. 1–16). Berlin: Springer-Verlag.

Hammond, K. R., Hamm, R. M., Grassia, J., & Pearson, T. (1987). Direct comparison of the efficacy of intuitive and analytical cognition in expert judgment. *IEEE Transactions on Systems, Man, and Cybernetics, SMC-17,* 753–770.

Hoffman, P. J. (1960). The paramorphic representation of clinical judgment. *Psychological Bulletin, 57,* 116–131.

Holland, J. H., Holyoak, K. J., Nisbett, R. E., & Thagard, P. R. (1986). *Induction: Processes of inference, learning, and discovery.* Cambridge, MA: MIT Press.

Johnson, E. J. (1980). Expertise in admissions judgment. Unpublished doctoral dissertation, Carnegie-Mellon University.

Johnson, E. J. (1988). Expertise and decision under uncertainty: Performance and process. In M. T. H. Chi, R. Glaser & M. J. Farr (Eds.), *The nature of expertise* (pp. 209–228). Hillsdale, NJ: Erlbaum.

Johnson, E. J., & Payne, J. (1985). Effort and accuracy in choice. *Management Science, 31,* 395–414.

Johnson, E. J., & Russo, J. E. (1984). Product familiarity and learning new information. *Journal of Consumer Research, 11,* 542–550.

Johnson, P. E., Hassebrock, F., Duran, A. S., & Moller, J. (1982). Multimethod study of clinical judgment. *Organizational Behavior and Human Performance, 30,* 201–230.

Jordan, M. I. (1986). An introduction to linear algebra in parallel distributed processing. In D. Rumelhart, Rumelhart, J. McClelland, & PDP Research Group (Eds.), *Parallel distributed processing: Explorations in the microstructure of cognition: Vol. 1. Foundations* (pp. 365–422). Cambridge, MA.: MIT Press.

Kahneman, D., Slovic, P., & Tversky, A. (1982). *Judgment under uncertainty: Heuristics and biases.* Cambridge University Press.

Keren, G. B. (1987). Facing uncertainty in the game of bridge: A calibration study. *Organizational Behavior and Human Decision Processes, 139,* 98–114.

Klayman, J. (1988). Cue discovery in probabilistic environments: Uncertainty and experimentation. *Journal of Experimental Psychology:: Learning, Memory, and Cognition, 14,* 317–330.

Klayman, J., & Ha, Y. (1985). Confirmation, disconfirmation, and information in hypothesis testing. *Psychological Review, 94,* 211–228.

Kleinmuntz, B. (1968). *Formal representation of human judgment.* New York: Wiley.

Kundel, H. L., & LaFollette, P. S. (1972). Visual search patterns and experience with radiological images. *Radiology, 103,* 523–528.

Larkin, J., McDermott, J., Simon, D. P., & Simon, H. A. (1980). Expert and novice performance in solving physics problems. *Science, 208,* 1335–1342.

Levenberg, S. B. (1975). Professional training, psychodiagnostic skill, and kinetic family drawings. *Journal of Personality Assessment, 39,* 389–393.

Libby, R. (1976). Man versus model of man: Some conflicting evidence. *Organizational Behavior and Human Performance, 16,* 1–12.

Libby, R., & Frederick, D. M. (1989, February). *Expertise and the ability to explain audit findings* (University of Michigan Cognitive Science and Machine Intelligence Laboratory Technical Report No. 21).

Lichtenstein, S., Fischhoff, B., & Phillips, L. D. (1977). Calibration of probabilities: The state of the art. In H. Jungermann & G. de Zeeuw (Eds.), *Decision making and change in human affairs*. Amsterdam: D. Reidel.

Meehl, P. E. (1954). *Clinical versus statistical prediction: A theoretical analysis and a review of the evidence*. Minneapolis: University of Minnesota Press.

Meehl, P. E. (1986). Causes and effects of my disturbing little book. *Journal of Personality Assessment, 50*, 370–375.

Meyer, R. J. (1987). The learning of multiattribute judgment policies. *Journal of Consumer Research, 14*, 155–173.

Murphy, A. H., & Winkler, R. L. (1977). Can weather forecasters formulate reliable probability forecasts of precipitation and temperature? *National Weather Digest, 2*, 2–9.

Philadelphia Inquirer. (1989, August 15). Personality test gets revamped for the '80s, pp. 1-D, 3-D.

Rumelhart, D., McClelland, J., & PDP Research Group (Eds.). (1986). *Parallel distributed processing: Explorations in the microstructure of cognition: Vol. 1. Foundations*. Cambridge, MA: MIT Press.

Sarbin, T. R. (1944). The logic of prediction in psychology. *Psychological Review, 51*, 210–228.

Sawyer J. (1966). Measurement and prediction, clinical and statistical. *Psychological Bulletin, 66*, 178–200.

Shanteau, J. (1988). Psychological characteristics and strategies of expert decision makers. *Acta Psychologica, 68*, 203–215.

Shortliffe, E. H., Buchanan, B. G., & Feigenbaum, E. A. (1979). Knowledge engineering for medical decision making: A review of computer-based decision aids. *Proceedings of the IEEE, 67*, 1207–1224.

Tversky, A., & Kahneman, D. (1973). Availability: A heuristic for judging frequency and probability. *Cognitive Psychology, 4*, 207–232.

Tversky, A., & Kahneman, D. (1982). Judgments of and by representativeness. In D. Kahneman, P. Slovic, & A. Tversky (Eds.), *Judgment under uncertainty: Heuristics and biases* (pp. 84–98). Cambridge: Cambridge University Press.

Voss, J. F., & Post, T. A. (1988). On the solving of ill-structured problems. In M. T. H. Chi, R. Glaser, & M. J. Farr (Eds.), *The nature of expertise* (pp. 261–285). Hillsdale, NJ: Erlbaum.

Wagenaar, W. A., & Keren, G. B. (1985). Calibration of probability assessments by professional blackjack dealers, statistical experts, and lay people. *Organizational Behavior and Human Decision Processes, 36*, 406–416.

Wiggens, N., & Kohen, E. S. (1971). Man vs. model of man revisited: The forecasting of graduate school success. *Journal of Personality and Social Psychology, 19*, 100–106.

Yntema, D. B., & Torgerson, W. J. (1961). Man–computer cooperation in decision requiring common sense. *IRE Transactions of the Professional Group on Human Factors in Electronics, 2*, 20–26.

9 Controlling complex systems; or, Expertise as "grandmother's know-how"

DIETRICH DÖRNER AND JULIA SCHÖLKOPF

INTRODUCTION

In this chapter we want to draw some comparisons between research activities that have been carried out in the general field of cognitive psychology (particularly the area of problem solving) and the expertise approach. Our focus will be on the study of problem solving in the context of complex and dynamic systems. Researchers interested in complex problem solving typically have used computer simulations of real-life problem tasks. Computer simulations allow a measure of control over the problem dimensions and their interactions. Computer simulations of complex tasks also provide an ideal context for collecting a variety of data concerning subjects' steps toward problem solutions. Depending on the extent to which a simulation resembles segments of real-life problems, researchers are able to tap into subjects' domain-relevant experience and factual knowledge, as well as their strategic capacities (procedural knowledge) to regulate their actions (cf. Eyferth, Schömann, & Widwoski, 1986).

One reason for the great interest in computer-simulated problem tasks is the fact that computer scenarios offer a much richer task environment than do traditional experimental problem-solving settings (Duncker, 1935) such as the Tower of Hanoi problem (Klix, 1971). Computer-implemented problem situations can be devised and presented to subjects in such a way that the tasks will be as complex, uncertain, "intransparent," and dynamic as real-life problems.

In the Anglo-American literature, an interest in simulating complex problem-solving situations began to evolve as early as 1970 (Bunderson, 1970), followed by the work of Broadbent and Aston (1978) and Sterman (1984, 1987). In the German-speaking countries, quite a few researchers are now using the computer-simulation approach to investigate the processes of problem solving in complex and dynamic task settings. The primary focus to date has been on the development of the computer-simulation programs. The following are some of the problem scenarios (Eyferth et al., 1986; Funke, 1984): "Aids" (Badke-Schaub & Dörner, 1987; Dörner, 1985, 1986a), "Dori" (Hesse, 1982), "Garden" (Schaub, 1989), "Kühlhaus" (Dörner & Reichert-Lieberknecht, 1991), "Lohhausen" (Dörner, Kreuzig, Reither, & Stäudel, 1983), "Manutex"

218

(Schaub & Tisdale, 1988), "Minisee" (Opwis, Spada, & Schwiersch, 1985), "Moon Landing" (Funke, 1981), "Moro" (Dörner, Stäudel, & Strohschneider, 1986), "Spacetrip" (Oesterreich, 1985), "Robi Otter" (Ackermann, 1984), "Sim002" (Kluwe & Reimann, 1983), "Summaria" (Gediga, Schöttke, & Tücke, 1983), "Tanaland" (Dörner & Reither, 1978), "Traveling Salesman" (Battmann, 1982), "Vektor" (Strohschneider, 1987), "World" (Eyferth et al., 1982). The merits of these systems currently are being widely discussed, particularly in regard to their different characteristics and demands; their complexity, transparency, and dynamics; their time frames and ecological validity; and the feasibility of their application to investigating the processes of problem solving (Eyferth et al., 1986; Funke, 1984; Reither & Stäudel, 1985).

Computer-simulated problem tasks are used for many purposes. Some research projects have compared performance on computer scenarios with performance in classical intelligence tests; some have investigated the effects of training; others have focused on measurement of transfer, learning, stress, and decision making. One of the most recent directions taken by this research is the use of computer simulations of complex and dynamic problem scenarios in connection with research on expertise.

This chapter is divided into four parts. First, a brief introduction to the computer scenario "Moro" is given. The Moro scenario is a simulation of the government of a seminomadic tribe. The subject's task is to care for the welfare of the tribe over a twenty-year period. Some results from the "governmental activities" of two subjects are reported to illustrate the type of data potentially collectable from this computer-simulation task. In the second part, we specify the demands of action situations – the roles of goal formulation, model design, data collection, prognoses, planning, decision making, and hypothesis testing – and describe some of the most important characteristics of the Moro system. In the third part, we discuss various success and failure strategies observed among subjects controlling complex systems and describe other relevant experiments (Badke-Schaub & Schaub, 1986; Putz-Osterloh & Lemme, 1987; Reichert & Dörner, 1988; Schaub & Strohschneider, 1989). In the fourth part, we talk about "grandmother's wisdom" – some of the contradictory strategies used and decisions made by subjects and their explanations of those decisions. Demonstrating expertise, in this approach, can be defined as being a *successful actor in a complex situation,* a player who pays close attention to the relative configuration of the facts at a given time, aiming all the while at adapting current behavior to the changing environment and constraints.

THE DEMANDS OF COMPLEX SYSTEMS

An example: government of the Moro tribe

We have used the computer scenario Moro in many experiments to determine how subjects cope with complex, dynamic, and "intransparent" systems (Stäudel, 1987; Strohschneider, 1986). The Moros are a seminomadic

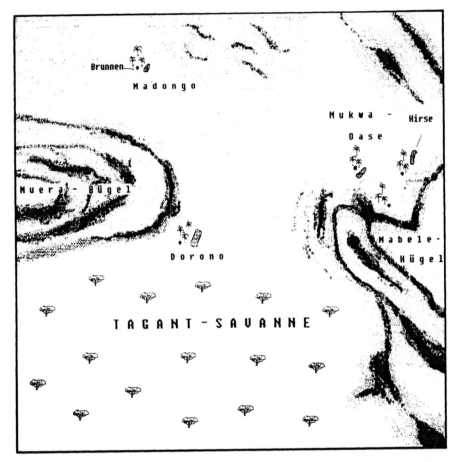

Figure 9.1. The territory of the Moros. In an experiment of this kind, the subject has the role of a development aid volunteer whose task is to create "better" living conditions for the Moros. In most of our experiments, the subjects were asked to decide on the fate of the Moros for a period of twenty simulated years.

tribe raising cattle. The men roam about with the cattle from one pasture to the next, and the women and children live in the villages at the oases and tend millet crops. The Moro tribe comprises some five hundred persons who somehow manage to survive in a barren region of Africa.

Figure 9.1 is a map representing the territory of the Moros, a geographical region, the Sahel Zone, south of the Sahara in Africa. The Sahel Zone consists predominantly of steppe, desert, dunes, and savanna regions. The map shows the isolated oases and watering places used by the Moros, as well as the farming areas they use to grow millet.

We simulated the Moros' living conditions on a computer. Our program simulates the tribe's demographic data: birth rate, death rate, susceptibility to illnesses, eating habits, and nutritional needs. In addition, it simulates the herds of cattle, the capacity of the watering places, precipitation, the growth of millet, the growth of grass on the grazing areas, pest populations (such as the tsetse fly) that afflict the cattle, and finally the Moros' trade contacts with the outside world.

In our experiments, the subject is given the role of a development aid volunteer whose task is to create "better" living conditions for the Moros. Typically, subjects are asked to decide on the fate of the Moros for a period of 20 (simulated) years. With a certain amount of money at their disposal, subjects are completely free to choose which measures to take and when to take them. The only condition, as they seek to improve the Moros' living conditions, is that the same amount of money available at the beginning must remain at the end of the twenty-year period.

The Moro problem is a "dynamic decision problem" (Brehmer & Allard, 1986). At any time during the experiment, the subjects may obtain information regarding the Moros' current situation in order to determine a course of action to be taken. They may decide, for example, to sink a deep well, or to buy tractors or storage buildings for the Moros. Subjects may create new trade contacts for the Moros, import fertilizers for the millet crops, attend to the Moros' medical care, or decide to combat pests. All measures taken are recorded and processed by the computer program, which then simulates the consequences for the Moros' living conditions. The program, however, provides only the most obvious features of the situation; for specific details, the subjects must ask more precise questions.

Figure 9.2 shows the results for two subjects. Obviously, the subject whose results are shown in the top graph did a good job. The stock of cattle grew, and the Moros increased in number. The groundwater supply remained unendangered. On the whole, this subject managed to maintain a continuous upward trend in development throughout the twenty-year period. The subject whose results are shown in the bottom graph was less successful. That subject's decisions resulted in a famine in the seventeenth year that extinguished the entire tribe. After the stock of cattle had become too large, the pastures were overgrazed and ruined by overuse. That inevitably led to famine. By and large, the subject's well-intentioned "policies for development aid" ended in disaster.

The demands of an action situation

What steps are necessary to solve a problem like that of the Moro scenario? What factors are decisive for the success or failure of individual subjects? Figure 9.3 shows the steps to be taken in coping with a complex system. The first important task is to formulate the goal, that is, to decide precisely what is to be achieved. Often the goal is described in general terms, rather than being clearly specified. In the Moro scenario, for example, the subjects are asked to "improve" the situation of the Moros – a rather vague

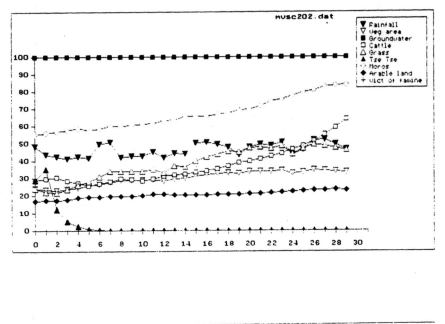

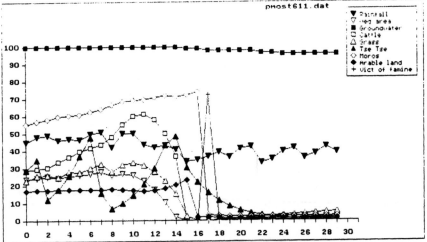

Figure 9.2. Results of the "governmental activities" of two subjects working with the Moros. The curve shows the states of important variables of the Moro system over a period of twenty years of "governmental" time and an additional ten-year period, showing the long-term effects of the subjects' actions.

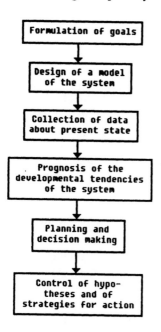

Figure 9.3. The demands of preparing to act and of acting in a complex system.

task description. Specific partial goals must be derived from the global goal. A subject, for instance, might reason thus: "I have to stock up the cattle; at least eight thousand head of cattle ought to be able to live in the region. By selling the cattle and the hides, it should be possible to provide the Moros with a regular income that will also allow them to finance adequate medical care."

To reach their goals, subjects have to develop a model of the system, analyzing its structure and defining the relevant variables as well as their interactions. Subjects can draw on previous knowledge to form hypotheses about the current problem, using the method of reasoning by analogy. These hypotheses, in turn, will have to be tested for their applicability in the current situation. Once a model of the situation has been developed, specific data on current conditions must be collected as a basis for future planning and actions.

The next step is to decide on the probable course of future developments, taking into account the current situation and the structure of the system. A detailed prognosis will facilitate coordination of the measures to be taken, with the aim of promoting desirable outcomes and preventing undesirable events.

Although careful, detailed planning is important, it is equally important that subjects make up their minds about the right time for action. While carrying out their project, subjects must continually control their chosen measures and, if necessary, adjust them appropriately in order to achieve the desired results. Reconsideration and modifications of strategies are necessities for coping with complex systems.

The demands of situation and system

We have outlined the necessary steps to be taken in coping with a complex system. These steps, however, can be handled in many different ways, and it is up to the subject to find the most appropriate method of dealing with the various situations most effectively.

In gathering information, for example, subjects may decide to collect a wide range of data in order to get a general idea of a situation, a bird's-eye view, or they may wish to dig up details and gather specific information on any given problem.

Likewise, one subject may prefer to plan each step carefully and precisely, in an effort to keep everything under control, whereas another may be more inclined to "play by ear," improvising rather than planning an appropriate course of action; compare, for example, the notion of "muddling-through behavior" (Lindblom, 1964).

Similarly, prognoses about future developments, on the basis of the data available, may be made on the basis of a simple linear extrapolation or, alternatively, a minute examination of possible changes and interactions. The choice of the most efficacious method will depend on the particular situation and the system being used. Subjects must be able to choose the right method at the right time and, if necessary, adapt their strategies to the requirements of the situation and the system.

The computer model of the world of the Moros is a model of a rather complex ecological system with feedback mechanisms and consequently many interrelated variables. The Moros' environment is a network of causal relations. Thus, any measure most likely will have unintended (and quite often undesirable) side effects. In addition, there may be unexpected and undesired long-term effects. Therefore, in working with the Moro system, success or failure will depend on a subject's ability to cope with the sometimes unpredictable consequences of a feedback system.

Furthermore, the Moro system is partly intransparent. Some variables are known and immediately accessible, whereas others, such as the groundwater supply, are hidden and can be assessed only by means of indicators.

Because of feedback mechanisms, the Moro system is also dynamic. It changes continually over the course of time, even without the subject's intervention. Therefore, subjects cannot rely on stable conditions but must always consider temporal developments in their prognoses for the future.

In addition, subjects have to plan cautiously, because in the Moro system many decisions are irreversible. This limits the possibility of making tentative test interventions merely to see what happens, because there is a high probability that undesirable consequences cannot be reversed.

Thus, in dealing with a complex system such as that of the Moro tribe and its territory, the success or failure of subjects will depend on their ability to adjust their measures to the characteristics of the system and the requirements of the actual situation. In the next section, we present two experiments to illustrate how individual subjects deal with the necessary operative flexibility, that is, how they manage to adjust continually the processes of planning, gathering information, forming hypotheses, making choices, and reconsidering decisions.

SOME EMPIRICAL RESULTS

Success and failure strategies in governing a complex system

Subjects can be classified as successful or unsuccessful in governing and maintaining the complex system of the Moro scenario. Two studies serve to illustrate such a classification. The first study was conducted by Schaub and Strohschneider (1989) using the Moro scenario; the second was by Putz-Osterloh (1987a), using Moro and "Tailor Shop" (another computer-simulated system from the field of economics).

Doing the right thing at the right time. Schaub and Strohschneider (1989) compared the various strategies used by a group of experienced executives from the industrial and commercial sectors with those used by a group of students. Forty-five directors and department managers from various companies in Switzerland and Germany were given the task of guiding the fate of the Moros for a period of two hours of experiment. The performances of these subjects were compared with those of forty-five students from the University of Bamberg.

Figure 9.4 shows the differences in the results for the executives and the students. It can be seen that the executives were considerably more successful in coping with the problems of the Moros than were the students. In the end, they had a greater supply of capital, a larger stock of cattle, a larger population, not significantly less groundwater, and a millet harvest that also was not significantly smaller. What were the reasons for these differences? Although we were not able to administer intelligence tests to executives in this experiment, it nevertheless seems reasonable to assume that the executives were no more intelligent (in terms of an intelligence test) than our student subjects. On the contrary, it seemed to us that the students reacted more quickly and more sensitively and that they displayed a more rapid mental grasp in assuming the role. But that, too, was merely an impression, not verifiable on the basis of data. It did not seem to us that the executives thought of details in any way fundamentally different from the way the students did. The executives did not display any special steps in thinking or modes of action that the students did not also use. Both groups formed ideas, asked questions, and drew conclusions from the data they had gathered; the individual components

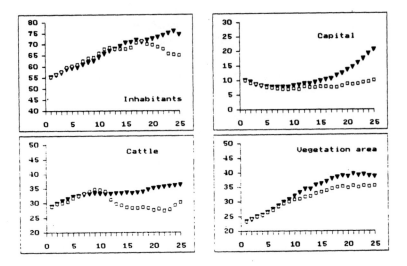

Figure 9.4. Final results for executives and students in the Moro game.

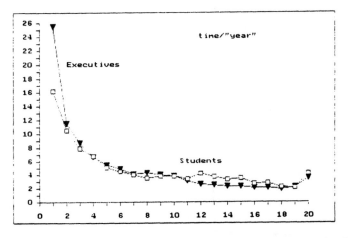

Figure 9.5. Investments of time for executives and students in the single years of the Moro simulation.

of thinking were not different for students and managers, insofar as that could be determined.

The main difference between the subjects in the two groups was that the executives were capable of doing the right thing at the right time. They were more likely than were the students to adjust their ways of acting to the requirements of the situation and the system. The pattern of their mental activities was different.

Let us consider two examples of this. Figure 9.5 shows the amounts of time

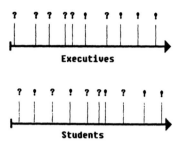

Figure 9.6. Sequencing of the questions and decision behaviors for executives and students.

invested by executives and students for each of the "years." It can be seen that the executives invested almost one-quarter of their total time working on the first year. At the outset, they spent significantly more time assessing the situation, setting their goals, and gaining an understanding of the system. The students spent less time on such endeavors. On average, the students began taking actions earlier; and only later, because of the failures that began to crop up, did they look toward deeper analysis of the system, usually too late. In Figure 9.5 it can be seen that they invested much time in years 12–15.

Figure 9.6 shows another difference between the way executives and students acted, having to do with the sequence of questions (?) and measures taken (!) in one phase of the Moro simulation, depicted in stylized form. At the left one sees a typical pattern for the students; at the right, a typical pattern for the executives. For the students, the questions and measures were mixed in various sequences. For the executives, on the other hand, the decisions regarding measures followed the questions. The executives first attempted to gain an overall picture by asking questions, and they did not act until that seemed to them to have been achieved.

The students, on the other hand, acted in a more ad hoc manner on the basis of both isolated findings and isolated answers to isolated questions. In Figure 9.6, to the right, the average relative distance between the time of the "mean question" in a phase and that of the "mean decision" can be seen. This difference amounts to 30.05% of the working time for the executives and 21.45% for the students. Thus, if one student and one executive each worked 30 minutes on a problem complex, and if the "mean question" was asked in the 15th minute, the "mean decision" was made by the student after 21 minutes and 24 seconds, whereas the executive made his decision after 24 minutes and 9 seconds. (The average difference with regard to this characteristic was highly significant when $z = 3.13$ at 19 degrees of freedom.) Thus, the executives were more likely than the students to coordinate the data before making a decision. They also gathered more information per decision. The number of questions per decision was an average of 3.12 for the executives and 2.67 for the students. This difference was likewise statistically highly significant.

Intensive analysis of the problem and self-reflexive modification of one's own mode of action. Experiments conducted by Putz-Osterloh yielded results similar to those just described. Two experiments (Putz-Osterloh, 1987a; Putz-Osterloh & Lemme, 1987) pursued the question of how experts and laypersons differed in coping with dynamic and intransparent systems. For these experiments, Putz-Osterloh employed two simulation scenarios: the Moro simulation and a simulation of a small textile factory. Professors, doctoral candidates, and graduate students in business did better than randomly selected students in coping with the textile factory. That, of course, is in part attributable to the experts' superior previous knowledge in the industrial sector. Yet previous knowledge was not the only reason the experts came off better.

As in Schaub and Strohschneider's experiment, the experts in Putz-Osterloh and Lemme's experiment (1987) also did better in dealing with the problems in the Moro scenario. That can hardly be attributed to differences in prior knowledge, as the business professors could not have known more about the Sahel Zone than the students could.

A detailed analysis of the subjects' performances showed that the experts consistently formed more hypotheses than the laypersons did. Laypersons analyzed the problems more intensely and did more planning. In so doing, they gained better-developed knowledge of the interrelations in the system. Another important difference to be dealt with later was the fact that the experts displayed more self-reflexive processes than the laypersons did, which was evident only in managing the Moro system – the one system in which it was less frequently possible to fall back on prior knowledge. It was not, however, possible for Putz-Osterloh to find any systematic correlations between the quality of problem solving and intelligence – as was the case in many preceding experiments (Dörner, 1986b; Dörner & Kreuzig, 1983; Putz-Osterloh, 1987a).

The differences between laypersons and experts in these experiments were found not in elementary intellectual abilities but in problem-solving strategies, in the domain of "heuristic knowledge" or "operative intelligence" (Dörner, 1986b). These are designations for the ability to execute in each case the right intellectual operation at the right time.

The same thing is not the same

The right operation at the right time – this also means that in different situations, and in coping with various systems, one may have to behave differently, perhaps even contradictorily. Let us consider a few examples of this.

Information gathering by acting and asking. Figure 9.7 shows the frequencies of questioning and decision behaviors in an experiment conducted by van der Weth (1989). The point of this experiment was to run a complicated produc-

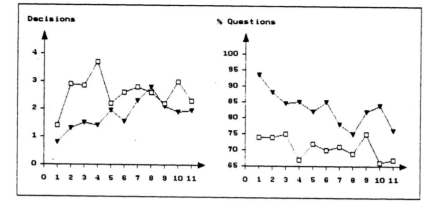

Figure 9.7. Frequencies of decisions and relative frequencies of questions for successful and unsuccessful subjects in a complex task.

tion plant, with the task of manufacturing three substances. Figure 9.7 shows the frequencies of questions and decisions for the subjects, who did well or poorly in the experiment. It can be seen that there were differences. The successful subjects asked substantially more questions at the beginning than the unsuccessful subjects. But the unsuccessful subjects made more decisions at the beginning than the successful ones.

In contrast, Badke-Schaub and Schaub (1986), in their experiment using the same system ("Machine") used by von der Weth, found that the successful subjects made more decisions at the beginning than the unsuccessful subjects (and asked exactly as many questions as those who performed poorly). In this example, therefore, we find contradictory behaviors for the ultimately successful subjects performing in the same system; however, that was not so for the unsuccessful subjects.

Why is this? The difference between the two experiments consisted in the fact that in von der Weth's experiment it was possible for the mode of production to result in massive, virtually irreversible damage to the environment, in the formation of citizens' interest groups against the enterprise and in strikes.

In view of the many consequences reversible only with great difficulty, it makes sense to orient oneself precisely before acting. The situation simulated in Badke-Schaub and Schaub's experiment was not embedded in the environment. For that reason, it definitely made sense there to carry out a great deal of explorative activity with the aim of gathering data on the system. The effects of the measures were in that situation not "externally" directed; they did not endanger the reputation of the firm and were easily reversible. In that situation, gathering information by trial and error was a sensible strategy.

Thus, in a range of studies, it has been found that successful subjects are capable of adapting their behavior to the circumstances in any given case.

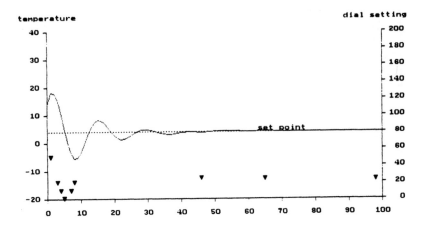

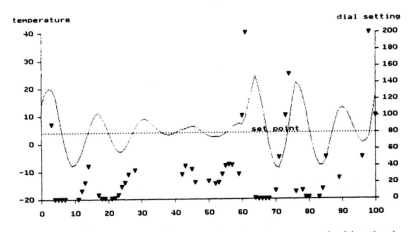

Figure 9.8. "Wait and see" and "doing" behaviors for one good subject (top) and one bad subject in the Kühlhaus experiment.

They are capable both of comprehending the requirements of the situation and of recognizing that gathering data by asking questions is reasonable in the one case, whereas in the other it makes sense to gather experience by testing, by taking action. Among the successful subjects, the individual phases of thinking and acting are then "conditionalized." They refer to the respective conditions. The successful subjects know when to act and what to do.

Wait and see instead of doing. Figure 9.8 shows two records of performance. At the top is the record of a successful subject's performance in Reichert's "Kühlhaus" experiment (Reichert & Dörner, 1988). At the bottom is an unsuccessful subject's record of performance. The point of the Kühlhaus experiment was for subjects to run a thermodynamic system, namely, a cold-storage depot. This system operates similarly to a thermostat for regulating heating. By dampened oscillations, one can make the system approximate the given nominal value. These oscillations have to be calculated while controlling the system. For a system of this kind, it hardly makes sense to respond only to the current state, that is, to the temperature at a particular time. It does, however, make sense to wait and observe the level about which the system oscillates. In this situation a wait-and-see strategy is correct; "doing" is wrong.

As can be seen, the subject whose results are shown at the top of Figure 9.8 realized this wait-and-see strategy after the first 9 phases. This subject did not do anything at all from the 9th to the 46th phase and intervened to make minor corrections only three times after that, thereby bringing the temperature relatively quickly to the desired value of 4° C. Not so for the subject whose results are shown at the bottom of Figure 9.8. Throughout the entire experiment this subject failed to understand that the point of the problem was to observe the level. This subject responded to each thermal state and thus caused the system to enter a mode of steadily increasing oscillations.

At the beginning, the successful subject, like the unsuccessful one, did not have the right knowledge. The successful subject also intervened relatively often. The difference between the two subjects was that the successful subject made a strategic switch from a status quo mode of action to a cautious, wait-and-see mode of action. Such a switch was never made by the subject at the bottom of Figure 9.8.

Let us now look at Figure 9.9, which shows the records of performance of one successful subject and one unsuccessful subject in an experiment conducted by Maas (1989). In this case the subjects had to manage an ecological system. This ecosystem consisted of a "predator population" and a "prey population." The subjects were to keep the prey population at a certain level by manipulating the predator population. The entire task was declared a task in "biologically combating pests."

It can be seen at the top of the figure that this subject coped rather well with the task. At the end, the prey population was stable at the desired value of 400. A strategic switch – like that seen in the Kühlhaus experiment – can also be attributed to this subject. Up to about phase 14, the subject behaved in an ad hoc manner: If the prey population was large, then a lot of predators were released; if the prey population was small, the predator population was drastically reduced so as to allow the prey population to recover. A pattern of rather troubled intervention behavior resulted. From phase 14 on, the subject learned to wait a long time and to take action extremely cautiously, thus managing to reach the goal. Not so for the subject at the bottom of Figure 9.9, who also responded in an ad hoc manner at first, but continued to do so

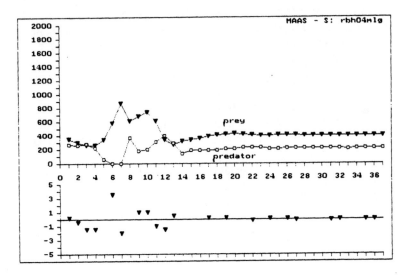

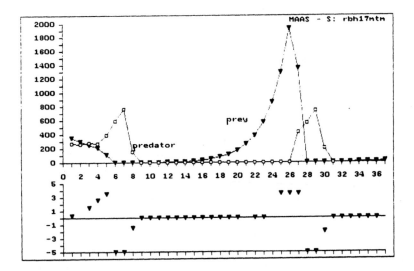

Figure 9.9. Performances of a good subject using a strategy change (top) and a bad subject without a strategy change in the predator–prey experiment (Maas, 1989).

throughout the experiment and never learned to understand the time characteristics of the development. No strategy change was evident for this subject.

In summarizing the differences between successful and unsuccessful subjects, a simple finding arises: The adept subjects wait and observe when that is appropriate. They develop a model of the system at the right time, not when it is already too late. They know how to do the right thing at the right time.

EXPERTISE IN COPING WITH COMPLEX SYSTEMS

Grandmothers' wisdom about solving problems

Everyday psychology has many maxims for thinking and acting while coping with problem situations. Here is a list of some of these rules for behavior:

- Get your goals clear in your mind.
- Don't allow yourself to be distracted by trivial details; concentrate on the most important problems. Develop areas of concentration. First things first.
- Always try to keep the overall picture in sight.
- Get your information straight before acting.
- Plan your course of action, your measures, carefully.
- Don't plan too long or too precisely. Everything will happen differently from what you expect anyway.
- Keep your eyes open for favorable opportunities, and seize them whenever they pop up.
- You have to know how to wait and see.
- You can't win if you don't risk anything.
- If you're going to do something, do it with gusto. Don't fiddle about. Fight it out.
- Always act cautiously. Better safe than sorry.
- If you don't know what to do, try anything at all. Muddle your way through. (See Lindblom, 1964, p. 36.) Recall Napoleon's motto: "On s'engage et puis on voit."
- Finish what you've started.
- One step at a time – all the time.
- In a complex situation you can never do just one thing.
- Look for simple explanations.
- Don't trust simple explanations.

These maxims are, for the most part, simply "grandmother's wisdom," familiar to everyone in one form or another. The term "grandmother's wisdom" has, on the one hand, a positive connotation, and, on the other, a negative connotation. Who would not appreciate the wisdom of the elderly? On the other hand, those pieces of wise advice listed are more often than not given a posteriori, that is, after the child has already fallen into the well. In this sort of a posteriori advice there is always a touch of malice and *Schadenfreude* (glee at someone else's misfortune), not so much knowing better as know-it-all-ism.

In taking a closer look at this list of maxims, it becomes obvious that many of them are mutually contradictory. How, for example, can you at the same time concentrate and "keep an overall picture"? How are you to "wait and see" and seize an opportunity simultaneously? And should you make exact plans or none at all? Should you get your goals clear in your mind or just "muddle your way through" without any clear goals? Should you act "in a flash" or take a long time gathering information and planning before acting? Should you interrupt your current intentions so as to grasp opportunities, or should you "finish what you've started"? Should you not let yourself be "distracted by trivial details," or should you "keep your eyes open for favorable opportunities"?

Several conclusions might be drawn from the obvious contradictions in such maxims. One might conclude that many of the contradictions simply reflect the fact that these pieces of grandmother's wisdom are not worth anything and merely indicate an after-the-fact, know-it-all attitude. Or one might conclude that the contradictions in these maxims reflect the fact that there are right and wrong maxims.

In our opinion, none of those conclusions is correct. All of these maxims are good for something, and not one of them is wrong. All are correct. But what they lack is information telling us when they are right. The maxims are useful when they are conceived of as conditionalized rules, that is, as rules to be followed under certain conditions but not under others.

In many situations it is reasonable to concentrate on a particular area, without looking to the right or left. In other situations, it is important to gain a broad orientation and, if need be, to let favorable opportunities distract you from pursuing the current intention. Sometimes it is reasonable to undertake long and meticulous planning. But sometimes it is reasonable not to plan at all, acting on the spur of the moment while "muddling along." Sometimes it makes sense to set your goals clearly in your mind. Sometimes it is reasonable just to get involved in something and play it by ear.

One must be strategically flexible to be successful in complex situations. One must know "when" and "what." This "when . . . what" knowledge constitutes the expertise needed to cope with complex systems. But what exactly does "strategic flexibility" mean? To which configurations does the expert pay attention when coping with a complex system? And how does one adapt one's modes of behavior to the demands of whichever situation is current? What is the difference between unreflective application of the grandmother rules and implementation of conditionalized rules?

The grandmother rules specify *what* is to be done but not *when* it must be done. They designate modes of behavior for coping with problem situations. These must, however, be linked to conditions so that they can be appropriately applied. There are two possible ways.

First, it is conceivable that the problem-solver will have in mind fixed decision rules for tackling the problem. One has, as it were, "set problem stereotypes" in mind that may or may not fit a given situation: "If time is pressing, I'd better not do any more planning (that only makes people more uncertain than they already are); it's better to wait and see what happens" – this is what a link between the actions taken and the characteristics of the situation might look like. The more sophisticated the set stereotypes for the problem situations, and the more sophisticated the thus-controlled inventory of procedures for acting, the greater the possibility for the problem-solver to respond adequately to the current situation. Possessing problem stereotypes with the appropriate modes of acting linked to them is, so to speak, "crystalline operative intelligence."

A second possibility involves conditionalizing the grandmother rules. This involves an ad hoc analysis of the requirements posed by the situation. Good problem-solvers consider the demands they face and develop strategy on the basis of these demands. This was illustrated, for example, in the "Lohhausen" experiment (Dörner et al., 1983), in which the subject, playing a mayor, had to determine the fate of a small town. In the Lohhausen experiment, the following kinds of "thinking aloud" were found: "First I have to gain an overall picture and discover what kinds of problems are actually facing me. Then I can look further." Or, later: "So I'm going to build new flats. But wait a minute! Before I make a final decision on that, I have to attend to the other things on the agenda. There may be something more important, and then I won't have any more money left for building flats anyway."

In the first case, at the beginning of the experiment, the subjects intructed themselves on the basis of an analysis of the facts: "Get an overall picture before you decide anything." In the second case, after the subjects had gained an overview and already knew what was at stake, they instructed themselves to coordinate the currently planned measure with possible other measures.

These instances of self-regulation occurred with appreciably greater frequently for successful subjects in the Lohhausen experiment than for unsuccessful subjects. By and large, successful subjects' actions were also considerably more consistent. A similar finding was reported in an experiment conducted by Tisdale (1988) that analyzed "thinking aloud" during planning processes. He was able to distinguish various modes of action. One of these was type "p," distinguished by the fact that the subject always regulated action via self-instruction, which was generated for each situation on the basis of an analysis of the given facts.

In working on a problem, the type "p" problem-solver follows a sequence of self-instructions like Ariadne's thread, while, however, constantly controlling the appropriateness of the strategy. If, for instance, type "p" problem-solvers have been intently gathering data on a particular topic for a period of time and reach a stopping point, they then first briefly recapitulate why they need the data, that is, what the original intention was. The type "p" problem-solver's thinking may thus jump from a current activity back to the superordinate goal. Subjects for whom such back-checks do not occur run the risk of getting bogged down and wasting a lot of time. If, for instance, in gathering their information they discover a new point, they respond ad hoc, without relating it to the superordinate goal.

Problem-solvers must, therefore, first be capable of programming their actions on the basis of an analysis of the facts of the situation and of the system, and do so by generating "self-instructions." Second, problem-solvers must not follow these self-instructions blindly; rather, they must continually check and recheck their actions by means of self-reflection. This is especially true for failures. Self-reflection means that one considers, checks, and, if necessary, modifies the "record" of one's own actions. And that was what the successful problem-solvers in the Lohhausen study and the experts in Putz-Osterloh's experiment (1987a) did more frequently than the unsuccessful subjects. By means of self-reflection, the problem-solvers acting in situations for which they did not possess any preconceived methods adapted their thinking processes to the current configuration and its demands.

Lumberjacks and reapers: an alternative view of expertise

The Prussian material theoretician Carl von Clausewitz (1880, pp. 139–140) wrote the following about war:

> War does not ultimately consist of an infinite set of minor events which may be passed on in their dissimilarities and which may therefore be controlled with greater or lesser difficulty by using better or worse methods. It rather consists of single great and decisive events which require attentive individual treatment. War is not a field full of stalks of grain which can, with greater or smaller degree of difficulty, be reaped by using a better or worse scythe, regardless of the shape of each single stalk; it is rather the big trees, to which the ax must be applied thoughtfully, paying attention to the composition and direction of each and every trunk.

What Clausewitz had to say about war can be transferred to complex situations of action in the following statement: Success is not simply a matter of paying attention to a few central features of a situation and of acting according to those features; it is, rather, a matter of paying attention to the configuration of the features, which in each case will be extremely specific and individual. There is a particular sequence of actions appropriate to each such configuration. "Methodologists" do not adapt to the requirements of each individual configuration. They have two or three methods, and these are applied in accordance with a few central indicators; the uniqueness of the situation found in the specific configuration of features is not taken into consideration.

It is a good idea to consider carefully Clausewitz's metaphor of felling trees. In felling a tree, one must carefully analyze whether or not the tree is situated on a slope, where it is situated relative to nearby trees, what the shape the tree is, from which direction the wind is coming, and whether the trunk is twisted or straight; all this must be known in order to determine where to begin cutting. The overall configuration of the features is significant. A change in one small detail can result in having to change completely where and how one begins cutting. It is possible to fell the stalks in a field of grain without paying attention to the structure of each individual stalk. That simply will not work with trees.

The expertise of a successful actor in a complex situation is that of the lumberjack, not that of the reaper. Nor is it the expertise of the "methodologist" who measures everything with the same yardstick. It is the expertise of one who pays close attention to the specific configuration of the facts at a given time, aiming all the while at adapting one's behavior accordingly.

REFERENCES

Ackermann, D. (1984). *Projektbericht "Robi Otter."* Lehrstuhl für Arbeits und Betriebspsychologie en der ETH Zürich.
Badke-Schaub, P., & Dörner, D. (1987). *Ein Simulationsmodell für die Ausbreitung von Aids – Erweiterte Fassung* (Memorandum No. 59, Lehrstuhl Psychologie II). Bamberg: Universität Bamberg.
Badke-Schaub, P., & Schaub, H. (1986). *Persönlichkeit und Problemlösen.* Diplomarbeit am Lehrstuhl Psychologie II, Universität Bamberg.
Battmann, W. (1982). *Planung und Belastung. Mentale und motivationale Konsequenzen.* Diplomarbeit, Institut für Psychologie der FU Berlin.
Brehmer, B., & Allard, R. (1986). *Dynamic decision making: A general paradigm and some experimental results.* Uppsala: Department of Psychology, University of Uppsala.
Broadbent, D. E., & Aston, B. (1978). Human control of a simulated economic system. *Ergonomics, 21,* 1035–1043.
Bunderson, C. V. (1970). The computer and instructional design. In W. H. Holtzman (Ed.), *Computer assisted instruction, testing and guidance* (pp. 45–73). New York: Harper & Row.
Clausewitz, C. von (1880). *Vom Kriege.* Berlin: Dümmler.
Dörner, D. (1985). *Modell der Ausbreitung von Aids in einer homogenen Population. Vorstudie zu einem Simulationsmodell* (Memorandum No. 38, Lehrstuhl Psychologie II). Bamberg: Universität Bamberg.
Dörner, D. (1986a). *Ein Simulationsprogramm zur Ausbreitung von Aids* (Memorandum No. 40, Lehrstuhl Psychologie II). Bamberg: Universität Bamberg.
Dörner, D. (1986b). Diagnostik der operativen Intelligenz. *Diagnostica, 32*(4), 290–308.
Dörner, D., & Kreuzig, H. W. (1983). Problemlösefähigkeit und Intelligenz. *Psychologische Rundschau, 34,* 185–192.
Dörner, D., Kreuzig, H. W., Reither, F., & Stäudel, T. (Eds.). (1983). *Lohhausen: Vom Umgang mit Unbestimmtheit und Komplexität.* Bern: Huber.
Dörner, D., & Reichert-Lieberknecht, U. (1991). *Kühlhaus.* Unpublished dissertation. Lehrstuhl Psychologie II. University of Bamberg, Germany.
Dörner, D., & Reither, F. (1978). Über das Problemlösen in sehr komplexen Realitätsbereichen. *Zeitschrift für Experimentelle und Angewandte Psychologie, 25,* 527–551.
Dörner, D., Stäudel, T., & Strohschneider, S. (1986). *MORO – Programmdoku-*

mentation (Memorandum No. 23, Lehrstuhl Psychologie II). Bamberg: Universität Bamberg.

Duncker, K. (1935). *Zur Psychologie des produktiven Denkens*. Berlin: Springer.

Eyferth, K., Hoffmann-Plato, I., Muchowski, L., Otremba, H., Rossbach, H., Spies, M., & Widowski, D. (1982). Handlungsorganisation. *Institut für Psychologie der TUB, Berlin: Forschungsbericht, 82*, 4.

Eyferth, K., Schömann, M., & Widwoski, D. (1986). Der Umgang von Psychologen mit Komplexität. *Sprache und Kognition, 1*, 11–26.

Funk, J. (1981). Mondlandung – ein neuer Aufgabentyp zur Erforschung komplexen Problemlösens. *Trierer Psychologische Berichte, 8*, 9.

Funke, J. (1984). *Komplexes Problemlösen. Kritische Bestandsaufnahme und weiterführende Perspektiven*. Dissertation, Universität Trier.

Gediga, G., Schöttke, H., & Tücke, M. (1983). Problemlösen in einer sehr komplexen Situation. *Archiv für Psychologie, 135*, 325–341.

Hesse, F. W. (1982). Effekte des semantischen Kontextes auf die Bearbeitung komplexer Probleme. *Zeitschrift für Experimentelle und Angewandte Psychologie, 29*, 62–91.

Klix, F. (1971). *Information und Verhalten*. Bern: Huber.

Kluwe, R., & Reimann, H. (1983). *Problemlösen bei vernetzten, komplexen Problemen. Effekte des Verbalisierens auf die Problemlöseleistung*. Bericht aus dem FB Pädagogik an der Bundeswehrhochschule Hamburg.

Lindblom, C. E. (1964). The science of "muddling through." In H. J. Leavitt & L. R. Pondy (Eds.), *Readings in managerial psychology* (pp. 61–78). University of Chicago Press.

Maas, W. (1989). *Manipulation eines Räuber-Beute-Systems*. Diplomarbeit im Fach Psychologie, Universität Bamberg.

Oesterreich, R. (1985). *Motivationale Aspekte des Handelns in simulierten Entscheidungsnetzen* (Projektbericht, Institut für Humanwissenschaft in Arbeit und Ausbildung der TU Berlin).

Opwis, K., Spada, H., & Schwiersch, M. (1985). *Erwerb und Anwendung von Wissen über ein ökologisches System* (Forschungsbericht Nr. 23 des Psychologischen Instituts der Albert-Ludwigs-Universität, Freiburg).

Putz-Osterloh, W. (1981). *Problemlöseprozesse und Intelligenztestleistung*. Bern: Huber.

Putz-Osterloh, W. (1987a). Komplexe Verhaltensmasse zur Erfassung von Hochbegabung. *Zeitschrift für differentielle und diagnostische Psychologie, 8*, 207–216.

Putz-Osterloh, W. (1987b). Gibt es Experten für komplexe Probleme? *Zeitschrift für Psychologie, 195*, 63–84.

Putz-Osterloh, W., & Lemme, M. (1987). Knowledge and its intelligent application to problem-solving. *German Journal of Psychology, 11*(4), 286–303.

Reichert, U. I., & Dörner, D. (1988). Heurismen beim Umgang mit einem "einfachen" dynamischen System. *Sprache und Kognition, 1*, 12–24.

Reither, F., & Stäudel, T. (1985). Thinking and action. In M. Frese & J. Sabini (Eds.), *Goal directed behavior: The concept of action in psychology* (pp. 110–122). Hillsdale, NJ: Erlbaum.

Schaub, H. (1989). *Garten: Verhaltenstypen beim Problemlösen*. Referat, gehalten auf der 31. TeaP, Bamberg, 20–23 März 1989.

Schaub, H., & Strohschneider, S. (1989). *Die Rolle heuristischen Wissens beim Umgang mit einem komplexen System – oder – sind Manager bessere Manager?*

(Memorandum No. 68, Forschungsbericht Lehrstuhl Psychologie II). Bamberg: Universität Bamberg.

Schaub, H., & Tisdale, T. (1988). *Institutsinterner Bericht* (Unpublished paper, Lehrstuhl Psychologie II). Bamberg: Universität Bamberg.

Stäudel, T. (1987). *Problemlösen, Emotionen und Kompetenz.* Regensburg: S. Roderer.

Sterman, J. D. (1984). *Instructions for running the beer distribution game.* (D-3674, MIT System Dynamics Group). Cambridge, MA: MIT.

Sterman, J. D. (1987). *Misconceptions of feedback in dynamic decision making* (Working Paper 1899–87, Sloan School of Management). Cambridge, MA: MIT.

Sterman, J. D., & Meadows, D. (1985). Strategem-2. A microcomputer simulation game of the Kondratiev cycle. *Simulation and Games, 16,* 174–202.

Strohschneider, S. (1986). Zur Stabilität und Validität des Handelns in komplexen Realitätsbereichen. *Sprache und Kognition, 1,* 42–48.

Strohschneider, S. (1987). *Vektor: Programmdokumentation (1)* (Memorandum No. 47, Lehrstuhl Psychologie II). Bamberg: Universität Bamberg.

Tisdale, T. (1988). *Planungs- und Entscheidungsprozesse von Individuen in komplexen Problemsituationen.* Diplomarbeit, Universität Bamberg.

van der Weth, R. (1989). *Zielbildung bei der Organisation des Handelns.* Frankfurt am Main: Lang.

10 Techniques for representing expert knowledge

JUDITH REITMAN OLSON AND KEVIN J. BIOLSI

At a high level, researchers investigating the nature of expertise want to know the same kinds of things. In the simplest terms, they want to know how the expert thinks. They want to know the *strategies* and *tactics* for interpreting a situation and how the appropriate responses are retrieved and enacted. And they want to know the content and organization of knowledge in that domain, the *concepts* and their categorical and causal *relationships*. Indeed, some of the continuing research themes have to do with how the organization of concepts for an expert differs from that for a novice, how the organization develops, and whether the strategies used by experts and novices to solve difficult problems differ.

The relevant technical literature for a given domain of expertise shows that the amount of knowledge available to experts is vast. If, in addition, we consider the large body of experiences and self-generated knowledge, as well as the acquired procedures, it is clear than an exhaustive enumeration of the relevant knowledge of even a single expert would be extremely difficult. It would become even more difficult if we wanted to make claims regarding how the experts' knowledge was internally represented and organized. Hence, researchers in expertise have designed specific tasks whereby experts as well as novices can be examined under more focused laboratory conditions.

For example, in their early studies of chess skill, Chase and Simon (1973) and de Groot (1965) asked experts and novices to reproduce chess positions after a single 5-second glance. They found that experts showed extraordinary skill at that task. Chase and Simon attributed that ability to experts' organization of knowledge of chess positions into meaningful "chunks," the chunks, in turn, being organized into hierarchies. Other researchers followed with a variety of analyses of special interviews (e.g., Patel, Evans, & Groen, 1988) and analyses of recall tasks (e.g., McKeithen, Reitman, Rueter, & Hirtle, 1981).

In the general literature on cognitive psychology, one can find a number of analysis techniques that were developed to display the content and organization of knowledge and to reveal the kinds of strategies people employ to solve problems. This chapter reviews a wide set of these techniques, with the goal of helping researchers who are concerned with the nature of expertise to select methods appropriate to their questions and their domains.

All research on expertise has shown that experts have a vast body of specific knowledge on which they consistently draw to generate efficient performance. The major challenge to investigators of expertise is to elicit and describe the content and the general organization of experts' knowledge, as well as to identify or infer their general strategies for operating with that knowledge to solve problems. The methods available to investigators can be organized along two dimensions: specific versus general and direct versus indirect. Some methods elicit specific knowledge and strategies in the context of accomplishing particular tasks, from which the investigator must identify potential general characteristics across different tasks by means of induction. Other methods, such as interviews, ask the experts themselves to identify their general strategies, as well as the general aspects of their knowledge.

A rather different approach is adopted by researchers who use any of the large class of indirect methods in which experts report ratings or recall based on their accumulated experiences. On the basis of large numbers of such ratings and recalls, it is possible to infer the general organization of a specified set of concepts using indirect computational methods. This chapter describes and reviews both direct and indirect techniques,[1] as well as those that are based on either specific or general knowledge. We compare the methods in terms of their advantages and disadvantages, highlighting their different underlying analytic assumptions and display representations.

In the discussion of these methods, we make distinctions among the ways in which information is *elicited* from the experts, the *summary form* of the data, the subsequent *analyses,* and the final *representations* of the information. In clearly distinguishing among these stages, we note that different methods share some stages, but differ in important assumptions in the other stages. This chapter ends with a suggestion for blending the techniques into a discovery cycle, providing the researcher with as rich a display of a person's knowledge as is currently feasible.

DIRECT METHODS

Figure 10.1 shows a map of the direct methods covered in this review, highlighting the connections among their various stages: elicitation, summary data, analysis, and final representation. This figure makes clear the common summary stage in most of these techniques, notably the common verbal transcript, which is analyzed to generate different final representations. Representations from direct methods include objects and their relationships, both categorical and causal, and global types of strategies, such as means–ends analysis and forward or backward chaining.

---

[1] These topics have been reviewed in much shorter form for the expert-system community by Olson and Rueter (1987) and Hoffman (1987).

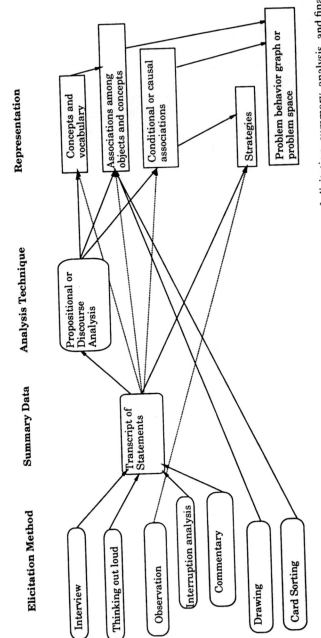

Figure 10.1. Diagram of the relationships among various *direct* methods in terms of elicitation, summary, analysis, and final representation.

Interviews: open form

An interview is the most common method for eliciting knowledge from people. The purpose is to engage in conversations with experts so that they can reveal the objects in their domains of expertise, how those objects are related or organized, and the processes used in making judgments, solving problems, or designing solutions. There are general, well-known problems involving the fact that the interviewer is not passive in this situation, making the technique ripe for bias. That is, the interviewer may interpret what the subject says in terms that are personally understandable, rather than in the way the subject intended it. But to get a fairly rough, rapid introduction to a domain – to identify the objects in which subjects code problem situations and to hear experts describe their perceptions and recall of how they approach their work – an interview is a good starting point.

Good seed questions for interviews include the following: "What kinds of things do you like to know about when you begin to ponder a problem?" "What facts or hypotheses do you try to establish when thinking about a problem?" "Does this factor depend on other factors being present?" Depending on the goal of the interview, the course of questioning and the amount of detail elicited can vary widely.

A principal problem with descriptions of general procedures elicited from interviews is that efficient performance by experts is observed on specific problems, where we see access to specialized knowledge and procedures. Hence, it is often unclear whether the statements about general knowledge are actually those stored and used or merely those described after the fact in response to the interviewer's questions. A large literature on postsession interviews regarding subjects' strategies in experiments shows that subjects' descriptions of their strategies correspond poorly to the observed performance aggregated across trials (Ericsson & Simon, 1984). In specific trials, however, subjects' immediate verbal reports on their thoughts are closely related to their actual performance. The methods involving immediate verbal reports are described in a later section.

Interviews: question answering

More specific information can be elicited by using questions of particular sorts. In an elegant, well-thought-out example, Patel and her colleagues (e.g., Joseph & Patel, 1990; Patel et al., 1988) asked medical experts for causal explanations of specific medical cases. In answering the questions, the subjects revealed both vocabulary and various kinds of learned and personally constructed connections included in the domain. From this set of sentences and interviewer responses, Patel and her colleagues then applied a combination of conversation analysis and protocol analysis (Ericsson & Simon, 1984) to identify objects and their causal, conditional, associative, equivalence, and category relationships. The resulting diagram of connections is quite rich in both its encoded information and the major clusters of ideas and concepts shown to the viewer. Examples of such representations are shown by Patel and Groen (chapter 4, this volume, Figures 4.4 and 4.5). It is important to note that Patel and her associates use specific clinical cases, as opposed to general probes, to elicit explanations. Inferences about general knowledge must be drawn by the analyst from the information gleaned from the specific cases.

In short, the technique of Patel and her associates presents the subject with some problem situations or diagnoses and elicits explanatory statements on how that situation may have arisen. The summary is a corpus of sentences that embody these concepts and a whole variety of relationships. A final representation is a labeled network of these concepts and relationships.

Interviews: probes of explicit relationships

A method called "inferential flow analysis" is a variant of the question-answering method that involves asking more pointed questions about general (not case-based) relationships (Salter, 1983). In general, like Patel, Salter draws a network diagram, but from particular answers to questions about the relationship between two objects or concepts in the domain of expertise. For example, in one study, Salter elicited laymen's views of the U.S. economic system. He first drew up a set of terms with which he thought laymen would be familiar, such as "personal savings interest rate," "productivity," and "business borrowing." He then asked specific questions about the relations between pairs of items; the subjects would answer in sets of sentences that included both the initial terms and others they thought it necessary to include in the explanation.

For example, he might ask, "What is the relationship between savings rate and inflation?" Answers might include such statements as this: "If inflation goes up, savings rates will go down, because savings interest rates are lower than the amount one can save by buying now instead of later." "Savings rate" and "inflation" are then linked with an inverse relationship, with "purchasing" identified as an intervening concept. A session begins with a set of seed questions, and over the course of the session new objects are included as they are mentioned by the subject. This corpus of sentences is then analyzed to reveal the subject's model of economic relationships. Salter then builds a diagram in the form of a network of causal links, with positive and negative weights associated with them indicating the direction of the relationship and the consistency with which explanatory statements are made. Figure 10.2 shows an example of a resulting network.

This method can be useful in studying straightforward, general underlying relationships, but it is likely to be inadequate when one is attempting to capture complex organizations or organizations that contain many exceptions arising from specific cases. It should not be assumed, however, that the expert has the more complex organization and the novice the simple organization.

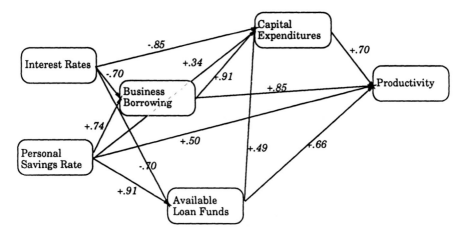

Figure 10.2. Inferential flow analysis made from statements regarding the relationships between concepts.

As will be shown later in discussing studies of indirect induction of networks of relationships, often it is the novice who has the less highly integrated, case-specific knowledge.

In short, inferential flow analysis begins with some concepts, elicits relationships and intervening concepts, and summarizes the set of sentences that contain the relationships. The analysis involves encoding the concepts, both probed and elicited, and the direction and frequency of elicited links between them. A final representation is a directed network of causal relationships.

Thinking out loud: protocol analysis

Because many people are not adept at recalling and explaining after the fact all of the associations or processes they normally use while performing a task, having them report their thoughts during task performance is believed to be a better way to acquire richer process information. This method asks people to report their current thoughts while they work through problems in their domains. They are instructed not to explain things or even use full sentences, but merely to "turn up the volume" on some of the associations or inferences made in the normal conduct of a task. Experts tend to report what they are trying to achieve, such as goals and subgoals, as well as the retrieved thoughts and knowledge that are helping them reach their goals.

From the set of utterances recorded, the objects are identified, along with their relationships and the causal inferences the expert drew moment by moment. Experts' think-aloud protocols reflect particular thoughts about specific problems. Hence, in order to identify the general characteristics of processes and retrieved knowledge, we need to rely on induction based on analyses of several protocols on similar tasks. Higher-level analyses are called in to

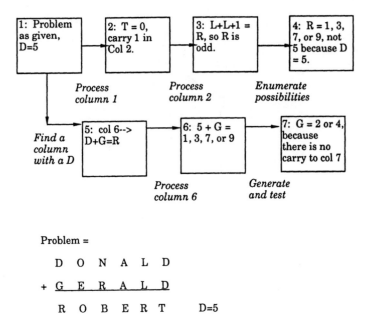

Problem =

```
    D   O   N   A   L   D
+   G   E   R   A   L   D
    R   O   B   E   R   T       D=5
```

Figure 10.3. Problem–behavior graph. Adapted from Lindsay & Norman (1977).

indicate the kinds of strategies people use. From the patterns of information as each new piece is discovered, the analyst can determine whether the person was working forward from the problem statement or backward from the goal, or was using some other strategy.

Two other representations can follow from the analyzed protocol. By identifying the individual pieces of information discovered at each successive moment, one can draw a summary figure called a *problem–behavior graph* (Newell & Simon, 1972), an example of which is shown in Figure 10.3. In these figures, time moves from left to right, and from top to bottom when there are no more moves to the right on a given row. This representation puts each piece of new information in a box and connects the boxes with labels indicating the operations that changed the person's state of knowledge. These operations include such acts as shifting attention to a new, related portion of the problem, making an inference from the current set of knowledge, and reviewing the collected bits of relevant knowledge for new inferences. The analyst then examines the overall series of operations and describes general characteristics of the person's behavior.

Figure 10.3 shows details of portions of the knowledge acquired while someone solves a cryptarithmetic problem. In this global view, there are annotations regarding the kinds of things the person seems to be doing at particular points. A more recent formalization of this kind of representation is the *problem space*, a collection of states of knowledge and "legal" operations that can advance the current state of knowledge into a new state. This is the representation used in the SOAR system (Laird, Newell, & Rosenbloom, 1987).

Capturing information from the process of thinking out loud has an advantage over interviewing and question answering in that there is no delay between the act of thinking of something and reporting it. But it is not appropriate for all kinds of tasks. Ericsson and Simon (1984) carefully detailed the kinds of tasks for which the thinking-out-loud protocol might provide acceptable, useful kinds of data. To summarize, the tasks for which verbalization is a natural part of thinking are the tasks for which the thinking-out-loud protocol is valid. That is, if verbal information is produced while one makes inferences to oneself, or identifies salient features of the objects in the situation, then the protocol provides acceptable data.

There are tasks that involve the use of idiosyncratic language in the process, and they can be difficult to analyze (e.g., in composing music, a composer often will have a special language for the part of the piece currently being written). And because social pressure in such a situation will encourage "explanation" to an outsider (the investigator), the protocol itself may either distort the process or be no better than after-the-fact descriptions, as in interviews. In general, however, there is good evidence that if a subject merely reports ongoing thoughts, the process followed is the same as that in silent conduct of the task. Highly routine, rapid tasks, such as perceptual motor activities in sports, do not typically involve verbal-based thinking, and therefore thinking-aloud verbalizations tend to be sparse and not highly informative.

Observation of task performance

If researchers want to avoid the distortions that can occur in thinking-out-loud tasks, they can merely observe performance. Researchers, however, have a more difficult time determining what the objects are in the domain, their relationships, and the inferences used in the situation. Two courses of action are common. First, the session can be videotaped and shown to the subject soon after the session. The tape can then be given a thorough commentary, with action stopped at critical points and the researcher interviewing the subject about certain detailed aspects of the behavior. This has the advantage of allowing commentary without interrupting the normal flow of work, a problem that can arise with concurrent verbalizing. It suffers, however, from potential distortion because of delay between the action and the report; such delay can lead to memory loss or can allow the subject time to begin explaining things in a way that will make the subject's actions appear less capricious and more rational.

A second option, particularly appropriate when a great deal of the expert's behavior is already accounted for, is to observe normal performance but interrupt at key moments when the behavior is either particularly puzzling or critical to a fuller understanding. The advantage of this is to capture immedi-

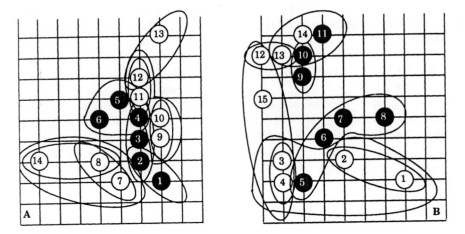

Figure 10.4. A pattern of stones from the game of Go for which the Go expert encircled those stones that "go together." The numbers on the stones represent the order in which the Go expert placed these stones on the board when recalling the position 6 months later.

ate memory for the situation, its antecedents, and the methods being used. But it has the obvious disadvantage of interrupting natural behavior, which is known to be difficult to resume, especially in difficult problem situations.

Special tasks: drawing "closed curves."   The foregoing methods attempt to reveal the contents of the thought processes during the solution of problems. These methods are free of assumptions about the form of the relations among the items, whether they are lists, tables, networks, or physical space. They do, however, require the subject to have in hand a vocabulary with which to describe the items and their relationships. This does not always suit those kinds of tasks that have elements encoded in nonverbal terms, as is likely in motor or perceptual tasks. The method of drawing "closed curves" is a specialized method for indicating the relationships among those objects that can be assumed to be encoded in a *physical-space representation.*

In the method of drawing closed curves, the expert is asked to indicate which of a collection of physical objects "go together," by encircling the related objects. This technique is applicable to any spatial representation, such as a typeset formula, an X-ray or CAT scan, or a position on a game board.

For example, Reitman (1976) asked a master of the game of Go to draw closed curves around related stones involved in a position in the game. Figure 10.4 illustrates several aspects of his responses. Two positions are displayed, with the master's encircling of related stones. In addition, each stone bears a number that represents the ordinal position in which that stone was placed on the board in a recall task six months later. Note that the recall order matches the closed curves to a remarkable degree: Nearly always, all stones of an encircled chunk were recalled before moving on to another chunk. This regularity of behavior supports claims for the validity of the information contained in the originally closed curves.[2]

Special tasks: hierarchical card sorting. The tasks of protocol analysis, observation and commentary, and drawing closed curves all elicit aspects of expertise in specific situations, from which the analyst then infers generalities. That is in contrast with both the interview technique and the next method to be described, both of which elicit generalities directly from the expert. Whereas interviews elicit verbal descriptions, the method to be discussed next is without verbalization.

In the method of hierarchical card sorting, investigators believe that subjects have information stored in hierarchies, and they ask their subjects to cluster items directly. In this method, the subject is given a stack of small cards, on each of which is written the name of one of the objects under study. Typically, subjects perform an initial sorting of the cards, either with or without instructions on how many piles are expected (Kellogg & Breen, 1987). Often, when the subject is unconstrained, the experimenter often then asks the subject to combine the clusters until they are all in one group (recording the contents at each level in the hierarchy as they go) or to take the original clusters and break them down into subclusters until there is no longer any natural, meaningful distinction among items in a category. This method requires that the analyst make the strong assumption that the information is stored in a hierarchy, and it suffers from the potential problem that the subject may make the organization more rational than the organization the subject has actually stored. It is, however, a quick method for beginning to understand the organization of information in memory.

INDIRECT METHODS

All of the previously described methods rely on the subject's reports. Most of them rely on the subject's ability to articulate information. It is not always the case, however, that experts have access to their knowledge. In many cases, objects are "seen" as related but the expert is not able to access the fleeting perception. Often inferences are drawn without the expert's knowing it.

In all of the following methods, experts are not asked for reports. Instead, they are asked to perform a variety of other tasks, such as rating how similar two objects are or recalling a set of objects several times from several starting points. From the regularities in the subject's set of behaviors in performing these tasks, the analyst infers underlying structure among the objects rated or

---

[2] This regular behavior also provided the core idea for the development of the Reitman-Rueter ordered-tree analysis (described later, in the section on indirect methods).

recalled. In most cases, there will be corroborating evidence from experimental studies that the structures thus uncovered have meaning and are likely to be used in some way by the subject in natural performance of the domain task. Again, these methods vary in regard to whether the experts (1) are given or are assumed to construct a specific context or case on which to base their judgments or (2) are assumed to be behaving on the basis of their internally generated principles. These variations are noted in the descriptions that follow.

Figure 10.5 shows the indirect methods and their elicitation procedures, their summary data, their algorithms, and the resulting representations, similar to those shown in Figure 10.1 for the direct methods. To allow the reader to evaluate and compare the representations from these methods informally for usefulness, we can use data from the same subjects judging the same items from their domain of expertise. We collected appropriate data from two subjects for use in a majority of the methods. These two subjects were instructors in an undergraduate laboratory course in experimental psychology at the University of Michigan. They were shown 16 terms used in the laboratory course, well known to them. On one occasion, they were asked to rate each pair of terms for similarity on a scale of 1–9; on another occasion they were asked to recall these 16 items 10 times from many different starting points. They were not interviewed for "repertory grid analysis"; we shall illustrate this method with hypothetical responses.

Multidimensional scaling

Multidimensional scaling (MDS) is a technique that assumes that the underlying mental representation is analogous to physical n-dimensional space (Kruskal, 1964; Shepard, 1962a, 1962b; Shepard, Romney, & Nerlove, 1972). The experimenter collects proximities (similarities) on all pairs of objects or concepts in the domain of inquiry. These proximities are assumed to be symmetric and graded; that is, A is as similar to B as B is to A, and the similarities take on a variety of continuous values, not just 0 or 1.

Commonly these proximities are obtained by asking the subject, for each pair, "How similar are A and B?" Other methods of obtaining proximities are described later. Figure 10.6 shows a small sample matrix for the similarities of 16 elementary concepts in experimental psychology. The matrix is then used as input to an analysis program that searches for the best placement of these objects in a space of analyst-specified dimensionality. Each solution associated with a potential dimensionality has an associated "stress" value, a measure of the deviation from a perfect fit. The analyst looks for solutions with low stress, with solutions on fewer dimensions preferred. The analyst then examines the plots to judge the best placement of the axes and a plausible labeling for them. Figure 10.7 shows the two-dimensional solution for the matrix in Figure 10.6, and a second solution for another subject judging the same terms.

This kind of display can reveal interesting clusters of objects, neighbor

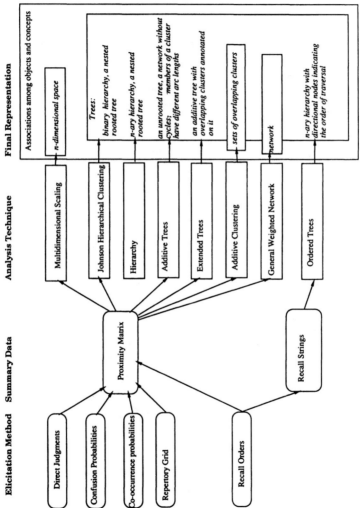

Elicitation Method **Summary Data** **Analysis Technique** **Final Representation**

Associations among objects and concepts

Direct Judgments

Confusion Probabilities

Co-occurrence probabilities

Repertory Grid

Proximity Matrix

Recall Orders

Recall Strings

Multidimensional Scaling → *n-dimensional space*

Johnson Hierarchical Clustering

Hierarchy

Additive Trees

Extended Trees

Additive Clustering

General Weighted Network

Ordered Trees

Trees:

binary hierarchy, a nested rooted tree

n-ary hierarchy, a nested rooted tree

an unrooted tree, a network without cycles;   members of a cluster have different arc lengths

an additive tree with overlapping clusters annotated on it

sets of overlapping clusters

network

n-ary hierarchy with directional nodes indicating the order of traversal

Figure 10.5. Diagram of the relationships among various indirect methods in terms of elicitation, summary, analysis, and final representation.

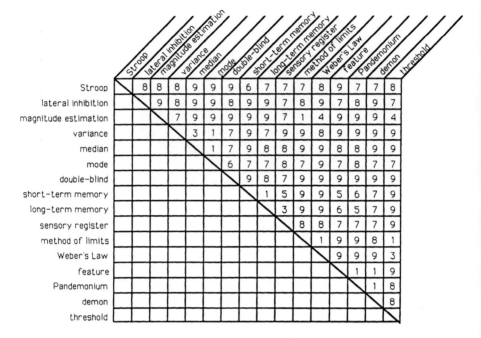

Figure 10.6. Distance matrix of judged similarities between pairs of items from a course in experimental psychology. These responses are from one subject.

relationships, and outliers. Further clarification of relationships can come from the subject's explanations of the reasons for certain clusterings or outlier relationships. One difficulty with this technique, however, is that elicitation of similarities from the subject is tedious if there are many objects; for n objects, $n(n - 1)/2$ judgments are required. Furthermore, there are no standard procedures to help the analyst find the dimensionality with the best stress value and then place the axes (moving them about the n-dimensional space) so that they can be meaningfully labeled. Use of the technique is straightforward; interpretation of the results is not.

Johnson hierarchical clustering

Like MDS, hierarchical clustering begins with a half-matrix of similarity judgments (Johnson, 1967). The assumptions for this technique, however, are in direct contrast to those for MDS. Whereas MDS assumes symmetric distances and graded properties, hierarchical clustering assumes that an item is or is not a member of a cluster. Judgments of similarity are assumed to be a function of the number of nested clusters that two items have in common, or the "height" at which two items become members of the same category.

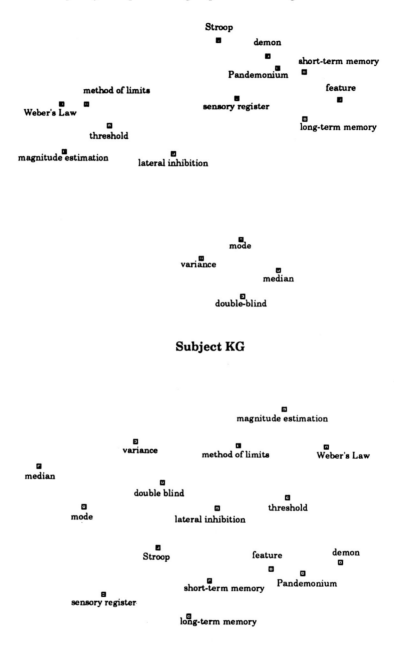

Subject KG

Subject CF

Figure 10.7. MDS solutions of similarity judgments from two different subjects.

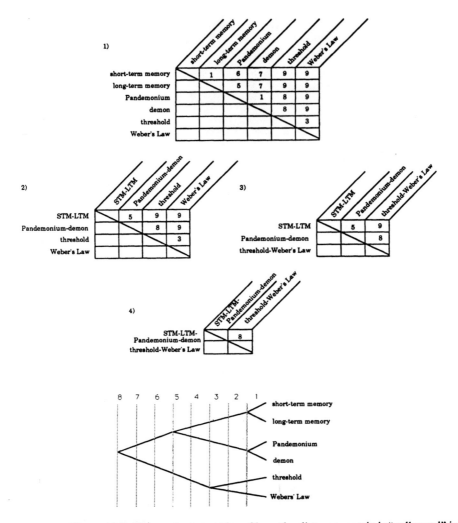

Figure 10.8. Illustrative examples of how the distance matrix is "collapsed" in the course of analyzing for a Johnson hierarchical clustering solution. The resulting tree is shown at the bottom.

Johnson hierarchical clustering is a fairly simple, straightforward algorithm that begins with the half-matrix of distances and ends with a hierarchical representation of the itcms. In broad strokes, pairs of items that are the closest in the matrix are joined into a single cluster. A new summary matrix is then drawn, with this cluster serving as a single item. This new matrix is then examined again for the closest pair; those items are joined, and a new matrix is drawn. Each time a new matrix is drawn, the interitem distances between unclustered items are copied from the original matrix; distances between items and the new clusters can be calculated as the *minimum* dis-

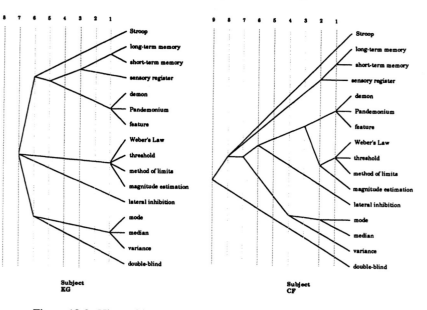

Figure 10.9. Hierarchical clustering solutions for two different subjects, using the single-link method.

tances from the unclustered items to the clustered items, or the *maximum*, or the *average*.

For example, in Figure 10.8, a small portion of the matrix from Figure 10.6 is collapsed using the minimum or single-link method, and the resulting tree is pictured. Notice that in moving from matrix 1 to matrix 2, we combine *short-term memory* and *long-term memory* into one cluster, and *Pandemonium* and *demon* into another, as these items are closest in the original matrix. The value in the rewritten matrix for the distance between two clusters is 5, the minimum of 5, 6, 7, and 7 (for *Pandemonium–long-term memory, Pandemonium–short-term memory, demon–long-term memory,* and *demon–short-term memory,* respectively). Solution hierarchies for our two subjects judging terms from experimental psychology are shown in Figure 10.9.

An advantage of hierarchical clustering is that it can be done with paper and pencil. A disadvantage is that it begins with a distance matrix that is just as tedious to collect as that for MDS. Furthermore, without some theoretical justification for choosing a particular joining algorithm (the minimum, maximum or average), one must choose arbitrarily; unfortunately, different algorithms can produce different hierarchies. For example, in Figure 10.10, where the minimum and maximum linkages were both used on the same proximity matrix to construct the hierarchy, note that in the single-link (minimum) method, *demon–Pandemonium–feature* belong to the cluster having to do with memory stores (*short-term memory , long-term memory, sensory register,* and *Stroop*), and in the complete-link (maximum) method it is unclustered.

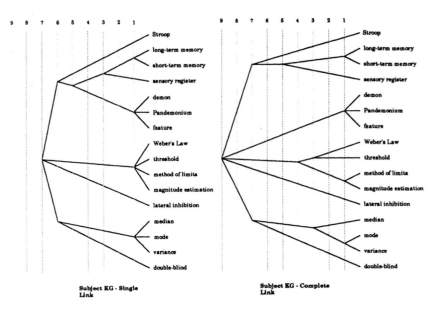

Figure 10.10. Two trees result from using different linking methods on the data from a given subject.

Repertory grid analysis

Repertory grid analysis is a blend of a novel elicitation technique based on interviews and the Johnson hierarchical clustering technique. The method has a procedure that produces the original distance matrix in a unique way (Boose, 1986). Repertory grid analysis has its origins in personal-construct theory in clinical psychology (Kelley, 1955), but has more recently been applied to the elicitation of expertise for building expert systems.

The elicitation session begins with an open interview of the subject, asking the subject to name some objects or concepts in the domain of interest. After a small set is generated, the analyst picks three of these items and asks, "What trait or dimension distinguishes any two of these items from the third?" The subject names a dimension in whatever terms are natural. The subject then indicates which of the three items are high on this trait, and which are low. The analyst records the responses, typically on a 1–3 or 1–5 scale, a rating for each of the three objects on that dimension. The analyst then picks three other objects and asks the same question about naming a trait that distinguishes one from the other two. This process of asking for salient dimensions or traits continues with a significant number of triples, enough so that the analyst is satisfied that the major dimensions of similarity and dissimilarity have been uncovered. The subject is then asked to rate all the remaining items on all the elicited dimensions, filling in the grid.

Having collected a grid with objects across the top and dimensions across

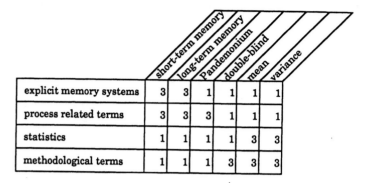

	short-term memory	long-term memory	Pandemonium	double-blind	mean	variance
explicit memory systems	3	3	1	1	1	1
process related terms	3	3	3	1	1	1
statistics	1	1	1	1	3	3
methodological terms	1	1	1	3	3	3

Figure 10.11. A portion of the repertory grid for a subject in which the dimensions were named by the subject, and various elements were rated on those dimensions.

the left border, as shown in Figure 10.11, the analyst then derives a proximity matrix. For each pair of objects, the analyst calculates the sum of the absolute differences of the ratings across dimensions. For example, for the grid in Figure 10.11, the distance between *double-blind* and *variance* is

$$0 + 0 + 2 + 0 = 2$$

The proximity matrix so calculated is then typically analyzed using Johnson hierarchical clustering.

This method also allows clustering of the *dimensions* elicited from the subject. A new proximity matrix is calculated from the repertory grid, this time finding distances between dimensions by summing the absolute differences across *items*. This proximity matrix then is analyzed using Johnson hierarchical clustering, with the resulting picture revealing the relationships between traits or categories that the subject uses to evaluate objects in the domain of expertise.

Additive trees

Johnson hierarchical clustering techniques impose the rather severe restriction that the distances from any nonterminal node to all terminal nodes below it are equal. That is, all within-cluster items are equidistant from each other and are also equidistant from any object outside the cluster.

Additive trees (Sattath & Tversky, 1977), also called weighted free trees (Cunningham, 1978) or path-length trees (Carroll, 1976), are not subject to the previously mentioned constraint. The additive-tree algorithm starts with a half-matrix of proximities and produces a set of nonoverlapping clusters such that the length of the segment joining any two objects represents the rated distance between the two objects. Because all stimulus objects need not be equidistant from the root node (in fact, there need be no distinctive root node), nonequivalent within-cluster distances can be preserved. Examples of two experts' additive trees for the 16 psychology terms are shown in Figure 10.12.

Extended trees

All of the clustering techniques described thus far represent the data as *nonoverlapping clusters*. However, often an object may potentially be considered as a member of more than one set of objects. Countries, for example, belong to clusters denoting their geographical neighborhoods, but also are associated with their former colonies or with other countries that have the same language or political orientation. Thus, Russia belongs with Finland and West Germany by geographical proximity, and until recently with Cuba by political proximity. Extended trees (Corter & Tversky, 1986) build upon additive-tree representations by allowing cluster overlap. Once the additive tree has been constructed, segments of the tree are *marked* to correspond to overlapping clusters. For example, in the extended trees in Figure 10.13, the term *long-term memory* has a strong link to *short-term memory* and *sensory register,* denoting traditional characterizations of memory stores. However, the model *Pandemonium,* a layered model of feature recognition, resides in *long-term memory* and is thus secondarily associated with it.

Additive clustering

Like the methods described thus far, additive clustering begins with a proximity matrix (Arabie & Carroll, 1980; Shepard & Arabie, 1979). The method, however, does not join items by finding clusters and linking them, but by merely joining one item to another in circled sets. The additive-clustering model assumes that a set of objects composes a nonempty set of properties and that the similarity between any two objects is simply an additive function of the weights associated with properties shared by the objects. Each recovered cluster of objects corresponds to one such shared property. As in the case of extended trees, items may belong to more than one cluster. The resulting diagram can be drawn in a variety of ways, the only constraint being that related items are enclosed in the same closed curve. Often these are drawn on top of another diagram, such as a two-dimensional MDS solution, making the joining of items visually compact.

General weighted networks (Pathfinder)

Schvaneveldt and his colleagues (Cooke, Durso, & Schvaneveldt, 1986; Schvaneveldt, Durso, & Dearholt, 1985a; Schvaneveldt et al., 1985b) have developed a technique that yields a network representation of a proximity matrix. Networks and trees both fall under the heading of *graphs,* connected sets of items through paths or links. However, network representations are less constrained in that cycles (more than one path connecting the items of a pair) are allowed.

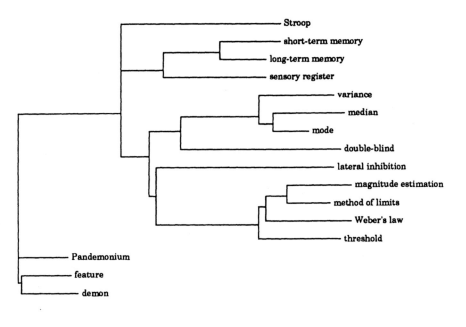

Subject KG

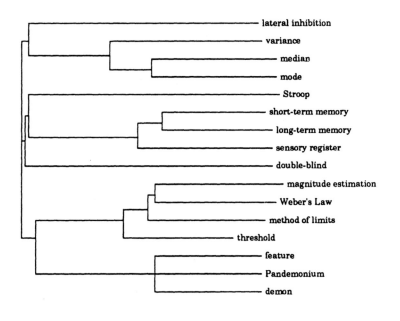

Subject CF

Figure 10.12. Additive-tree solutions for two subjects.

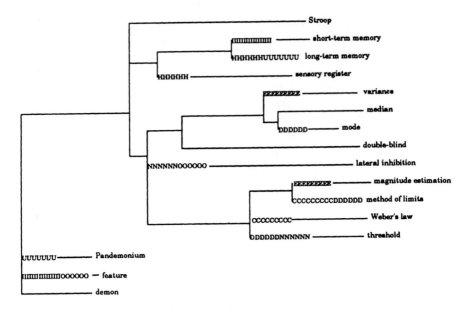

Subject
KG

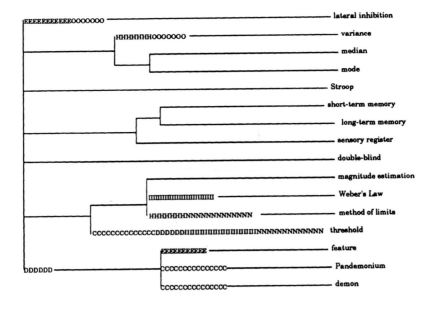

Subject
CF

Figure 10.13. Extended-tree solutions for two subjects.

Pathfinder starts with the full network defined by the data, in which links are placed between *all* pairs of objects for which proximities have been obtained.[3] The initial link weights are given by the original distance estimates. Once the algorithm has been applied, a link remains in the network only if it is on the *shortest* path connecting two objects. Path length can be defined in either of two ways. The first relies on the Minkowski *r*-metric:

$$\text{length}(P) = (\textstyle\sum l_i^r)^{1/r}$$

where l_i is the weight of the *i*th link in path *P*, and $1 \le r \le \infty$. Thus, the interpretation of path length varies with *r*. For example, if $r = 1$, then path length is simply the sum of the link weights along the path; if $r = \infty$, then path length is equal to the maximum link weight along the path.

The second method for computing path length is based on spreading-activation theories of memory (Collins & Loftus, 1975; Meyer & Schvaneveldt 1976). To compute the path length between two items, link weights are summed, starting at each of the items, until these two summed paths intersect at some third item. The path length is taken as the maximum of the two summations to the intersecting item. Traversing the distances in parallel from the two ends of the path is analogous to activation spreading through the network.

Pathfinder is a powerful representation of associations among items because it has the fewest constraints to satisfy. It does not require that items belong or not belong to a cluster (the items need not be strictly nested), and there can be several connect items, representing different dimensions of commonality and different kinds of associations. An example solution for the 16 items from psychology is shown in Figure 10.14.[4] Unlike the other methods described earlier, Pathfinder does not require that distances between objects be symmetric. For asymmetric proximity matrices, Pathfinder will construct a *directed graph,* such that a link between two objects may be traversed in only one direction. For symmetric proximity matrices, the solution will be an *undirected graph,* such that links may be traversed in either direction.

Pathfinder has been used in a variety of studies, including explorations of expert–novice differences (Schvaneveldt et al., 1985a). Among other differences, Schvaneveldt and associates found that experts' structures had fewer links (more consistently rated items in various combinations in the matrix), and they could easily label the links (as "is a," or "causes," for example).

Ordered trees from recall

Ordered trees come from work by Reitman and Rueter (1980) in their exploration of how memory organizations differ among experts and

---

[3] Pathfinder does not require that *all* pairwise estimates be obtained.
[4] This graphic was made from a proximity matrix that was an aggregate over five subjects. If the matrix for a single subject has a number of ties in it (as ours did), the Pathfinder solution is very complicated, with many links connecting many items, a veritable spaghetti bowl.

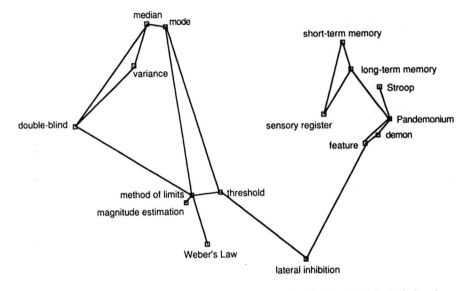

Figure 10.14. The general weighted network solution (Pathfinder) for data aggregated over a number of subjects.

novices. Ordered trees begin not with a distance matrix but with recall trials. The technique assumes that objects belong to a cluster or do not belong, similar to the assumption of hierarchical clustering. Unlike hierarchical clustering, however, this technique is built on a model of how the data are produced by the subject; it assumes that subjects recall items from a stored cluster before recalling items from another cluster. This assumption builds on data from people recalling from known (learned) organizations (Bower & Springston, 1970). Regularities found over a set of recall orders are assumed to reflect memory organization.

The following list shows several recall orders from subjects recalling elementary concepts from experimental psychology, the same set of items used in the foregoing similarity matrices, but from a different elicitation task (the asterisks indicate the trials in which the subject was asked to begin with that first word):

1. *feature, demon, Pandemonium, Stroop, magnitude estimation, method of limits, threshold, Weber's law, median, mode, variance, double-blind, lateral inhibition, sensory register, long-term memory, short-term memory

2. magnitude estimation, method of limits, threshold, Weber's law, median, mode, variance, double-blind, lateral inhibition, feature, demon, Pandemonium, Stroop, sensory register, long-term memory, short-term memory

3. *Weber's law, magnitude estimation, threshold, method of limits, median, mode, variance, double-blind, lateral inhibition, feature, demon, Pandemonium, Stroop, sensory register, long-term memory, short-term memory

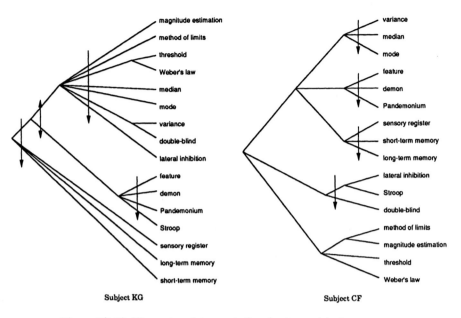

magnitude estimation
method of limits
threshold
Weber's law
median
mode
variance
double-blind
lateral inhibition
feature
demon
Pandemonium
Stroop
sensory register
long-term memory
short-term memory

variance
median
mode
feature
demon
Pandemonium
sensory register
short-term memory
long-term memory
lateral inhibition
Stroop
double-blind
method of limits
magnitude estimation
threshold
Weber's law

Subject KG   Subject CF

Figure 10.15. The ordered-tree solution for two subjects.

4. *median, mode, variance, double-blind, magnitude estimation, method of limits, threshold, Weber's law, feature, demon, Pandemonium, Stroop, lateral inhibition, sensory register, long-term memory, short-term memory

Typically, the subject is asked to recall the well-learned set of items many times from many different starting points. These recall strings are then examined for regularities; all sets of items that are recalled contiguously are identified as chunks, the chunks being written into a lattice (with inclusion being the covering relationship). This lattice is then redrawn into an ordered-tree structure, such as those in Figure 10.15, where arrows (either unidirectional or bidirectional) are drawn over the chunk elements that were recalled consistently in a particular order (or one order and its reverse).

One variant of the ordered-tree method releases the requirement that the subjects recall these items from memory. Instead, subjects sort cards with the individual items on them and then construct an order through the cards, either reporting this order to an analyst or writing the items down in a single order on paper. This variant has the advantage of ensuring that the subject records all items on each trial, but it has the disadvantage that the subject can make a more thoughtful progression and comparison of concepts, rather than a simple retrieval path from the organization as stored in memory.

This technique has been used to study expert–novice differences in several domains, such as computer programming (McKeithen et al., 1981), concepts in an undergraduate psychology course (Naveh-Benjamin, McKeachie, Lin,

& Tucker, 1986), and formulas and concepts from physics (J. Larkin, personal communication, 1978).

ANALYSIS AND COMPARISON OF METHODS

All of these methods progress through four distinct stages: They *elicit* behavior from the subject (e.g., ask the subject to rate the similarities of all pairs of items), *summarize* that behavior in a form that can be analyzed from different algorithmic perspectives (e.g., enter the judgments in a proximity half-matrix), *analyze* the data using one of a variety of algorithms or methods, and *display* the resulting regularities (e.g., in a multidimensional space or a hierarchy). Figures 10.1 and 10.5 illustrate the four stages of analysis of mental representation covered by both the direct and indirect methods reviewed here.

The methods have theoretically important differences involving the final form of the representation and the underlying assumptions about how the subject's knowledge is organized. But, surprisingly, as shown in this analysis, many of them share intermediate stages. For example, most of the direct methods involve categorizing utterances from a verbal transcript, and many of the indirect methods pass through a stage of summarizing data in a similarity matrix. By comparing the methods on these stages, we can better understand such things as the assumptions made about the relationship between the elicitation task and the final representation, the ease with which subjects can perform the important initial behaviors, and the algorithms that construct the final display for the analyst. Also, by showing the commonalities and links, the analyst can better select the proper elicitation and display methods to fit the underlying assumptions about the domain of expertise.

Elicitation methods

A number of methods can be used to elicit behavior from subjects so that we can infer the content and organization of their knowledge and the strategies they use to operate on that knowledge.

Interview and other retrospective reports. The most basic method is to interview the subjects, using free-form discussion of how they think about their domains, by asking for rationales and explanations, or by asking questions directly about particular relationships. These methods have the advantage of providing rich information, but they suffer from well-known limitations having to do with the accuracy of retrospective reports.

Thinking out loud during task performance. A second common elicitation method is to have subjects report their verbalizations during the course of performing tasks in their areas of expertise. In response to the general question, "What are you thinking about?" the subject has the opportunity to report the quick associations, inferences, and so forth, that arise during the normal course of work. Clearly there are tasks for which that would be inappropriate, such as tasks in which a person does not normally verbalize, as in highly perceptual and motor tasks. In addition, even when the task is primarily verbal, there is the persistent worry that the aspects reported will be different from the "normal" course of work and that the amount of mental effort expended in verbalizing, and therefore not available for the task itself, will change the way the subject is thinking. However, in a number of cases in which the performance of subjects who gave thinking-out-loud protocols was compared with the performance of those who did not verbalize, the processes were identical (Ericsson & Simon, 1984). It is important to have this kind of check on the potential distortion imposed by the concurrent task.

Drawing and card sorting. Drawing closed curves around items that "go together" and sorting cards with the items printed on them are direct elicitation methods. Although in some cases the subjects find such tasks quite natural and easy to do (e.g., the Go master in the Reitman, 1976, study), there can be situations in which a subject will not think of things on the basis of contiguity. It could be, for example, that the major determinant of items "going together" in Go is not close proximity in various arrangements, but distant loose associations, in which sets of stones conspire to force moves in a separate area. The recommendation in the use of this elicitation method is to be sensitive to the subject's reports of ease or naturalness.

In card sorting, we similarly recommend that the analyst note the ease with which the subject does the task as an indication that the results are or are not meaningful. Furthermore, constraining subjects to an initial fixed number of categories can be argued to be unnatural, in that if researchers know enough beforehand to designate a good number of categories, they probably also know what the categories will be. Also, there are data to suggest that instructing subjects to begin with a few categories that will then be successively broken into smaller and smaller subcategories will result in an organization different from what will be seen in the situation in which subjects begin with many small categories and progressively join them into higher-level groups. The first case accentuates differences; the second accentuates commonalities (Chin, 1988).

Direct and derived judgments of pairwise similarities. For these methods, subjects are required to compare selected objects and rate their similarity or relatedness. Among the direct judgment methods are ratings on a specified scale, rank orderings of pairs of items, triadic methods (i.e., in which subjects are asked which two of three items are more similar), and dyadic methods (i.e., in which subjects are presented with two pairs of items and asked to determine which of the pairs has greater similarity between its two members).

All of these methods of direct elicitation can be time-consuming if there are substantial numbers of items to be judged. If we use pairwise similarities, they will require $n(n - 1)/2$ judgments. If we assume that it takes about 10 sec for each judgment, a set of 50 will take 3.5 hours.

A more serious issue concerns the way in which people make these judgments and the matching of that process to the algorithm that uncovers the final representation. Each of these direct elicitations of proximities has implicit in it a theory that maps the process by which subjects go from an underlying mental representation (an n-dimensional space, a hierarchy, a network) into a set of judgments. Few have made these theories explicit, although Rips, Shoben, and Smith (1973) provided a notable exception. Because the algorithms by which the proximity matrices are transformed into representations differ markedly, it is important that researchers inventing or using these techniques make their theories of behavior explicit. Once explicit, the theories can then be verified by converging operations.

For example, there is some evidence that people do not weigh all the possible dimensions of similarity when generating a similarity-scale value, an assumption that is key to the use of MDS algorithms. Instead, people focus on one or two salient dimensions (salient at the time, depending on context) and use a simple aggregating function to summarize to one number. This suggests, then, that if similarity ratings are elicited, they are heavily dependent on the current context. In fact, as an example, there is evidence that the ratings and thus the final representation of the number system will be heavily dependent on the context in which the judgments are elicited (whether the numbers are in Roman numerals or series of dots, for example) (Shepard, Kilpatric, & Cunningham, 1975).

Furthermore, there is additional evidence to suggest that each pair presented to a subject elicits its own context or reminds the expert of a specific case. For example, when one is asked to judge the similarity between Russia and Finland, geographical proximity becomes salient; when one is asked about Cuba and Russia, the context of political orientation becomes salient, and striking current events can alter basic knowledge built up over a longer period of time. A matrix of similarities is more likely to be a large set of more localized judgments on pairs of items than to be a single, stable composite of many simultaneous dimensions. When MDS solutions have low stress values only when there are many dimensions or the dimensions are difficult to label, that may be a symptom of this effect of context. More locally sensitive representation algorithms, such as Johnson hierarchical clustering or Pathfinder, are on firmer psychological ground in this sense.

Confusion and co-occurrence probabilities. Distances or proximities can be derived from tasks other than direct judgments. For example, if people have a difficult time distinguishing two items, then those items are likely to be similar in some respects. For example, when subjects are asked to echo spoken letters, and *B* and *V* are often reported for each other, we say that to the subject they seem similar on some dimension, likely because they share a major vowel sound, "ee." Thus, confusion probabilities are taken as measures of similarity and can be used in proximity matrices to infer mental organization.

Similar to the use of confusions as measures of similarity is the use of the number of times that items are grouped together, either in a card-sorting task (in which several people are sorting the cards, or one person is sorting them several times) or in a task such as free association or sentence construction. The analyst counts the number of times that two items appear in the same cluster or sentence, or are reported as associates to a stimulus item. These elicitation techniques have the advantage of having similarities derived from other behaviors, perhaps skirting the issues of context outlined earlier.

Repertory grid. The use of the interview technique and triadic judgment task in the elicitation phase of repertory grid analysis is an interesting blend of a direct report and a derived measure: Subjects are asked to name the dimension on which they are judging the items in the current triple, then rate the items for their strength on that dimension. The overall similarity of two items comes from a simple summary of the absolute differences among two items' values on all the dimensions elicited over all items. There are many different ways in which similarity can be derived from the rating grid, such as a weighted sum, a squared variance, or a Minkowski metric with different powers.

This raises the issue of which summary statistic is "right." How do people judge similarities across many dimensions or characteristics? As mentioned earlier, there is some suggestion that people do not make formal distance calculations when considering items that vary on many dimensions. Whatever statistic is used in the repertory grid analysis to convert judgments of dimensional ratings into a single similarity measure should be based on the kinds of processes assumed to be used by the subject to generate and combine these dimensions in real task settings.

Recall orders. Recall orders as data for inferring mental organization are unlike those discussed earlier in that there is no calculation of a single number or judgment made by the subject. The subject merely reports out loud the next association after having recalled the previous items. Although this is more natural than the similarity measures described earlier, with better psychological coupling to its representation algorithm, the method has its distortions and limitations as well.

In the Reitman and Rueter method, subjects are required to recall all the items in the designated set, without missing any and without repeating any. This has proved to be a difficult constraint for some; often an item is recalled after a pause at the end, because the subject forgot it when recalling its clustermates. Subjects often report that they think of a single item twice, having to suppress it from overt recall the second time. Furthermore, recall orders, being difficult, often tend to emphasize one or at most two salient dimensions that organize the whole set of items. For example, in determining the organization of the names of 50 countries, subjects often adopted a traversal path reflecting geographical neighbors, reporting that if they deviated into other strong local associations (e.g., Russia and Cuba having similar political bases), they risked having an incomplete recall trial. Thus, the requirement to recall all items will inhibit some existing but inconvenient associations, even strong ones, in favor of paths that will assure compliance with the requirement to be complete and not repeat any items.

Recall orders do provide a practical benefit to the analyst, however. As mentioned earlier, the time to elicit all pairwise similarity ratings from subjects for a set of 50 items can take longer than 3 hours. Recalling 50 items in a sufficient number of trials (with different items serving as starting cues) will require far less than 3 hours. Assuming that a subject reports two words per second, 20 recall trials will take less than 20 minutes, even allowing for 30-second pauses between trials.

Summary methods

Once elicited, these behaviors are summarized into one of three major forms: a transcript of retrospective verbal description or concurrent thinking aloud, a proximity matrix, or a set of orders. Only the drawing and card-sorting data are directly represented in a final hierarchy without an intermediate processing step.

Transcript. Often the subject's answers in an interview, answers to special questions, or thinking-out-loud utterances are tape-recorded and transcribed for further analysis. This works well when all of the subject's thinking is being done "in the head." However, it is becoming increasingly clear that most expert behaviors rely heavily on external aids, such as drawings, notes, and even extensive information compendia ready at hand (Norman, 1988). It is thus critical to an understanding of an expert's behavior to note in the transcript the use of external information and explanatory gestures, as well as verbalizations. Indeed, expertise such as that in industrial design and some software design situations is composed of equal parts drawing, pointing, and gesturing, as well as verbal descriptions (Tang, 1989). Making videotapes is thus critical to capturing this important information, and finding a way to note it in the transcript and incorporate it in final representations is similarly important.

Proximity matrix. Confusion probabilities, co-occurrence counts, and direct judgments are all items that fill the cells of the proximity matrix. The repertory grid elicitation technique provides judgments of strengths of items on different attributes or dimensions that are then summarized (by one of a variety of possible methods) into a single pairwise similarity measure. Recall orders can be converted to proximity scores by counting the average number of items that intervene between the recalls of two items.

Strings. Only two elicitation methods are summarized into ordered strings. The Reitman and Rueter method elicits recall orders, strings themselves, which are analyzed directly. Orders produced from card sorting have also provided the basis for analysis into ordered trees. That is, subjects are asked to sort cards first, then to produce an order through the items by pointing to successive items. The subject is assumed to choose the item that is closest to the one just reported, finishing all items of a cluster before moving to another cluster. Further, it is assumed that the next cluster chosen will be near the one just finished. Both recall orders and orders produced from card sorting are direct reports of associations, within the constraint that subjects not repeat themselves.

Analyses

After summarizing the elicited behaviors, analyses and algorithms are used to produce various representations of the regularities found. The direct methods provide a base from which analysts can extract both knowledge organization and strategies; the indirect methods serve only to uncover the organization of knowledge.

Formal analyses of transcripts. There are several ways in which the utterances from either an interview or a thinking-out-loud protocol can be extracted and coded to indicate a subject's knowledge and its organization, as well as the strategies the subject seems to be using with that knowledge. Most of them begin by segmenting the utterances into episodes, sentences, or fragments.

If the transcript comes from an interview, one must separate the statements made to query the interviewer or to move the "conversation" forward and the statements that center on explaining the core knowledge. There are various ways to do this with "conversation analysis" and "interaction analysis," in which each utterance is examined for its *purpose* in the conversation (Searle, 1969; Winograd & Flores, 1986). Often, the most useful of these categories separates out the statements of *negotiation* (i.e., promising or refusing to do something) and *orientation* (i.e., requesting clarification from someone else) from those of *clarification* (i.e., in which subjects say more of what they are thinking, perhaps repeating, but often expanding on earlier ideas) and *possibilities* (i.e., in which subjects are associating things that they know to further explore the chain of reasoning).

From the core set, again there are various coding schemes that can help illuminate a subject's knowledge, its organization, and the strategies used. From elicited explanations of phenomena, one can look for concepts and their relationships, indicating which of the relationships are causal, conditional, associative, equivalence, and categorical relationships (Patel & Groen, chapter 4, this volume). One can find evidence regarding a subject's strategies, such as working forward through the problem (from fact to hypothesis) or working backward (from hypothesis to fact), by tracing the order in which the subject worked through this associative structure.

The most common method for analyzing thinking-out-loud protocols is *protocol analysis* (Ericsson & Simon, 1984). Protocol analysis is a systematic way of identifying the subject's current state of knowledge about a given problem and the way the subject progresses to discover new knowledge (not necessarily correct) by retrieval of new inferences or use of more formal operators specific to the domain of investigation. The exact vocabulary used to identify this evolving state of knowledge will vary from one domain to another. However, the point is to discover the subject's knowledge (in terms of retrieved inferences and associations), as well as the methods or approaches that the subject takes to gain an understanding of the problem. For example, a subject under study may be seen to encode certain aspects of the situation and to freely associate among the possible explanations, then select them one by one to be examined and tested. The analyst often seeks evidence of the expert working forward or backward or using simple methods like means–ends analysis or a generate-and-test protocol.

Other analyses are possible. In the domain of design, for example, one could adopt a coding scheme that would identify the issues in the problem, their possible solutions, and the evaluations and decisions on those issues as they emerge over time. That is what is done in the "Issue Based Information System" (IBIS) introduced by Rittal and Kunz (1970), a prescriptive scheme that was developed to help designers keep track of and evaluate their emerging design ideas.[5] Furthermore, if one records in the transcript the ways in which the expert uses materials, they can also be classified on the basis of their functions during the course of expert problem solving. For example, an artifact can serve to *store* partial or intermediate information, to *trigger* new associations or check inferences that come to mind, and so forth (Tang, 1989).

Algorithms on proximities. The algorithms used to uncover structure in a proximity matrix differ markedly in regard to whether they assume that the subject has a global scheme under which similarities are generated or assume that similarities reflect local, context-driven associations. For example, MDS assesses "stress" as a weighted sum of the deviations between original distances and solution distances. It carries a hidden assumption that the subject is able to generate each pairwise similarity by calculating the Euclidean distance between two objects on all their n-dimensions of distinct characteristics.

In contrast, Johnson hierarchical clustering adds items to clusters on a one-by-one basis, assuming that the distances generated by the subject were simple pairwise associations on one or two dimensions triggered in the current context. Similarly, Pathfinder locates the single path that is shortest (in some declared metric), searching local pairwise distances. Additive trees and extended trees are constructed to most closely satisfy a particular semilocal distance constraint (known as the *four-point condition*). Additive clustering

---

[5] Furthermore, IBIS has been made into graphic, hypertext interactive form on a workstation for designers in a system called gIBIS (Conklin & Begeman, 1988).

seeks to find the smallest set of overlapping clusters, based on shared properties between objects, that will provide a satisfactory fit to the data. Because items can belong to more than one category, it is a solution that reflects local properties.

These distinctions in how the algorithms work are important if the analyst wants to fit the representation to the processes that are assumed to have been operative when the subject produced the data.

Algorithms on strings. The algorithm that uncovers the chunks in the ordered-tree analysis looks for sets of items that "go together" in all the strings, regardless of the order of the constituents. Because this search is done without regard for the consistency of the overall fit, such as "stress," this makes it a local algorithm. However, if one considers the task that the subject performed, this is more likely a global picture. In order for subjects to recall consistently the items designated and only those items, they most likely will have to adopt a single, all-encompassing categorization scheme. As mentioned earlier, subjects might be tempted to use some strong local associations, but are likely to avoid such associations for fear of losing track of the path that takes them through remaining items.

Forms of representation

The right-hand columns in Figures 10.1 and 10.5 list the kinds of representations that result from application of the various analysis methods to the elicited summary data. The direct methods are useful for discovery of the objects and their relationships. The secondary analyses of the order in which the subject discovers new knowledge indicate the kinds of strategies used. Several investigators have used diagrams to represent the flow of discovery over time, such as the problem–behavior graph of Newell and Simon (1972). Others have chosen to represent the relationships among the concepts reported in terms of a network, with links named according to the kind of association reported (causal, associative, etc.), ignoring the time dimension in the diagram. These two diagrams lend themselves to different conclusions, with the network being more amenable to comparisons of organizations among individuals, and the problem–behavior graphs better showing the strategies and paths of analysis taken by the subject.

The indirect methods are much more richly detailed in displaying a variety of forms of mental organization for the concepts involved in expertise. There are several distinct categories: *n*-dimensional space (MDS), nested structures (Johnson hierarchical clustering, direct hierarchies, additive trees, and ordered trees), overlapping clusters (extended trees and additive clustering, and, to some extent, ordered trees), and networks (general weighted networks). If there is no theory about which of these representations map well to the ways in which the information is stored, and no theory about how well the eliciting technique matches the stored representation, then these pictures of

associations are merely summaries of the regularities. They variously emphasize different aspects – their graded properties, their inclusion in categories,
or their association paths. If there is a theory about how the information is
stored, then we should expect evidence of its validity from converging operations, as discussed in a later section.

Hierarchies constructed from ordered trees are somewhat different from
the solutions derived with the other methods. Ordered trees are strict representations of all the order or clustering relationships found to exist on all
trials. There may be more regularities than are represented by the final ordered tree; a simple error or perturbation will violate the strict rule that only
those regularities found on all trials are represented in the final solution.[6]

Recombining the stages

All these methods have four explicit stages. Depending on the circumstances and assumptions, the analyst can use an eliciting method and combine it
with any summary or final representation on the path. For example, the repertory grid technique traditionally displays the proximities, derived from the
interview, in a hierarchy. This is not an absolute requirement. If one believes
that an extended tree will better display overlapping clusters that may be inherent in the mental representation, one can choose to combine the interview
method of elicitation from traditional repertory grid analysis with a final representation in an extended tree. We encourage deliberate decisions at each of the
four stages regarding which method will best capture the underlying representation, and which eliciting method will most closely match the abilities and natural behavior of the subject who holds that underlying representation.

More globally, the direct and indirect methods can be combined in a cycle
of discovery. After eliciting the objects in the subject's vernacular from an
interview and a thinking-out-loud protocol, one can then understand the relationships between the objects using some indirect methods. Additionally,
because often it is difficult after the representation is displayed for the analyst
to infer the dimensions that were used during the elicitation stage, perhaps
these judgments can be collected while the subject thinks out loud. That is, as
subjects form their single proximity judgments, they can report on what aspects of similarity they are thinking about. This will help both with identifying
the dimensions after the fact and with choosing methods of analysis that will
fit the kind of processes that subjects were using to generate the proximities.
After the analysis and display of the inferred organization of these objects, we
can interview the subjects again, having them explain the displayed relationships and the strategies they used in solving particular example problems.

---

[6] To avoid the cases in which solutions "blow up" to reveal no regularity at all, certain cleaning-up
procedures prepare the initial data. Trials are "jackknifed" so as to identify single-outlier trials
or items (trials that destroy clusters that appear on all other trials, or items that "wander" the
organization), setting them aside while the remaining regularities are summarized in the
ordered-tree solution.

WHICH METHOD FITS WHAT KIND OF
ASSUMED REPRESENTATION?

Several authors have commented on the appropriateness of the final representations – how well it fits the assumptions about the underlying organization of knowledge.

> It would be a mistake to ask which of these various scaling, tree-fitting, or clustering methods is based on *the* correct model . . . different models may be more appropriate for different sets of stimuli or types of data. Even for the same set of data, moreover, different methods of analysis may be better suited to bring out different but equally informative aspects of the underlying structure. (Shepard, 1980, p. 397)

Recognizing from the preceding section that these methods involve different explicit or implicit theories of either behavior or underlying representation, we have summarized these relationships. Table 10.1 shows a mapping between the kind of underlying representation an expert may be assumed to have and the method or methods that will best fit that assumption. Although there is no large body of evidence to confirm the validity of this mapping, we have used our collective experience and analysis of the details of the methods and algorithms to suggest these mappings as appropriate.

The column headings of Table 10.1 show the different kinds of underlying representations that subjects can be assumed to have for various kinds of knowledge. The methods that utilize the organizations of concepts (primarily indirect methods) reviewed earlier are listed in the left column. The capital letters X indicate a strong association between assumption and method, and small letters x indicate possible relationships. The importance of fitting the method to the assumptions about the underlying representation has been illustrated most strongly in a set of studies comparing two methods. Although there seems to have been no comprehensive critical comparison of all the techniques described here, several experimenters have compared subsets of these techniques on various criteria, among them the amount of variance explained by the fitted solution, the extent to which the solutions explain or predict future behavior, and the degree to which data sets satisfy the particular model assumptions.

Holman (1972) proved that any data set that exactly fits a hierarchical tree representation cannot be accurately represented by MDS in a small number of dimensions. However, Kruskal (1977) suggested that for real data, which are unlikely to be exactly represented by any method, each technique may provide useful information. Although it is not clear whether that is because of shortcomings in the models, variability in solutions, or something else, the analyst may benefit from exploratory analysis using different methods. If a choice between methods must be made, however, the choice should rest on the assumptions one has about the underlying representation producing the observed behavior.

Table 10.1. *Mapping between methods and underlying representations*

Method	List	Table	Hierarchy	Flow	Network	Physical space	Physical model
MDS	x	x				X	
Johnson clustering			X				
Hierarchical card sort			X				
Repertory grid			X	x			
Additive tree			X				
Extended tree	x	x	X		x		
Additive clustering		x	X		x		
General weighted network	x	x	x	x	X		x
Ordered tree	x		X	x			x

Several investigators have evaluated different methods in terms of goodness of fit to the original data. For example, Pruzansky, Tversky, and Carroll (1982) compared additive-tree solutions and MDS solutions. For artificially generated data, they found, not surprisingly, that the tree solutions better fit the data generated from a tree, whereas MDS solutions better fit the data generated from a plane. Those authors also applied the two techniques to 20 real data sets. They found that semantic stimuli (e.g., animals, occupations) were better represented by trees, whereas perceptual stimuli (e.g., colors, sounds) were better fit by MDS.

Cooke et al. (1986) compared Pathfinder solutions to MDS solutions in predicting both serial recall and free recall of lists of words. For the serial-recall task, the authors constructed several lists of concepts that had previously undergone both Pathfinder and MDS analysis. The lists were constructed to be either network-organized, such that successive concepts in the list were linked in the Pathfinder solution, but distant in the MDS solution, or the reverse. They found that free recall for both those lists was better than for control (random) lists, but that serial recall was better only for the list generated from the network, not for the list from the MDS distances.

Walker and Kintsch (1985, pp. 269–270) compared the results of a sorting task with the results of clustering from retrieval and found only a 19% overlap in clusters: "Apparently, the principles of organization in the clustering task were quite different from those operative in the retrieval task. . . . When sorting the items, subjects tended to rely on context-free, semantic dimensions. But when they were asked to retrieve members of those categories, their tendency was to rely on episodic retrieval cues." Clearly, the context of the task is itself a major determinant of the kinds of behaviors and thus the representations found.

Gammack (1987) described an extensive body of work involving the application of several of the techniques described earlier to concepts from three different domains: steam-locomotive classification, information sciences, and statistical analysis. In particular, he used card sorting to construct hierarchical trees and applied MDS, single-link cluster analysis, and Pathfinder to sets of similarity ratings. Additionally, he applied these same methods to proximities derived from repertory grid analysis. Finally, he constructed proximity matrices from cued-recall orders (cf. Friendly, 1977) and again applied the same methods. Five experts provided all data, one for the steam-locomotive domain, and two each for the other two domains.

Gammack found considerable agreement across the different elicitation methods (i.e., similarity ratings, repertory grid, and cued recall), suggesting that "stabilized knowledge underlies task performance" (1987, p. 169). He also found considerable agreement among the experts within the information sciences and within the statistical-analysis domain. With regard to the value of the three indirect methods – MDS, clustering, and Pathfinder – Gammack emphasized the local–global distinction described earlier. More precisely, he asserted that MDS provides global representation, that clustering highlights "natural groupings" (possibly within that more global, spatial structure), and that the Pathfinder networks preserve the pairwise associations between elements.

Sullivan, Hirtle, Olson, and Rueter (1980) collected both pairwise similarities and recall orders for 50 country names. Although the MDS solutions and the ordered-tree solutions were describably similar, there were some interesting mismatches. Some of the similarity ratings (and thus the MDS solution distances) expressed dimensions of comparison that the recall orders did not. For example, Russia and Cuba were consistently given ratings suggesting similarity, whereas they were distant in the ordered-tree solution. As mentioned earlier, it appears that subjects will adopt a single focus or dimension with which to report (traverse) their associations to perform well in the recall task. When faced with only a pair of items in the similarity-rating task, they can base their judgments not on all possible dimensions but on a particularly salient dimension for that pair in that part of the data-collection sequence (e.g., here noting the political alliance, even though the two countries are geographically distant).

Because different methods make different assumptions about the underlying representations, various properties of the data may suggest the more appropriate method. Pruzansky et al. (1982) proposed two measures for identifying whether a particular data set is more likely to have been generated by a tree representation or by a spatial representation. The first of these, *skewness*, reflects the distribution of pairwise distances in the original proximity data. Earlier work by Sattath and Tversky (1977) suggested that spatial representations tend to produce many small distances and fewer large distances, whereas tree representations produce more large distances and fewer small distances. Therefore, the skewness of the proximities should provide a useful starting point for determining whether the proximities are more likely to be produced by a tree or by a Euclidean space.

The second measure proposed by Pruzansky and associates is the *elongation* of a data set. Each triple of objects in a binary tree will tend to form a subtree such that two of the items belong to a cluster that does not contain the third. For example, in both trees in Figure 10.9, consider the items *mean, median,* and *short-term memory. Mean* and *mode* both belong to clusters that do not include *short-term memory.* Because within-cluster distances tend to be smaller, on average, than between-cluster distances, the three pairwise distances associated with any three objects will tend to be such that the larger two of the distances will be more nearly equal than the smaller two. That is, each triple of objects forms a triangle such that the longer two sides are more nearly equal in length than the shorter two sides. Elongation is the proportion of the triangles whose middle side is closer in length to the larger side than to the smaller side. Tree-generated proximities should exhibit more elongation than should spatially generated proximities.

Several general results have emerged from the few studies that have compared subsets of the different techniques. Network solutions better represent local (e.g., pairwise) relations, whereas MDS solutions emphasize global (dimensional) relations among stimulus items. In addition, perceptual stimuli such as colors and sounds are better represented by spatial solutions, whereas discrete solutions are more appropriate for semantic stimuli. Furthermore, certain statistical properties like elongation and skewness may help determine which is the more appropriate representation and analysis method.

ARE THESE REPRESENTATIONS REAL?

Because we are using these techniques to better understand the nature of expertise, it is important to know if these are just convenient pictures of regularities in the data or if they correspond to the ways in which people store information for use in expert tasks. If they are real, we should be able to use them to predict related behavior. We next address both the face validity of the resulting displays and two studies of converging evidence.

Face validity

Many of the displayed organizations that have been reported have been accompanied by descriptions that have seemed reasonable. For example, McKeithen et al. (1981) explored the differences between the memory representations of Algol-W programmers at three levels of skill using the Reitman-Rueter ordered-tree analysis. The experts had organizations that not only looked alike (discussed later in the section on individual differences) but also were reasonable clusters of terms specific to programming. For example, whereas novices clustered words such as *if, and,* and *for* together because they are all short words, experts clustered *if* with *then* and *else, and* with *or,* and *for* with *while* – all parts of known functional chunks in Algol-W.

Similarly, Naveh-Benjamin et al. (1986) explored the ordered-tree representations of students and their instructors in a class on the psychology of aging. They found that beginning students organized the items as small stories or alphabetical sublists, whereas the advanced students organized the concepts into meaningful clusters having to do with concepts and theories learned in class. Furthermore, converging evidence was found in that those students whose representations were more like those of their instructor received higher grades.

Expert pilots participating in a study of Schvaneveldt et al. (1985a, 1985b) produced Pathfinder displays of terms related to flying that were different from those produced by novices in three ways: The numbers of links were fewer (indicating stable relationships across larger sets of items), the cycles were identifiable clusters of flying terms and skills, and experts had no trouble labeling the links displayed.

Converging evidence

Explainability is not a strong test of the reality of these representations. As in the case of Rorschachs, experts can find meaning in nearly any nonsensical display of relationships. A stronger test would involve predictions of related behaviors that would follow the inferred structure. The most comprehensive examination of converging evidence was reported for MDS solutions (Rips et al., 1973) and for ordered trees (McKeithen et al., 1981; Reitman & Rueter, 1980). In those cases, reaction times and judgment accuracies or recall latencies were measured and compared with the distances between items in the inferred representations.

The subjects of Rips et al. (1973) first provided similarity ratings for bird and mammal names, then made a series of judgments about the category memberships of the items. The reaction times to the judgments were highly related to the distances between the items and their category names in the MDS solution. Furthermore, the abilities of the subjects to complete analogies involving the items in the two categories (birds and mammals) were predicted by the distances between the items in the spaces.

Reitman and Rueter (1980) and McKeithen et al. (1981) conducted the most extensive explorations of converging evidence for the existence of ordered trees. They found that the pauses between successively recalled items were highly correlated with the inferred distances in the tree. Furthermore, those clusters that were designated as "ordered," meaning that the subjects consistently recalled items in a single order (unidirectional) or in an order and its reverse (bidirectional), were recalled significantly faster than were clusters that were recalled together but in mixed orders. Additional detailed analysis

(Hirtle, Olson, & Rueter, 1989) showed that subjects' regularity in pauses could be modeled to follow one of two retrieval methods: In one, subjects seemed to retrieve the hierarchy from the top down, saving higher-order nodes in short-term memory to be unpacked and recalled later. Other subjects seemed to recall item by item, pausing to check at the end of the cluster to see if it was complete. This body of work suggests that, at least for ordered trees, there is substantial evidence that the representations are reflecting an aspect of the stored information, not just summarizing in a picture the regularities found in a highly contrived task.

HOW DO WE IDENTIFY EXPERTS USING THESE METHODS? CAN WE COMPARE INDIVIDUAL SOLUTIONS?

In addition to being able to specify when one scaling method might be more appropriate than another for a given data set, we would like to be able to compare individual solutions produced by a given method. For example, we might want to compare a given individual's network of relationships among concepts with that from a textbook or from an expert, or compare the ordered-tree solutions of two different individuals in order to assess their similarities in regard to domain knowledge. We might also be interested in comparison techniques in order to determine the things that constitute expert structures, as well as to isolate *where* expert–novice differences lie.

Patel, Evans, and Kaufman in 1989 compared a simple count of the propositions generated in protocols by medical students to the counts from two different kinds of texts, a basic science text and a clinical text. There were interesting differences among the groups, depending on their years in medical school, with older students showing a shift toward using clinical information, both from the book and from other sources.

Unfortunately, few psychological studies have been reported that have compared individuals' representations from indirect methods. This probably is largely because of the mathematical and/or computational complexity of many of the comparison methods. In the interest of clarity for researchers' use, we review here only some of the more easily understood correlational methods (which can be applied to any of the scaling methods) and methods specifically applicable to ordered-tree analysis. We focus on ordered trees primarily because there have been several studies that have used the comparison methods in the context of expert–novice differences. Comparison methods applicable to the other scaling techniques will be discussed only briefly, mainly to point to relevant source material.

The matrix correlation is a straightforward similarity measure that can be applied to any of the techniques described earlier that use a proximity matrix as summary data. In brief, this measure is simply the matrix correlation of the *derived* distances for two individual structures. For example, we might take the distances implied by the hierarchical trees of two different subjects and correlate these distances to provide a measure of similarity between subjects.

However, correlation as a measure of structure similarly has its critics. Hirtle (1982) questioned the use of correlations for ordered trees because of the ad hoc nature of deriving a distance matrix from these structures. Gower (1971) criticized the use of correlations in general because of the possibility of exaggerated correlations when there is lack of independence. Holgersson (1978) discussed the limitations of matrix correlations in hierarchical tree structures.

Ordered-tree solutions have been compared in several studies (McKeithen et al., 1981; Naveh-Benjamin et al., 1986). McKeithen and associates defined the similarity of two trees to be a function of the number of chunks in common between the two ordered trees. More precisely,

$$\text{similarity} = \frac{\ln(\text{number of chunks two trees have in common} + 1)}{\ln(\text{total number of chunks contained in both trees} + 1)}$$

Using this measure (which ranges between 0 and 1), those authors were able to compare the structures of expert and novice Algol programmers. They filled a proximity matrix of *distances between subjects* and performed several analyses on that matrix. First, they found a three-dimensional MDS solution in which subjects were spread out in a cone shape, where the vertical axis denoted expertise, and the planar dimensions denoted aspects of the various organization principles. Experts were clustered more tightly at the top of the cone; intermediates and novices were moved down the axis and were spread out more. Other summary statistics on the nature of expertise indicated that there was greater similarity among the experts, on average, than among the members of any other group. And, interestingly, novices were more similar to experts than they were to each other.

Naveh-Benjamin et al. (1986) also used this measure of similarity to compare the ordered trees of students in an introductory psychology course to the ordered-tree structure of the course instructor. They found that similarity to the instructor correlated positively with scores on the final exam, as well as with final course grades.

Hirtle (1982) suggested that the measure of tree similarity described earlier suffers from at least two problems. First, whereas the logarithmic transformation removes a bias resulting from a positive correlation between the total number of chunks and the ratio of shared chunks to total chunks, it also disturbs the metric properties of the distance measure. Second, this method treats unidirectional and bidirectional chunks identically, so that directionality, an important piece of the ordered tree, is underemphasized. As an alternative, Hirtle proposed two similarity measures that build on the lattice structure of the ordered trees. In brief, these measures reflect the number of moves required to transform one tree into the other by stepwise traversal of the lattice. The differences between the measures are based on the specific routes taken through the lattice.

Several additional methods for computing similarities between structures have been described in the literature. MDS solutions can be compared by calculating the optimal agreement of the solutions subject to certain rotations and scale changes (Peay, 1988; Schonemann & Carroll, 1970). Hierarchical trees can be compared using lattice theory and partitioning methods (Arabie & Boorman, 1973; Boorman & Arabie, 1972). In addition, Fowlkes and Mallows (1983) described a profile method for hierarchical trees in which similarities are calculated at each distinct partitioning of the data, thus providing a *set* of numbers for each pair of trees, rather than one global measure. Finally, Gammack (1987) described several statistical techniques that can be used to compare different network structures.

With few exceptions (e.g., the profile method of Fowlkes and Mallows), most of the comparison techniques described earlier have a common short-coming: They provide a single, global measure of similarity. There is no suggestion of where the similarities arise. In trying to isolate domain expertise, we are likely to be interested in specifically what experts share and what they do not share. For example, in Figure 10.9 the two instructors agree that *demon, Pandemonium,* and *feature* are strongly related, but they do not treat terms such as *double-blind, Stroop,* and *lateral inhibition* in the same way. Finer-grained analyses are needed to reveal such local relationships across structures.

The one method that can show some of the aspects of similarity is the ordered-tree analysis. By comparing the chunks that two individuals have in common, one can either derive a single similarity measure, as described earlier, or list the chunks they have in common. Some work in progress (Olson, Nilsen, Biolsi, & Jong, 1989) is using this approach to diagnose the knowledge that a person acquires in software (the concepts in Lotus 1-2-3) that grows more similar to the knowledge of the expert. It attempts to identify the order in which concepts are learned (identified by the congruence of a subject's chunks with those of the expert) and the consequent performance changes in using the piece of software.

If such analysis can show which chunks are in common, it can also display the chunks that are not in common. There is no convenient single picture of this, because all nonexperts seem to organize their novice knowledge in their own unique ways. However, any technique that can identify the nature of expert organization, as well as compare the individual's growth toward expert organization, can lead to new inferences about how experts develop. In particular, such a technique could point toward an answer to the question whether expertise in a particular domain is the result of simple, hard-earned accretion or whether it involves a major reorganization of concepts.

NEW DIRECTIONS

This chapter has reviewed the methods currently available to researchers interested in the nature of expertise, attempting to help them make inferences about the nature of the expert's knowledge in a domain and the kinds of reasoning strategies used when approaching a difficult problem. In brief, direct methods, such as interviews and thinking-out-loud protocols, reveal some of the expert's concepts and the organization of those concepts and give some indication of the approaches used in problem solving. These methods are the only ways currently available for discovering the expert's concepts and strategies. Because they either may tap knowledge about specific cases in which the investigator must induce the generalities or may ask for generalities that may or may not reflect knowledge used in thinking, we recommend that the conclusions reached with these methods be confirmed with other, more subtle, converging measures.

There are numerous methods, which we call indirect methods, that are at the same time more detailed in process and narrower in their conclusions. They extract more fine-grained behavior from the expert and use more complicated algorithms to make inferences about the nature of the organization of knowledge. However, they show only the organization of concepts already identified by some other means; they show nothing about the kinds of thinking processes involved in actual problem solving.

For the researcher who is interested in building expert systems or simulating expert behavior in some other form, who may not be concerned with exactly how the expert has the information stored nor with exactly what methods the expert uses to solve domain problems, there is a rich set of methods that can help. We would recommend a combination of the thinking-out-loud protocol and interview to uncover the objects, followed by the use of several members of the set of indirect methods to discover the ways in which those concepts are related.

Care should be taken to choose methods that will fit the kinds of assumptions one has about the ways in which experts have their information organized. That is, for domains in which objects can be assumed to be encoded on continuous dimensions, MDS is appropriate. For those in tidy categories, hierarchical clustering is appropriate. For domains in which there is a variety of associations among objects, either network analysis (such as Pathfinder) or a method that can uncover overlapping categories would seem best.

Because some of the indirect methods produce results that are difficult to interpret, we further recommend having the expert think out loud while making the judgments or recall. These extra thoughts can help the analyst interpret the relationships, identify the characteristics of the objects to which the expert attends, and understand more completely how the objects are related. Furthermore, the representation of the organization of the concepts can be shown to the expert for interpretation, in much the same way a videotape of problem-solving behavior can be shown to the expert for explanation and interpretation. Once the concept knowledge base is understood, the analyst then can use thinking out loud in a problem-solving situation once again to make inferences about what strategies the expert uses.

For the researcher concerned with strong inferences about the exact processes used by an expert and the precise form in which this knowledge is encoded, these methods, though rich, are not as well founded as one might hope. Each of these methods involves a theory about how the information is stored and how the person acts on that information to produce the responses. For example, MDS assumes that information is stored in a form that encodes all the features of an object. Furthermore, in order to produce a single number rating for the similarity between two objects, the person is assumed to calculate the straight-line distance between those objects in the n-dimensional space. Other research has indicated that this probably is not the process that people use in generating a similarity judgment. People reduce the complexity of the task by attending to only a few of the many dimensions and calculating a rating from them. Thus, the conclusions drawn about the final array of objects in an n-dimensional space are suspect.

Thus, to have confidence in the conclusions drawn from any of these methods, one must consider the implicit assumptions about the stored representation, the process that produced the judgment or other behavior, and the kinds of information used in the algorithm that produced the final representation. There are myriad interesting *basic* research questions about the nature of mental representation and the nature of expertise that have been highlighted by detailed comparisons of the various components of these methods.

ACKNOWLEDGMENTS

This chapter benefited greatly from careful comments from and ensuing discussions with Anders Ericsson. He was an exemplary editor.

REFERENCES

Arabie, P., & Boorman, S. A. (1973). Multidimensional scaling of distances between partitions. *Journal of Mathematical Psychology, 10,* 148–203.

Arabie, P., & Carroll, J. D. (1980). MAPCLUS: A mathematical programming approach to fitting the ADCLUS model. *Psychometrika, 45,* 211–235.

Boorman, S. A., & Arabie, P. (1972). Structural measures and the method of sorting. In R. N. Shepard, A. K. Romney, S. B. Nerlove (Eds.), *Multidimensional scaling: Theory and applications in the behavioral sciences* (Vol. 1) (pp. 225–249). New York: Seminar Press.

Boorman, S. A., & Olivier, D. C. (1973). Metrics on spaces of finite trees. *Journal of Mathematical Psychology, 10,* 26–59.

Boose, J. H. (1986). *Expertise transfer for expert system design.* New York: Elsevier.

Bower, G., & Springston, F. (1970). Pauses as recoding points in letter series. *Journal of Experimental Psychology, 80*(2, Pt. 2).

Carroll, J. D. (1976) Spatial, non-spatial, and hybrid models for scaling. *Psychometrika, 41,* 439–463.

Chase, W. G., & Simon, H. A. (1973). Perception in chess. *Cognitive Psychology, 4,* 55–81.

Chin, J. (1988, May). *Scripts in fixed and dynamic computer menu systems: A theory-based approach to categorization.* Paper presented at the doctoral consortium at CHI '88: Human Factors in Computing Systems, Washington, D.C.

Collins, A. M., & Loftus, E. F. (1975). A spreading activation theory of semantic processing. *Psychological Review, 82,* 407–428.

Conklin, J., & Begeman, M. (1988). gIBIS: A hypertext tool for exploratory policy discussion. In I. Grief (Ed.), *Proceedings of the Conference on Computer Supported Cooperative Work* (pp. 140–152). New York: Association for Computing Machinery.

Cooke, N. M., Durso, F. T., & Schvaneveldt, R. W. (1986). Recall and measures of memory organization. *Journal of Experimental Psychology: Learning, Memory, and Cognition, 12,* 538–549.

Corter, J. E., & Tversky, A. (1986). Extended similarity trees. *Psychometrika, 51,* 429–451.

Cunningham, J. P. (1978). Free trees and bidirectional trees as representations of psychological distances. *Journal of Mathematical Psychology, 17,* 165–188.

de Groot, A. D. (1965). *Thought and choice in chess.* Paris: Mouton.

Ericsson, K. A., & Simon, H. A. (1984). *Protocol analysis: Verbal reports as data.* Cambridge, MA: MIT Press.

Fowlkes, E. B., & Mallows, C. L. (1983). A method for comparing two hierarchical clusterings. *Journal of the American Statistical Association, 78,* 553–569.

Friendly, M. J. (1977). In search of the M-gram: The structure of organization in free-recall. *Cognitive Psychology, 9,* 188–249.

Gammack, J. G. (1987). *Eliciting expert conceptual structure using converging techniques.* Unpublished doctoral dissertation, Darwin College, Cambridge University.

Gower, J. C. (1971). Statistical methods of comparing different multivariate analyses of the same data. In F. R. Hodson, D. G. Kendall, & P. Tautu (Eds.), *Mathematics in the archaeological and historical sciences* (pp. 138–149). Edinburgh: Edinburgh University Press.

Hirtle, S. C. (1982). Lattice-based similarity measures between ordered trees. *Journal of Mathematical Psychology, 25,* 206–225.

Hirtle, S. C., Olson, J. R., & Rueter, H. R. (1989). *Free recall timing reveals free recall strategies* (Technical Report). University of Michigan.

Hoffman, R. R. (1987). The problem of extracting the knowledge of experts from the perspective of experimental psychology. *AI Magazine 8*(2), 53–67.

Holgersson, M. (1978). The limited value of cophenetic correlation as a clustering criterion. *Pattern Recognition, 10,* 287–295.

Holman, E. W. (1972). The relation between hierarchical and Euclidean models for psychological scaling. *Psychometrika, 37,* 417–423.

Johnson, S. C. (1967). Hierarchical clustering schemes. *Psychometrika, 32,* 241–254.

Joseph, G.-M., & Patel, V. L. (1990). Domain knowledge and hypothesis generation in diagnostic reasoning. *Journal of Medical Decision Making, 10,* 31–46.

Kelley, G. A. (1955). *The psychology of personal constructs.* New York: Norton.

Kellogg, W. A., & Breen, T. J. (1987). Evaluating user and system models: Applying scaling techniques to problems in human-computer interaction. In R. Baecker & W. Buxton (Eds.), *CHI '87: Human factors in computing systems* (pp. 303–308). New York: Association for Computing Machinery.

Kruskal, J. B. (1964). Multidimensional scaling by optimizing goodness of fit to a nonmetric hypothesis. *Psychometrika, 29,* 1–27.

Kruskal, J. B. (1977). The relationship between multidimensional scaling and clustering. In J. Van Ryzin (Ed.), *Classification and clustering* (pp. 17–44). New York: Academic Press.

Laird, J. E., Newell, A., & Rosenbloom, P. S. (1987). SOAR: An architecture for general intelligence. *Artificial Intelligence, 33*(1), 1–64.

Lindsay, P. H., & Norman, D. A. (1977). *Human information processing: An introduction to psychology.* New York: Academic Press.

McKeithen, K. B., Reitman, J. S., Rueter, H. H., & Hirtle, S. C. (1981). Knowledge organization and skill differences in computer programmers. *Cognitive Psychology, 13,* 307–325.

Meyer, D. E., & Schvaneveldt, R. W. (1976). Meaning, memory structure, and mental processes. *Science, 192,* 27–33.

Naveh-Benjamin, M., McKeachie, W. J., Lin, Y., & Tucker, D. G. (1986). Inferring students' cognitive structures and their development using the "ordered tree technique." *Journal of Educational Psychology, 78,* 130–140.

Newell, A., & Simon, H. A. (1972). *Human problem solving.* Englewood Cliffs, NJ: Prentice-Hall.

Norman, D. A. (1988). *The psychology of everyday things.* New York: Basic Books.

Olson, J. R., Nilsen, E., Biolsi, K., & Jong, H. (1989). *The growth of expertise in human–computer interaction* (Technical Report). University of Michigan.

Olson, J. R., & Rueter, H. H. (1987). Extracting expertise from experts: Methods for knowledge acquisition. *Expert Systems, 4,* 152–168.

Patel, V. L., Evans, D. A., & Groen, G. J. (1988). Biomedical knowledge in clinical reasoning. In D. Evans & V. Patel (Eds.), *Cognitive science in medicine: Biomedical modeling* (pp. 207–251). Cambridge, MA: MIT Press.

Peay, E. R. (1988). Multidimensional rotation and scaling of configurations to optimal agreement. *Psychometrika, 53,* 199–208.

Pruzansky, S., Tversky, A., & Carroll, J. D. (1982). Spatial versus tree representations of proximity data. *Psychometrika, 47,* 3–19.

Reitman, J. S. (1976). Skilled perception in Go: Deducing memory structures from inter-response times. *Cognitive Psychology, 8,* 336–356.

Reitman, J. S., & Rueter, H. H. (1980). Organization revealed by recall orders and confirmed by pauses. *Cognitive Psychology, 12,* 554–581.

Rips, L. J., Shoben, E. J., & Smith, E. E. (1973). Semantic distance and the verification of semantic relations. *Journal of Verbal Learning and Verbal Behavior, 12,* 1–20.

Rittal, H., & Kunz, W. (1970). *Issues as elements of information systems* (Working Paper No. 131, Institut für Grundlagen der Planug I.A., University of Stuttgart, Germany).

Salter, W. J. (1983). Tacit theories of economics. In *Proceedings of the 5th Annual Conference of the Cognitive Science Society.* Rochester, NY: Cognitive Science Society.

Sattath, S., & Tversky, A. (1977). Additive similarity trees. *Psychometrika, 42,* 319–345.

Schonemann, P. H., & Carroll, R. M. (1970). Fitting one matrix to another under choice of a central dilation and a rigid motion. *Psychometrika, 35,* 245–255.

Schvaneveldt, R. W., Durso, F. T., & Dearholt, D. W. (1985a). *Pathfinder: Scaling with network structures* (Memorandum in Computer and Cognitive Science No. MCCS-85-9). Las Cruces: New Mexico State University, Computing Research Laboratory.

Schvaneveldt, R. W., Durso, F. T., Goldsmith, T. E., Breen, T. J., Cooke, N. M., Tucker, R. G., & DeMaio, J. C. (1985b). Measuring the structure of expertise. *International Journal of Man–Machine Studies, 23,* 699–728.

Searle, J. (1969) *Speech acts*. Cambridge: Cambridge University Press.

Shepard, R. N. (1962a). Analysis of proximities: Multidimensional scaling with an unknown distance function. I. *Psychometrika, 27,* 125–140.

Shepard, R. N. (1962b). Analysis of proximities: Multidimensional scaling with an unknown distance function. II. *Psychometrika, 27,* 219–246.

Shepard, R. N. (1980). Multidimensional scaling, tree-fitting, and clustering. *Science, 210,* 390–398.

Shepard, R. N., & Arabie, P. (1979). Additive clustering: Representation of similarities as combinations of discrete overlapping properties. *Psychological Review, 86,* 87–123.

Shepard, R. N., Kilpatric, D. W., & Cunningham, J. P. (1975). The internal representation of numbers. *Cognitive Psychology, 7,* 82–138.

Shepard, R. N., Romney, A. K., & Nerlove, S. B. (1972). *Multidimensional scaling: Theory and applications in the behavioral sciences, Vol. 1.* New York: Seminar Press.

Sullivan, J. M., Hirtle, S. C., Olson, J. R., & Rueter, H. H. (1980). *Semantic similarity and the mental organization of country names: A comparison of tasks.* Unpublished manuscript, Department of Psychology, University of Michigan.

Tang, J. C. (1989). *Listing, drawing, and gesturing in design: A study of the use of shared workspaces by design teams* (Xerox Tech Report P89-00032). Dissertation, Department of Mechanical Engineering, Stanford University.

Walker, W. H., & Kintsch, W. (1985). Automatic and strategic aspects of knowledge retrieval. *Cognitive Science, 9,* 261–283.

Winograd, T., & Flores, C. F. (1986). *Understanding computers and cognition: A new foundation for design.* Norwood, NJ: Ablex.

11 *Expertise as the circumvention of human processing limitations*

TIMOTHY A. SALTHOUSE

The term "expertise" has a number of popular definitions, but all are somewhat vague, and none lends itself to concrete suggestions about how one might be able to become an expert. For example, according to one popular definition, an expert is anyone who is holding a briefcase and is more than 50 miles from home. Reliance on that definition presumably would imply that the way to become an expert is to travel widely and carry a briefcase, but it is not clear what should be put in the briefcase or where one should travel. By another definition, an expert is anyone who has the self-confidence to consider himself or herself an expert. That interpretation also does not immediately suggest any strategies for acquiring expertise, except perhaps by emulating extremely arrogant people, such as certain physicians who seem to specialize in communicating self-confidence. A third definition of an expert, which again is not particularly useful for the purpose of learning how to acquire expertise, is that an expert is someone who continually learns more and more about less and less. Of course, the problem with relying on that definition to guide the acquisition of expertise is that it is difficult to determine when one's area of specialization has become narrow enough so that whatever knowledge one possesses will be sufficient for one to be considered an expert.

Because these popular definitions of expertise appear to provide little insight into the nature of expertise, or into the manner in which it might be acquired, it is desirable to begin by outlining a somewhat more precise definition. Virtually everyone would agree that the term "expertise" connotes extreme or exceptional performance. It therefore seems reasonable to suggest that in terms of a normal distribution of performances or competences such as that shown in Figure 11.1, experts fall in the rightmost, or highest-scoring, region of the distribution.

Although admittedly a rather gross oversimplification, Figure 11.1 is useful for making two important methodological points. The first is that the dimension along which expertise is most appropriately evaluated should represent some measure of actual competence, rather than a possible correlate of competence such as amount of experience or social consensus. Measures of real competence should be used to assess expertise, rather than an index of experience, because, as Ericsson and Smith point out (chapter 1, this volume), mere

286

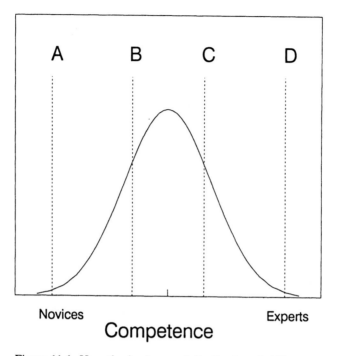

Novices   Experts
Competence

Figure 11.1. Hypothesized normal distribution of skill or expertise.

experience may not be sufficient to produce high levels of proficiency. Consensual judgments of expertise should also be avoided, because they can be influenced by a variety of characteristics other than true competence, such as popularity or reputation. Individuals' amounts of experience and peer ratings frequently can be correlated with their levels of competence, but it seems preferable, whenever possible, to use more precise criteria to document the competences of individuals suspected of differing in expertise. In particular, reliance on amount of experience, academic credentials, or professional classification (such as student compared with teacher, or trainee compared with supervisor) as the sole basis for categorizing people as experts or nonexperts probably should be avoided in research on the nature of expertise.

The second point that can be illustrated with the aid of Figure 11.1 is that categorization of an individual as an expert is relatively arbitrary, in that there is a range of positions along the hypothesized competence continuum at which individuals can be placed. Patel and Groen (chapter 4, this volume) propose that the competence dimension be partitioned into six categories – layperson, beginner, novice, intermediate, subexpert, and expert – but the problem remains of determining the locations of the boundaries between categories. It seems likely that inconsistencies among researchers in regard to the level of competence that qualifies one as expert, as well as inconsistencies in regard to the region of the competence distribution from which individuals are drawn to be compared with experts, may be hampering progress in understanding expertise.

One means of dealing with the classification problem is to restrict usage of the term "expertise" to individuals in the highest percentiles of the distribution of competence for a given activity. This distribution-referenced interpretaton of expertise obviously conflicts with Sloboda's suggestion (chapter 6, this volume) that virtually everybody has some degree of expertise in certain domains, such as music or proficiency in one's own language. Sloboda's view seems to imply an all-or-none conceptualization of expertise based on absolute standards of proficiency, whereas my proposal assumes that there is nearly always a continuum of competence or expertise, regardless of the absolute levels of performance. Because of the difficulty of achieving agreement on the absolute standards of performance associated with the expertise threshold in different domains, and because expertise generally has a connotation of exclusivity, I prefer a relativistic definition of expertise.

If it is accepted that experts can be identified in virtually any domain for which suitable criterion measures of competence are available, we can turn our attention to one of the major themes of this volume, namely, whether or not there are commonalities in the nature of expertise across different domains of activity. It is not at all obvious on a priori grounds that this question can be answered in the affirmative, because of the great diversity of activities in which expertise can be manifested. Nevertheless, there appear to be at least two different approaches that could be pursued to determine if there are similarities in the processes associated with expertise in different domains. The two approaches are loosely based on bottom-up and top-down strategies, in that they differ primarily with respect to the starting place for identifying, or confirming, possible commonalities across domains of expertise. I shall discuss these approaches in some detail because they provide a useful framework for organizing research in expertise, as well as a larger context within which to place my comments on other chapters in this volume.

The bottom-up approach to investigating the nature of expertise can be viewed as involving three major steps. The first step consists of conducting detailed analyses of the processes associated with expertise in a given domain and the mechanisms responsible for implementing those processes. At least initially, these analyses will be of the case-study variety, in that relatively small numbers of individuals will be studied intensively in order to gather as much information as possible about how experts in a given domain differ from nonexperts.

The second step in the bottom-up strategy is to test and verify the hypotheses generated during the initial investigations. This generally will entail recruiting moderate numbers of individuals in both the expert and nonexpert groups and collecting data that can be evaluated with conventional inferential statistical procedures. The use of formal quantitative techniques to assess statistical significance is important, because much of the early research on expertise can be criticized for having failed to document the reliability of the observations.

Also to be examined in the second phase is the generality of the proposed expertise characteristics across individuals, across degrees of expertise, and across experimental situations. That is, an explicit focus of research in this second stage should be to determine whether or not the inferred principles apply to different samples of experts, to people at different positions along the competence continuum, and to observations derived from different procedures and paradigms.

The issue of generalizability across experts should be examined because a question of considerable theoretical interest is whether there are multiple routes to naturally occurring expertise or whether all experts in a given domain necessarily achieve their expertise in the same manner. If the former is true, then one might expect experts to be less similar to one another than novices are to each other, whereas if the latter is the case, then interindividual variability might be expected to decrease as the level of competence increases. I am unaware of any systematic data on this topic, though Olson and Biolsi (chapter 10, this volume) suggest that there seems to be greater similarity in the knowledge organizations of expert programmers than in the organizations of novice programmers.

Generalizability of the findings across different phases of skill acquisition is also important because, as suggested by Charness (chapter 2, this volume) and by Patel and Groen (chapter 4, this volume), it is possible that different mechanisms or principles may be operative at different phases in the acquisition of expertise. For example, the characteristics distinguishing individuals at positions A and D in Figure 11.1 may not be the same as those distinguishing individuals at other positions, such as C and D. Only when we have systematic comparisons of individuals at many different levels of competence can this question of the monotonicity (invariance across levels) of expertise mechanisms be resolved. It may also be desirable in this phase to conduct longitudinal analyses, as well as cross-sectional analyses, to minimize the possibility that the expertise-related differences that are observed might be attributable to selection differences. A particularly valuable type of longitudinal study is that in which the expertise is engineered in the laboratory, thereby demonstrating relatively complete understanding of the processes responsible for the expertise. Kliegl, Baltes, and their colleagues (e.g., Kliegl, Smith, & Baltes, 1989; Kliegl, Smith, Heckhausen, & Baltes, 1987) have described an impressive example of this approach, using the activity of memorizing long sequences of digits, and other longitudinal studies of the acquisition of cognitive skills have been reported by Charness and Campbell (1988), Chase and Ericsson (1981), and Staszewski (1988).

Examination of the generality of expertise-related phenomena across procedures is valuable because confidence in one's conclusions obviously increases with the amount and diversity of the relevant evidence. Replicating the major results with different experimental tasks and procedures is particularly desirable in cognitive studies because the linkages between theoretical constructs and observable variables often are quite speculative in this research area.

The third and final step in my ideal bottom-strategy involves examining the results from the first two phases across several different domains to determine if there are common principles underlying expertise in different classes of activities. Although the primary purpose of this phase is the abstraction of possible commonalities, it can also be viewed as another assessment of generalizability. Charness (chapter 2, this volume) refers to chess as a prototypical or model domain for the study of expertise. Although it is certainly true that chess has received considerable attention by researchers interested in expertise, it is still necessary to explore other domains to have confidence that what is true for chess is also true for other types of activities. Attribution of prototypicality should be on the basis of shared characteristics and should not simply reflect priority or preferences on the part of certain researchers.

I have stressed the importance of the second phase in this bottom-up approach to research on expertise because it is critical for the ultimate success of this strategy that researchers have considerable confidence in the observations about the nature of expertise within each domain. In my opinion, such a degree of confidence currently is not justified for most of the activity domains in which expert performance has been analyzed, because few studies have met the criteria of what I have termed stage 2 research. Specifically, there is a lack of information about the statistical significance of many of the observations, and there has been only limited examination of the generalizability of the findings across different experts, different levels of expertise, and different methods of observation.

For the reasons mentioned, it may not yet be practical to rely on a bottom-up approach in attempting to reach definitive conclusions about what is common across expert levels of performance in different domains. An attractive alternative may therefore be the top-down approach, in which one begins by speculating about rather general characteristics of expertise and then uses those speculations as guidelines to systematic investigation. In fact, I shall devote the remainder of my comments to the elaboration of one particular top-down speculation, namely, the idea that it might be productive to view expertise as the process or processes of circumventing normal limitations on human information processing.

According to the perspective of expertise as consisting of the circumvention of normal human limitations, the major reason that expert performance is impressive is that it seems less constrained, and sometimes completely unconstrained, by the limitations on human information processing that serve to restrict the performances of nonexperts. Of course, it is likely that different domains vary in terms of the types of limitations that must be overcome in order to achieve expertise, and perhaps also in terms of the specific manner in which those limitations are circumvented. However, at least as a first approximation, it seems reasonable to suggest that a common characteristic of expertise in virtually every domain is that high levels of performance are accomplished by overcoming limitations that serve to restrain the performances of most people.

An objection could be raised that an interpretation of expertise as the circumvention of limitations is merely a trivial restatement of the fact that experts perform better than nonexperts in the relevant activity. However, I would argue that the view of expertise as freedom from certain constraints is not simply a restatement of the defining performance differences, because it forces the researcher to be explicit in specifying what these constraints are and how they are circumvented by experts in the domain. These points will be elaborated, first by considering several general reasons why the limitations may not apply to experts, and then by examining the nature of the limitations in progressively more detail for a few sample domains.

There appear to be three alternative possibilities that might explain why experts are not constrained by the presumably natural limitations that restrict the performances of most members of the population. These explanations are not unique to the limitations perspective, and indeed they are closely related to the inherited/acquired and general/specific distinctions discussed by Ericsson and Smith (chapter 1, this volume). One interpretation or explanation is that the experts have always been superior in the relevant abilities and that their advantage is attributable to genetic factors rather than to any type of learning. This alternative seems unlikely to be the primary explanation in knowledge-rich domains, but it may be plausible in other domains, particularly if the genetic contribution is viewed as a predisposition or an aptitude rather than a completely developed skill.

A second possible explanation for why experts seem less constrained by processing limitations than novices is that an individual's level of certain general abilities may improve as a function of experience within the activity domain. That is, as an individual develops expertise, there may be an alteration in one or more relevant abilities, such that expert performance is no longer constrained by the types of limitations affecting people with lower levels of ability in the given domain. An implication of this alternative is that experts should be found to be superior to nonexperts in a variety of relatively broad measures of ability, not simply in aspects of performance restricted to particular tasks.

A third possible interpretation of how experts seem to escape normal limitations on human information processing is that expertise may develop through the acquisition of mechanisms or processes specific to particular tasks or activities. As Ericsson and Smith point out (chapter 1, this volume), this is the alternative usually favored in contemporary discussions of the nature of expertise. Of course, the challenge from this perspective is to indicate exactly what it is that experts acquire and to specify how it is acquired.

The simplest way of confronting this challenge might be to begin by identifying processing limitations that seem to be characteristic of different activity domains. The chapters in this volume reflect the wide diversity of activity

Table 11.1. *Performance limitations of nonexperts, by activity domain*

Activity domain	Hypothesized processing limitations
Planning/managing	Not knowing what to do and when to do it Not knowing what to expect Lack of knowledge of interrelations among variables
Decision making and medical diagnosis	Not knowing what information is relevant and why Lack of knowledge of interrelations among variables Difficulty in combining or integrating information
Chess	Not knowing what to do Not knowing what to expect
Physics	Not knowing what information is relevant and why Lack of knowledge of interrelations among variables
Music	Not knowing what to expect in musical sequences Insensitivity to sensory/perceptual discriminations (pitch, timing, etc.) Lack of proficiency in production of pitch, rhythm, intensity, etc.
Sports	Not knowing what to expect from one's own actions, or from one's opponent Not knowing what action to perform and when Insensitivity to sensory/perceptual discrimination (e.g., dynamic aspects of the environment, such as trajectories of moving objects) Lack of proficiency in performing actions

domains in which expertise has been investigated by contemporary researchers, and hence they can be used to illustrate the range of limitations that might be circumvented by individuals achieving expertise in different domains. Six activity domains discussed by the authors of other chapters are listed in Table 11.1, along with initial speculations about the limitations that might be restricting the performances of nonexperts attempting to perform that activity. There are at least three important qualifications regarding the limitations listed in Table 11.1. The first is that the list of limitations was not produced in any systematic manner, but instead was generated by imagining myself, as someone with nearly impeccable credentials as a novice in virtually all demanding human activities, attempting to perform an activity within the domain and trying to think of the factors that would limit my performance. It is quite possible that others, perhaps experts in the respective domains, would produce a somewhat different set of limitations. The important point, however, is that regardless of the specific composition of the list, it does appear meaningful to refer to factors that limit the performances of nonexperts in nearly every domain in which expertise can be achieved.

A second qualification regarding the limitations in Table 11.1 is that the list is static, rather than dynamic, in that the limitations are assumed to apply equally at all stages during the acquisition of expertise. This is undoubtedly an oversimplification because research by Fleishman (1972), and more recently by Ackerman (1988), suggests that different combinations of abilities contribute to proficiency at different phases of skill acquisition. It therefore seems likely that the particular limitations that serve to constrain the acquisition of expertise change as an individual becomes progressively more competent in a given activity. Because there has been no attempt to incorporate this dynamic aspect into Table 11.1, the entries must be viewed as incomplete and tentative.

The third qualification regarding the limitations listed in Table 11.1 is that the limitations are described in broad, general terms. This has been done deliberately, because I suspect that precise specification of the exact nature of the limitations will be possible only as research within a given domain progresses and more detailed information about the characteristics of expertise becomes available. Examples of this progression toward greater specificity of the nature of the limitations, and explicit hypotheses about the manner in which they might be circumvented, will be discussed shortly.

Although the entries in Table 11.1 must be qualified in several respects, they do suggest a number of possible commonalities across different domains of expertise in regard to the types of limitations that must be overcome to achieve high levels of proficiency in those domains. These hypothesized commonalities can be clarified by rearranging the entries in Table 11.1 according to type of limitation, as has been done in Table 11.2. Knowledge factors clearly dominate the entries, but there are interesting similarities in the types of domains. For example, in many of the domains it seems that a major limitation constraining the performances of novices is that they are unable to determine which pieces of information are relevant to their tasks and how different kinds of information are interrelated. Another fairly common type of limitation is that novices in a given activity do not know what to expect, either as a consequence of their own actions or from external sources, such as changes in the task environment or unpredictable actions on the part of opponents.

It is interesting to speculate about the number of different types of knowledge that must be acquired to overcome the limitations listed in Tables 11.1 and 11.2. One possibility is that most of the cognitive factors are mediated by the same type of knowledge, which simply becomes more extensive and better

Table 11.2. *Activity domains, by processing limitation of nonexperts*

Hypothesized processing limitation	Activity domain
Not knowing what to expect	Planning/managing Chess Music Sports
Not knowing what to do and when to do it	Planning/managing Chess Sports
Lack of knowledge of interrelations among variables	Planning/managing Decision making Physics
Not knowing what information is relevant	Decision making Physics
Difficulty in combining information	Decision making
Insensitivity to sensory/perceptual discriminations	Music Sports
Lack of production proficiency	Music Sports

organized as greater degrees of expertise are acquired. For example, if the knowledge is structured according to the major principles within a given domain, then this will (1) indicate how different variables are interrelated, (2) facilitate recognition of what information is relevant, and (3) support the formation of internal representations that suggest the actions to be performed and lead to expectations about the consequences of these actions. Well-structured knowledge may also enhance the rapid encoding of domain-specific information by providing a framework within which the information can be easily assimilated. Given this hypothesized importance of knowledge structure, the excellent review by Olson and Biolsi (chapter 10, this volume) of techniques for investigating knowledge structures should prove extremely valuable for future research on the nature of expertise.

However, it should not be assumed that possession of greater amounts of knowledge invariably or automatically confers all of the powers of an expert. Scardamalia and Bereiter (chapter 7, this volume) mention that expert writers appear to work harder than novice writers. Situations can also be imagined, and sometimes documented (e.g., Adelson, 1984; Britton & Tesser, 1982), in which there are disadvantages of too much knowledge because of the more extensive search requirements and the greater difficulty of discriminating between relevant and irrelevant information. It seems quite likely that knowledge plays an important role in the acquisition of expertise, but it will be the task of future research to describe the mechanisms by which knowledge exerts both beneficial and detrimental effects.

The categorizations in Tables 11.1 and 11.2 are still quite gross, and it will be essential to pursue research within each domain in order to determine the reasonableness of the initial categorization of processing limitations and then to specify the limitations in a manner precise enough to allow testable hypotheses about how they might be circumvented by experts in that domain. I shall illustrate how this research might progress with two examples, one from the familiar domain of chess, and the other from a less familiar domain, namely, transcription typing.

The major limitations listed in Table 11.1 as constraints on high levels of performance in chess are lack of knowledge concerning what actions to perform and not knowing what to expect from one's opponent. Further consideration of the game of chess reveals that these limitations exist because there are far too many sequences of possible moves, each followed by many potential countermoves by one's opponent, to permit an exhaustive search to identify the optimal move in any given situation. To illustrate, Charness (chapter 2, this volume) estimates that there are more than 9 million alternatives when considering three moves from the initial position, and that number increases substantially as one progresses further into the game. The overall complexity of chess is so great that a complete or exhaustive search-and-evaluation process for all possible moves is beyond the capabilities of all humans, and apparently even the fastest contemporary computers.

As most of us are aware, and as briefly reviewed by Charness (chapter 2, this volume) and Ericsson and Smith (chapter 1, this volume), Chase and Simon proposed that an extensive search may not be necessary to select effective moves in chess, because with experience there is considerable accumulation of knowledge concerning the relations between specific configurations of chess pieces and the consequences of particular moves. The number and strength of these pattern–action associates gradually increase to the point that among individuals with 10 years or more of experience, it is hypothesized that an appropriate action may be elicited almost automatically simply by recognizing the relevant pattern of chess pieces. An obvious advantage of this type of automatic elicitation of good moves on the basis of pattern recognition is that many of the slow and laborious processes of search and evaluation can be avoided. That, in turn, may allow greater time and effort to be devoted to the unfamiliar or unusually difficult situations that still require careful analysis and deliberation.

Both Charness (chapter 2, this volume) and Ericsson and Smith (chapter 1, this volume) point out that the Chase and Simon proposal is still a hypothesis in need of refinement and further investigation. However, it is an elegant example of how the limitations confronting novice chess players might be overcome to achieve extremely high levels of proficiency.

The second example of how research might proceed from the perspective of expertise as the circumvention of limitations is based on some of my own research in the domain of transcription typing. Transcription typing is an interesting activity from the limitations perspective, because measurements of several perceptual motor processes imply that there should be severe constraints on the maximum speed at which effective typing can occur. For example, reaction times to successively presented stimuli in a recent study (Salthouse, 1984) averaged more than 550 msec per response, which, assuming 5 characters per word, would correspond to a maximum typing rate of less than 22 words per minute. Even the rate of repetitive finger tapping, without any requirement to choose among alternative stimuli or to select among distinct responses, seems to place severe constraints on maximum speeds of typing. As an illustration, in the same study in which reaction times were measured, I found that the interval between successive finger taps averaged 163 msec, which would yield a typing rate of less than 74 words per minute.

Highly skilled typists apparently have developed some means of overcoming these perceptual motor limitations, because their typing speeds, adjusted to reflect correct processing of the characters, often exceed 75 words per minute. Based on my research and the research of others (e.g., Gentner, 1988), it appears that one of the major things acquired by typists as they develop proficiency in typing is an ability to capitalize on the simultaneous availability of relevant information to convert what might be a slow, discrete task into a fast and continuous one. That is, reaction-time tasks are necessarily discrete, because the second stimulus is not presented until a response has been registered to the first stimulus. Under these circumstances the individual is constrained to respond in a serial, or reactive, basis. However, in normal typing, the material to be typed is almost always visible, and therefore it is possible for processing of subsequent stimuli to begin before all of the processing of easier stimuli has been completed.

In my research I have obtained two types of evidence that a major factor contributing to proficiency in transcription typing is the development of overlapped or parallel processing. One set of evidence derives from manipulations of the number of characters visible during typing. When the number of to-be-typed characters visible on a computer screen is progressively reduced, the rate of typing decreases dramatically, until reaching the level of reaction time when the letters are presented one at a time. Moreover, by measuring the average interval between keystrokes at each level of preview for individual typists, it is possible to obtain estimates of the number of characters that each individual normally processes by determining the largest number of characters at which typing rate is first disrupted. Because typing is disrupted when less than this number of characters is presented, it can be inferred that the typist processes at least this number of characters during normal typing. Figure 11.2 illustrates, with data from 29 typists ranging between 18 and 43 years of age (Salthouse, 1985), the relation between typing skill and this measure of eye–hand span, represented by the number of preview characters needed to maintain normal rate of typing. Notice that greater skill is associated with larger eye–hand spans, indicating that faster typists begin processing the to-be-typed

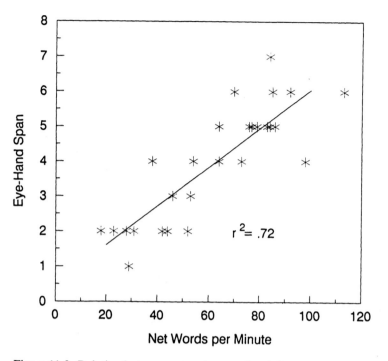

Figure 11.2. Relation between net typing speed and the number of characters that must be visible on the screen to maintain one's normal rate of typing (eye–hand span). Data from Salthouse (1984).

text several characters in advance of slower typists. A nearly identical relationship, with approximately one additional character of eye–hand span with each increase of 20 net words per minute, was observed in another study involving 74 typists ranging from 19 to 72 years of age (Salthouse, 1984).

The significant relation between typing skill and eye–hand span implies that the more skilled typists are processing information farther in advance of the keystroke than are the less skilled typists. How is this advance processing beneficial? There probably are numerous advantages from this extended anticipation in the form of overlapping or parallel execution of several processing operations. Results from my studies provide evidence for one type of parallel processing that seems to be acquired as typists become more expert. This concerns the relative efficiencies of two types of keystrokes – repetitions of the same letter, as in *t-t* or *I-I*, and letters preceded by keystrokes on the opposite hand, as in *t-h* or *i-s*. Little or no advance processing is possible when a given keystroke is repeated, because the first keystroke must be completed before the second can be initiated. However, considerable advance processing is possible when successive keystrokes are typed with fingers of different hands, because the finger and hand to be used for the second keystroke can be moved into optimal positions during the execution of the first keystroke.

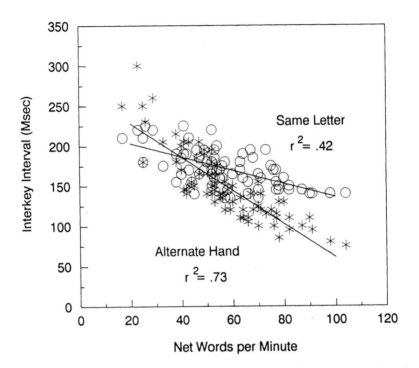

Figure 11.3. Median interkey interval for repetitions of a given keystroke and for successive keystrokes using alternate hands. Data from Salthouse (1985).

Figure 11.3 illustrates the mean speeds of these two types of keystrokes for the 74 typists mentioned earlier (Salthouse, 1984). Notice that the speeds for both types of keystrokes are greater with increased skill, but that the skill–speed relation is greater with keystrokes from alternate hands. It is particularly interesting to note that the relative speeds of the two types of keystrokes actually reverse as the level of skill increases, in that for slow typists repetition of a given letter is faster than is the typing of two letters by the fingers of alternate hands, but the opposite is true for fast typists.

The hypothesis suggested by the preceding two sets of results is that skilled typists rely on at least two mechanisms for circumventing the perceptual motor limitations that might otherwise restrict typing speed. First, as typists become more skilled, they tend to expand their eye–hand span, such that they begin processing characters up to seven in advance of the current keystroke. Second, one of the benefits of this advance information is that it allows typists to overlap their processing of successive keystrokes, with the consequence that their greatest speed is achieved with keystrokes in which there is the greatest opportunity for overlapped processing. Taken together, then, the results are quite consistent with the hypothesis that an important factor contributing to proficient typing is development of the ability to overlap the processing of successive keystrokes, thereby converting a serial and discrete task, subject to severe processing limitations, into a dynamic and continuous task in which those constraints are relatively unimportant.

These are only two examples, but additional instances of how expertise might productively be viewed as the circumvention of limitations on processing could certainly be identified. In fact, I did not even discuss what may be the most dramatic example of this phenomenon, that of skilled memory in which the normal limits of remembering less than 10 digits are exceeded by a factor of about 10 in carefully studied memory experts (e.g., Chase & Ericsson, 1981; Kliegl et al., 1987; Kliegl et al., 1989).

CONCLUSION

I conclude by briefly summarizing the major advantages of the circumvention-of-limitations perspective on expertise. A primary advantage is that a focus on the limitations that must be overcome to achieve expertise should make it easier to identify commonalities across activity domains sharing similar types of limitations. In other words, if the information in Tables 11.1 and 11.2 has any validity, then there should be important similarities in how expertise is achieved in various domains.

A second advantage of this view of expertise is that it encourages a coherent and systematic approach to the investigation of expertise. That is, the limitations perspective suggests that research should begin by asking what factors constrain the performances of novices, next considering how the identified limitations are overcome, and finally examining the manner in which the relevant mechanisms for circumventing limitations are acquired.

Many questions remain to be answered in regard to this perspective of expertise, and hence they might serve as productive topics for future research. Among the most interesting are these: (1) What are the specific mechanisms responsible for dealing with each type of limitation, and are there different ways of circumventing a given limitation? (2) Does the possession of expertise in one activity confer advantages in acquiring expertise in another activity that has similar limitations? (3) What are the prerequisites for circumventing limitations on performance?

REFERENCES

Ackerman, P. L. (1988). Determinants of individual differences during skill acquisition: Cognitive abilities and information processing. *Journal of Experimental Psychology: General, 117,* 288–318.

Adelson, B. (1984). When novices surpass experts: The difficulty of a task may increase with expertise. *Journal of Experimental Psychology: Learning, Memory, and Cognition, 10,* 483–495.

Britton, B. K., & Tesser, A. (1982). Effects of prior knowledge on use of cognitive capacity in three complex cognitive tasks. *Journal of Verbal Learning and Verbal Behavior, 21,* 421–436.

Charness, N., & Campbell, J. I. D. (1988). Acquiring skill at mental calculation in adulthood: A task decomposition. *Journal of Experimental Psychology: General, 117*, 115–129.

Chase, W. G., & Ericsson, K. A. (1981). Skilled memory. In J. R. Anderson (Ed.), *Cognitive skills and their acquisition* (pp. 141–189). Hillsdale, NJ: Erlbaum.

Fleishman, E. A. (1972). On the relation between abilities, learning, and human performance. *American Psychologist, 27*, 1017–1032.

Gentner, D. R. (1988). Expertise in typewriting. In M. T. H. Chi, R. Glaser, & M. J. Farr (Eds.), *The nature of expertise* (pp. 1–21). Hillsdale, NJ: Erlbaum.

Kliegl, R., Smith, J., & Baltes, P. B. (1989). Testing-the-limits and the study of adult age differences in cognitive plasticity of a mnemonic skill. *Developmental Psychology, 25*, 247–256.

Kliegl, R., Smith, J., Heckhausen, J., & Baltes, P. B. (1987). Mnemonic training for the acquisition of skilled digit memory. *Cognition and Instruction, 4*, 203–223.

Salthouse, T. A. (1984). Effects of age and skill in typing. *Journal of Experimental Psychology: General, 113*, 345–371.

Salthouse, T. A. (1985). Anticipatory processing in transcription typing. *Journal of Applied Psychology, 70*, 264–271.

Staszewski, J. J. (1988). Skilled memory and expert mental calculation. In M. T. H. Chi, R. Glaser, & M. J. Farr (Eds.), *The nature of expertise* (pp. 71–128). Hillsdale, NJ: Erlbaum.

12 *Symbolic connectionism: toward third-generation theories of expertise*

KEITH J. HOLYOAK

In discussing literary expertise, Scardamalia and Bereiter (chapter 7, this volume) mention an intellectual who was accused of not actually reading books, but of raiding them. I must confess that I have similarly raided the chapters in this book, and other sources as well, looking for clues to the directions that new theories of expertise are likely to take. Furthermore, given my entering biases, I no doubt was primed to value some clues more than others. In any case, I found that certain conjectures began to coalesce around the themes linking the diverse approaches to expertise reflected in this volume. In this chapter I shall review the themes that caught my attention and suggest what our current knowledge of expertise implies about the likely course of future theory development in this area. I realize this is a dangerous enterprise, for without a reliable crystal ball, today's predictions can easily turn into tomorrow's embarrassments. Still, the sweeping scope of this collection of reports on the state of the art in expertise research, delivered as they are at the turn of a decade and in the midst of theoretical ferment in cognitive science, surely justifies the risk.

THE FIRST TWO GENERATIONS

Theories of expertise have now passed through two generations. The first generation centered on the early insights of Newell and Simon (1972; Newell, Shaw, & Simon, 1958): their conceptualization of problem solving as search, and their specification of a small number of heuristic methods for serial search (e.g., means–ends analysis and hill climbing) that could be applied across an indefinitely broad range of domains, with minimal knowledge about the specific content of any particular domain. The first fruits of work on artificial intelligence – the "Logic Theorist" and the "General Problem Solver" – were based on general methods for heuristic search. The obvious first conjecture about expertise was that an expert was someone particularly skilled at general heuristic search.

That conjecture was short-lived. First in chess (Chase & Simon, 1973; de Groot, 1965), then in physics (Chi, Feltovich, & Glaser, 1981; Larkin, McDermott, Simon, & Simon, 1980), and then in myriad other domains it became

301

apparent that expertise depended crucially on detailed domain knowledge, reflected in specialized memory abilities and inference patterns. Heuristic search methods were general but weak, characteristic of novice rather than expert performance. "Knowledge is power" was the slogan that captured the essence of the second generation of theories of expertise, which dominated both cognitive psychology and artificial intelligence throughout the 1970s and 1980s; for a capsule history, see Feigenbaum (1989).

The second generation of expertise theories transformed the study of cognition, bringing the study of high-level problem solving – the "prototype" area for expertise research – to a prominence it had not enjoyed since the era of Gestalt psychology early in this century. Complex problem solving was seen as a particularly worthy proving ground for cognitive theories, as it necessarily required integration of assumptions about the basic component processes of memory, attention, and reasoning. Complex problem solving has real-world importance and ecological validity as an area of research. Expertise obviously depends on learning how to do something well; hence, the study of procedural learning (rather than only declarative memory) became a crucial area for research. The sophisticated methodology of protocol analysis (Ericsson & Simon, 1980) was developed in conjunction with the second generation of theories. Perhaps most important, second-generation theories were based on a particular canonical cognitive architecture – serial production systems (Newell, 1973) – that created direct ties between cognitive psychology and artificial intelligence and hence contributed to the rise of interdisciplinary cognitive science. In artificial intelligence, production systems became the basis for expert systems, the first major commercial applications of the field. In cognitive psychology, production systems provided the core of Anderson's evolving ACT theory (Anderson, 1976, 1983, 1987), which became the first grand, overarching theory of cognition since the Hull-Spence theories of the 1940s and 1950s.

Second-generation theories of expertise provide a fundamentally simple picture of the development of expertise, which has been most clearly articulated and empirically motivated in Anderson's (1983, 1987) theory of knowledge compilation. Similar principles provide the basis for the Rosenbloom and Newell (1986) theory of chunking. The central idea of knowledge compilation is that operator sequences that yield a successful solution to a problem can be "cached" as new, specialized production rules that will lead to more efficient solutions of similar problems in the future. Compilation can be viewed as an instantiation of Chase and Simon's (1973) hypothesis that expertise involves the acquisition of large integrated "chunks" of knowledge. In knowledge compilation, chunks take the form of larger, more detailed conditions and actions of production rules. Larger conditions provide more precise specification of the circumstances under which the action is appropriate; larger actions allow more to be accomplished by a single "rule-firing." In addition, compilation involves a reduction in the need to access declarative memory, as well as speeded-up rule-firing due to increases in the strengths of rules with each successful application. Knowledge compilation is closely related to Shiffrin and Schneider's (1977) theory of the development of automaticity with practice at a consistent task. The general picture is that a novice first solves problems by weak methods (often working backward from the goal), and successful solutions result in automatic generation of specialized productions (often allowing forward progress from the initial problem state toward the goal). Relative to the novice, the expert is able to reach the correct solution more quickly and efficiently.

WHY A THIRD GENERATION?

As Kuhn (1962) and others have told us, two great pressures drive scientific change: problems encountered in using current theories to explain empirical findings, and the rise of theoretical alternatives. Both of these conditions are evident in the field of expertise research. The chapters in this volume, and other recent papers, describe findings about expert performance that are unexplained and in some cases anomalous from the perspective of second-generation theories. Many authors express dissatisfaction with the current theoretical understanding (e.g., Lesgold, 1989), and Patel and Groen (chapter 4, this volume) and Sloboda (chapter 6, this volume) allude to the potential of an alternative theoretical paradigm – connectionism – that has invigorated other areas of cognitive science in recent years (Feldman & Ballard, 1982; Rumelhart, McClelland, & PDP Research Group, 1986b). I shall first survey the reasons for unease about our current understanding of expertise, and then sketch an emerging framework that may yield a third generation of theories of expertise.

Empirical inconsistencies and theoretical anomalies of expertise

The canonical second-generation view of expert preformance suggests some major uniformities in the nature of expert performance and its acquisition across different domains. Among the supposed commonalities widely cited in textbook treatments are the following: (1) experts perform complex tasks in their domains much more accurately than do novices; (2) experts solve problems in their domains with greater ease than do novices; (3) expertise develops from knowledge initially acquired by weak methods, such as means–ends analysis; (4) expertise is based on the automatic evocation of actions by conditions; (5) experts have superior memory for information related to their domains; (6) experts are better at perceiving patterns among task-related cues; (7) expert problem-solvers search forward from given information rather than backward from goals; (8) one's degree of expertise increases steadily with practice; (9) learning requires specific goals and clear feedback; (10) expertise is highly domain-specific; (11) teaching expert rules results in expertise; (12) performances of experts can be predicted accurately from knowledge of the rules they claim to use. These predicted characteristics of expertise have received empirical support in varying degrees; nonetheless, surveys of expertise research (e.g., Waldmann & Weinert, 1990) reveal that none provides a universal characterization of expert performance. Although not all of these inconsistencies are incompatible with second-generation theories, none seems clearly illuminated by them. Let us examine some exceptions that have been reported.

Experts sometimes achieve mediocrity. Camerer and Johnson, in their review of research on expert clinical decision making (chapter 8, this volume), provide the following summary: Expert decision-makers appear to do remarkably well, "generating hypotheses and inducing complex decision rules. The result is a more efficient search of the available information directed by goals and aided by the experts' superior store of knowledge. Unfortunately, their knowledge and rules have little impact on experts' performances. Sometimes experts are more accurate than novices (though not always), but they are rarely better than simple statistical models."

Experts sometimes feel more pain. Scardamalia and Bereiter (chapter 7, this volume) point out that studies of writing provide important exceptions to the idea that experts always accomplish with ease what novices do only with difficulty. As they summarize the field, "expert writers generally are found to work harder at the same assigned tasks than are nonexperts, engaging in more planning and problem solving, more revision of goals and methods, and in general more agonizing over the task." The reason, as Scardamalia and Bereiter point out, is that writing tasks are inherently ill-defined problems. The result is that expert writers tend to define the task in such a way that it is problematic, so that it cannot be accomplished by routine application of available skills, but instead requires them to work at the edge of their competence. This situation, of course, is not unique to expert writers; laborious extended efforts have been documented through the notebooks of scientists (e.g., Tweney's, 1985, analysis of the work of Faraday) and in the verbal protocols of physicists attempting to solve nonroutine problems (Clement, 1989).

Means–ends analysis can impair learning. According to second-generation theories, problem solutions initially attained by weak methods, most notably means–ends analysis, provide the grist for knowledge compilation and hence expertise development. But the work of Sweller and his colleagues (Owen & Sweller, 1985; Sweller, Mawer, & Ward, 1983) has shown that having subjects solve algebra-word problems by means–ends analysis actually impairs their performances on subsequent transfer tests. A more effective initial learning strategy involves free forward search from the given information in the absence of an explicit goal.

Conditions and actions sometimes can be flexibly recoupled. In second-generation theories, expertise is viewed as the result of automatic evocation of specialized actions in response to specialized conditions, a connection typically formalized with production rules. However, Allard and Starkes (chapter 5, this volume) report a series of studies of motor performance in which subjects displayed striking abilities to adjust to altered condition–action links. Their evidence indicates that the greater the skill level of the performer, the less the performance decrement resulting from being forced to alter the action required by a given condition – opposite to the prediction that would seem to follow from the hypothesis that expertise involves increasingly automated firing of condition–action rules. Such evidence is reminiscent of classic demonstrations that visual perception adapts quite rapidly to the effects of distorting prisms, with minimal aftereffects when the prisms are removed (Stratton, 1897). In a more cognitive procedural task, learning to use a text editor, Anderson (1987) reported that subjects were able to switch from one text editor to another with relative ease.

Expertise sometimes can be decoupled from memory performance. Ever since the seminal work of de Groot (1965) and Chase and Simon (1973) on chess expertise, a standard finding has been that experts have superior memory for stimuli related to their domains. This is, of course, especially the case when the domain of expertise is actually memory performance, as documented in the work of Ericsson and Staszewski (1989) on skilled memory. Nonetheless, expertise and memory performance sometimes are decoupled. Perhaps the most striking example was provided by a study of computer programmers by Adelson (1984), in which she found that novices actually had better memory for details of code than did experts. The reason appeared to be that experts attended more to the overall goal structure of the programming task, rather than to actual code. The experts found it easier to solve a programming task again rather than memorize a detailed solution, whereas the reverse was the case for novices.

Other dissociations of problem-solving and memory performances are reported by Patel and Groen (chapter 4, this volume) for medical diagnosis and by Charness (chapter 2, this volume) for chess. Patel and Groen report that memory for clinical cases does not always increase (and may even be nonmonotonic) with medical expertise. In studies of chess, Holding and Reynolds (1982) found that skilled players chose better moves for disorganized but legal chess positions, even though they showed no recall advantage for such positions; and Charness (1981) found that older players had poorer memory for board positions than did equivalently skilled younger players. Such exceptions call into question the common assumption that domain-specific memory skill is directly related to expert problem solving.

Expertise sometimes can be decoupled from pattern perception. Closely related to the typically superior memory performances of experts is their greater ability to perceive patterns in stimuli drawn from their domains (e.g., the chess expert can more quickly detect a potential fork). But Allard and Starkes (chapter 5, this volume) report an exception for expert volleyball players (in contrast to experts in dance, basketball, and hockey, who show the typical expertise advantage in processing structured stimuli). Better volleyball players do not show a consistent advantage over weaker players in perceiving offensive volleyball patterns; however, they do show an advantage in sheer speed of detecting a volleyball (but not a referee!) in photographic slides showing game positions. Allard and Starkes argue that this exception arises because in volleyball, offensive positions typically are designed to deceive the defenders and hence are best ignored in favor of continuous focus on the ball.

Expert search strategies are extremely varied. Work on solving routine physics problems indicates that acquisition of expertise is accompanied by a shift from backward search to forward search. In computer programming, however, both novices and experts emphasize backward search from goals (Anderson, Farrell, & Sauers, 1984; Jeffries, Turner, Polson, & Atwood, 1981). The reason appears to be that in computer programming, unlike routine physics problem solving, the initial state places few constraints on the solution path. The search processes are not simply identical for novice and expert programmers; experts do a kind of breadth-first search for a global program design, whereas novices tend to get lost in depth-first searches. Even in physics, nonroutine problems evoke backward search by experts (Tweney, 1985). More generally, expertise in complex tasks often is distinguished not by some single canonical search strategy but by flexible switching among alternative strategies (Dörner & Schölkopf, chapter 9, this volume).

Performance may not show continuous improvement with practice. Performances on many tasks seem to improve smoothly with practice, typically following a power function. Yet exceptions are common for complex tasks. As Scardamalia and Bereiter (chapter 7, this volume) put it, "vague notions of 'experience' and 'practice' obscure what is undoubtedly the socially most significant issue in the study of expertise, the issue of why there are such great differences in competence among people with equivalent amounts of experience and practice. No one is disturbed by the fact that experienced physicians are better at diagnosis than interns. We are all disturbed by the possibility that our health may fall into the hands of physicians whose diagnostic expertise has not kept pace with their years of experience."

The acquisition of expertise, even when it does not prematurely "asymptote," does not always follow a smooth path. Ericsson and Staszewski (1989) describe the development of memory skill in their subject SF, who was able to dramatically improve his short-term memory ability by using specialized strategies. His learning curve exhibited flat periods followed by dramatic increments corresponding to qualitative changes in his evolving strategy. Higher levels of expertise may sometimes require not just greater speed and efficiency in processing but a more radical restructuring of the task itself (Cheng, 1985). The development of typing skill, for example, depends on a shift from serial to parallel planning and execution of finger movements (D. R. Gentner, 1983; Salthouse, chapter 11, this volume).

Learning need not require goals or feedback, The canonical second-generation account of skill acquisition emphasizes that learning depends on clear feedback about the success or failure of attempts to achieve goals (Anderson, 1987), and in many contexts there is good evidence in favor of this view. However, studies of the acquisition of musical expertise (Sloboda, chapter 6, this volume) suggest that children typically learn the basic chordal structure of music by age 7 simply from exposure to music and that premature stress on achievement of goals in musical performance may actually be detrimental. Such complex forms of perceptual learning seem to lie outside the scope of second-generation theories. In a much more explicit problem-solving context, Koedinger and Anderson (1989) found that subjects skilled in geometry solved proof problems on the basis of perceptual chunks related to canonical diagrams. The subjects planned solutions in considerably fewer steps than were actually required to execute the proofs, and the nature of the abbreviated planning phase was inconsistent with standard models of knowledge compilation.

Knowledge can be transferred across domains. A central tenet of second-generation theories has been that high levels of performance reflect specialized domain knowledge that by its very nature is of little or no use in performing tasks in other domains (or even novel tasks within the same domain). And, indeed, demonstrations of failure to achieve transfer of solution methods across domains are commonplace in the problem-solving literature; for a recent review, see Gick and Holyoak (1987). Nonetheless, there is a growing body of evidence to indicate that with appropriate instruction, knowledge often can be transferred effectively to novel problems (e.g., Brown, Kane, & Echols, 1986; Catrambone & Holyoak, 1989; Gick & Holyoak, 1983). Dörner and Schölkopf (chapter 9, this volume) report that experienced executives were more successful than college students in coping with an unfamiliar problem involving management of a complex dynamic environment. This finding is consistent with other evidence that abstract types of reasoning skills acquired through systematic training can be applied in contexts quite different from that in which training occurred. Nisbett and his colleagues (Cheng, Holyoak, Nisbett, & Oliver, 1986; Fong, Krantz, & Nisbett, 1986; Nisbett, Fong, Lehman, & Cheng, 1987) have found that training in statistics or in everyday deductive reasoning can improve performances on problems with novel content. Theorists such as D. Gentner (1983) and Holyoak (1985) have emphasized the power of analogical thinking as a tool for transfer of knowledge across domains.

Scardamalia and Bereiter (chapter 7, this volume) raise the possibility that expert writing is really a kind of expert thinking, which could have a direct impact on performances at the frontiers of an indefinitely wide range of disciplines. Another candidate source of broad expertise is knowledge of mathematics, which provides formal representations of wide potential applicability. Bassok and Holyoak (1989) found training in algebraic sequences (by direct instruction in the relevant concepts and equations, coupled with practice in solving example word problems) was sufficient to allow most students to recognize immediately the relevance of the learned procedures to isomorphic problems with novel content (constant-acceleration problems in physics). Novick (1988; Novick & Holyoak, 1991) found that high levels of expertise in mathematics (as indexed by high scores on the quantitative section of the Scholastic Aptitude Test) was predictive of successful analogical transfer of a novel mathematical procedure. Anzai (chapter 3, this volume) describes a transfer study in which a subject was able to apply general procedures for constructing diagrams to novel types of physics problems. All of these demonstrations of relatively flexible transfer seem to require explanations that go beyond a characterization of expertise as the product of increasingly specialized domain knowledge.

Teaching expert rules may not yield expertise. If expert knowledge can be fundamentally represented as a set of production rules, as second-generation theories assume, then the most direct way to improve students' expertise would seem to be to teach them the experts' rules. The "overlay" paradigm for building intelligent tutoring systems assumes that a student's state of knowledge at any time is a subset of that of the expert and that a tutor should incrementally add expert rules to the student's knowledge base (Carr & Goldstein, 1977). In fact, however, several researchers in the area of automated tutoring systems have argued that the overlay paradigm is inadequate (e.g., Clancey, 1986; Wenger, 1987).

Rules elicited from experts may not predict their performance. An even more obvious prediction of the view that expertise can be represented by a set of production rules is that if we know what rules experts are using to perform a task, we should be able to predict their performances. This prediction has been challenged by the findings in a study by Lundell (1988; Hunt, 1989): University students were exposed to five hundred displays representing possible readings of instruments for an imaginary but realistic power plant; they were asked to provide a diagnosis for each display and were then told the correct diagnosis. By the end of the session the subjects were accurate on 75% of trials (as opposed to initial chance performance of 25%). Using structured interviews based on techniques for knowledge engineering, Lundell developed a rule-based system to represent each subject's knowledge. The rule-based system for each student was then used to predict the student's performance on a set of new transfer cases. The programs produced the correct diagnoses for just 55% of the new cases, whereas the students were again correct 75% of the time; but worse, the system tailored to an individual student was no more predictive of that student's performance than were systems tailored to other students. In contrast, Lundell found that connectionist networks constructed for each student by an incremental error-correction algorithm classified 72% of the transfer trials correctly, and each student's performance tended to be better predicted by his or her own network than by someone else's.

Caution is clearly called for in generalizing from Lundell's results, as the amount of training used was modest, and the validity of the method used to extract rules from subjects could be questioned. Nonetheless, the greater predictive success of the connectionist networks is at least suggestive.

Summary. When we survey the overall field of expertise research, we find what is surely a disconcerting lack of constancy in the correlates of expertise. There appears to be no single "expert way" to perform all tasks. Perhaps the most apt general characterization of expert performance is that suggested by Dörner and Schölkopf (chapter 8, this volume): An expert is someone capable of doing the right thing at the right time. This characterization is, of course, nearly vacuous; nonetheless, it does suggest a way of understanding some of the variations noted earlier. In general, an expert will have succeeded in adapting to the inherent constraints of the task. If the task can be done most efficiently by forward search, the expert will search forward; if backward search is better, the expert will search backward. If certain patterns of cues are crucial to performing the task well, the expert likely will perceive and remember them; if patterns are not so important, the expert will not selectively process them. The tendency of experts to adapt to task constraints would account for the fact that whereas novices differ widely in the way they organize domain-relevant concepts, experts tend to resemble each other (and differ from novices) in their conceptual organizations (McKeithen, Reitman, Rueter, & Hirtle, 1981; Olson & Biolsi, chapter 10, this volume).

Given the importance of task constraints, as emphasized many years ago by Simon (1969), it might be useful to analyze expertise systematically in terms of the kind of "rational analysis" proposed by Anderson (1990), which attempts to eliminate the need to specify process models. But even this general approach must confront the unfortunate experts at clinical diagnosis, whose adaptation to their task fell short of that afforded by simple linear regression models. It may well be the case that their failures can be explained as the products of generally useful learning strategies that have been confounded by the inherent randomness and poor feedback associated with their target task. But if so, a complete model of expertise acquisition will necessarily require a clear account of human learning mechanisms and their processing limitations, rather than rational analysis alone.

Second-generation theories certainly are capable of explaining some of the diversity in expert performance surveyed earlier. However, to do so they must be elaborated to incorporate learning mechanisms other than knowledge compilation and its variants. A number of researchers have suggested that expertise depends largely on the induction, retrieval, and instantiation of schematic knowledge structures (e.g., Gick & Holyoak, 1983; Koedinger & Anderson,

1989; Schank, 1982; Sweller et al., 1983). Such processes seem quite different from the acquisition and use of specialized production rules. In addition, a great deal of evidence suggests that skilled performance in tasks ranging from the perceptuomotor level (e.g., word recognition and typing) to higher cognitive levels (e.g., discourse comprehension and analogical reasoning) depends on the parallel integration of multiple sources of information. This style of processing cannot be gracefully implemented in serial production systems, the typical architecture for second-generation models.

Routine versus adaptive expertise

The diversity of expert learning and performance suggests the importance of distinguishing qualitatively different varieties of expertise. As Ericsson and Smith (chapter 1, this volume) have argued, it is likely that "research on superior expert performance is benefited more by the development of a taxonomy of different types of mechanisms acquired through different types of learning and adaptation processes than by restricting the definition of expertise to a specific type of acquisition through learning."

A broad distinction between two classes of expertise is suggested by two tentative definitions of expertise raised by Sloboda (chapter 6, this volume). One possible definition is that expert performance involves "the reliable attainment of specific goals within a specific domain." A more demanding definition is that "an expert is someone who can make an appropriate response to a situation that contains a degree of unpredictability." These alternatives correspond to the distinction drawn by Hatano and Inagaki (1986; Hatano, 1988) between *routine* expertise and *adaptive* expertise. (Salomon & Perkins, 1989, elucidated a related distinction between "low-road" and "high-road" mechanisms of transfer.) Whereas routine experts are able to solve familiar types of problems quickly and accurately, they have only modest capabilities in dealing with novel types of problems. Adaptive experts, on the other hand, may be able to invent new procedures derived from their expert knowledge. Hatano and Inagaki (1986) suggested that the key to adaptive expertise is the development of deeper conceptual understanding of the target domain. Such understanding, they argued, is heavily dependent on the conditions under which learning takes place. Understanding is more likely to result when the task is variable and in some degree unpredictable, rather than stereotyped, and when the task is explored freely without heavy pressure to achieve an immediate goal. Understanding can result from sensitivity to internally generated feedback, such as surprise at a predictive failure, perplexity at noticing alternative explanations for a phenomenon, and discoordination due to lack of explanatory links between pieces of knowledge that apparently should be related. Understanding is also fostered by social support and encouragement of deeper comprehension, and by efforts to explain a task to others.

Hatano (1988) exemplified the distinction between routine and adaptive expertise with a cross-cultural contrast between two forms of mathematical calculation skills: use of the abacus in Japan and other Asian cultures (e.g.,

Hatano & Osawa, 1983) and the "street math" of Brazilian children working as vendors. Expertise in use of the abacus leads to extremely rapid calculations and to increased digit span; however, such knowledge cannot readily be generalized to repair "buggy" pencil-and-paper arithmetic procedures (Amaiwa, 1987) or to use nonconventional abacuses with a different base value. In contrast, unschooled Brazilian children who acquire arithmetic skills in the context of selling merchandise on the street can adapt general components of their procedures, such as decomposition and regrouping, to solve novel problems both on the street and in classroom mathematics (Carraher, Carraher, & Schliemann, 1987; Saxe, 1988). The primary difference between the two skills, according to Hatano, is that representations of number relations on the abacus are impoverished in meaning, whereas those used in street math are semantically transparent, analogous to the wider range of activities involving goods and money. In addition, abacus use is basically a solitary skill in which speed and accuracy are the dominant goals, whereas street math is a social enterprise in which transparency to the customer, rather than speed, is crucial.

Other researchers have also noted that learning directed toward understanding is associated with more adaptive forms of expertise. The advantage of learning through free forward search, rather than through goal-dominated means–ends analysis (Sweller et al., 1983), is consistent with this pattern. Both scientific discovery (Clement, 1989) and advanced skills in writing (Scardamalia & Bereiter, chapter 7, this volume) emphasize understanding as an overarching goal. The kind of cognitive knowledge acquired in "open" motor skills (Allard & Starkes, chapter 5, this volume) presumably reflects the inherent variety of the performances through which learning takes place. Skill at jazz improvisation (Sloboda, chapter 6, this volume) seems to be acquired in the context of supportive social interaction involving free exploration rather than fixation on a precise goal.

Hatano (1988) emphasized cases in which an entire skill lent itself more to the acquisition of routine (abacus) or adaptive (street math) expertise. However, it is quite likely that individual differences in the acquisition of a given basic skill may reflect differences in learning styles. For example, Chi, Bassok, Lewis, Reimann, and Glaser (1989) found that better students of physics took a more active approach to learning from worked examples of word problems than did weaker students. The better students continually tried to explain *why* the steps of the illustrated solutions were required. As other investigators have argued, motivation and ability to monitor one's own comprehension seem to be crucial to the acquisition of flexible expertise (Dörner & Schölkopf, chapter 9, this volume; Scardamalia & Bereiter, chapter 7, this volume).

The second-generation theories of expertise, with their emphasis on the acquisition of more specialized production rules through knowledge compilation, can be characterized as attempts to explain routine expertise. As Ericsson and Smith (chapter 1, this volume) point out, most empirical and theoretical work has been directed at accounting for stable superior performance on representative tasks, for which reproductive methods and specific knowledge are in fact central. Indeed, such theories typically are described as models of "skill acquisition," which, as Wenger (1987) has pointed out, is not coextensive with expertise: "Whereas skill acquisition can be tested by straightforward performance measures, expertise is a much more subtle notion. . . . [It] must also be evaluated by the capacity to handle novel situations, to reconsider and explain the validity of rules, and to reason about the domain from first principles" (p. 302). In Hatano's terminology, skill acquisition results in routine expertise; adaptive expertise requires something else. The second generation of expertise theories was born of the hope that domain-specific knowledge, built up on top of a foundation of weak methods for serial heuristic search, would have the power to fully model human expertise. For some researchers in the area of expertise that hope has now faded, and their loss of innocence is accompanied by theoretical quandaries and increasing openness to new directions. A full account of expertise, it seems, will require a new generation of theories.

THE THIRD GENERATION: SYMBOLIC CONNECTIONISM

I am, of course, trying merely to predict the future, not to describe a present reality; thus, I intend to sketch not a new theory of expertise, or even a framework for a theory, but simply an evolving paradigm within which I conjecture that new theories of expertise will eventually emerge. The name I give to this paradigm is "symbolic connectionism." The knowledgeable reader may find the label internally contradictory; there has been much discussion of whether or not connectionism will allow cognitive science to do away with symbolic representations altogether. In agreement with the severest critics of connectionism (Fodor & Pylyshyn, 1988; Pinker & Prince, 1988), I believe that reports of the demise of symbols are premature. In particular, adaptive expertise in tasks requiring high-level reasoning appears to require representations that by any reasonable definition are inherently symbolic, just as does the ability to speak and comprehend a human language. But unlike its severest critics, I believe that connectionism offers important new insights into information processing that will sufficiently change the character of cognitive theories that it will be reasonable to speak of a generational change. As was the case in the second generation, these third-generation theories will first arise as models of aspects of the human cognitive architecture, rather than of expertise per se, but then will be tested in part by their ability to account for various forms of expertise.

Symbolic connectionism, as the name implies, will be based on the integration of theoretical ideas drawn from symbolic models (including second-generation models of expertise) and connectionist models. I shall first describe connectionism and its apparent implications for understanding expertise and then provide some reasons why symbolic representations are also required. I shall then briefly describe some early examples of symbolic connectionist models that may point the way toward new treatments of expertise.

The connectionist view of expertise

Connectionist representations consist of networks of relatively simple processing units connected by links. Processing involves a series of cycles in which in each cycle the units take on new states of activation as a function of their own prior activations, the prior activations of units to which they are connected, and the weights on the interconnecting links. Weights can be either excitatory (tending to make the receiving unit active when the sending unit is active) or inhibitory (tending to make the receiving unit inactive when the sending unit is active). Connectionist models embody three central ideas. First, decision making it based on *parallel constraint satisfaction:* A cycle of processing tends to converge on an activation pattern over units that best satisfies the constraints embodied in the weights on links. The units with the highest asymptotic activations will tend to support each other and to inhibit their competitors. Second, knowledge is, to varying extents, *distributed* over sets of units, rather than identified with single units. Third, learning consists in *incremental revision of weights* on the basis of internally or externally generated feedback concerning the performance of the network. For detailed introductions to connectionism, see Feldman and Ballard (1982) and Rumelhart et al. (1986b).

The parallelism of connectionist networks supports a style of knowledge representation in which decisions are based not on individual rules with large conditions and actions, as is suggested by the notion of knowledge compilation, but rather on interactions between multiple, simpler connections. An example of a connectionist network is depicted in Figure 12.1, which shows the representation of knowledge used in a model of the generation of musical expectations (Bharucha, 1987a, 1987b). The network consists of layers of units representing different types of musical units, such as tones and chords, densely interconnected by links.

There are general advantages to having smaller units of knowledge operating in parallel relative to having larger units of knowledge (such as compiled rules) operating individually. A rule with multiple clauses in its condition is likely to be "brittle," providing no information on how to behave in slightly different situations. And because a rule with a highly specific condition will be less likely to be tested than a rule (or connection) with a more general trigger, any validity estimate will tend to be less reliable for the more specific rule, simply because of the smaller associated sample size (Camerer & Johnson, chapter 8, this volume). Complex rules of the sort produced by knowledge compilation may indeed be useful for performing routine tasks efficiently (see Miyata, 1989, for a connectionist version of knowledge compilation); however, such rules are not likely to provide the key to adaptive expertise.

The connectionist perspective offers a number of possible insights into the nature of expertise (Rumelhart, Smolensky, McClelland, & Hinton, 1986c; Smolensky, 1986). Parallel constraint satisfaction can in principle capture the most striking aspect of human expert performance: Experts tend to arrive

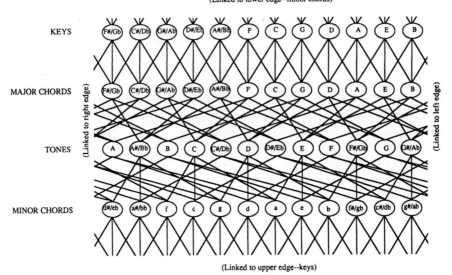

Figure 12.1. A network representing relationships among tones, chords, and keys. Links between units reflect the memberships of tones in chords and of chords in keys. A musical context activates tone units, and the activation spreads through the network, reverberating until it settles into a state of equilibrium. The pattern of activation at equilibrium represents the array of chordal expectations and key implications and influences the consonance and recognition of events that follow. From Bharucha (1987a). Copyright by the Cognitive Science Society Incorporated. Used by permission.

quickly at a small number (sometimes one) of the best solutions to a problem, without serial search through alternative possibilities (de Groot, 1965; Patel & Groen, chapter 4, this volume). Fundamentally, expertise is the product of the acquisition of task-appropriate constraints. A "chunk" of knowledge will correspond to a tightly connected excitatory subnet of mutually supportive units. In contrast to the standard conception of chunking as an all-or-none phenomenon, from the connectionist perspective it may be viewed as a matter of degree of excitatory connectivity. Research has shown that multiple, possibly overlapping chunks appear to form the cores of expert representations of board positions in chess and other games (Chase & Simon, 1973; Reitman, 1976). It is natural, from the connectionist view, for a unit to participate in multiple chunks, and several chunks may be active simultaneously to represent a complex, possibly unique, problem situation. If units representing board positions are connected to units representing possible moves, then the weights on links connecting units for chunks with units for moves will provide constraints that can be used to generate plausible moves in response to particular board configurations.

Connectionist principles provide mechanisms for implementing a parallel, content-addressable memory-retrieval system (Hinton & Anderson, 1981). Thus, any component of the representation of a problem situation can potentially provide access to similar structures in memory that may provide information relevant to a solution. The more links that connect problem cues to representations of relevant prior knowledge, the more likely it is that such knowledge will be activated. In addition, connectionist processing provides automatic pattern completion, reflecting top-down processing and its interactions with bottom-up processing. Thus, partial cues in the problem situation may activate a cluster of units representing one or more schemes for interpreting the situation, which will in turn provide a richer interpretation of the problem.

A number of connectionist learning schemes have been devised to adaptively modify the weights on links. These learning rules, in effect, pick out statistical regularities among clusters of inputs (Rumelhart & Zipser, 1986) or among reinforced input–output relations (Rumelhart, Hinton, & Williams, 1986a). Schemes of this nature may play an important role in the basic processes of perceptual learning (e.g., the process by which children learn musical patterns from exposure to music; Bharucha, in press), motor learning (e.g., the gradual shift from serial to parallel movement planning in typing; Miyata, 1989), and more central associative learning.

The idea that states of networks have varying degrees of "harmony" or coherence (Smolensky, 1986) suggests that networks can be augmented with mechanisms that allow sensitivity to internal states of the system, thus generating internal feedback. For example, a network may preactivate units representing potential perceptual inputs; deviations of the internally generated activation pattern from actual perceptual inputs may trigger a "surprise" reaction. An asymptotic activation pattern in which active units are inhibiting each other is a sign that contradictory interpretations are simultaneously supported, triggering "perplexity." Such information about the state of the system could potentially contribute to learning by understanding.

The need for symbolic representations

The reader will doubtless have noticed that the foregoing sketch of connectionism as an approach to understanding expertise is laden with promissory notes. There are as yet no serious connectionist models of expertise in chess, physics, or any other domain involving high-level cognition. Furthermore, there are significant impediments to the development of such models. Connectionist theorists are grappling with difficult questions concerning the representational adequacy of their networks. The problems they face have been articulated by critics ranging from the sympathetic (Dyer, 1991; Norman, 1986) to the highly skeptical (Fodor & Pylyshyn, 1988).

The central difficulties all hinge on the need to represent various types of knowledge that are inherently *relational*. To take a simple example, one might suppose that the proposition "the dog chased the cat" could be represented by the simultaneous activation of units representing the concepts "dog," "chase," and "cat." However, this pattern would be indistinguishable from that activated by the proposition "the cat chased the dog," or for that matter by the word list "chase, cat, dog." Keeping variable bindings straight, as is required to use simple inference rules, poses similar problems. For example, if we know the rule that "if a seller sells a possession to a buyer, then the buyer comes to own the possession," and find out that Bob sold a bicycle to Helen, we can readily conclude that Bob is the seller, the bicycle is the possession, Helen is the buyer, and therefore it is Helen who ends up owning the bicycle. However, this inference requires more than simply activating the relevant concepts; in addition, roles must be represented and bound to the appropriate individuals. Although there have been serious attempts to deal with relational knowledge in connectionist terms (e.g., Hinton, 1981; Smolensky, 1987; Touretsky & Hinton, 1988), fully satisfactory solutions have yet to emerge.

The absence of such solutions makes it difficult for connectionist models to provide accounts of many cognitive abilities that are linked to expertise, such as learning from verbal instructions, representing goal hierarchies (Anderson, 1987; Newell & Simon, 1972), computing analogical mappings (D. Gentner, 1983), assessing similarity of relational structures (Goldstone, Gentner, & Medin, 1989), and accounting for the role of relations in memory retrieval (Ratcliff & McKoon, 1989). A general account of expertise, especially if it is to account for cross-domain transfer of knowledge, will require such inherently relational constructs as goals, types of solution methods, abstract inference rules, and metacognitive procedures.

These representational problems are related to the basic questions of what a unit in a connectionist network can represent. The fact that knowledge is distributed over a set of units does not in itself constrain the "grain size" of what can be represented as a unit. Connectionist theorists have often been extremely vague in defining what a unit can represent. For example, McClelland and Rumelhart (1986) suggested that "a unit may correspond to a neuron, a cluster of neurons, or a conceptual entity related in a complex way to actual neurons" (p. 329). Although radical proponents of parallel distributed processing (PDP) often stress that units represent subsymbolic "microfeatures," many of the most successful connectionist cognitive models have included units representing such complex elements as lexical entries, concepts, or propositions. For example, Bharucha's (1987a) model of musical expectations (Figure 12.1) includes units for abstract musical structures (chords and keys), which are inherently relational in nature, in addition to units for simple tones. It has for some time been recognized that the most serious issues of representational adequacy arise in networks in which concepts that must have a complex internal structure are represented by diffuse, overlapping sets of units (Feldman & Ballard, 1982). Localist connectionist networks, of the sort proposed by Feldman and Ballard, represent individual concepts by a small number of units (a dozen or less, and often just one). Such networks can more readily perform symbolic functions.

The lack of constraint placed on what a unit can represent might be interpreted as a weakness of the connectionist research program; however, it might instead be taken as a clue that representational and processing issues can usefully be separated. As I have noted elsewhere,

> for many purposes it is useful to extract the essential properties of connectionist models from their metaphorical neural trappings. In general terms, units represent hypotheses, and connections capture inferential dependencies among hypotheses. Thus if one unit has an excitatory connection to another, this indicates that support for the first hypothesis provides some degree of positive evidence for the second. . . . Summation of activation at each unit serves to integrate multiple sources of converging or contradictory evidence regarding a hypothesis. . . . [M]any of the processing principles embodied in PDP models can be readily incorporated into models that choose to represent hypotheses as symbol structures rather than primitive units. [Holyoak, 1987, p. 994]

The symbolic connectionist paradigm simply accepts that units can potentially represent "hypotheses" with substantial internal complexity. Standard techniques for symbolic representation (or more connectionist-style techniques, as these are developed) can be used to represent relational information; at the same time, connectionist processing techniques can be used to manipulate the units to accomplish such cognitive tasks as memory retrieval and decision making. Such models attempt to capitalize on the complementary strengths of symbolic representation and connectionist processing. As we shall see, this integrated approach proves to be especially useful in deriving inferences from complex relational knowledge. Symbolic connectionist models can make inferences that standard symbolic systems often are too brittle to derive, using knowledge that diffuse connectionist systems cannot readily represent.

Symbolic connectionism: case studies

A number of artificial-intelligence models have been proposed to reflect various hybridizations of symbolic representations and connectionist processing (e.g., Ajjanagadde & Shastri, 1989; Cottrell, 1985; Dolan & Dyer, 1988; Dolan & Smolensky, 1988; Hendler, 1989; Lange & Dyer, 1989; Shastri, 1988; Shastri & Ajjanagadde, 1990; Touretsky & Hinton, 1988). These models are aimed at the development of new, connectionist-style techniques for symbol processing. Another group of models, which I shall sketch here, can combine standard symbolic representations with connectionist constraint-satisfaction procedures to account for psychological data concerning human performance of high-level cognitive tasks, such as discourse comprehension, analogical thinking, and evaluation of explanations. These models suggest the potential breadth of the domains to which symbolic connectionism can be applied, as well as some important commonalities in theoretical mechanisms.

Discourse comprehension. Most of us have some degree of expertise at understanding spoken or written discourse. Comprehension typically succeeds with little apparent effort, despite the fact that discourse is fraught with lexical and syntactic ambiguities, as well as lacunae that must be filled by inference processes. Traditional symbolic models typically have depended on the use of parsing and inference rules carefully tailored to produce "correct" interpretations, leading just as typically to various forms of nonhumanlike brittleness. Kintsch (1987) has developed a symbolic connectionist model that appears to circumvent some of these difficulties. His "construction-integration" model has four main components: (1) initial parallel activation of memory concepts corresponding to words in the text, together with formation of propositions by parsing rules; (2) spreading of activation to a small number of close associates of the text concepts; (3) inferring additional propositions by inference rules; and (4) creating excitatory and inhibitory links, with associated weights, between units representing activated concepts and propositions, and allowing the network to settle. The entire process is iterative. A small portion of text is processed, the units active after the settling process are maintained, and then the cycle is repeated with the next portion of text.

The central characteristic of the model is that it allows the parsing and inference rules to apply in a loose, error-prone fashion, overgenerating concepts and propositions that initially form an incoherent representation of the discourse. For example, a parser is given this text: "The lawyer discussed the case with the judge. He said 'I shall send the defendant to prison.' " The parser will create rival propositions that respectively will represent the judge and the lawyer as the referent of "he." The constraint network that is constructed will then use parallel constraint satisfaction to identify a coherent subset of the units, deactivating possible interpretations that do not fit the discourse context.

In addition to accounting for psycholinguistic data on text comprehension, the construction-integration model has recently been extended to account for levels of expertise in planning routine computing tasks (Doane, Kintsch, & Polson, 1990; Mannes & Kintsch, 1989).

Analogical thinking. One of the central mechanisms for transfer of knowledge is reasoning by analogy. Two of the basic components of analogical thinking are retrieval of useful analogies from memory and mapping of the elements of a known situation (the source) and a new situation (the target) to identify useful correspondences. Both of these components can be challenging, especially when the analogues have few direct similarities between their elements. People often fail to retrieve potentially useful source analogues (Gick & Holyoak, 1980, 1983), but performance improves when multiple analogues allow induction of a more abstract schema (Bassok & Holyoak, 1989; Brown et al., 1986; Catrambone & Holyoak, 1989; Gick & Holyoak, 1983). Also, once people are directed to relate two analogues, they often succeed in using remote analogues effectively. Indeed, cross-domain analogies are routinely used as devices to aid in teaching new concepts (e.g., Thagard, Cohen, & Holyoak, 1989).

Because analogical mapping sometimes requires finding relational correspondences in the absence of overt similarities, diffuse connectionist models lack the requisite representational tools. Purely symbolic models have difficulty avoiding combinatorial explosion in searching either for possible analogues in a large memory store or for optimal mappings between two analogues, without being forced to impose unduly limiting restrictions on the search process. Paul Thagard and I, together with our colleagues, have recently constructed symbolic connectionist models of both mapping and analogue retrieval (Holyoak & Thagard, 1989a; Thagard, Holyoak, Nelson, & Gochfeld, 1990). Both the mapping model, ACME, and the retrieval model, ARCS, operate by taking symbolic, predicate-calculus-style representations of situations as inputs, applying a small set of abstract constraints to build a network of units representing possible mappings between elements of two analogues, and then allowing parallel constraint satisfaction to settle the network into a stable state in which asymptotic activations of units reflect the degrees of confidence in possible mappings. The constraints on mapping lead to preference for sets of mapping hypotheses that yield isomorphic correspondences, link similar elements, and map elements of special importance. These same constraints (with differing relative impacts) operate in both the mapping and retrieval models.

As in Kintsch's model of discourse comprehension, ACME and ARCS first overgenerate a large pool of potential candidate hypotheses, and then use constraint satisfaction to select a coherent subset. As an example, the Appendix presents two mathematical word problems that were used by Novick and Holyoak (1991) to investigate analogical transfer in mathematical problem solving. College students first studied the "garden problem," plus a solution to it based on finding least common multiples. They then attempted to solve the target "band problem" using the garden problem as a source analogue. In addition, some subjects were explicitly asked to state the correct mapping for various key concepts and numbers in the band problem. For example, the band members should map onto plants, the number of members in a row or column onto the number of plants of a kind, and the successful divisor in the band problem (5, which leaves a zero remainder) onto the successful divisor (6) in the garden problem. Note that the two problems have many surface dissimilarities (e.g., band members have no obvious resemblance to plants), contain some misleading similarities (e.g., the divisor 5 in the band problem should map onto 6, not 5, in the garden problem), and are far from isomorphic (e.g., the band problem involves two people who consider a single total number of band members, whereas the garden problem involves three people who consider two different possible total numbers of plants). There was therefore good reason to expect that mapping these two analogues would be challenging for either a person or a computational model.

The ACME model was applied to predicate-calculus representations of the two problems. Each representation was quite detailed, requiring about 70 propositions to represent the band problem and over 80 to represent the garden problem and its solution. The program proceeded to construct a constraint network consisting of over 1,600 units representing mapping hypotheses (e.g., "band members = plants") interconnected by over 30,000 excitatory and inhibitory links. After about 200 cycles of settling, the network converged on a set of best mappings for the elements of the band problem that were consistent with the intuitively correct set of mappings. These included the optimal mappings between dissimilar concepts, such as band members and plants, and between specific numerical values, such as 5 and 6.

Similarly, the college subjects tested by Novick and Holyoak (1991) achieved over 80% accuracy in providing the correct mappings for the key concepts and numbers. Oral protocols collected from some subjects revealed few overt signs of the mapping process, consistent with the use of a parallel and relatively fast mapping mechanism. Interestingly, knowing the correct mapping did not guarantee successful transfer of the solution method, as about a third of the subjects who had appropriate mappings still failed to develop the analogous solution; furthermore, protocols consisted largely of laborious efforts to work out the *implications* of the correspondences found between the two analogues, after the initial mapping process was apparently completed. These results suggest that general skill in analogical mapping develops quite naturally, but is only one component of skill in analogical transfer. An implication is that adaptive expertise in humans is in part built on powerful constraint-satisfaction mechanisms for finding mappings between complex representations.

Explanatory coherence. The problem of evaluating competing explanations arises in an enormous range of domains, including medical diagnosis (Patel & Groen, chapter 4, this volume), legal reasoning, science (Anzai, chapter 3, this volume), and everyday language comprehension and reasoning. A long-standing problem in arriving at criteria for preferring one explanation to a rival is that observations and their relations to possible explanations often are intertwined in complex ways. As Quine put it, "our statements about the external world face the tribunal of sense experience not individually but only as a corporate body" (1961, p. 41). This extreme interdependence has defeated attempts to formulate strict rules for assessing explanatory adequacy.

Thagard (1989) has shown that the problem of evaluating competing explanations can be addressed by a symbolic connectionist model of explanatory coherence: ECHO. The model takes as inputs symbolic representations of basic explanatory relations among propositions corresponding to data and explanatory hypotheses. The system then builds a constraint network linking units representing the propositions. As in ACME and ARCS, a few very general constraints are used in network construction. In ECHO, the constraints support explanations with greater explanatory breadth (more links to data), greater simplicity (fewer constituent assumptions), and greater correspon-

Table 12.1. *Input propositions for ECHO analysis of phlogiston and oxygen explanations*

Evidence
  (proposition 'E1 "In combustion, heat and light are given off.")
  (proposition 'E2 "Inflammability is transmittable from one body to another.")
  (proposition 'E3 "Combustion only occurs in the presence of pure air.")
  (proposition 'E4 "Increase in weight of a burned body is exactly equal to weight of air absorbed.")
  (proposition 'E5 "Metals undergo calcination.")
  (proposition 'E6 "In calcination, bodies increase weight.")
  (proposition 'E7 "In calcination, volume of air diminishes.")
  (proposition 'E8 "In reduction, effervescence appears.")

Oxygen hypotheses
  (proposition 'OH1 "Pure air contains oxygen principle.")
  (proposition 'OH2 "Pure air contains matter of fire and heat.")
  (proposition 'OH3 "In combustion, oxygen from the air combines with the burning body.")
  (proposition 'OH4 "Oxygen has weight.")
  (proposition 'OH5 "In calcination, metals add oxygen to become calxes.")
  (proposition 'OH6 "In reduction, oxygen is given off.")

Phlogiston hypotheses
  (proposition 'PH1 "Combustible bodies contain phlogiston.")
  (proposition 'PH2 "Combustible bodies contain matter of heat.")
  (proposition 'PH3 "In combustion, phlogiston is given off.")
  (proposition 'PH4 "Phlogiston can pass from one body to another.")
  (proposition 'PH5 "Metals contain phlogiston.")
  (proposition 'PH6 "In calcination, phlogiston is given off.")

Source: From Thagard (1989).

dence to analogous explanations of other phenomena. Relations of mutual coherence (modeled by symmetrical excitatory links) hold between hypotheses and the data they explain; relations of mutual incoherence (inhibitory links) hold between competing hypotheses. The resulting network thus typically contains multiple contradictory propositions. Parallel constraint satisfaction then settles the network into an asymptotic state in which units representing the most mutually coherent hypotheses and data are active, and units representing inconsistent rivals are deactivated.

As an example, Table 12.1 lists the sets of propositions relevant to Lavoisier's eighteenth-century arguments comparing the phlogiston and oxygen theories of such phenomena as combustion and respiration. These consist of sets of propositions representing observed evidence and sets representing the compo-

Table 12.2. *Input explanations and*
contradictions for phlogiston and oxygen
explanations

Oxygen explanations
(explain '(OH1 OH2 OH3) 'E1)
(explain '(OH1 OH3) 'E3)
(explain '(OH1 OH3 OH4) 'E4)
(explain '(OH1 OH5) 'E5)
(explain '(OH1 OH4 OH5) 'E6)
(explain '(OH1 OH5) 'E7)
(explain '(OH1 OH6) 'E8)

Phlogiston explanations
(explain '(PH1 PH2 PH3) 'E1)
(explain '(PH1 PH3 PH4) 'E2)
(explain '(PH5 PH6) 'E5)

Contradictions
(contradict 'PH3 'OH3)
(contradict 'PH6 'OH5)

Data
data '(E1 E2 E3 E4 E5 E6 E7 E8))

Source: From Thagard (1989).

nent hypotheses for the two theories. Table 12.2 lists the explanatory relations
among the propositions that serve as the input to ECHO, and Figure 12.2
depicts a portion of the resulting constraint network. The solid lines represent
excitatory links between cohering propositions, and the inhibitory link exemplifies a relation of contradiction, here between the rival hypotheses that oxygen
or phlogiston is the product of combustion. After about 100 cycles, the network
settles into an asymptotic state in which the oxygen hypotheses are active and
the phlogiston hypotheses have been deactivated, reflecting Lavoisier's conclusion that the oxygen theory was globally superior. Thagard (1989) showed that
ECHO is able to model a number of realistic cases of explanation evaluation in
both scientific and legal contexts. The basic idea that explanations are evaluated on the basis of their internal coherence and completeness is quite consistent with findings concerning the reasoning of doctors performing medical
diagnoses (Patel & Groen, chapter 4, this volume).

Commonalities among the models

Although the examples of symbolic connectionist models described
earlier span quite different tasks and differ in many important ways, some
major commonalities are evident, and they distinguish these models from

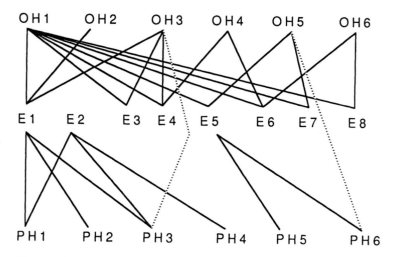

Figure 12.2. A portion of the constraint network formed by ECHO to represent Lavoisier's argument comparing the oxygen and phlogiston theories. From Thagard (1989).

those typical of strictly connectionist or symbolic approaches (Thagard et al., 1990). First, all use highly general constraints, potentially applicable to an unlimited range of examples, to transform symbolic structures into specific constraint networks. The constraints may take the form of parsing rules, inference rules, or other procedures for forming interconnected hypotheses. This on-line construction process is quite different from typical connectionist algorithms for building networks by learning algorithms operating incrementally on numerous examples. A second, related commonality is that the resulting constraint networks are essentially ephemeral. They are built to find a coherent interpretation and then are discarded (although the asymptotic states might readily be used for learning). In this respect these symbolic connectionist models resemble connectionist models of perception (in which ephemeral networks are formed in the process of interpreting sensory inputs) more than typical connectionist models of learning. Third, all the models allow the network-construction procedure to operate in a loose and uncritical manner, overgenerating a set of inconsistent hypotheses; they then rely on parallel constraint satisfaction to select a coherent subset of the hypotheses and discard the rest. This aspect of the models frees them from much of the brittleness that plagues purely symbolic treatments of similar cognitive tasks.

THE FUTURE OF THE THIRD GENERATION

I hope I am not mistaken in taking these examples of symbolic connectionist models as evidence that the third generation of theories of expertise, though still in its infancy, has in fact been born. Although none of these models addresses the nature of expertise directly, they offer theoretical mechanisms for modeling aspects of higher-level cognition that must surely figure prominently in any model of expert performance. The most salient gap in the current models is that none addresses the crucial issue of learning. Nonetheless, it seems reasonable to expect that learning models can be developed within the symbolic connectionist paradigm. Connectionist schemes for associative learning could readily be incorporated, as could more knowledge-intensive mechanisms associated with symbolic models. The potential of learning mechanisms based on selective recombination of useful existing representations (Holland, 1986; Holland, Holyoak, Nisbett, & Thagard, 1986) deserves exploration. Such mechanisms might, for example, help account for the flexible repairing of conditions and actions found in studies of procedural transfer (e.g., Allard & Starkes, chapter 5, this volume).

The coordination of multiple approaches to learning may in fact yield synergistic benefits. For example, simple models of generalization operate by identifying similarities between elements in successive positive examples of a category. A major limitation of this approach is that in complex relational structures (as opposed to simple feature vectors of the sort typically provided as inputs to connectionist learning algorithms), it is difficult to identify which elements ought to be compared. However, a model of analogical mapping, such as ACME, can in effect force previously unrelated elements (such as band members and plants in the algebra-word problems discussed earlier) into correspondence, making salient the common relational roles that link them. This information could readily be used to guide the process of generalization in the aftermath of analogical transfer (Holyoak & Thagard, 1989b).

Inconsistencies and anomalies revisited

Symbolic connectionism, in its current natal stage, certainly offers no panacea for our incomplete understanding of the inconsistencies and anomalies of expertise reviewed earlier. Still, it may be worthwhile to briefly reconsider these phenomena and offer some very preliminary speculations as to what each may imply about future theoretical developments related to expertise. In some cases the phenomena suggest potential applications of connectionist mechanisms, in other cases the need for symbolic components, and in some cases possible interactions between symbolic representations and connectionist processing.

Experts sometimes achieve mediocrity. The deficiencies of experts in clinical decision making, relative to simple statistical models that are closely related to some connectionist learning procedures, suggest some important ways in which these connectionist schemes may require modification or augmentation to account for human learning. The most salient characteristics of the learning situation confronting decision-makers in many areas, such as personnel selection, is that the pool of relevant features is poorly constrained, and feedback on accuracy of predictions is delayed, intermittent, and sometimes unreliable. Such learning situations are known to impair covariation detection (Holland et al., 1986, chapter 5). It is possible that people often assume that they are correct when feedback is lacking (thus potentially reinforcing flawed decisions). They may also switch attention to new cues when an established regularity is shown to lead to an error, fostering the learning of special-case exceptions, rather than the correction of erroneous weights relating old cues to predictions. In addition, top-down expectations generated by prior beliefs, to the extent they are invalid, may impair bottom-up contingency learning.

Experts sometimes feel more pain. The extended efforts at problem reformulation, planning, and revision of goals and methods that characterize experts working at their creative edge remain poorly understood.

Means–ends analysis can impair learning. The work of Sweller and his colleagues indicates that free forward search from the given information in the absence of an explicit goal, rather than means–ends analysis, can lead to superior subsequent problem-solving performance. Relatively free problem exploration would be expected to foster the acquisition of broad knowledge of problem constraints and regularities, perhaps using prediction-based learning procedures. Such learning would yield a rich constraint network, which in turn would facilitate the solution of relatively novel problems in the domain.

Conditions and actions sometimes can be flexibly recoupled. Such results may have implications for the acquisition of constraint networks. For example, consider the situation facing a macrosurgeon learning to perform microsurgery (Allard & Starkes, chapter 5, this volume). The visual cues that elicit a certain pattern of macromovements must now come to elicit a totally different set of micromovements; yet the old condition–action links must be preserved to allow continued skill in macrosurgery. A connectionist-style solution to this problem in skill acquisition might be to preserve the existing excitatory connections among related visual cues, add new excitatory connections from the visual cues to the required micromovements, and at the same time add inhibitory links between the two sets of visual-to-motor connections, so that the context would be able to "flip a switch" to choose which set of connections would be allowed to operate at a given time. The new skill thus would build on the old (by using preexisting connections among condition cues) while minimizing interference between the two. Similar mechanisms might allow useful but imperfect generalizations to be preserved by coupling them to more specific exception conditions that would override the default when they conflicted (Fahlman, 1979; Holland et al., 1986).

Most connectionist learning schemes have not built new knowledge on top of prior knowledge in this sense; rather, new learning using these algorithms has involved explicit "unlearning" of existing connections, creating interference. However, recent proposals for learning mechanisms of a more incremental sort, in which established connections are "frozen" before new connections are added to the network, show promise of being better able to capture humanlike flexibility in building new knowledge (Fahlman & Lebiere, 1990).

Expertise sometimes can be decoupled from memory performance. From the symbolic connectionist perspective, routine expert performance is basically controlled by the activity of constraint networks. The same networks of constraint relations may help experts to form new memory representations for problems, producing the typical expert advantage in memory tests (Chase & Simon, 1973). However, such memory advantages may be fundamentally incidental in nature. If the expert's constraint network does not include nonessential problem-specific details (as may be the case in expert medical diagnosis; see Patel & Groen, chapter 4, this volume), or if other factors interfere with setting up new memory representations (such as the effects of aging; Charness, 1981), then expert problem solving may be decoupled to some extent from expert memory performance.

Expertise sometimes can be decoupled from pattern perception. Similarly, changes in pattern perception may accompany expertise only to the extent the new patterns are required by the constraint network developed to perform the task. In cases such as expertise in volleyball (Allard & Starkes, chapter 5, this volume), a game in which some patterns may actually be misleading, the constraint network of the expert player may not facilitate (or even may inhibit) their detection.

Expert search strategies are extremely varied. If high-level heuristics and strategies are represented by units in a constraint network, then contextual cues provided by problem situations can potentially drive the flexible selection of search strategies.

Performance may not show continuous improvement with practice. Although connectionist learning algorithms typically are slow and incremental in nature, constraint-satisfaction models of decision processes can undergo relatively radical reorganizations (e.g., Rumelhart et al., 1986c). A change in activation of a unit at one place in the constraint network can trigger a major revision in the overall state of the network. Such rapid changes can be observed in the ECHO model of explanatory coherence when new evidence overturns a crucial assumption of a previously dominant theory (Thagard, 1989). Such rapid changes in network states may underlie major conceptual shifts that sometimes accompany changes in levels of expertise.

Learning need not require goals or feedback. Some connectionist learning schemes can identify regularities in inputs without overt feedback (Rumelhart

& Zipser, 1986); see Bharucha (in press) for an application to the learning of musical chords.

Knowledge can be transferred across domains. Symbolic connectionist models of analogical reasoning provide potential mechanisms for cross-domain knowledge transfer (Holyoak & Thagard, 1989a).

Teaching expert rules may not yield expertise. The knowledge embodied in a constraint network typically will involve subtle interactions and contextual shading that "expert" rules often may miss.

Rules elicited from experts may not predict their performance. For the same reason, experts may be unable to articulate the complex interactions between small pieces of knowledge embodied in their constraint networks and thus will be unable to provide accurate descriptions of the basis for their superior task performances. A constraint network can represent the kind of difficult-to-verbalize knowledge associated with expert "intuition."

CONCLUSION

Although still more speculative than substantive, the symbolic connectionist paradigm appears to have at least the potential to blossom into a new generation of models of cognition and expertise. Whether or not it will in fact do so, and what it will mean if it does, remain open questions. If more radical connectionists are right, elegant general solutions to the kinds of representational issues discussed earlier will quickly enable them to sweep aside the final vestiges of symbol systems, rendering hybrid systems obsolete. But if such solutions come slowly (or not at all), then symbolic connectionism offers at least pragmatic advantages for those trying to construct models of expertise in high-level cognitive tasks. Symbolic connectionists have the luxury of remaining officially agnostic regarding the "ultimate" resolution of debates about the status of symbolic representation. The pragmatic position is that by incorporating symbolic representations as needed, we can take advantage of connectionist processing mechanisms to build models with more of the flexibility in dealing with novelty and complexity that characterizes adaptive expertise. If the radical connectionists are fundamentally right, but overly optimistic about the time scale of their progress, then the symbolic part of symbolic connectionism will serve as a useful stopgap, slowly being replaced by "pure" connectionist mechanisms as these are discovered.

There are, of course, other possibilities. In particular, perhaps the radicals are wrong; perhaps human intelligence is based in part on mental representations that by any reasonable set of criteria are symbol systems. As I survey the current work directed at allowing connectionist networks to perform symbolic functions, my impression is that the more promising lines of attack are better characterized as connectionist-style implementations of symbolic representations, rather than connectionist eliminations of symbols. This is not in any way to slight the importance of such efforts; on the contrary, new implementations of symbolic functions may have important psychological (and perhaps biological) implications we cannot yet fully anticipate. However, these new symbolic connectionist models will have identifiable components that will perform such symbolic functions as representing variables and their bindings, objects of belief, and other abstract types of knowledge; they will postulate processes by which knowledge can become available for structured recombination and self-reflection. At the same time, these models will use connectionist principles to allow decisions about novel situations to emerge from the graceful integration of multiple constraints. In this possible future for models of high-level cognition, symbolic connectionism will flourish. Time will tell.

APPENDIX: ANALOGOUS MATHEMATICAL WORD PROBLEMS USED IN MAPPING EXPERIMENT[1]

Garden problem (source)

Mr. and Mrs. Renshaw were planning how to arrange vegetable plants in their new garden. They agreed on the total number of plants to buy, but not on how many of each kind to get. Mr. Renshaw wanted to have a few kinds of vegetables, and 10 of each kind. Mrs Renshaw wanted more different kinds of vegetables, so she suggested having only four of each kind. Mr. Renshaw did not like that, because if some of the plants died, there would not be many left of each kind. So they agreed to have five of each vegetable. But then their daughter pointed out that there was room in the garden for two more plants, although then there would not be the same numbers of all kinds of vegetables. To remedy this, she suggested buying six of each vegetable. Everyone was satisfied with this plan. Given this information, what is the fewest number of vegetable plants the Renshaws can have in their garden?

Solution. Because at the beginning Mr. and Mrs. Renshaw agreed on the total number of plants to buy, 10, 4, and 5 must all go evenly into that number, whatever it is. Thus, the first thing to do is to find the smallest number that is evenly divisible by those three numbers, which is 20. So the original number of vegetable plants the Renshaws were thinking of buying could have been any multiple of 20, that is, 20 or 40 or 60 or 80, and so forth. But then they decided to buy two additional plants that they had not been planning to buy originally, so the total number of plants they actually end up buying must be 2 more than the multiples of 20 listed earlier, that is, 22 or 42 or 62 or 82, and so forth. This means that 10, 4, and 5 will now no longer go evenly into the total number of plants. Finally, the problem states that they agree to buy six of each vegetable, so the total number of plants must be evenly divisible by 6. The

---

[1] Adapted from Novick and Holyoak (1991).

smallest total number of plants that is evenly divisible by 6 is 42, and that is the answer.

Band problem (target)

Members of the West High School band were hard at work practicing for the annual homecoming parade. First they tried marching in rows of 12, but Andrew was left by himself to bring up the rear. The band director was annoyed because it did not look good to have one row with only a single person in it, and of course Andrew was not pleased either. To get rid of this problem, the director told the band members to march in columns of eight. But Andrew was still left to march alone. Even when the band marched in rows of three, Andrew was left out. Finally, in exasperation, Andrew told the band director that they should march in rows of five in order to have all the rows filled. He was right. This time, all the rows were filled, and Andrew was not alone any more. Given that there were at least 45 musicians on the field, but fewer than 200 musicians, how many students were there in the West High School band?

ACKNOWLEDGMENTS

Preparation of this chapter was supported by contract MDA903-89-K-0179 from the Army Research Institute. Miriam Bassok, Patricia Cheng, K. Anders Ericsson, Laura Novick, Paul Thagard, and Michael Waldmann provided helpful comments on earlier drafts.

REFERENCES

Adelson, B. (1984). When novices surpass experts: The difficulty of a task may increase with expertise. *Journal of Experimental Psychology: Learning, Memory, and Cognition, 10,* 483–495.

Ajjanagadde, V., & Shastri, L. (1989). Efficient inference with multi-place predicates and variables in a connectionist system. In *Proceedings of the 11th Annual Meeting of the Cognitive Science Society* (pp. 396–403). Hillsdale, NJ: Erlbaum.

Amaiwa, S. (1987). Transfer of subtraction procedures from abacus to paper and pencil (in Japanese with English summary). *Japanese Journal of Educational Psychology, 35,* 41–48.

Anderson, J. R. (1976). *Language, memory, and thought.* Hillsdale, NJ: Erlbaum.

Anderson, J. R. (1983). *The architecture of cognition.* Cambridge, MA: Harvard University Press.

Anderson, J. R. (1987). Skill acquisition: Compilation of weak-method problem solutions. *Psychological Review, 94,* 192–210.

Anderson, J. R. (1990). *The adaptive character of thought.* Hillsdale, NJ: Erlbaum.

Anderson, J. R., Farrell, R., & Sauers, R. (1984). Learning to program in LISP. *Cognitive Science, 8,* 87–129.

Bassok, M., & Holyoak, K. J. (1989). Interdomain transfer between isomorphic topics in algebra and physics. *Journal of Experimental Psychology: Learning, Memory, and Cognition, 15,* 153–166.

Bharucha, J. J. (1987a). A connectionist model of musical harmony. In *Proceedings of the 9th Annual Conference of the Cognitive Science Society* (pp. 508–517). Hillsdale, NJ: Erlbaum.

Bharucha, J. J. (1987b). Music cognition and perceptual facilitation: A connectionist framework. *Music Perception, 5,* 1–30.

Bharucha, J. J. (in press). Tonality, expectation and learnability. In M. R. Jones & S. Holleran (Eds.), *Cognitive bases of musical communication.* Washington, DC: American Psychological Association.

Brown, A. L., Kane, M. J., & Echols, C. H. (1986). Young children's mental models determine analogical transfer across problems with a common goal structure. *Cognitive Development, 1,* 103–121.

Carr, B., & Goldstein, I. P. (1977). Overlays: A theory of modeling for computer-aided instruction (AI Lab Memo 406, Logo Memo 45). Cambridge, MA: MIT, Artificial Intelligence Laboratory.

Carraher, T. N., Carraher, D. W., & Schliemann, A. D. (1987). Written and oral mathematics. *Journal for Research in Mathematics Education, 18,* 83–97.

Catrambone, R., & Holyoak, K. J. (1989). Overcoming contextual limitations on problem-solving transfer. *Journal of Experimental Psychology: Learning, Memory, and Cognition, 15,* 1147–1156.

Charness, N. (1981). Visual short-term memory and aging in chess players. *Journal of Gerontology, 36,* 615–619.

Chase, W. G., & Simon, H. A. (1973). Perception in chess. *Cognitive Psychology, 4,* 55–81.

Cheng, P. W. (1985). Restructuring versus automaticity: Alternative accounts of skill acquisition. *Psychological Review, 92,* 414–423.

Cheng, P. W., Holyoak, K. J., Nisbett, R. E., & Oliver, L. M. (1986). Pragmatic versus syntactic approaches to training deductive reasoning. *Cognitive Psychology, 18,* 293–328.

Chi, M. T. H., Bassok, M., Reimann, P., & Glaser, R. (1989). Self-explanations: How students study and use examples in learning to solve problems. *Cognitive Science, 13,* 145–182.

Chi, M. T. H., Feltovich, P. J., & Glaser, R. (1981). Categorization and representation of physics problems by experts and novices. *Cognitive Science, 5,* 121–152.

Clancey, W. (1986). Qualitative student models. *Annual Review of Computational Science, 1,* 381–450.

Clement, J. (1989). Learning via model construction and criticism: Protocol evidence on sources of creativity in science. In J. Glover, R. Ronning, & C. Reynolds (Eds.), *Handbook of creativity: Assessment, theory, and research* (pp. 341–381). New York: Plenum.

Cottrell, G. W. (1985). Connectionist parsing. In *Proceedings of the 7th Annual Conference of the Cognitive Science Society* (pp. 201–211). Hillsdale, NJ: Erlbaum.

de Groot, A. D. (1965). *Thought and choice in chess.* The Hague: Mouton.

Doane, S. M., Kintsch, W., & Polson, P. G. (1990). Modeling UNIX command production: What experts must know (ICS Technical Report 90-1). Institute of Cognitive Science, University of Colorado.

Dolan, C., & Dyer, M. G. (1988). Parallel retrieval and application of conceptual knowledge (Technical Report UCLA-AI-88-3). Department of Computer Science, UCLA.

Dolan, C., & Smolensky, P. (1988). Implementing a connectionist production system using tensor products (Technical Report UCLA-AI-88-15). Department of Computer Science, UCLA.

Dyer, M. G. (1991). Symbolic NeuroEngineering for natural language processing: A multilevel research approach. In J. Barnden & J. Pollack (Eds.), *Advances in connectionist and neural computation theory.* Vol. 1: *High level connectionist models* (pp. 32–86). Norwood, NJ: Ablex.

Ericsson, K. A., & Simon, H. A. (1980). Verbal reports as data. *Psychological Review, 87,* 215–251.

Ericsson, K. A., & Staszewski, J. J. (1989). Skilled memory and expertise: Mechanisms of exceptional performance. In D. Klahr & K. Kotovsky (Eds.), *Complex information processng: The impact of Herbert A. Simon* (pp. 235–267). Hillsdale, NJ: Erlbaum.

Fahlman, S. (1979). *NETL: A system for representing and using real-world knowledge.* Cambridge, MA: MIT Press.

Fahlman, S., & Lebiere, C. (1990). The cascade-correlation learning architecture (Technical Report CMU-CS-90-100). School of Computer Science, Carnegie-Mellon University.

Feigenbaum, E. A. (1989). What hath Simon wrought? In D. Klahr & K. Kotovsky (Eds.), *Complex information processing: The impact of Herbert A. Simon* (pp. 165–182). Hillsdale, NJ: Erlbaum.

Feldman, J. A., & Ballard, D. H. (1982). Connectionist models and their properties. *Cognitive Science, 6,* 205–254.

Fodor, J. A., & Pylyshyn, Z. W. (1988). Connectionism and cognitive architecture: A critical analysis. In S. Pinker & J. Mehler (Eds.), *Connections and symbols* (pp. 3–71). Cambridge, MA: MIT Press.

Fong, G. T., Krantz, D. H., & Nisbett, R. E. (1986). The effects of statistical training on thinking about everyday problems. *Cognitive Psychology, 18,* 253–292.

Gentner, D. (1983). Structure-mapping: A theoretical framework for analogy. *Cognitive Science, 7,* 155–170.

Gentner, D. R. (1983). The acquisition of typing skill. *Acta Psychologica, 54,* 233–248.

Gick, M. L., & Holyoak, K. J. (1980). Analogical problem solving. *Cognitive Psychology, 12,* 306–355.

Gick, M. L., & Holyoak, K. J. (1983). Schema induction and analogical transfer. *Cognitive Psychology, 15,* 1–38.

Gick, M. L., & Holyoak, K. J. (1987). The cognitive basis of knowledge transfer. In S. M. Cormier & J. D. Hagman (Eds.), *Transfer of training: Contemporary research and applications* (pp. 9–46). New York: Academic Press.

Goldstone, R. L., Gentner, D., & Medin, D. L. (1989). Relations relating relations. In *Proceedings of the 11th Annual Meeting of the Cognitive Science Society* (pp. 131–138). Hillsdale, NJ: Erlbaum.

Hatano, G. (1988). Social and motivational bases for mathematical understanding. In G. B. Saxe & M. Gearhart (Eds.), *Children's mathematics* (pp. 55–70). San Francisco: Jossey-Bass.

Hatano, G., & Inagaki, K. (1986). Two courses of expertise. In H. Stevenson, H. Azuma, & K. Hakuta (Eds.), *Child development and education in Japan* (pp. 262–272). San Francisco: Freeman.

Hatano, G., & Osawa, K. (1983). Digit memory of grand masters in abacus-derived mental calculation. *Cognition, 15,* 95–110.

Hendler, J. A. (1989). Marker-passing over microfeatures: Towards a hybrid symbolic/connectionist model. *Cognitive Science, 13,* 79–106.

Hinton, G. E. (1981). Implementing semantic networks in parallel hardware. In G. E. Hinton & J. A. Anderson (Eds.), *Parallel models of associative memory* (pp. 191–217). Hillsdale, NJ: Erlbaum.

Hinton, G. E., & Anderson, J. A. (Eds.). (1981). *Parallel models of associative memory.* Hillsdale, NJ: Erlbaum.

Holding, D. H., & Reynolds, R. I. (1982). Recall or evaluation of chess positions as determinants of chess skill. *Memory & Cognition, 10,* 237–242.

Holland, J. H. (1986). Escaping bitterness: The possibilities of general purpose machine learning algorithms applied to parallel rule-based systems. In R. S. Michalski, J. G. Carbonell, & T. M. Mitchell (Eds.), *Machine learning: An artificial intelligence approach* (Vol. 2, pp. 593–623). Los Altos, CA: Morgan Kaufmann.

Holland, J. H., Holyoak, K. J., Nisbett, R. E., & Thagard, P. R. (1986). *Induction: Processes of inference, learning, and discovery.* Cambridge, MA: MIT Press.

Holyoak, K. J. (1985). The pragmatics of analogical transfer. In G. H. Bower (Ed.), *The psychology of learning and motivation* (Vol. 19, pp. 59–87). New York: Academic Press.

Holyoak, K. J. (1987). A connectionist view of cognition [Review of *Parallel distributed processing* by D. E. Rumelhart, J. L. McClelland, & PDP Research Group]. *Science, 236,* 992–996.

Holyoak, K. J., & Thagard, P. (1989a). Analogical mapping by constraint satisfaction. *Cognitive Science, 13,* 295–355.

Holyoak, K. J., & Thagard, P. (1989b). A computational model of analogical problem solving. In S. Vosniadou & A. Ortony (Eds.), *Similarity and analogical reasoning* (pp. 242–266). Cambridge University Press.

Hunt, E. (1989). Connectionist and rule-based representations of expert knowledge. *Behavior Research Methods, Instruments, & Computers, 21,* 88–95.

Jeffries, R., Turner, A. T., Polson, P. G., & Atwood, M. E. (1981). The processes involved in designing software. In J. R. Anderson (Ed.), *Cognitive skills and their acquisition* (pp. 255–283). Hillsdale, NJ: Erlbaum.

Kintsch, W. (1987). The role of knowledge in discourse comprehension: A construction-integration model. *Psychological Review, 95,* 163–182.

Koedinger, K. R., & Anderson, J. R. (1989). Perceptual chunks in geometry problem solving: A challenge to theories of skill acquisition. In *Proceedings of the 11th Annual Meeting of the Cognitive Science Society* (pp. 442–449). Hillsdale, NJ: Erlbaum.

Kuhn, T. S. (1962). *The structure of scientific revolutions.* University of Chicago Press.

Lange, T., & Dyer, M. G. (1989). High-level inferencing in a connectionist network. *Connection Science, 1,* 181–217.

Larkin, J. H., McDermott, J., Simon, D., & Simon, H. A. (1980). Expert and novice performance in solving physics problems. *Science, 208,* 1335–1342.

Lesgold, A. (1989). Context-specific requirements for models of expertise. In D. Evans & V. L. Patel (Eds.), *Cognitive science in medicine: Biomedical modeling* (pp. 373–400). Cambridge, MA: MIT Press.

Lundell, J. W. (1988). *Knowledge extraction and the modelling of expertise in a diagnostic task.* Unpublished Ph.D. dissertation, University of Washington.

McClelland, J. L., & Rumelhart, D. E. (1986). Introduction to Part V. In J. L. Mc-Clelland, D. E. Rumelhart, & PDP Research Group (Eds.), *Parallel distributed processing: Explorations in the microstructure of cognition* (Vol. 2, pp. 327–331). Cambridge, MA: MIT Press.

McKeithen, K. B., Reitman, J. S., Rueter, H. H., & Hirtle, S. C. (1981). Knowledge organization and skill differences in computer programmers. *Cognitive Psychology, 13,* 307–325.

Mannes, S. M., & Kintsch, W. (1989). *Planning routine computing tasks: Understanding what to do* (ICS Technical Report 89-9). Institute of Cognitive Science, University of Colorado.

Miyata, M. (1989). A PDP model of sequence learning that exhibits the power law. In *Proceedings of the 11th Annual Meeting of the Cognitive Science Society* (pp. 9–16). Hillsdale, NJ: Erlbaum.

Newell, A. (1973). Production systems: Models of control structures. In W. G. Chase (Ed.), *Visual information processing* (pp. 463–526). New York: Academic Press.

Newell, A., Shaw, J. C., & Simon, H. A. (1958). Elements of a theory of human problem solving. *Psychological Review, 65,* 151–166.

Newell, A., & Simon, H. A. (1972). *Human problem solving.* Englewood Cliffs, NJ: Prentice-Hall.

Nisbett, R. E., Fong, G. T., Lehman, D. R., & Cheng, P. W. (1987). Teaching reasoning. *Science, 238,* 625–631.

Norman, D. A. (1986). Reflections on cognition and parallel distributed processing. In J. L. McClelland, D. E. Rumelhart, & PDP Research Group (Eds.), *Parallel distributed processing: Explorations in the microstructure of cognition* (Vol. 2, pp. 531–546). Cambridge, MA: MIT Press.

Novick, L. R. (1988). Analogical transfer, problem similarity, and expertise. *Journal of Experimental Psychology: Learning, Memory, and Cognition, 14,* 510–520.

Novick, L. R., & Holyoak, K. J. (1991). Mathematical problem solving by analogy. *Journal of Experimental Psychology: Learning, Memory, and Cognition.*

Owen, E., & Sweller, J. (1985). What do students learn while solving mathematics problems? *Journal of Educational Psychology, 77,* 272–284.

Pinker, S., & Prince, A. (1988). On language and connectionism: Analysis of a parallel distributed processing model of language acquisition. In S. Pinker & J. Mehler (Eds.), *Connections and symbols* (pp. 73–193). Cambridge, MA: MIT Press.

Quine, W. V. O. (1961). *From a logical point of view* (2nd ed.). New York: Harper Torchbooks.

Ratcliff, R., & McKoon, G. (1989). Similarity information versus relational information: Differences in the time course of retrieval. *Cognitive Psychology, 21,* 139–155.

Reitman, J. S. (1976). Skilled perception in go: Deducing memory structures from inter-response times. *Cognitive Psychology, 8,* 336–356.

Rosenbloom, P. S., & Newell, A. (1986). The chunking of goal hierarchies: A generalized model of practice. In R. S. Michalski, J. G. Carbonell, & T. M. Mitchell (Eds.), *Machine learning: An artificial intelligence approach* (Vol. 2, pp. 247–288). Los Altos, CA: Morgan Kaufmann.

Rumelhart, D. E., Hinton, G. E., & Williams, R. J. (1986a). Learning internal representations by error propagation. In D. E. Rumelhart, J. L. McClelland, & PDP Research Group (Eds.), *Parallel distributed processing: Explorations in the microstructure of cognition* (Vol. 1, pp. 318–362). Cambridge, MA: MIT Press.

Rumelhart, D. E., McClelland, J. L., & PDP Research Group. (Eds.). (1986b). *Paral-

lel distributed processing: Explorations in the microstructure of cognition (2 vols.). Cambridge, MA: MIT Press.

Rumelhart, D. E., Smolensky, P., McClelland, J. L., & Hinton, G. E. (1986c). Schemata and sequential thought processes in PDP models. In J. L. McClelland, D. E. Rumelhart, & PDP Research Group (Eds.), *Parallel distributed processing: Explorations in the microstructure of cognition* (Vol. 2, pp. 7–57). Cambridge, MA: MIT Press.

Rumelhart, D. E., & Zipser, D. (1986). Feature discovery by competitive learning. In D. E. Rumelhart, J. L. McClelland, & PDP Research Group (Eds.), *Parallel distributed processing: Explorations in the microstructure of cognition* (Vol. 1, pp. 151–193). Cambridge, MA: MIT Press.

Salomon, G., & Perkins, D. N. (1989). Rocky roads to transfer: Rethinking mechanisms of a neglected phenomenon. *Educational Psychologist, 24,* 113–142.

Saxe, G. B. (1988). Candy selling and math learning. *Educational Researcher, 17,* 14–21.

Schank, R. C. (1982). *Dynamic memory.* Cambridge: Cambridge University Press.

Shastri, L. (1988). A connectionist approach to knowledge representation and limited inference. *Cognitive Science, 12,* 331–392.

Shastri, L., & Ajjanagadde, V. (1990). *From simple associations to systematic reasoning: A connectionist representation of rules, variables and dynamic bindings* (Technical Report MS-CIS-90-05). Computer and Information Science Department, University of Pennsylvania.

Shiffrin, R. M., & Schneider, W. (1977). Controlled and automatic information processing: II. Perceptual learning, automatic attending, and a general theory. *Psychological Review, 84,* 127–190.

Simon, H. A. (1969). *The sciences of the artificial.* Cambridge, MA: MIT Press.

Smolensky, P. (1986). Information processing in dynamical systems: Foundations of harmony theory. In D. E. Rumelhart, J. L. McClelland, & PDP Research Group (Eds.), *Parallel distributed processing: Explorations in the microstructure of cognition* (Vol. 1, pp. 194–281). Cambridge, MA: MIT Press.

Smolensky, P. (1987). *On variable binding and the representation of symbolic structures in connectionist systems* (Technical Report CU-CS-355-87). Department of Computer Science, University of Colorado.

Stratton, G. M. (1897). Vision without inversion of the retinal image. *Psychological Review, 4,* 341–360, 463–481.

Sweller, J., Mawer, R. F., & Ward, M. R. (1983). Development of expertise in mathematical problem solving. *Journal of Experimental Psychology: General, 112,* 639–661.

Thagard, P. (1989). Explanatory coherence. *Behavioral and Brain Sciences, 12,* 435–467.

Thagard, P., Cohen, D. M., & Holyoak, K. J. (1989). Chemical analogies: Two kinds of explanation. In *Proceedings of the 11th International Joint Conference on Artificial Intelligence* (pp. 818–824). San Mateo, CA: Morgan Kaufmann.

Thagard, P., Holyoak, K. J., Nelson, G., & Gochfeld, D. (1990). Analog retrieval by constraint satisfaction. *Artificial Intelligence.*

Touretsky, D., & Hinton, G. (1988). A distributed connectionist production system. *Cognitive Science, 12,* 423–466.

Tweney, R. (1985). Faraday's discovery of induction: A cognitive approach. In D.

Goodling & F. James (Eds.), *Faraday rediscovered: Essays on the life and work of Michael Faraday, 1791–1867* (pp. 189–209). New York: Stockton Press.

Waldmann, M. R., & Weinert, F. E. (1990). *Intelligenz und Denken* [Intelligence and thinking]. Göttingen: Hogrefe.

Wenger, E. (1987). *Artificial intelligence and tutoring systems: Computational and cognitive approaches to the communication of knowledge.* Los Altos, CA: Morgan Kaufmann.

Index